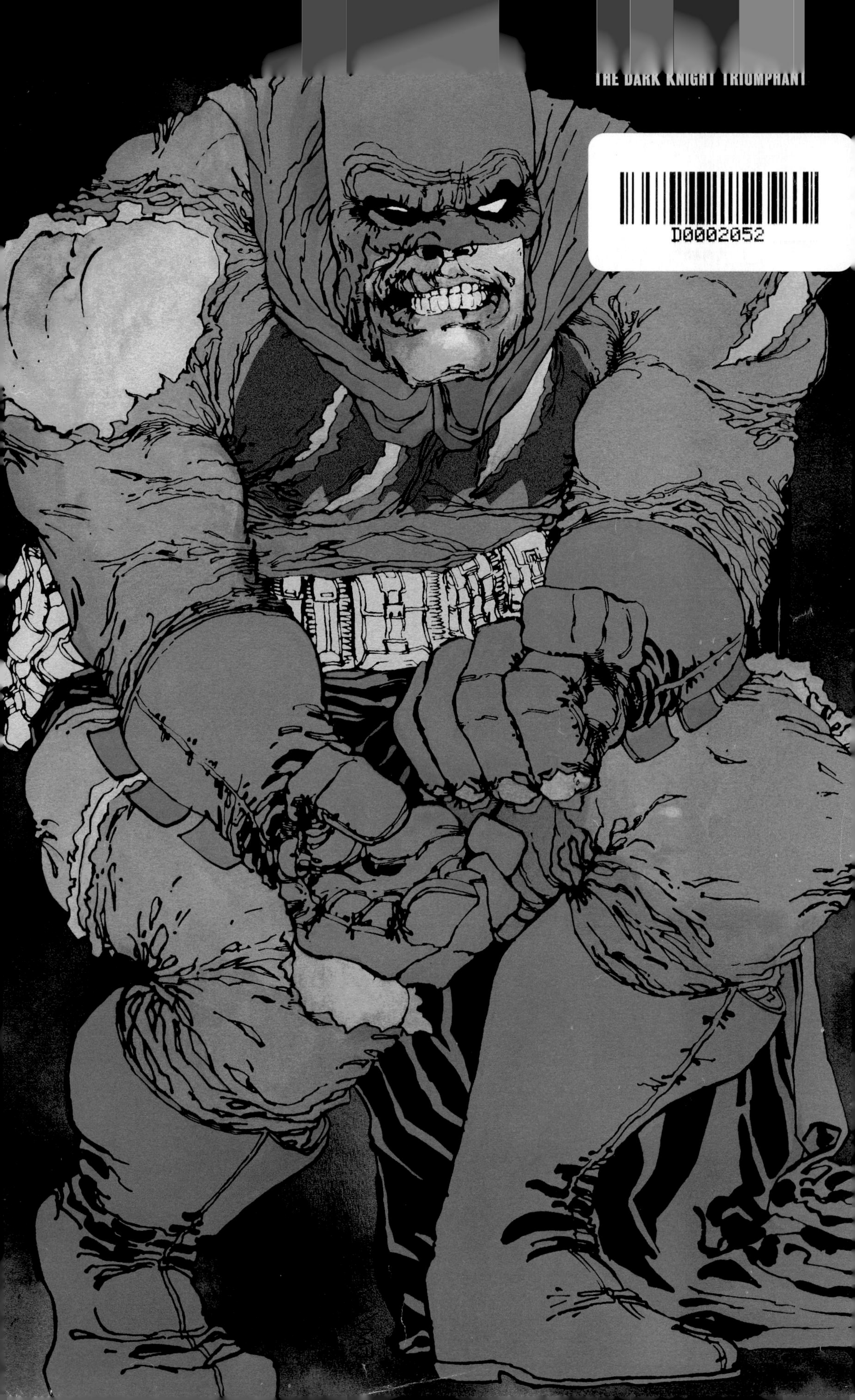
THE DARK KNIGHT TRIUMPHANT

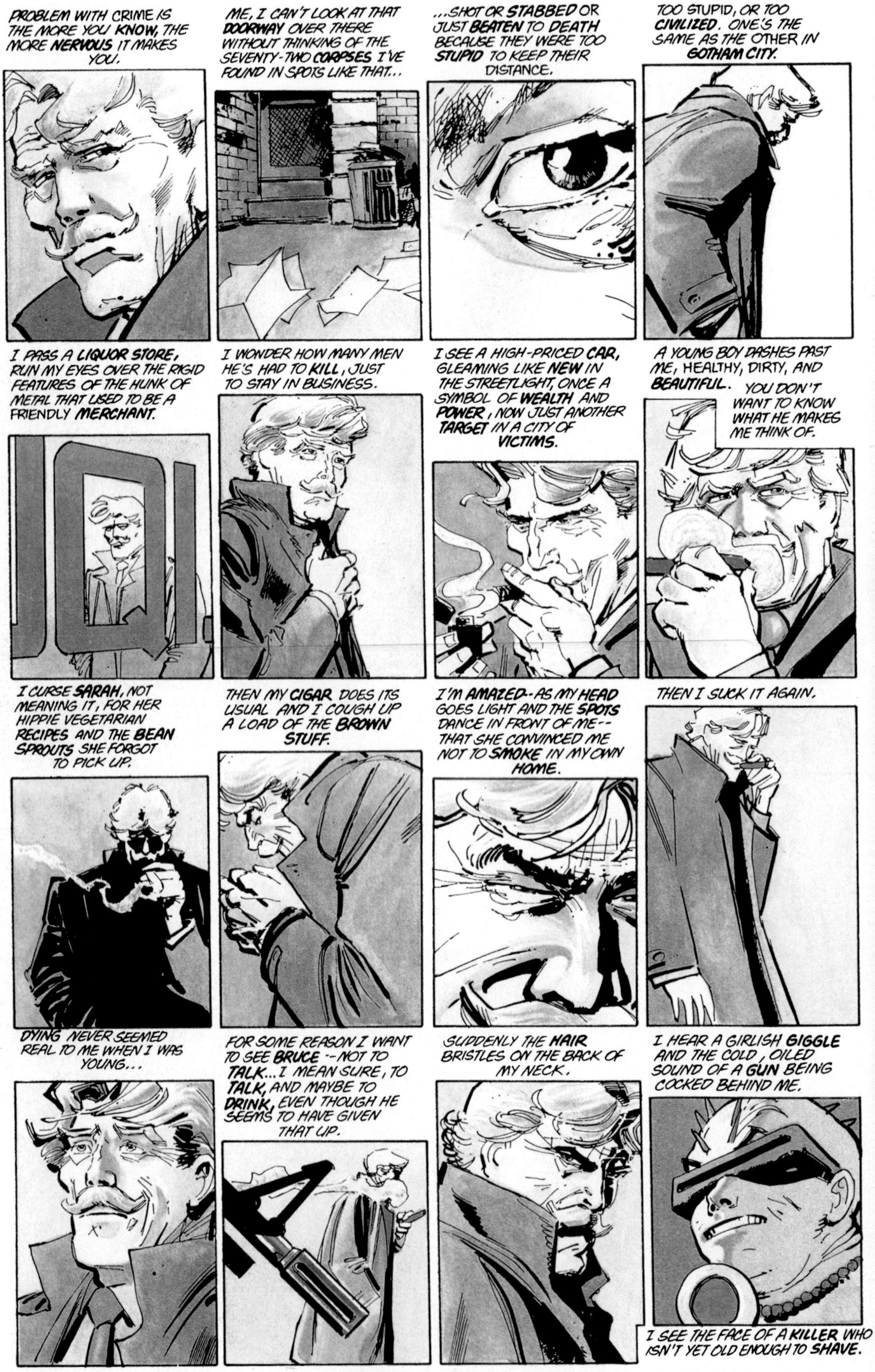
PROBLEM WITH CRIME IS THE MORE YOU KNOW, THE MORE NERVOUS IT MAKES YOU.
ME, I CAN'T LOOK AT THAT DOORWAY OVER THERE WITHOUT THINKING OF THE SEVENTY-TWO CORPSES I'VE FOUND IN SPOTS LIKE THAT...
...SHOT OR STABBED OR JUST BEATEN TO DEATH BECAUSE THEY WERE TOO STUPID TO KEEP THEIR DISTANCE.
TOO STUPID, OR TOO CIVILIZED. ONE'S THE SAME AS THE OTHER IN GOTHAM CITY.
I PASS A LIQUOR STORE, RUN MY EYES OVER THE RIGID FEATURES OF THE HUNK OF METAL THAT USED TO BE A FRIENDLY MERCHANT.
I WONDER HOW MANY MEN HE'S HAD TO KILL, JUST TO STAY IN BUSINESS.
I SEE A HIGH-PRICED CAR, GLEAMING LIKE NEW IN THE STREETLIGHT, ONCE A SYMBOL OF WEALTH AND POWER, NOW JUST ANOTHER TARGET IN A CITY OF VICTIMS.
A YOUNG BOY DASHES PAST ME, HEALTHY, DIRTY, AND BEAUTIFUL.
YOU DON'T WANT TO KNOW WHAT HE MAKES ME THINK OF.
I CURSE SARAH, NOT MEANING IT, FOR HER HIPPIE VEGETARIAN RECIPES AND THE BEAN SPROUTS SHE FORGOT TO PICK UP.
THEN MY CIGAR DOES ITS USUAL AND I COUGH UP A LOAD OF THE BROWN STUFF.
I'M AMAZED-- AS MY HEAD GOES LIGHT AND THE SPOTS DANCE IN FRONT OF ME-- THAT SHE CONVINCED ME NOT TO SMOKE IN MY OWN HOME.
THEN I SUCK IT AGAIN.
DYING NEVER SEEMED REAL TO ME WHEN I WAS YOUNG...
FOR SOME REASON I WANT TO SEE BRUCE --NOT TO TALK... I MEAN SURE, TO TALK, AND MAYBE TO DRINK, EVEN THOUGH HE SEEMS TO HAVE GIVEN THAT UP.
SUDDENLY THE HAIR BRISTLES ON THE BACK OF MY NECK.
I HEAR A GIRLISH GIGGLE AND THE COLD, OILED SOUND OF A GUN BEING COCKED BEHIND ME.
I SEE THE FACE OF A KILLER WHO ISN'T YET OLD ENOUGH TO SHAVE.

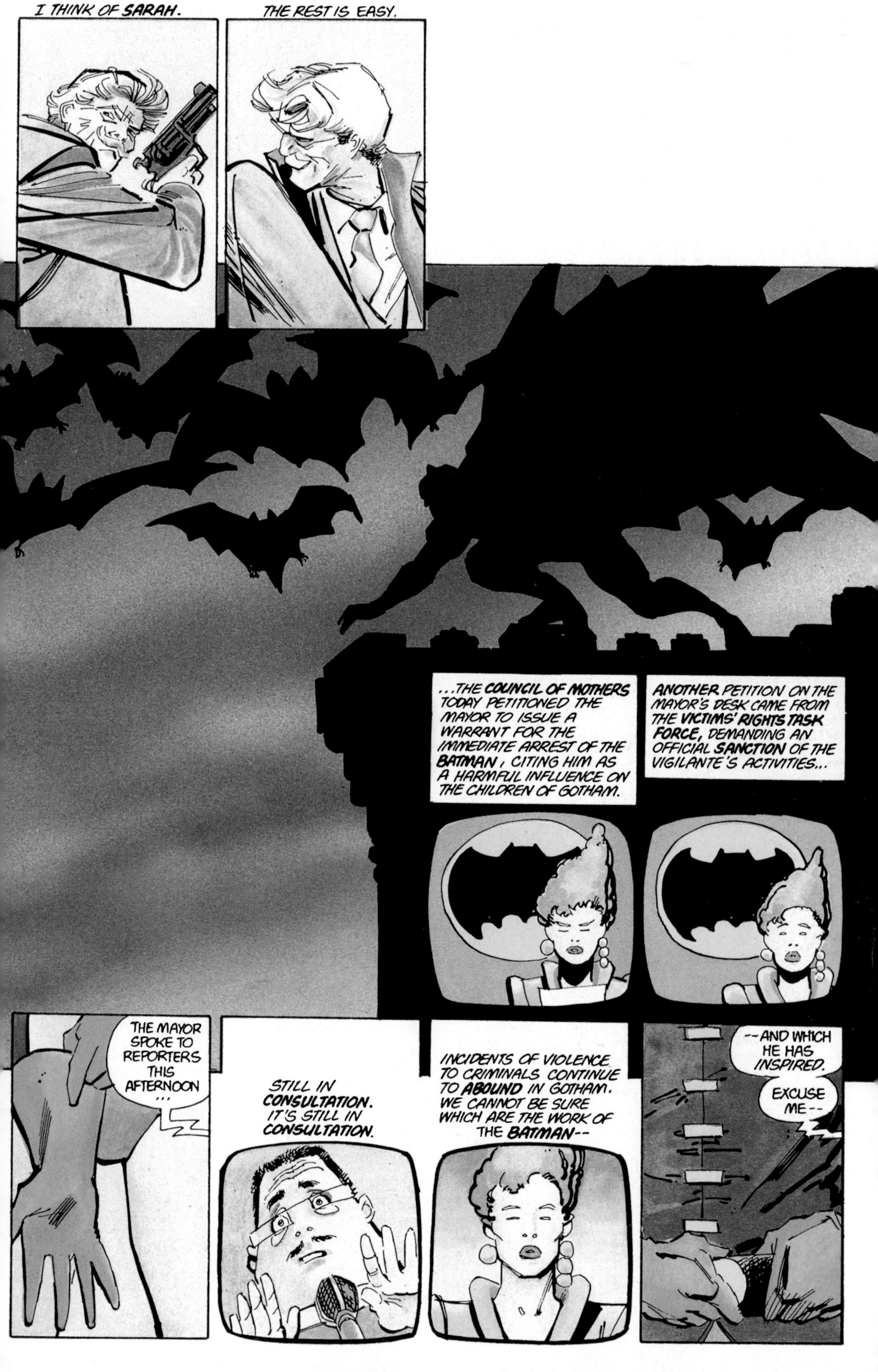
I THINK OF SARAH.
THE REST IS EASY.
...THE COUNCIL OF MOTHERS TODAY PETITIONED THE MAYOR TO ISSUE A WARRANT FOR THE IMMEDIATE ARREST OF THE BATMAN, CITING HIM AS A HARMFUL INFLUENCE ON THE CHILDREN OF GOTHAM.
ANOTHER PETITION ON THE MAYOR'S DESK CAME FROM THE VICTIMS' RIGHTS TASK FORCE, DEMANDING AN OFFICIAL SANCTION OF THE VIGILANTE'S ACTIVITIES...
THE MAYOR SPOKE TO REPORTERS THIS AFTERNOON ...
STILL IN CONSULTATION. IT'S STILL IN CONSULTATION.
INCIDENTS OF VIOLENCE TO CRIMINALS CONTINUE TO ABOUND IN GOTHAM. WE CANNOT BE SURE WHICH ARE THE WORK OF THE BATMAN--
--AND WHICH HE HAS INSPIRED.
EXCUSE ME--

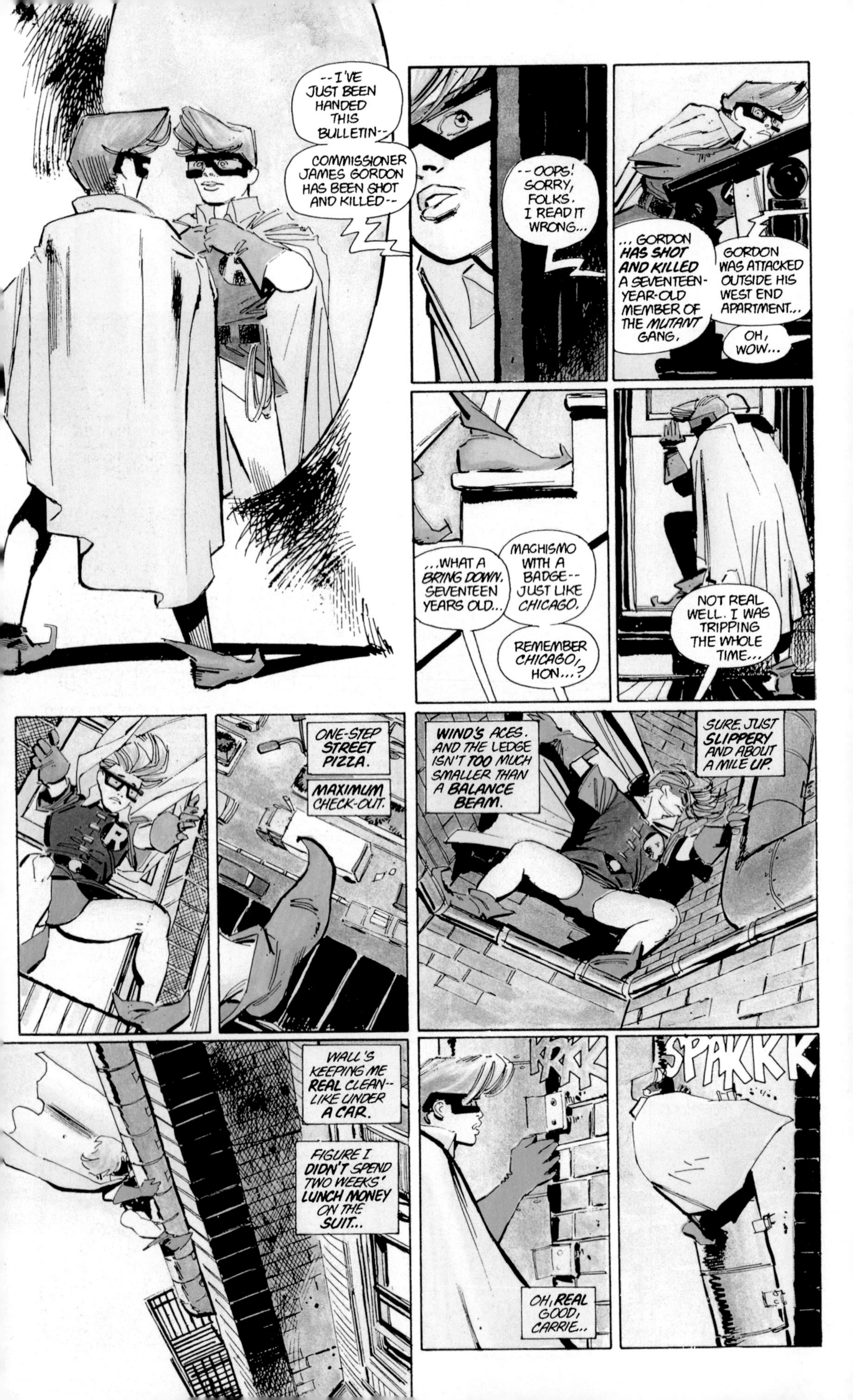
--I'VE JUST BEEN HANDED THIS BULLETIN--
COMMISSIONER JAMES GORDON HAS BEEN SHOT AND KILLED--
--OOPS! SORRY, FOLKS. I READ IT WRONG...
..., GORDON HAS SHOT AND KILLED A SEVENTEEN-YEAR-OLD MEMBER OF THE MUTANT GANG.
GORDON WAS ATTACKED OUTSIDE HIS WEST END APARTMENT...
OH, WOW...
...WHAT A BRING DOWN. SEVENTEEN YEARS OLD...
MACHISMO WITH A BADGE--JUST LIKE CHICAGO.
REMEMBER CHICAGO, HON...?
NOT REAL WELL. I WAS TRIPPING THE WHOLE TIME...
ONE-STEP STREET PIZZA.
MAXIMUM CHECK-OUT.
WIND'S ACES. AND THE LEDGE ISN'T TOO MUCH SMALLER THAN A BALANCE BEAM.
SURE. JUST SLIPPERY AND ABOUT A MILE UP.
WALL'S KEEPING ME REAL CLEAN--LIKE UNDER A CAR.
FIGURE I DIDN'T SPEND TWO WEEKS' LUNCH MONEY ON THE SUIT...
KRKK
OH, REAL GOOD, CARRIE...
SPAKKK

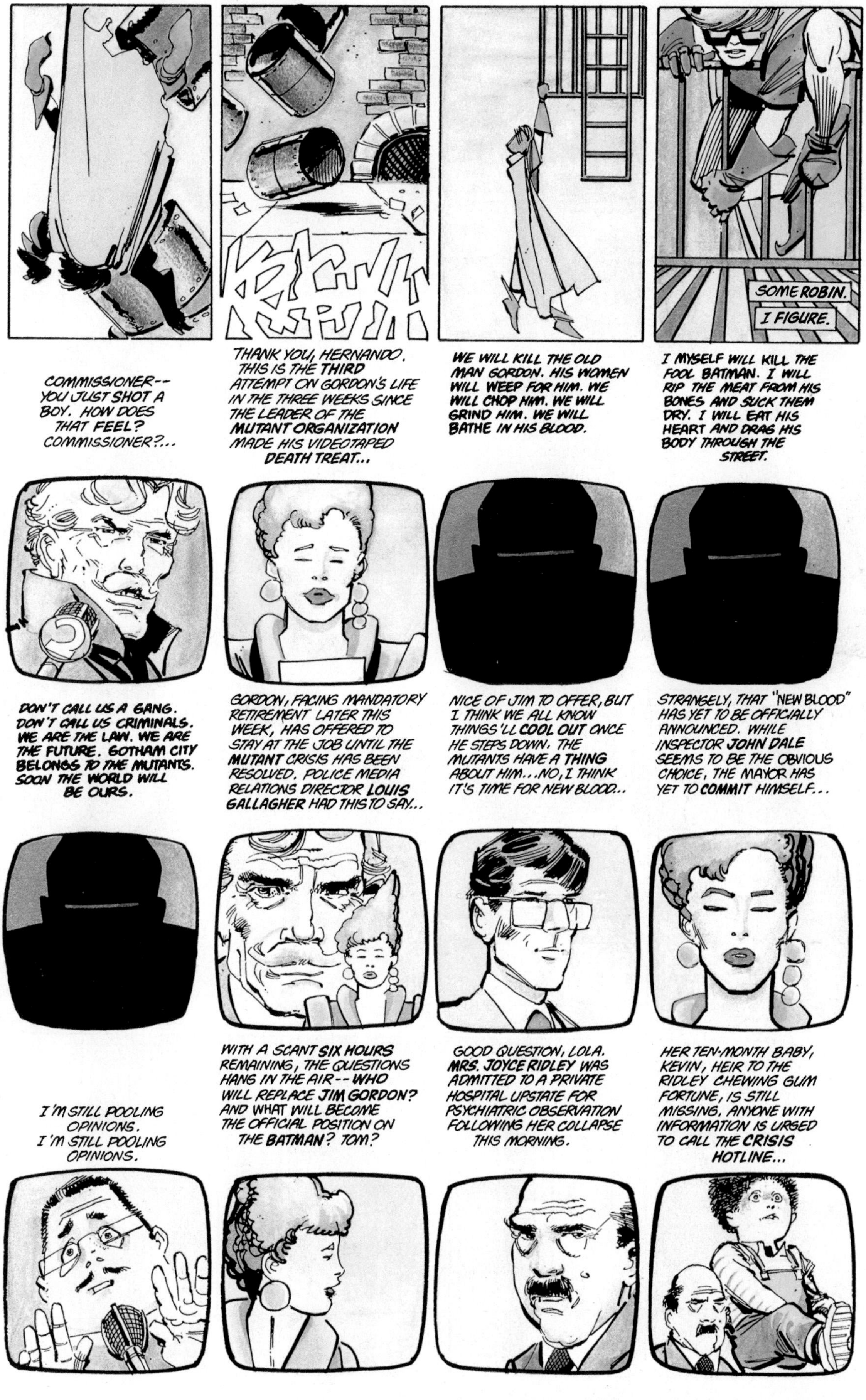
SOME ROBIN.
I FIGURE.
COMMISSIONER-- YOU JUST SHOT A BOY. HOW DOES THAT FEEL? COMMISSIONER?...
THANK YOU, HERNANDO. THIS IS THE THIRD ATTEMPT ON GORDON'S LIFE IN THE THREE WEEKS SINCE THE LEADER OF THE MUTANT ORGANIZATION MADE HIS VIDEOTAPED DEATH TREAT...
WE WILL KILL THE OLD MAN GORDON. HIS WOMEN WILL WEEP FOR HIM. WE WILL CHOP HIM. WE WILL GRIND HIM. WE WILL BATHE IN HIS BLOOD.
I MYSELF WILL KILL THE FOOL BATMAN. I WILL RIP THE MEAT FROM HIS BONES AND SUCK THEM DRY. I WILL EAT HIS HEART AND DRAG HIS BODY THROUGH THE STREET.
DON'T CALL US A GANG. DON'T CALL US CRIMINALS. WE ARE THE LAW. WE ARE THE FUTURE. GOTHAM CITY BELONGS TO THE MUTANTS. SOON THE WORLD WILL BE OURS.
GORDON, FACING MANDATORY RETIREMENT LATER THIS WEEK, HAS OFFERED TO STAY AT THE JOB UNTIL THE MUTANT CRISIS HAS BEEN RESOLVED. POLICE MEDIA RELATIONS DIRECTOR LOUIS GALLAGHER HAD THIS TO SAY...
NICE OF JIM TO OFFER, BUT I THINK WE ALL KNOW THINGS'LL COOL OUT ONCE HE STEPS DOWN. THE MUTANTS HAVE A THING ABOUT HIM... NO, I THINK IT'S TIME FOR NEW BLOOD...
STRANGELY, THAT "NEW BLOOD" HAS YET TO BE OFFICIALLY ANNOUNCED. WHILE INSPECTOR JOHN DALE SEEMS TO BE THE OBVIOUS CHOICE, THE MAYOR HAS YET TO COMMIT HIMSELF...
I'M STILL POOLING OPINIONS. I'M STILL POOLING OPINIONS.
WITH A SCANT SIX HOURS REMAINING, THE QUESTIONS HANG IN THE AIR-- WHO WILL REPLACE JIM GORDON? AND WHAT WILL BECOME THE OFFICIAL POSITION ON THE BATMAN? TOM?
GOOD QUESTION, LOLA. MRS. JOYCE RIDLEY WAS ADMITTED TO A PRIVATE HOSPITAL UPSTATE FOR PSYCHIATRIC OBSERVATION FOLLOWING HER COLLAPSE THIS MORNING.
HER TEN-MONTH BABY, KEVIN, HEIR TO THE RIDLEY CHEWING GUM FORTUNE, IS STILL MISSING. ANYONE WITH INFORMATION IS URGED TO CALL THE CRISIS HOTLINE...

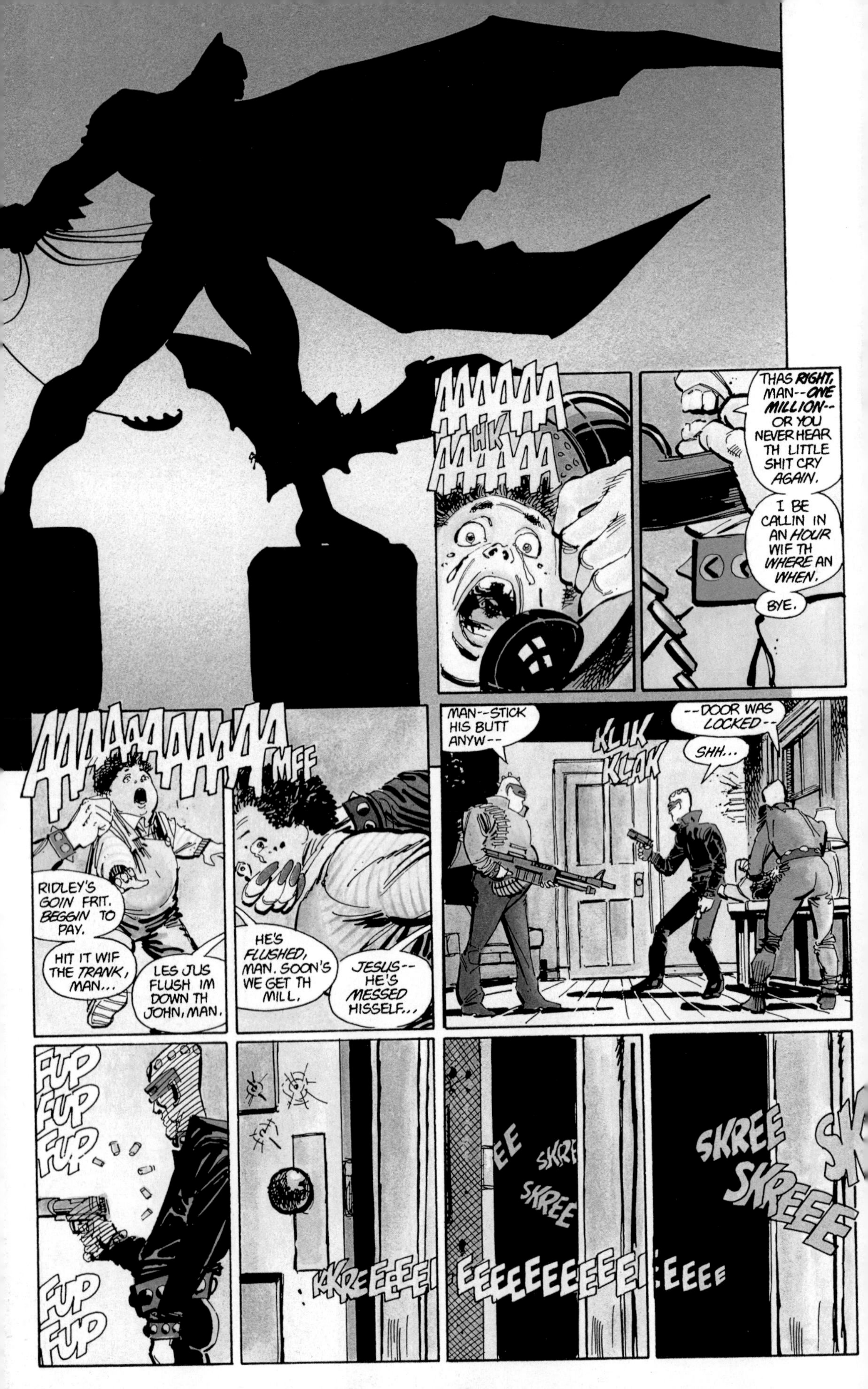
AAAAAA AHK AAAAAA
THAS RIGHT, MAN--ONE MILLION--OR YOU NEVER HEAR TH LITTLE SHIT CRY AGAIN.
I BE CALLIN IN AN HOUR WIF TH WHERE AN WHEN.
BYE.
AAAAAAAAAAA MFF
RIDLEY'S GOIN FRIT. BEGGIN TO PAY.
HIT IT WIF THE TRANK, MAN...
LES JUS FLUSH IM DOWN TH JOHN, MAN.
HE'S FLUSHED, MAN. SOON'S WE GET TH MILL.
JESUS--HE'S MESSED HISSELF...
MAN--STICK HIS BUTT ANYW--
KLIK KLAK
--DOOR WAS LOCKED--
SHH...
FUP FUP FUP
FUP FUP
KKREEEEEEEEEEEEEEEEEEEEEE
SKREE
SKREE
SKREE
SKREE
SKREEEE

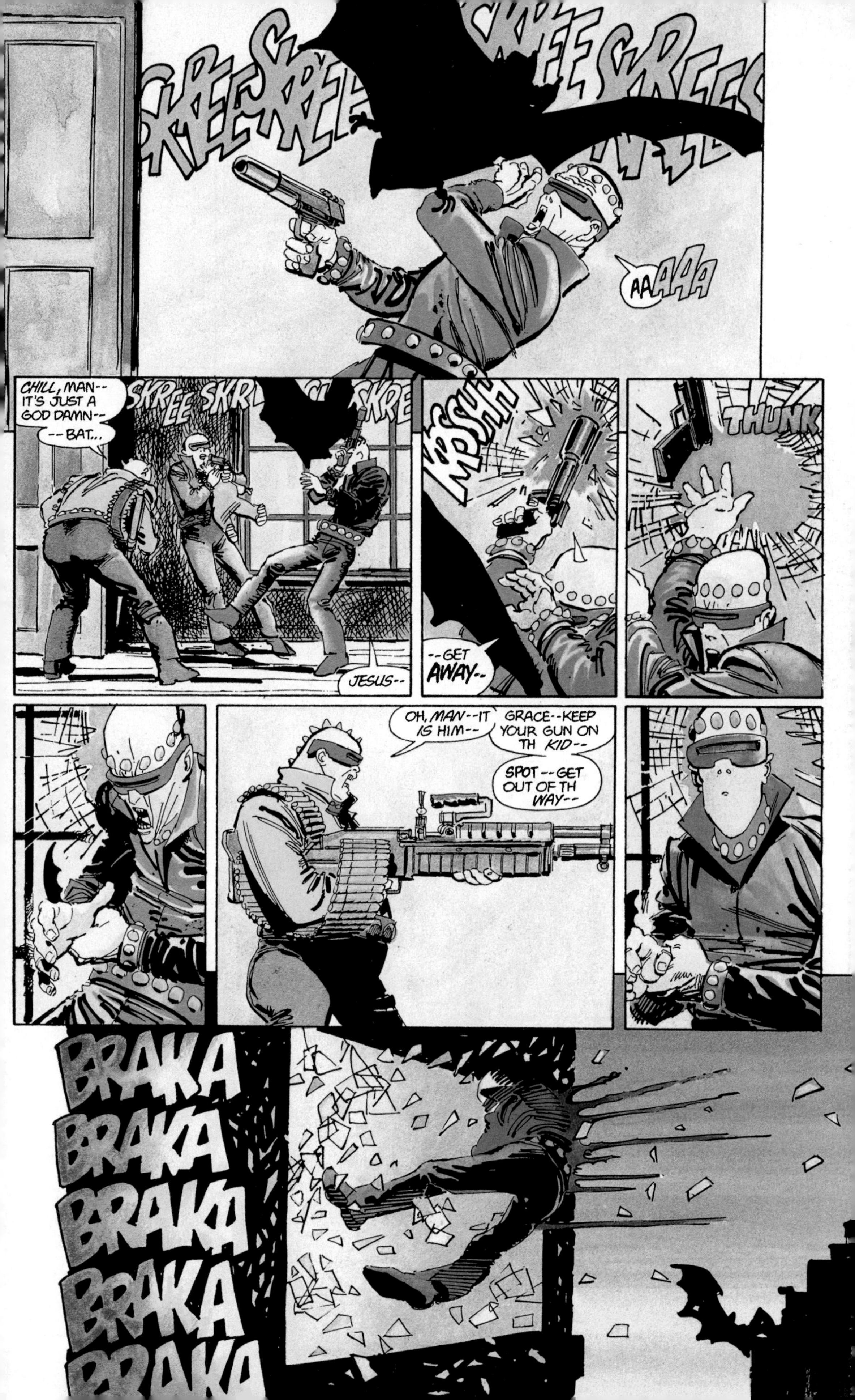

SKREE SKREE SKREE SKREE
AAAAAA
CHILL, MAN-- IT'S JUST A GOD DAMN--
--BAT...
SKREE SKR SKRE
JESUS--
WHSSH
--GET AWAY--
THUNK
OH, MAN--IT IS HIM--
GRACE--KEEP YOUR GUN ON TH KID--
SPOT--GET OUT OF TH WAY--
BRAKA
BRAKA
BRAKA
BRAKA
BRAKA

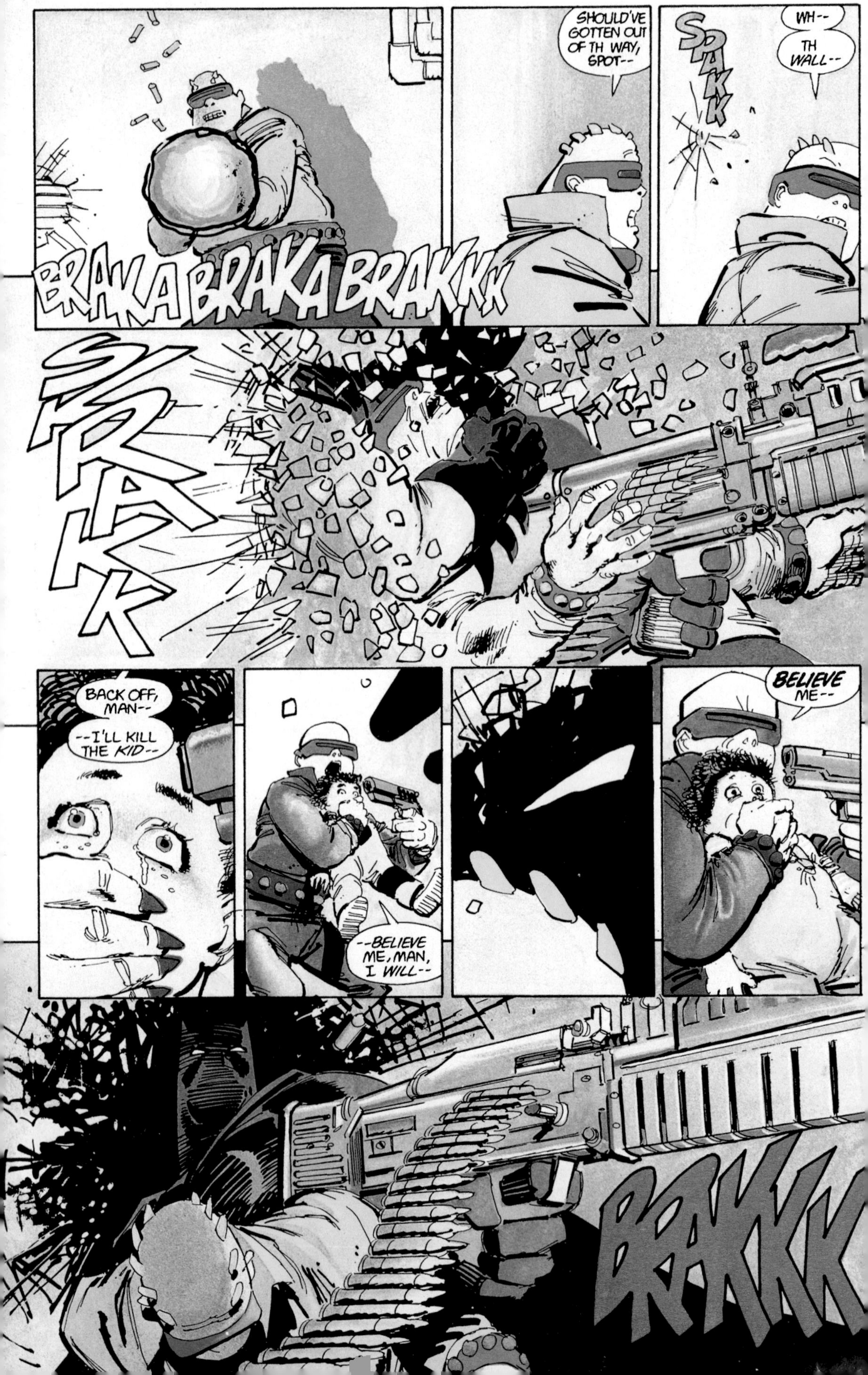
BRAKA BRAKA BRAKKK
SHOULD'VE GOTTEN OUT OF TH WAY, SPOT--
SPAKK
WH--
TH WALL--
SPRAKK
BACK OFF, MAN--
--I'LL KILL THE KID--
--BELIEVE ME, MAN, I WILL--
BELIEVE ME--
BRAKKK

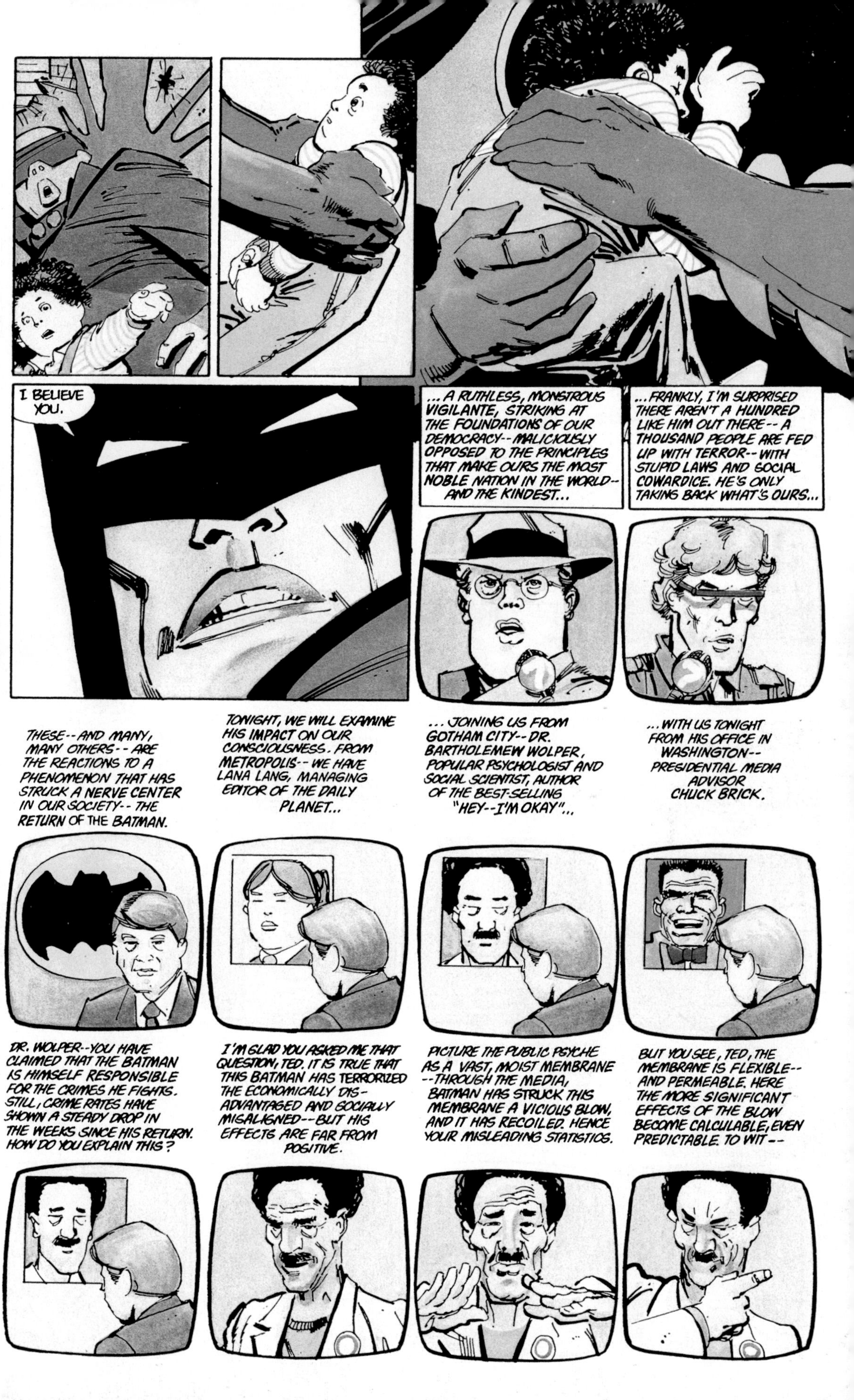
I BELIEVE YOU.
...A RUTHLESS, MONSTROUS VIGILANTE, STRIKING AT THE FOUNDATIONS OF OUR DEMOCRACY--MALICIOUSLY OPPOSED TO THE PRINCIPLES THAT MAKE OURS THE MOST NOBLE NATION IN THE WORLD--AND THE KINDEST...
...FRANKLY, I'M SURPRISED THERE AREN'T A HUNDRED LIKE HIM OUT THERE--A THOUSAND PEOPLE ARE FED UP WITH TERROR--WITH STUPID LAWS AND SOCIAL COWARDICE. HE'S ONLY TAKING BACK WHAT'S OURS...
THESE--AND MANY, MANY OTHERS--ARE THE REACTIONS TO A PHENOMENON THAT HAS STRUCK A NERVE CENTER IN OUR SOCIETY--THE RETURN OF THE BATMAN.
TONIGHT, WE WILL EXAMINE HIS IMPACT ON OUR CONSCIOUSNESS. FROM METROPOLIS--WE HAVE LANA LANG, MANAGING EDITOR OF THE DAILY PLANET...
...JOINING US FROM GOTHAM CITY--DR. BARTHOLEMEW WOLPER, POPULAR PSYCHOLOGIST AND SOCIAL SCIENTIST, AUTHOR OF THE BEST-SELLING "HEY--I'M OKAY"...
...WITH US TONIGHT FROM HIS OFFICE IN WASHINGTON--PRESIDENTIAL MEDIA ADVISOR CHUCK BRICK.
DR. WOLPER--YOU HAVE CLAIMED THAT THE BATMAN IS HIMSELF RESPONSIBLE FOR THE CRIMES HE FIGHTS. STILL, CRIME RATES HAVE SHOWN A STEADY DROP IN THE WEEKS SINCE HIS RETURN. HOW DO YOU EXPLAIN THIS?
I'M GLAD YOU ASKED ME THAT QUESTION, TED. IT IS TRUE THAT THIS BATMAN HAS TERRORIZED THE ECONOMICALLY DIS-ADVANTAGED AND SOCIALLY MISALIGNED--BUT HIS EFFECTS ARE FAR FROM POSITIVE.
PICTURE THE PUBLIC PSYCHE AS A VAST, MOIST MEMBRANE--THROUGH THE MEDIA, BATMAN HAS STRUCK THIS MEMBRANE A VICIOUS BLOW, AND IT HAS RECOILED. HENCE YOUR MISLEADING STATISTICS.
BUT YOU SEE, TED, THE MEMBRANE IS FLEXIBLE--AND PERMEABLE. HERE THE MORE SIGNIFICANT EFFECTS OF THE BLOW BECOME CALCULABLE, EVEN PREDICTABLE. TO WIT--

EVERY ANTI-SOCIAL ACT CAN BE TRACED TO *IRRESPONSIBLE MEDIA INPUT*. GIVEN THIS, THE PRESENCE OF SUCH AN ABERRANT, VIOLENT FORCE IN THE MEDIA CAN ONLY LEAD TO ANTI-SOCIAL *PROGRAMMING*.

JUST AS *HARVEY DENT*-- WHO'S RECOVERING STEADILY, THANKS FOR ASKING-- ASSUMED THE ROLE OF *IDEOLOGICAL DOPPELGANGER* TO THE BATMAN, SO A WHOLE NEW *GENERATION*, CONFUSED AND ANGRY--

-- WILL BE BENT TO THE MATRIX OF BATMAN'S PATHOLOGICAL SELF-DELUSION. BATMAN IS, IN THIS CONTEXT-- AND PARDON THE TERM-- A SOCIAL *DISEASE*...

THAT'S THE *DUMBEST* LOAD OF...

LANA-- PLEASE-- THE *NETWORK*--

DIDN'T *SUCK.*

MR. BRICK-- THE PRESIDENT HAS REMAINED *SILENT* ON THIS ISSUE. DON'T YOU--AND HE-- FEEL THAT THE NATIONAL *UPROAR* OVER THE BATMAN WARRANTS, IF NOT ACTION, A STATEMENT OF *POSITION?*

HECK, TED. HE'LL GET AROUND TO A *PRESS CONFERENCE* SOONER OR LATER. BUT THE PRESIDENT'S GOT TO KEEP HIS EYE ON THE *BIG PICTURE*, Y'KNOW? AND THIS *BATMAN* FLAPTRAP, WELL...

...IT'S NOISY, ALL RIGHT. THAT BIG *CAPE* AND POINTY *EARS* -- IT'S GREAT *SHOW BIZ.* AND YOU KNOW THE *PRESIDENT* KNOWS HIS *SHOW BIZ*. YOU JUST KEEP YOUR *SHORTS* ON, TED...

...PRETTY SOON NOW THE *RATINGS'LL* DROP ON THIS ONE AND IT'LL BLOW *OVER.* BESIDES, I THINK THE WHOLE THING'S JUST AS LIKELY A *HOAX*. NETWORKS'VE DONE *WORSE.*

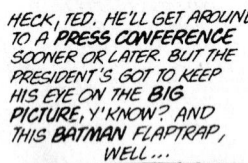 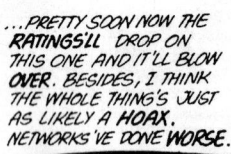

I MEAN, BATBOY'D BE PUSHING *SIXTY* BY NOW-- IF HE EVER WAS REAL. FUNNY NOBODY'S EVER TAKEN A *PICTURE* OF HIM... *MIGHTY* FUNNY, I SAY...

MISS LANG, YOU ARE THE BATMAN'S MOST *VOCAL* SUPPORTER. HOW CAN YOU CONDONE BEHAVIOR THAT'S SO BLATANTLY *ILLEGAL?* WHAT ABOUT *DUE PROCESS--CIVIL RIGHTS?*

WE LIVE IN THE *SHADOW* OF CRIME, TED, WITH THE UNSPOKEN UNDERSTANDING THAT WE ARE *VICTIMS*-- OF *FEAR*, OF *VIOLENCE*, OF SOCIAL *IMPOTENCE*.

A *MAN* HAS RISEN TO SHOW US THAT THE POWER IS, AND ALWAYS HAS BEEN, IN *OUR* HANDS. WE ARE UNDER *SIEGE* -- HE'S SHOWING US THAT WE CAN *RESIST.*

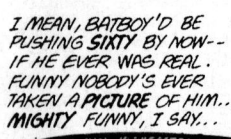   

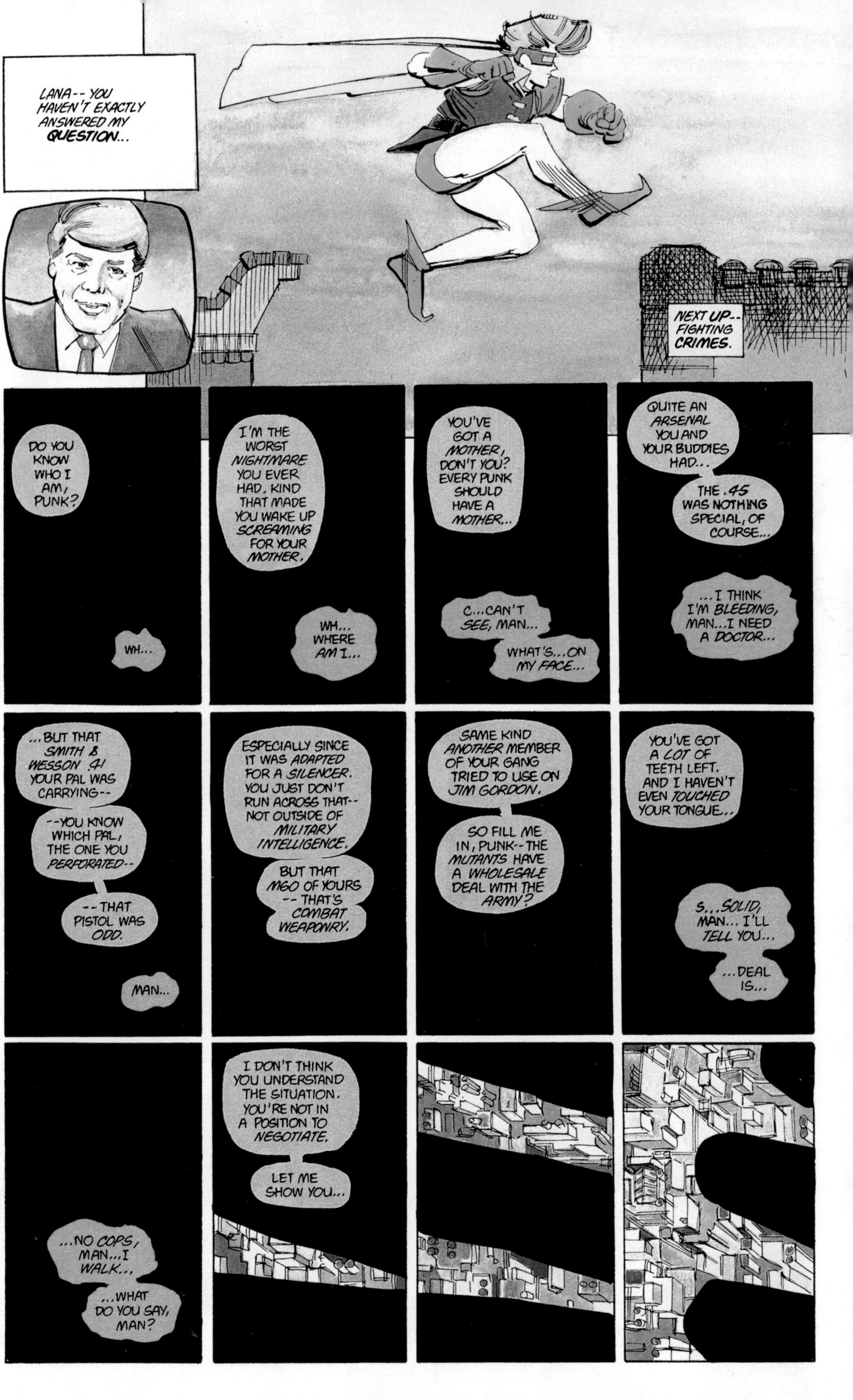
LANA-- YOU HAVEN'T EXACTLY ANSWERED MY QUESTION...
NEXT UP-- FIGHTING CRIMES.
DO YOU KNOW WHO I AM, PUNK?
WH...
I'M THE WORST NIGHTMARE YOU EVER HAD. KIND THAT MADE YOU WAKE UP SCREAMING FOR YOUR MOTHER.
WH... WHERE AM I...
YOU'VE GOT A MOTHER, DON'T YOU? EVERY PUNK SHOULD HAVE A MOTHER...
C...CAN'T SEE, MAN...
WHAT'S...ON MY FACE...
QUITE AN ARSENAL YOU AND YOUR BUDDIES HAD...
THE .45 WAS NOTHING SPECIAL, OF COURSE...
...I THINK I'M BLEEDING, MAN...I NEED A DOCTOR...
...BUT THAT SMITH & WESSON .41 YOUR PAL WAS CARRYING--
--YOU KNOW WHICH PAL, THE ONE YOU PERFORATED--
--THAT PISTOL WAS ODD.
MAN...
ESPECIALLY SINCE IT WAS ADAPTED FOR A SILENCER. YOU JUST DON'T RUN ACROSS THAT-- NOT OUTSIDE OF MILITARY INTELLIGENCE.
BUT THAT M60 OF YOURS -- THAT'S COMBAT WEAPONRY.
SAME KIND ANOTHER MEMBER OF YOUR GANG TRIED TO USE ON JIM GORDON.
SO FILL ME IN, PUNK-- THE MUTANTS HAVE A WHOLESALE DEAL WITH THE ARMY?
YOU'VE GOT A LOT OF TEETH LEFT. AND I HAVEN'T EVEN TOUCHED YOUR TONGUE...
S...SOLID, MAN... I'LL TELL YOU...
...DEAL IS...
...NO COPS, MAN...I WALK...
...WHAT DO YOU SAY, MAN?
I DON'T THINK YOU UNDERSTAND THE SITUATION. YOU'RE NOT IN A POSITION TO NEGOTIATE.
LET ME SHOW YOU...

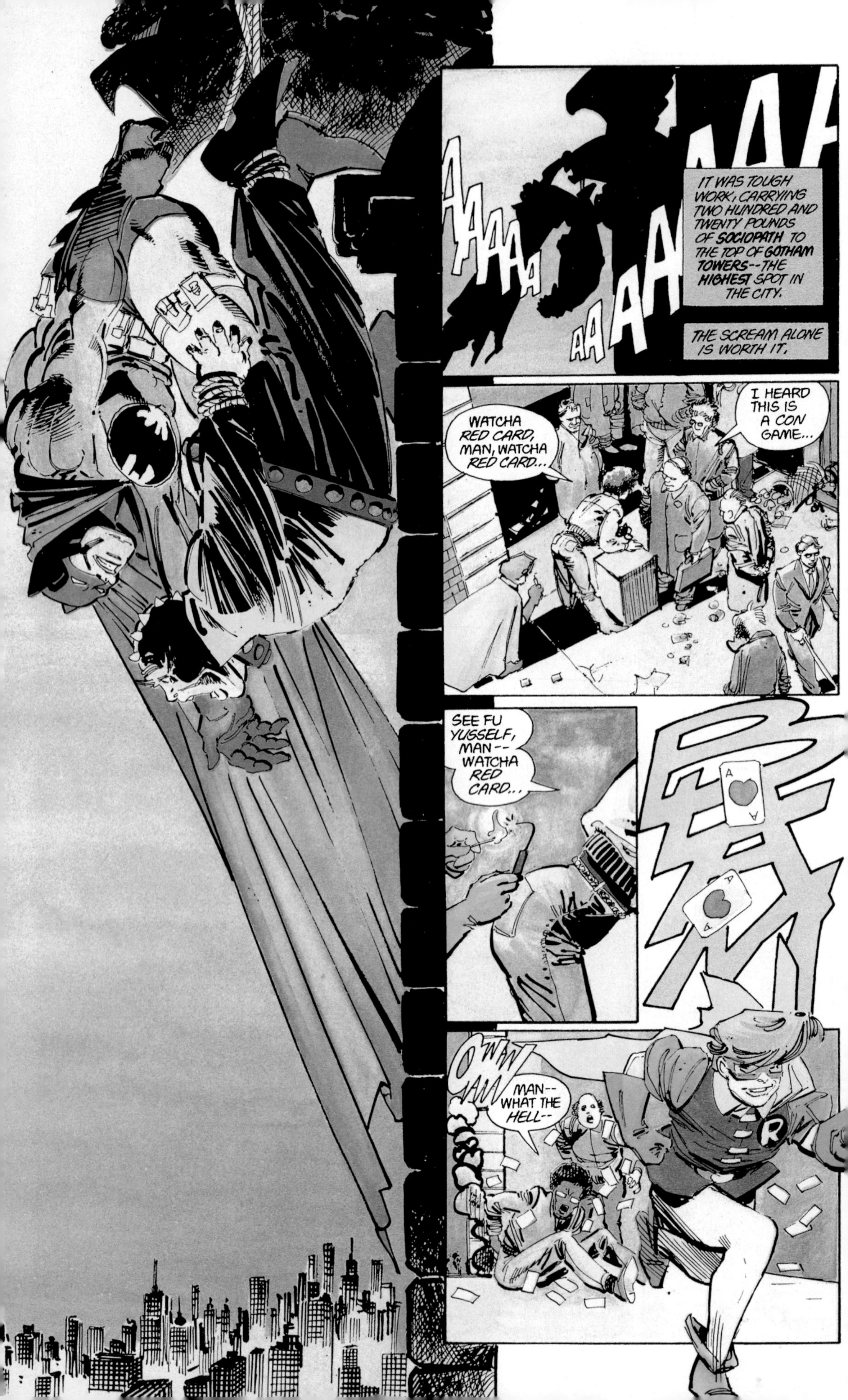
AAAAAAAAAAAAAAA
IT WAS TOUGH WORK, CARRYING TWO HUNDRED AND TWENTY POUNDS OF SOCIOPATH TO THE TOP OF GOTHAM TOWERS--THE HIGHEST SPOT IN THE CITY.
THE SCREAM ALONE IS WORTH IT.
WATCHA RED CARD, MAN, WATCHA RED CARD...
I HEARD THIS IS A CON GAME...
SEE FU YUSSELF, MAN-- WATCHA RED CARD...
OWAN GAAA
MAN-- WHAT THE HELL--
R

IT'S THE **TRAIN**, THINKS MARGARET CORCORAN, MY LEGS NEVER HURT LIKE THIS WHEN I WAIT THE TABLES.

THE **TRAIN**-- IT WON'T LET THE PAIN LIE IN MY **CALVES** WHERE I'M **USED** TO IT.

VARICOSE VEINS, THE DOCTOR SAID. EASY FOR HIM TO TELL HER TO QUIT HER JOB. EASY FOR **HIM** TO TALK ABOUT **SURGERY.**

SURGERY. WITH NO INSURANCE AND TWO PAYMENTS LEFT ON JAMIE'S BRACES AND THE TURN-OFF NOTICE FROM THE ELECTRIC COMPANY WITH WINTER ON ITS WAY,

SHE FEELS THE METAL SQUARE INSIDE HER PURSE AND SMILES.

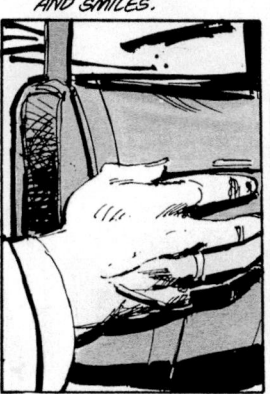

ALMOST NOBODY TIPS ANYMORE, BUT AN UPTOWN DRUNK LEFT TEN DOLLARS ON THE TABLE TONIGHT. WHAT WITH THE TURN-OFF NOTICE IT WAS WRONG TO SPEND THE TIP ON THE PAIN.

BUT YOUNG ROBERT'S **ART TEACHER** SAYS HE HAS **TALENT**...

SHE PICTURES ROBERT'S ABLE LITTLE HANDS, HIS EAGER SMILE...

HER **PURSE STRAP** BITES INTO HER SHOULDER...

...AND MARGARET CORCORAN, WHO HAD NOT PLEADED WITH BLUE CROSS WHEN THEY CANCELLED HER INSURANCE OR WITH **CITICORP** WHEN THEY REPOSSESSED HER CAR...

...BEGS LIKE A WINO FOR A TEN-DOLLAR PAINT SET.

SHE FEELS HER PURSE HIT HER STOMACH AS THE TRAIN RUMBLES TO A STOP. SHE HEARS THEM LAUGH.

SHE LANDS HARD ON THE CEMENT, BUT IT ONLY HURTS.

SHE FEELS THE SQUARE OF METAL AND THANKS GOD AND CAN'T HELP BUT CRY.

THEN SHE FEELS SOMETHING HEAVY AND ROUND LIKE AN APPLE IN HER PURSE...

WOMAN EXPLODES IN SUBWAY STATION-- FILM AT ELEVEN.

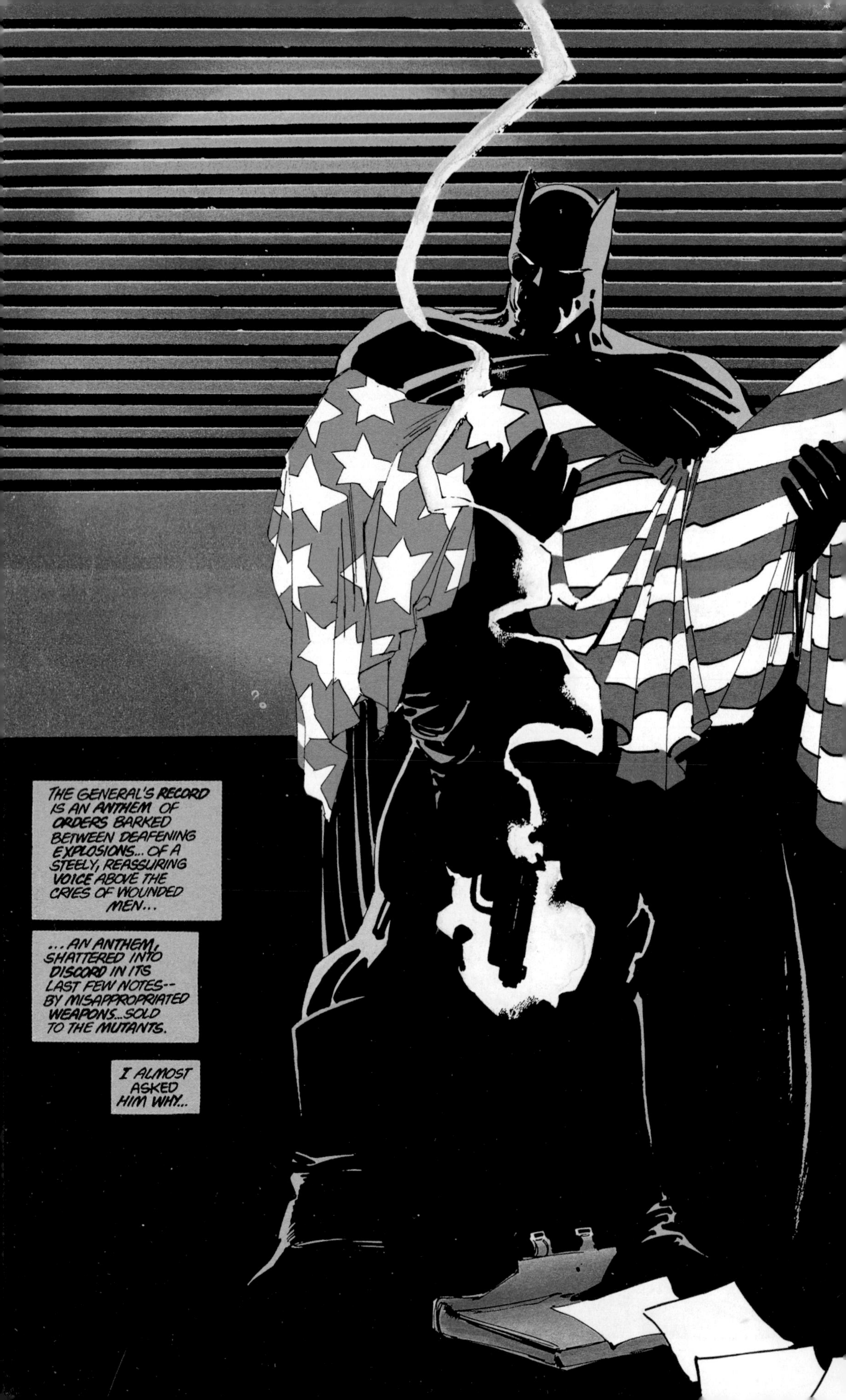
THE GENERAL'S RECORD IS AN ANTHEM OF ORDERS BARKED BETWEEN DEAFENING EXPLOSIONS... OF A STEELY, REASSURING VOICE ABOVE THE CRIES OF WOUNDED MEN...
... AN ANTHEM, SHATTERED INTO DISCORD IN ITS LAST FEW NOTES-- BY MISAPPROPRIATED WEAPONS...SOLD TO THE MUTANTS.
I ALMOST ASKED HIM WHY...

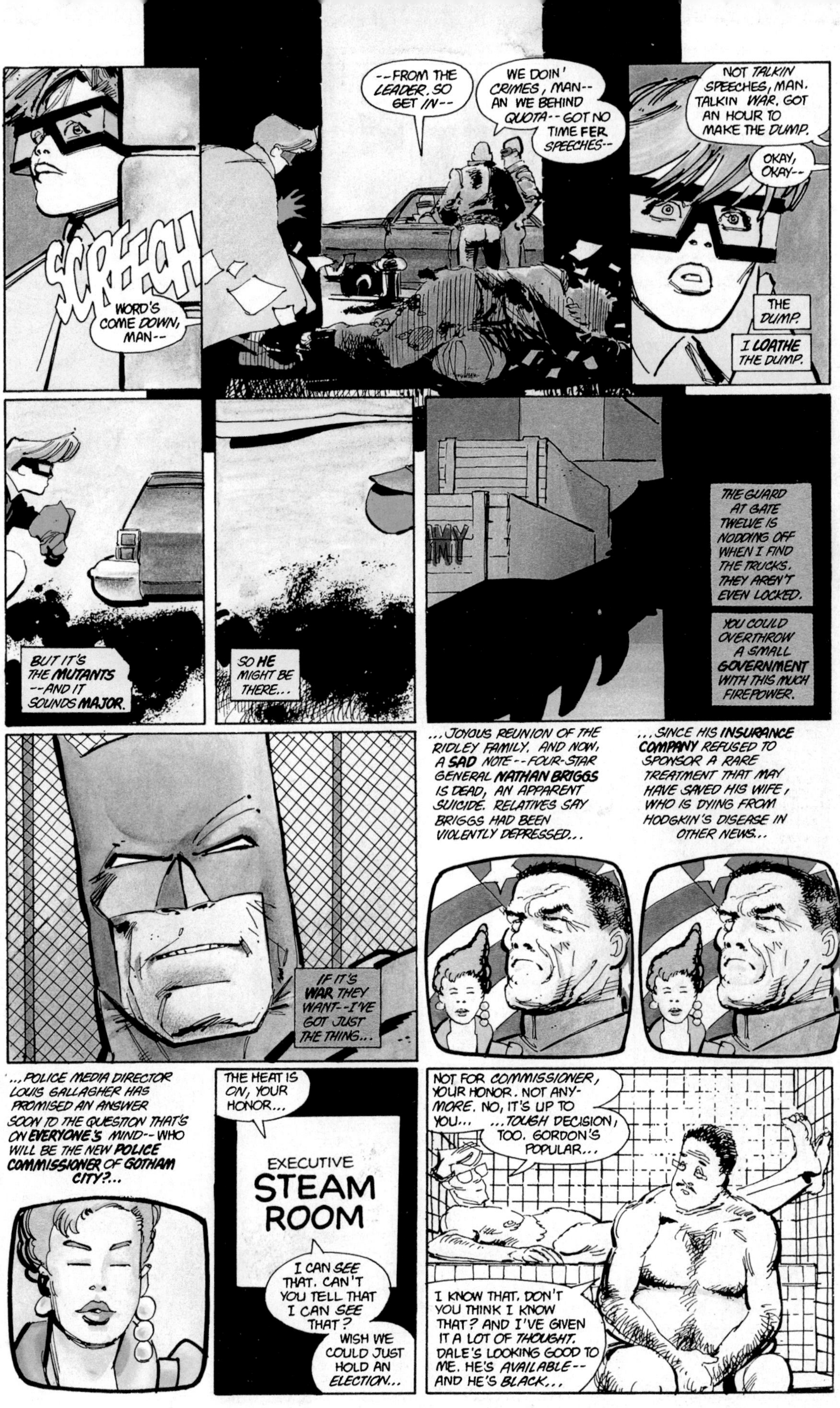
SCREECH
WORD'S COME DOWN, MAN--
--FROM THE LEADER. SO GET IN--
WE DOIN' CRIMES, MAN-- AN WE BEHIND QUOTA--GOT NO TIME FER SPEECHES--
NOT TALKIN SPEECHES, MAN. TALKIN WAR. GOT AN HOUR TO MAKE THE DUMP.
OKAY, OKAY--
THE DUMP.
I LOATHE THE DUMP.
BUT IT'S THE MUTANTS --AND IT SOUNDS MAJOR.
SO HE MIGHT BE THERE...
THE GUARD AT GATE TWELVE IS NODDING OFF WHEN I FIND THE TRUCKS. THEY AREN'T EVEN LOCKED.
YOU COULD OVERTHROW A SMALL GOVERNMENT WITH THIS MUCH FIREPOWER.
IF IT'S WAR THEY WANT--I'VE GOT JUST THE THING...
...JOYOUS REUNION OF THE RIDLEY FAMILY. AND NOW, A SAD NOTE--FOUR-STAR GENERAL NATHAN BRIGGS IS DEAD, AN APPARENT SUICIDE. RELATIVES SAY BRIGGS HAD BEEN VIOLENTLY DEPRESSED...
...SINCE HIS INSURANCE COMPANY REFUSED TO SPONSOR A RARE TREATMENT THAT MAY HAVE SAVED HIS WIFE, WHO IS DYING FROM HODGKIN'S DISEASE. IN OTHER NEWS...
...POLICE MEDIA DIRECTOR LOUIS GALLAGHER HAS PROMISED AN ANSWER SOON TO THE QUESTION THAT'S ON EVERYONE'S MIND--WHO WILL BE THE NEW POLICE COMMISSIONER OF GOTHAM CITY?...
THE HEAT IS ON, YOUR HONOR...
EXECUTIVE STEAM ROOM
I CAN SEE THAT. CAN'T YOU TELL THAT I CAN SEE THAT?
WISH WE COULD JUST HOLD AN ELECTION...
NOT FOR COMMISSIONER, YOUR HONOR. NOT ANY-MORE. NO, IT'S UP TO YOU...
...TOUGH DECISION, TOO. GORDON'S POPULAR...
I KNOW THAT. DON'T YOU THINK I KNOW THAT? AND I'VE GIVEN IT A LOT OF THOUGHT. DALE'S LOOKING GOOD TO ME. HE'S AVAILABLE-- AND HE'S BLACK...

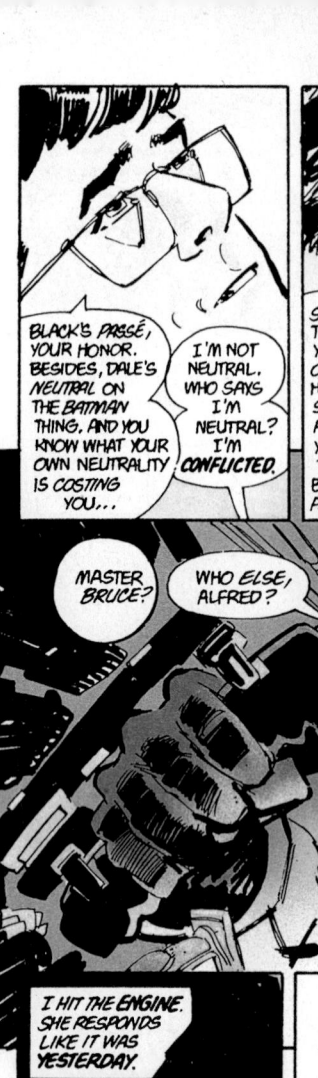

BLACK'S *PASSÉ,* YOUR HONOR. BESIDES, DALE'S *NEUTRAL* ON THE *BATMAN* THING, AND YOU KNOW WHAT YOUR OWN NEUTRALITY IS COSTING YOU...

I'M NOT NEUTRAL. WHO SAYS I'M NEUTRAL? I'M *CONFLICTED.*

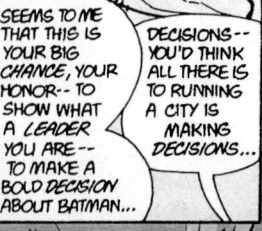

SEEMS TO ME THAT THIS IS YOUR *BIG CHANCE,* YOUR HONOR-- TO SHOW WHAT A *LEADER* YOU ARE-- TO MAKE A BOLD *DECISION* ABOUT BATMAN...

DECISIONS-- YOU'D THINK ALL THERE IS TO RUNNING A CITY IS MAKING DECISIONS...

WELL, ALL *RIGHT,* GALLAGHER-- I'LL MAKE A *DECISION.* I'LL *SHOW* THEM WHO'S BOSS. ON MY OWN PRIVATE *AUTHORITY*-- --I ASSIGN YOU THE TASK OF FINDING ME A POLICE COMMISSIONER.

I ALREADY *HAVE,* SIR.

MASTER BRUCE?

WHO *ELSE,* ALFRED?

OF COURSE, SIR. IT'S JUST THAT THE SIGNAL IS COMING FROM INSIDE THE--

THAT'S *RIGHT,* ALFRED. I'M TAKING HER *OUT.*

I HIT THE *ENGINE.* SHE RESPONDS LIKE IT WAS *YESTERDAY.*

IT *IS* YESTERDAY...

I AM EXCITED--NO, *THRILLED*--CAN'T YOU TELL I'M THRILLED?--TO GIVE YOU THE NEXT *POLICE COMMISSIONER* OF GOTHAM CITY...

...CAPTAIN ELLEN YINDEL.

THE *YOUNGEST* EVER TO HOLD THE OFFICE--AND, OF COURSE, THE FIRST *WOMAN*-- ELLEN YINDEL BRINGS WITH HER AN *ASTONISHING* ARREST RECORD FROM *CHICAGO.* SHE WAS QUICK TO ANSWER ON THE SUBJECT OF *BATMAN*...

I'M SURPRISED THERE *IS* A CONTROVERSY. HIS ACTIONS ARE CATEGORICALLY *CRIMINAL.* I WILL HAVE HIM BROUGHT TO TRIAL. EXCUSE ME?...

...YES. I'LL BE SPECIFIC. MY FIRST ACT AS *POLICE COMMISSIONER* WILL BE TO ISSUE AN *ARREST WARRANT* FOR THE BATMAN ON CHARGES OF *ASSAULT, BREAKING AND ENTERING, CREATING A PUBLIC HAZARD*...

LITTLE MORE THAN *HALF* THE AGE OF THE MAN SHE'S *REPLACING,* ELLEN YINDEL IS--

A WOMAN. CHRIST ALMIGHTY...

KLIK

DID YOU SAY SOMETHING, JIM?

...NOTHING, SWEETHEART...

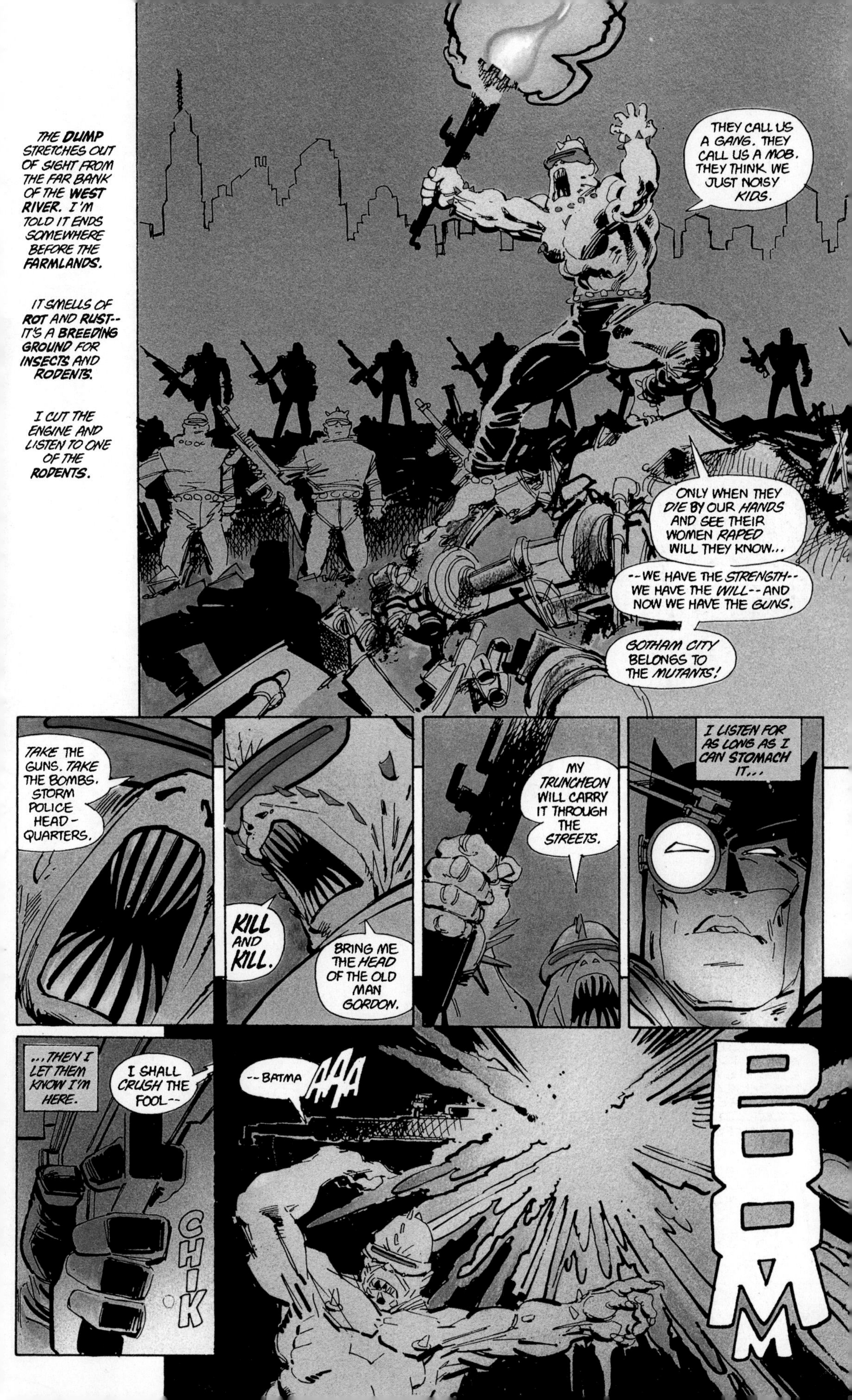
THE DUMP STRETCHES OUT OF SIGHT FROM THE FAR BANK OF THE WEST RIVER. I'M TOLD IT ENDS SOMEWHERE BEFORE THE FARMLANDS.
IT SMELLS OF ROT AND RUST-- IT'S A BREEDING GROUND FOR INSECTS AND RODENTS.
I CUT THE ENGINE AND LISTEN TO ONE OF THE RODENTS.
THEY CALL US A GANG. THEY CALL US A MOB. THEY THINK WE JUST NOISY KIDS.
ONLY WHEN THEY DIE BY OUR HANDS AND SEE THEIR WOMEN RAPED WILL THEY KNOW...
--WE HAVE THE STRENGTH-- WE HAVE THE WILL--AND NOW WE HAVE THE GUNS.
GOTHAM CITY BELONGS TO THE MUTANTS!
TAKE THE GUNS. TAKE THE BOMBS. STORM POLICE HEAD-QUARTERS.
KILL AND KILL.
BRING ME THE HEAD OF THE OLD MAN GORDON.
MY TRUNCHEON WILL CARRY IT THROUGH THE STREETS.
I LISTEN FOR AS LONG AS I CAN STOMACH IT...
...THEN I LET THEM KNOW I'M HERE.
I SHALL CRUSH THE FOOL--
CHIK
--BATMA AAA
BOOM

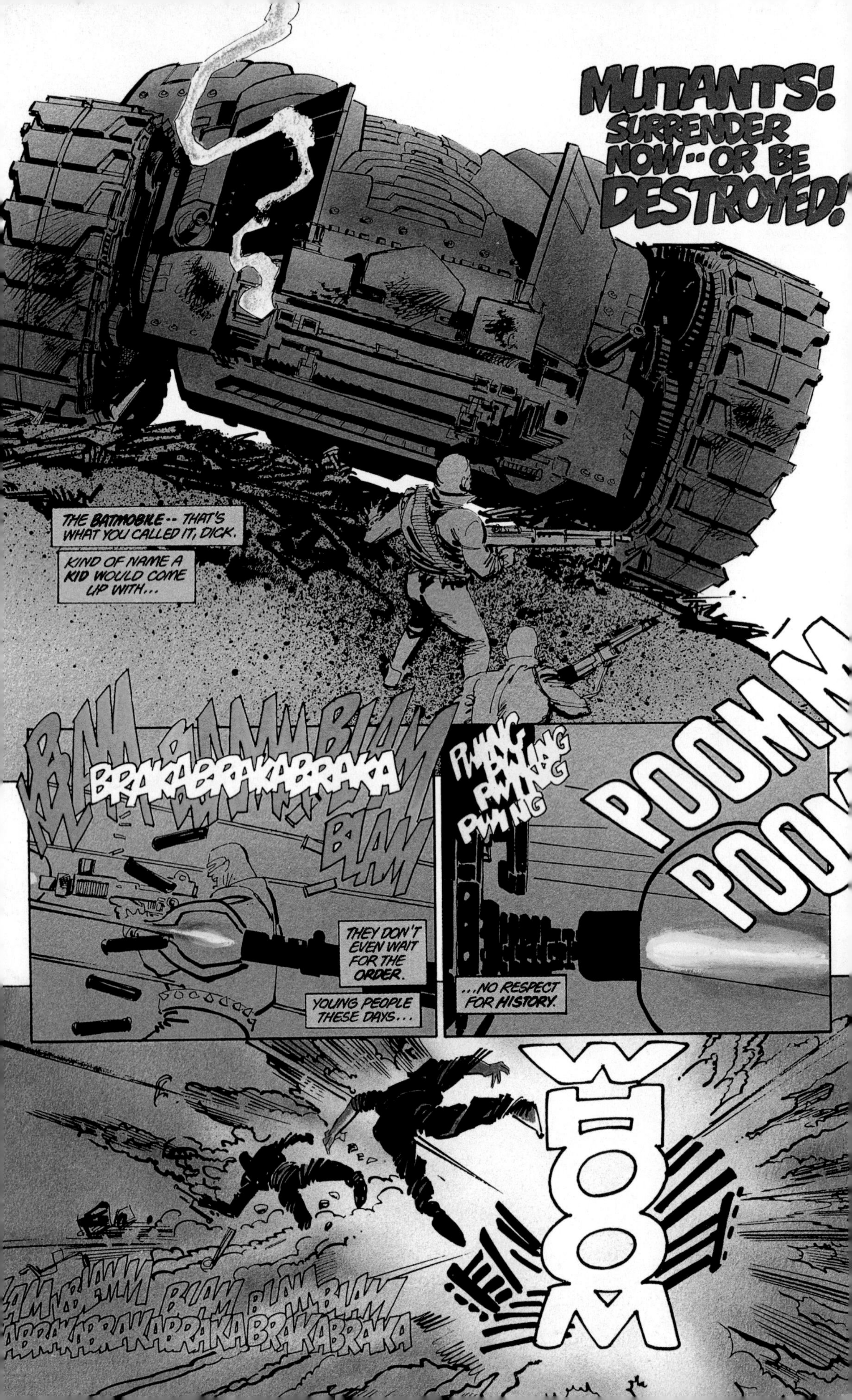

MUTANTS! SURRENDER NOW -- OR BE DESTROYED!
THE BATMOBILE -- THAT'S WHAT YOU CALLED IT, DICK.
KIND OF NAME A KID WOULD COME UP WITH...
BRAKABRAKABRAKA
BLAM
THEY DON'T EVEN WAIT FOR THE ORDER.
YOUNG PEOPLE THESE DAYS...
PWING
PWING
PWING
PWING
POOMM
...NO RESPECT FOR HISTORY.
WHOOM
BLAM
BLAM BLAM
BRAKABRAKABRAKABRAKABRAKA

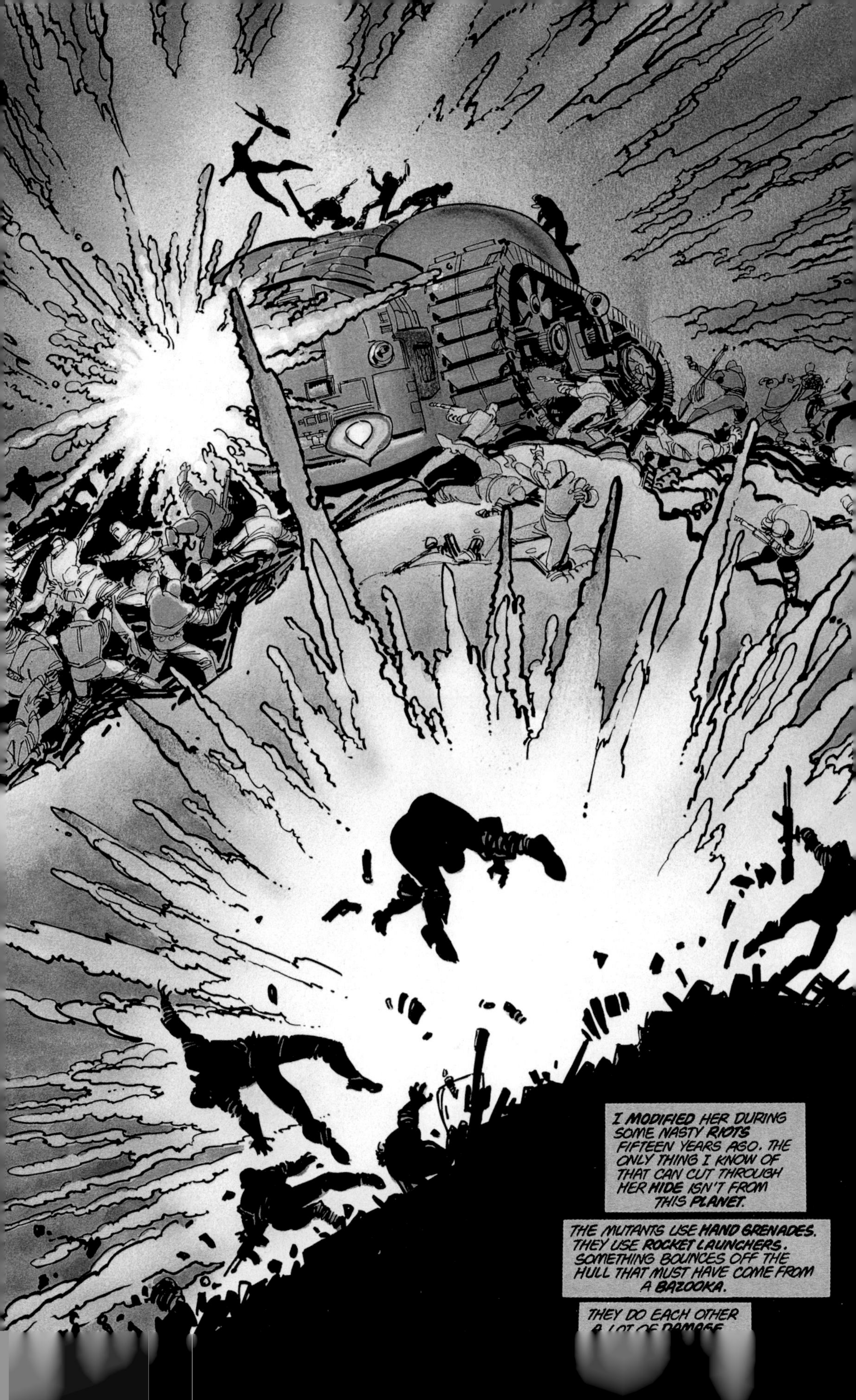
I MODIFIED HER DURING SOME NASTY RIOTS FIFTEEN YEARS AGO. THE ONLY THING I KNOW OF THAT CAN CUT THROUGH HER HIDE ISN'T FROM THIS PLANET.
THE MUTANTS USE HAND GRENADES. THEY USE ROCKET LAUNCHERS. SOMETHING BOUNCES OFF THE HULL THAT MUST HAVE COME FROM A BAZOOKA.
THEY DO EACH OTHER

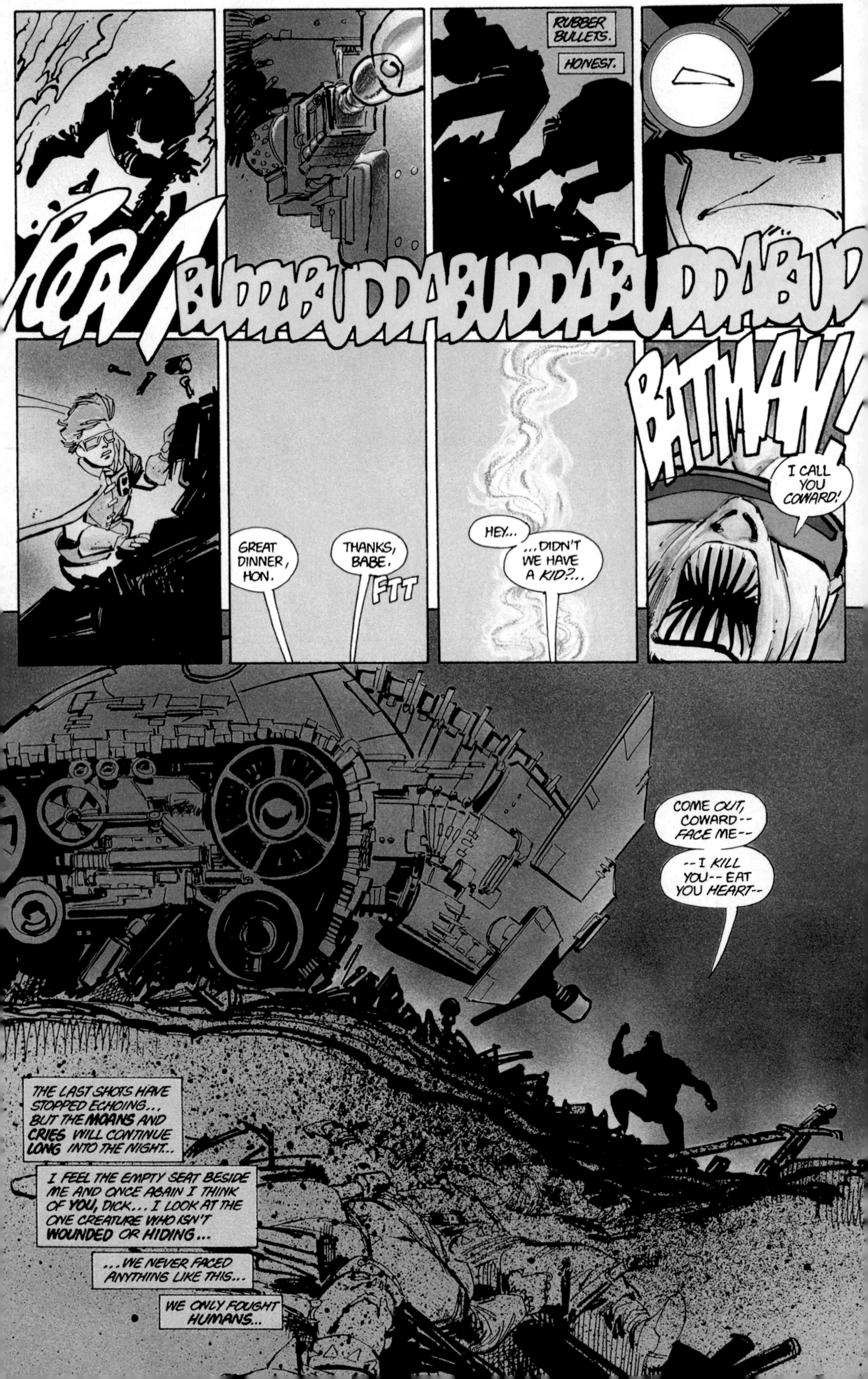

POW
RUBBER BULLETS.
HONEST.
BUDDABUDDABUDDABUDDABUD
GREAT DINNER, HON.
THANKS, BABE.
FTT
HEY...
...DIDN'T WE HAVE A KID?...
BATMAN!
I CALL YOU COWARD!
COME OUT, COWARD-- FACE ME--
--I KILL YOU-- EAT YOU HEART--
THE LAST SHOTS HAVE STOPPED ECHOING... BUT THE MOANS AND CRIES WILL CONTINUE LONG INTO THE NIGHT...
I FEEL THE EMPTY SEAT BESIDE ME AND ONCE AGAIN I THINK OF YOU, DICK... I LOOK AT THE ONE CREATURE WHO ISN'T WOUNDED OR HIDING...
...WE NEVER FACED ANYTHING LIKE THIS...
WE ONLY FOUGHT HUMANS...

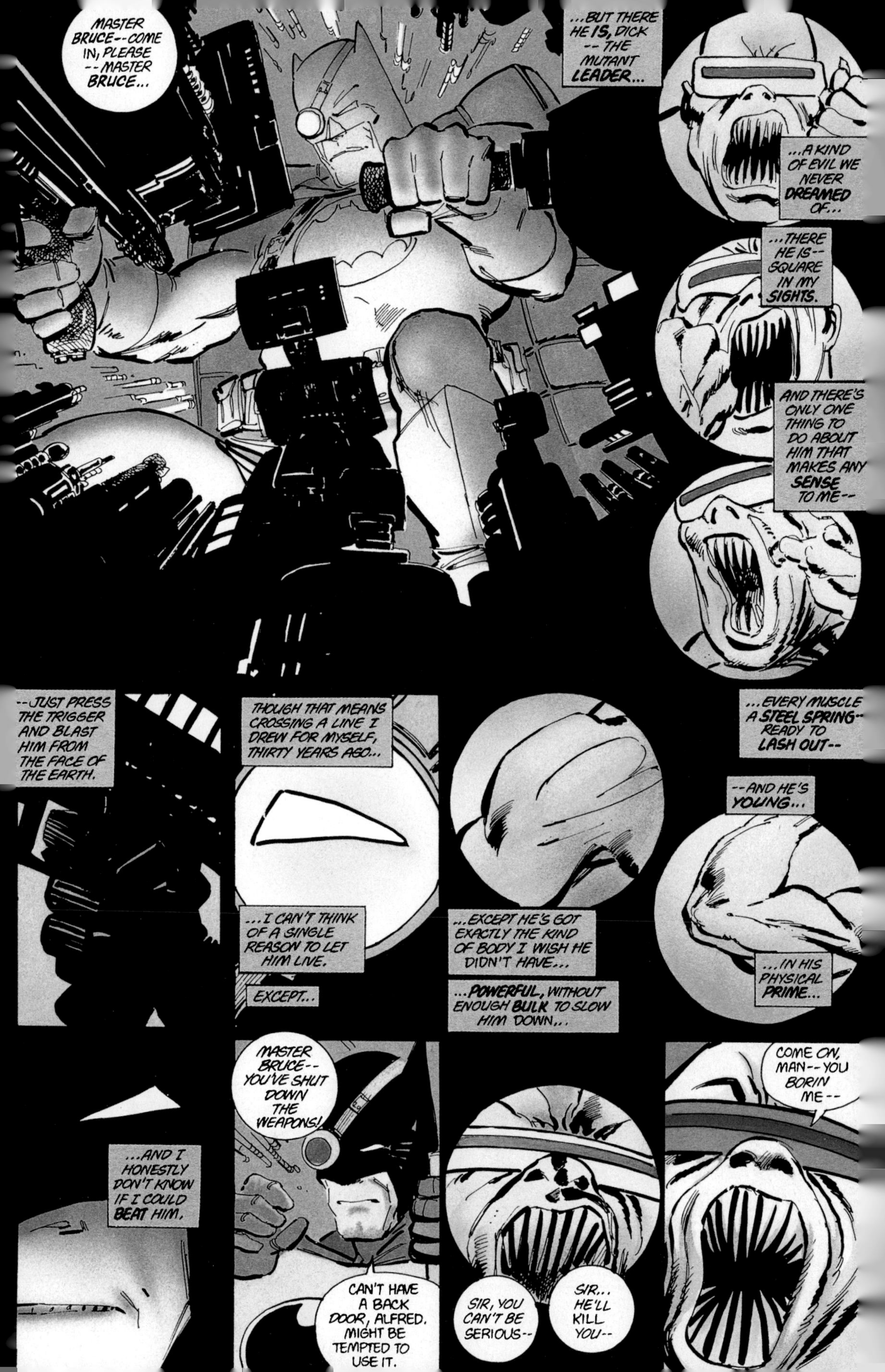
MASTER BRUCE--COME IN, PLEASE --MASTER BRUCE...
...BUT THERE HE IS, DICK -- THE MUTANT LEADER...
...A KIND OF EVIL WE NEVER DREAMED OF...
...THERE HE IS-- SQUARE IN MY SIGHTS.
AND THERE'S ONLY ONE THING TO DO ABOUT HIM THAT MAKES ANY SENSE TO ME--
--JUST PRESS THE TRIGGER AND BLAST HIM FROM THE FACE OF THE EARTH.
THOUGH THAT MEANS CROSSING A LINE I DREW FOR MYSELF, THIRTY YEARS AGO...
...I CAN'T THINK OF A SINGLE REASON TO LET HIM LIVE.
EXCEPT...
...EXCEPT HE'S GOT EXACTLY THE KIND OF BODY I WISH HE DIDN'T HAVE...
...POWERFUL, WITHOUT ENOUGH BULK TO SLOW HIM DOWN...
...EVERY MUSCLE A STEEL SPRING-- READY TO LASH OUT--
--AND HE'S YOUNG...
...IN HIS PHYSICAL PRIME...
...AND I HONESTLY DON'T KNOW IF I COULD BEAT HIM.
MASTER BRUCE-- YOU'VE SHUT DOWN THE WEAPONS!
CAN'T HAVE A BACK DOOR, ALFRED. MIGHT BE TEMPTED TO USE IT.
SIR, YOU CAN'T BE SERIOUS--
SIR... HE'LL KILL YOU--
COME ON, MAN--YOU BORIN ME--

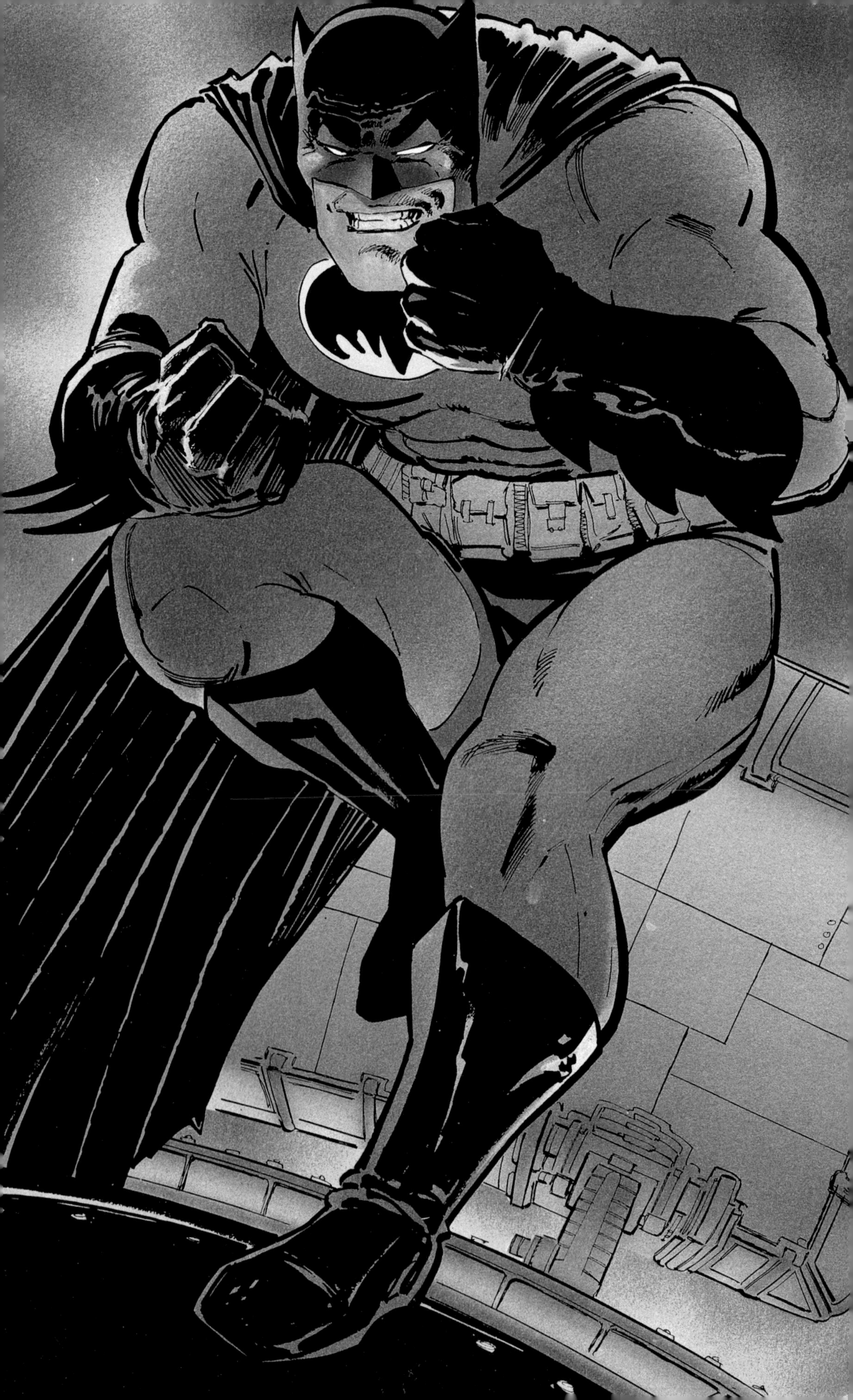

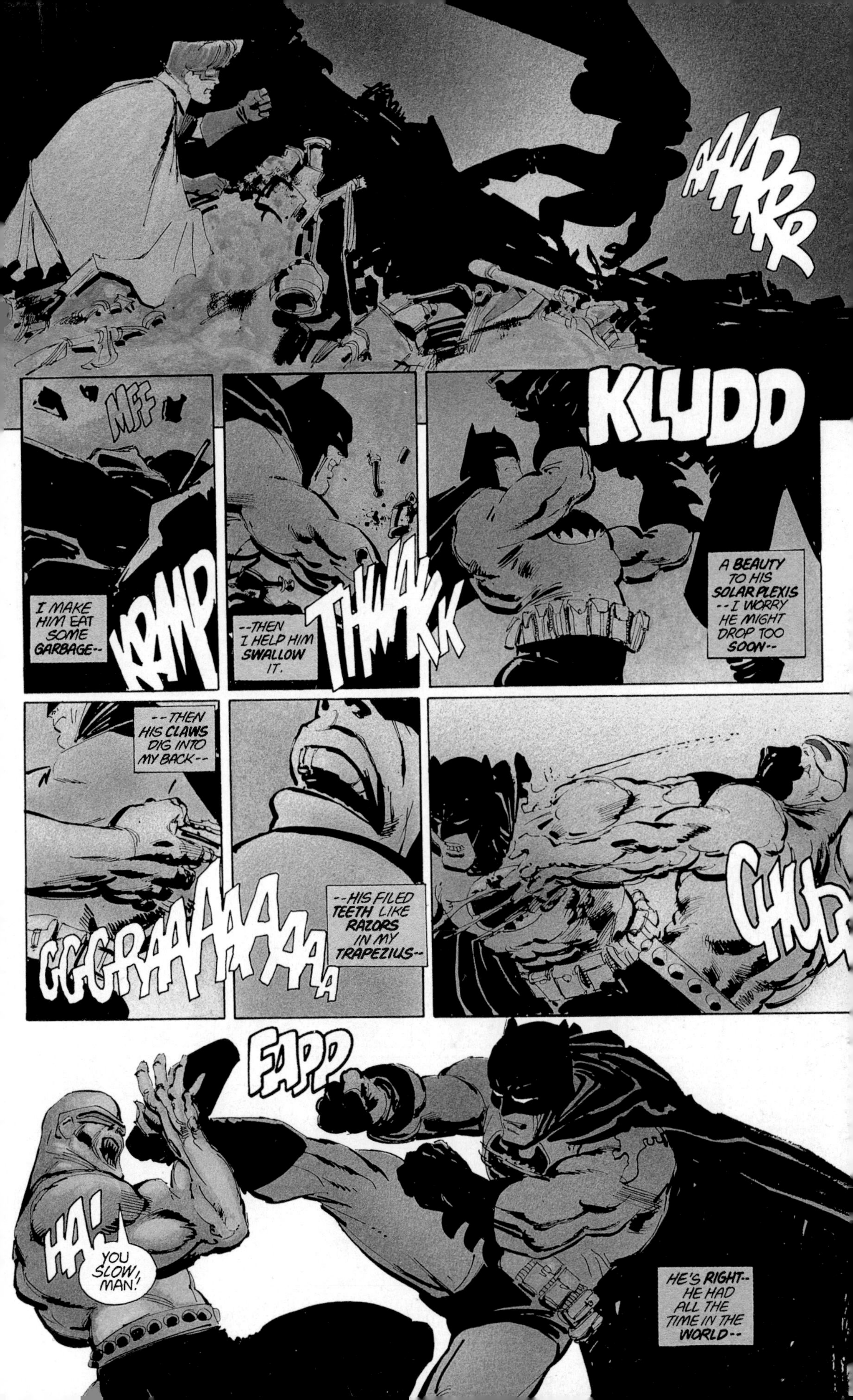

RAAARRR
MFF
I MAKE HIM EAT SOME GARBAGE--
KRAMP
--THEN I HELP HIM SWALLOW IT.
THWAKK
KLUDD
A BEAUTY TO HIS SOLAR PLEXIS --I WORRY HE MIGHT DROP TOO SOON--
--THEN HIS CLAWS DIG INTO MY BACK--
GGGRAAAAAAAAAA
--HIS FILED TEETH LIKE RAZORS IN MY TRAPEZIUS--
FAPP
HA!
YOU SLOW, MAN!
HE'S RIGHT-- HE HAD ALL THE TIME IN THE WORLD--

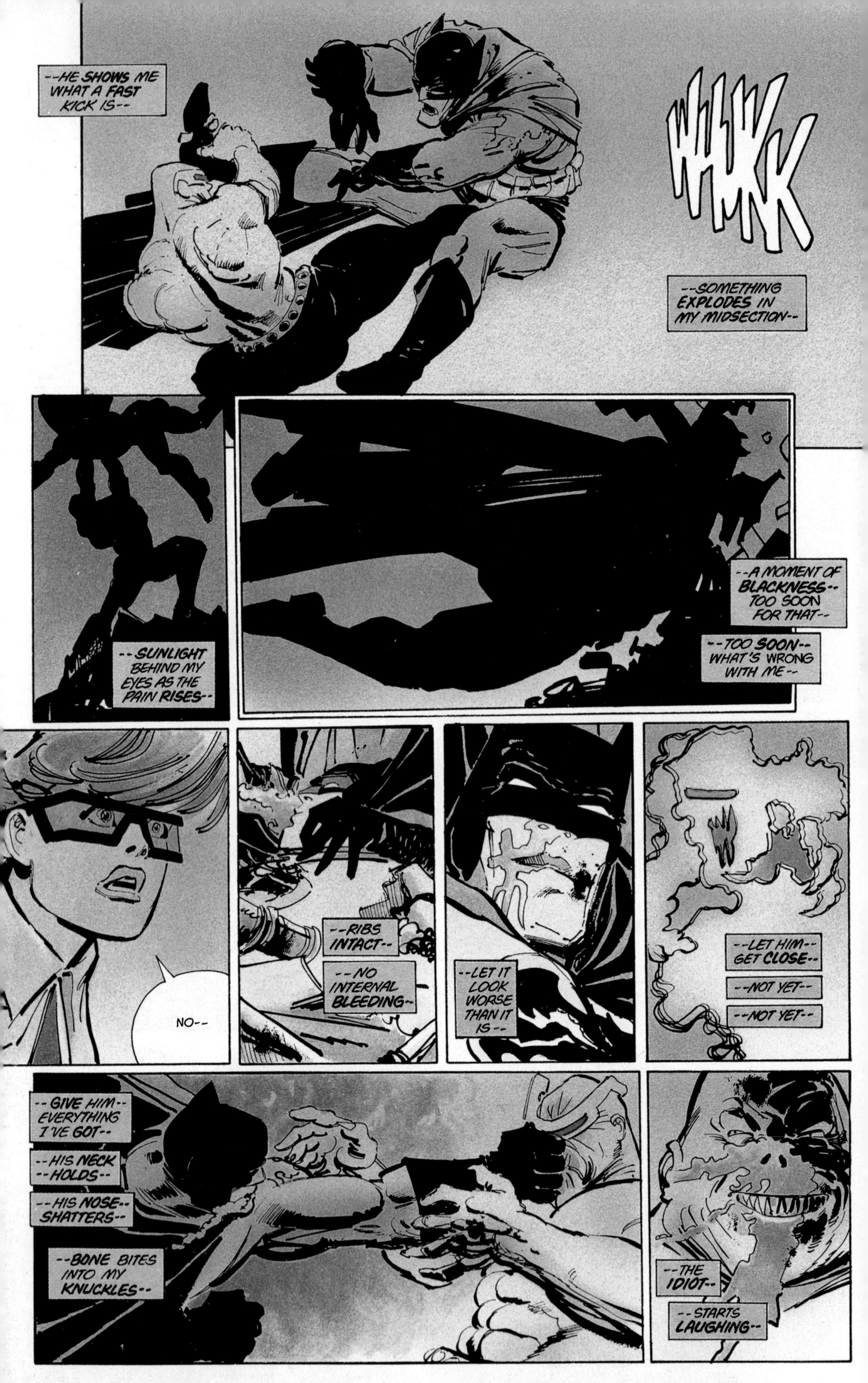
--HE SHOWS ME WHAT A FAST KICK IS--
WHUK
--SOMETHING EXPLODES IN MY MIDSECTION--
--SUNLIGHT BEHIND MY EYES AS THE PAIN RISES--
--A MOMENT OF BLACKNESS-- TOO SOON FOR THAT--
--TOO SOON-- WHAT'S WRONG WITH ME--
NO--
--RIBS INTACT--
--NO INTERNAL BLEEDING--
--LET IT LOOK WORSE THAN IT IS--
--LET HIM-- GET CLOSE--
--NOT YET--
--NOT YET--
--GIVE HIM-- EVERYTHING I'VE GOT--
--HIS NECK --HOLDS--
--HIS NOSE-- SHATTERS--
--BONE BITES INTO MY KNUCKLES--
--THE IDIOT--
--STARTS LAUGHING--

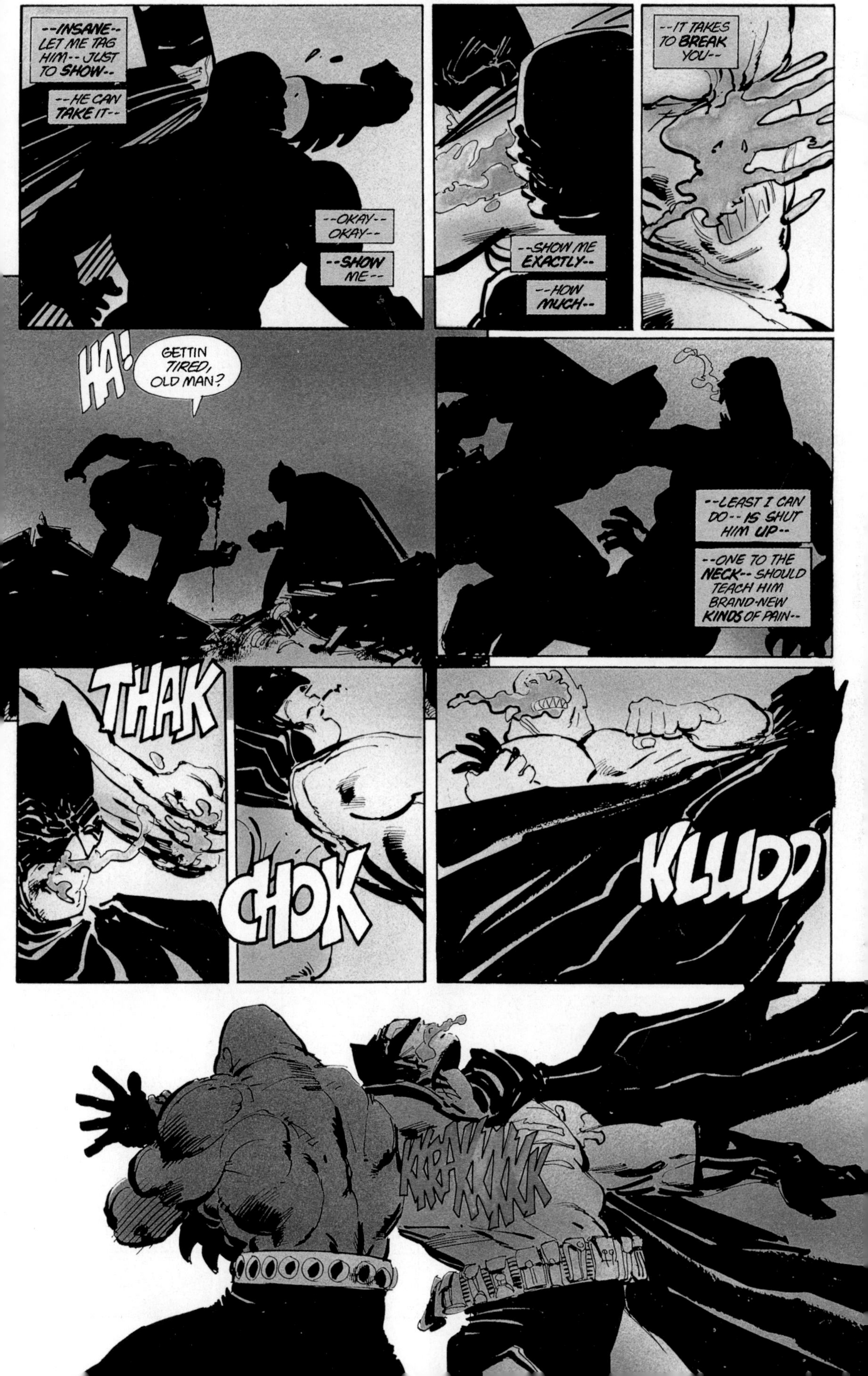
--INSANE-- LET ME TAG HIM-- JUST TO SHOW--
--HE CAN TAKE IT--
--OKAY-- OKAY--
--SHOW ME--
--SHOW ME EXACTLY--
--HOW MUCH--
--IT TAKES TO BREAK YOU--
HA!
GETTIN TIRED, OLD MAN?
--LEAST I CAN DO-- IS SHUT HIM UP--
--ONE TO THE NECK-- SHOULD TEACH HIM BRAND-NEW KINDS OF PAIN--
THAK
CHOK
KLUDD
KRAKAKAKK

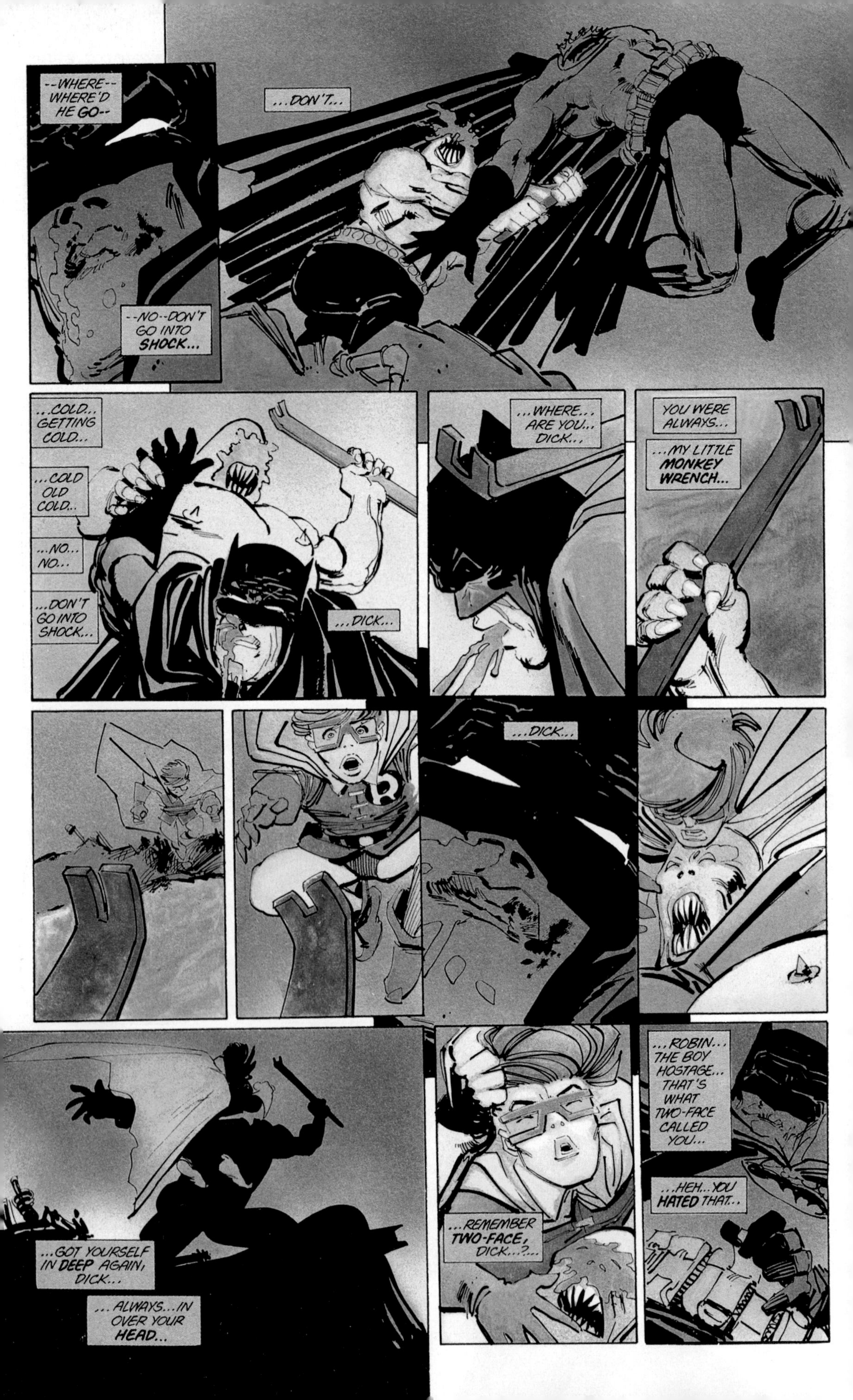

--WHERE--
WHERE'D HE GO--
...DON'T...
--NO--DON'T GO INTO SHOCK...
...COLD... GETTING COLD...
...COLD OLD COLD...
...NO... NO...
...DON'T GO INTO SHOCK...
...DICK...
...WHERE... ARE YOU... DICK...
YOU WERE ALWAYS...
...MY LITTLE MONKEY WRENCH...
...DICK...
...GOT YOURSELF IN DEEP AGAIN, DICK...
...ALWAYS...IN OVER YOUR HEAD...
...REMEMBER TWO-FACE, DICK...?...
...ROBIN... THE BOY HOSTAGE... THAT'S WHAT TWO-FACE CALLED YOU...
...HEH...YOU HATED THAT...

LUCKY...YOU'RE LUCKY I'M ALWAYS HERE...

...TO BAIL YOU OUT...

...DICK...

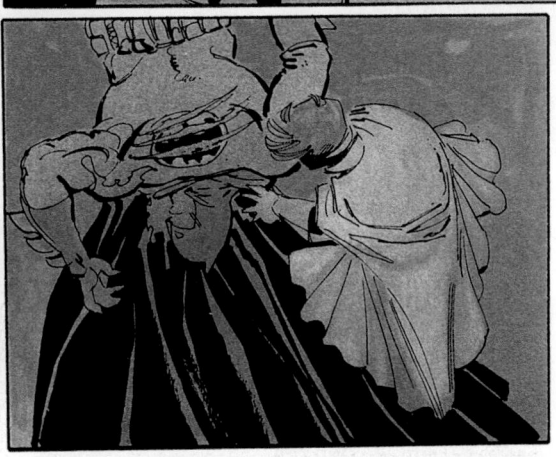

STILL ALIVE--

PORN STAR **HOT GATES** TODAY SIGNED A TWELVE-MILLION-DOLLAR CONTRACT WITH **LANDMARK FILMS** TO STAR IN A SCREEN VERSION OF **SNOW WHITE.** "I'M DOING IT FOR THE KIDS," SAYS GATES...

IN OTHER NEWS, GALAXY BROADCASTING PRESIDENT JAMES OLSEN ASSURED VIEWERS THAT THE TELEVISION WRITERS' STRIKE, NOW IN ITS FOURTH YEAR, WILL NOT AFFECT THE YEAR'S PROGRAMMING...

...THE **POLITICAL PERFORMANCE COMMISSION** HAS AWARDED THE **PRESIDENT** AN UNPRECEDENTED **FIVE CREDIBILITY POINTS** FOR HIS HANDLING OF PUBLIC PERCEPTION DURING THE ECONOMIC CRISIS...

...THIS JUST IN--EYEWITNESSES REPORT EXPLOSIONS RIPPING ACROSS THE **GOTHAM DUMP.** A NEWS FOUR **HELICOPTER** IS ON ITS WAY, FOLKS...

GENTLY, NOW. GENTLY. GOOD GIRL.

NOW YOU JUST RUN ALONG HOME...

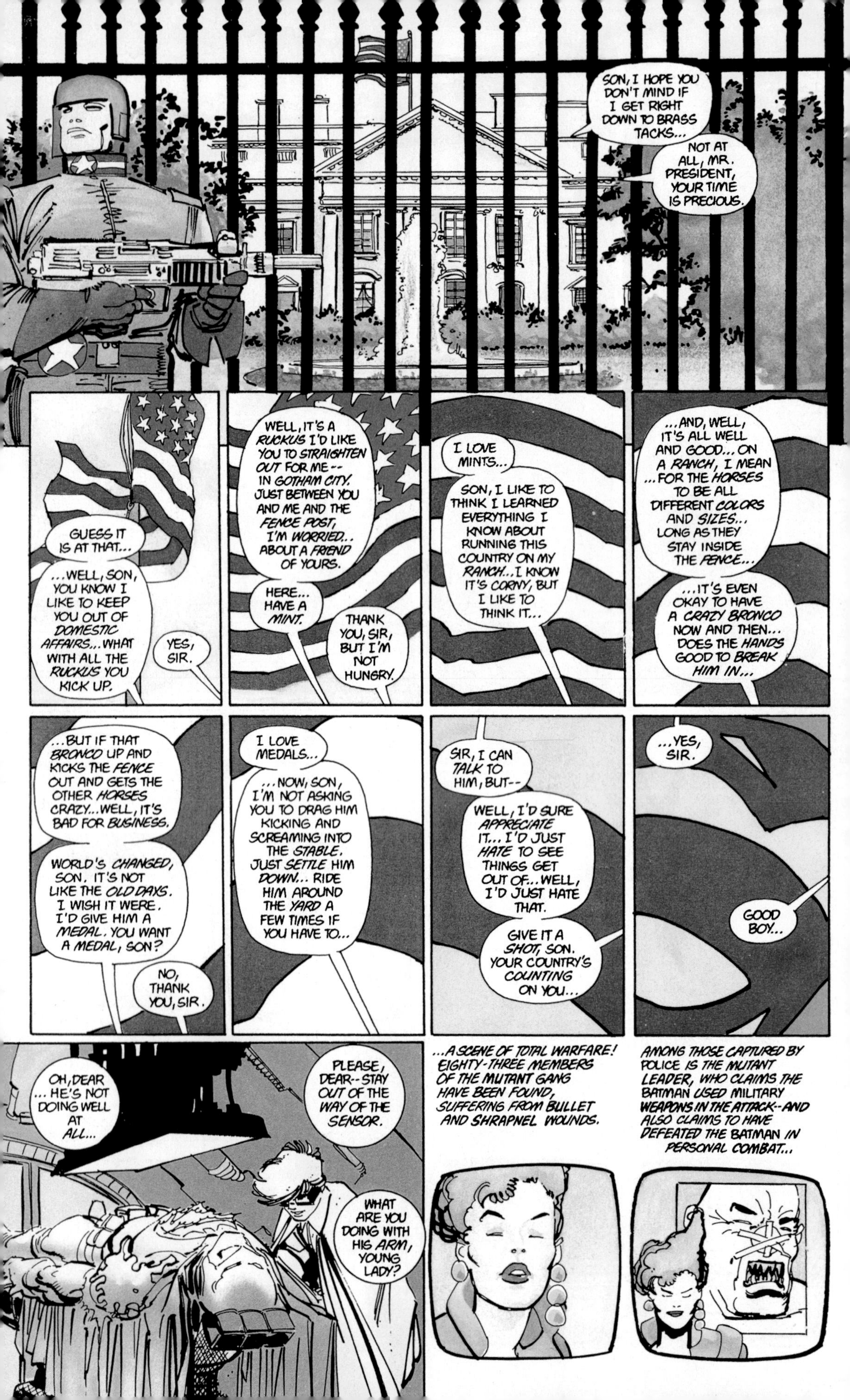
SON, I HOPE YOU DON'T MIND IF I GET RIGHT DOWN TO BRASS TACKS...
NOT AT ALL, MR. PRESIDENT, YOUR TIME IS PRECIOUS.
GUESS IT IS AT THAT...
...WELL, SON, YOU KNOW I LIKE TO KEEP YOU OUT OF DOMESTIC AFFAIRS... WHAT WITH ALL THE RUCKUS YOU KICK UP.
YES, SIR.
WELL, IT'S A RUCKUS I'D LIKE YOU TO STRAIGHTEN OUT FOR ME-- IN GOTHAM CITY. JUST BETWEEN YOU AND ME AND THE FENCE POST, I'M WORRIED... ABOUT A FRIEND OF YOURS.
HERE... HAVE A MINT.
THANK YOU, SIR, BUT I'M NOT HUNGRY.
I LOVE MINTS...
SON, I LIKE TO THINK I LEARNED EVERYTHING I KNOW ABOUT RUNNING THIS COUNTRY ON MY RANCH... I KNOW IT'S CORNY, BUT I LIKE TO THINK IT...
...AND, WELL, IT'S ALL WELL AND GOOD... ON A RANCH, I MEAN ...FOR THE HORSES TO BE ALL DIFFERENT COLORS AND SIZES... LONG AS THEY STAY INSIDE THE FENCE...
...IT'S EVEN OKAY TO HAVE A CRAZY BRONCO NOW AND THEN... DOES THE HANDS GOOD TO BREAK HIM IN...
...BUT IF THAT BRONCO UP AND KICKS THE FENCE OUT AND GETS THE OTHER HORSES CRAZY... WELL, IT'S BAD FOR BUSINESS.
WORLD'S CHANGED, SON. IT'S NOT LIKE THE OLD DAYS. I WISH IT WERE. I'D GIVE HIM A MEDAL. YOU WANT A MEDAL, SON?
NO, THANK YOU, SIR.
I LOVE MEDALS...
...NOW, SON, I'M NOT ASKING YOU TO DRAG HIM KICKING AND SCREAMING INTO THE STABLE. JUST SETTLE HIM DOWN... RIDE HIM AROUND THE YARD A FEW TIMES IF YOU HAVE TO...
SIR, I CAN TALK TO HIM, BUT--
WELL, I'D SURE APPRECIATE IT... I'D JUST HATE TO SEE THINGS GET OUT OF... WELL, I'D JUST HATE THAT.
GIVE IT A SHOT, SON. YOUR COUNTRY'S COUNTING ON YOU...
...YES, SIR.
GOOD BOY...
OH, DEAR ... HE'S NOT DOING WELL AT ALL...
PLEASE, DEAR-- STAY OUT OF THE WAY OF THE SENSOR.
WHAT ARE YOU DOING WITH HIS ARM, YOUNG LADY?
...A SCENE OF TOTAL WARFARE! EIGHTY-THREE MEMBERS OF THE MUTANT GANG HAVE BEEN FOUND, SUFFERING FROM BULLET AND SHRAPNEL WOUNDS.
AMONG THOSE CAPTURED BY POLICE IS THE MUTANT LEADER, WHO CLAIMS THE BATMAN USED MILITARY WEAPONS IN THE ATTACK--AND ALSO CLAIMS TO HAVE DEFEATED THE BATMAN IN PERSONAL COMBAT...

BATMAN IS A COWARD. I BROKE HIS BONES. I CONQUERED THE FOOL. I MADE HIM BEG FOR MERCY. ONLY BY CHEATING DID HE ESCAPE ALIVE.
LET HIM GO TO HIS WOMEN. LET HIM LICK HIS WOUNDS. HIS DAY IS DONE. GOTHAM CITY BELONGS TO THE MUTANTS.
CAREFUL, MAN--YOU'RE BOUNCING AROUND TOO--
NO... ...NOT... BOUNCING ME... DON'T WORRY...
SKREEECH
STRETCHER'S... ON A GYROSCOPE... STAYS LEVEL... NO MATTER WHAT...
THAT'S KEEN.
NOW DON'T YOU STRAIN YOURSELF, SIR. YOU'VE QUITE A LOT OF INTERNAL BLEEDING.
THIS YOUNG LADY WAS KIND ENOUGH TO HELP YOU ABOARD...
I... KNOW WHAT SHE DID, ALFRED.
WHERE... DID YOU LEARN TO SET AN ARM... MAKE A SPLINT...?
GIRL SCOUTS.
WHAT'S... YOUR NAME...
CARRIE. CARRIE KELLEY.
ROBIN.
MINE'S BRUCE...
SIR! YOU'RE DELIRIOUS, SIR. YOU JUST REST NOW--DON'T TRY TO SPEAK--
WE'RE ONLY MOMENTS FROM THE HOSPITAL--
NO... HOSPITAL, ALFRED...
...THE CAVE...
BUT SIR--
THE CAVE...
..., AND ROBIN... COMES WITH US...
SOON MY ARMY WILL STORM GOTHAM CITY. SOON THE HEAD OF GORDON WILL BE CARRIED THROUGH THE STREETS. THEN I WILL HUNT YOUR NEW COP--YOUR WOMAN COP--AND I WILL

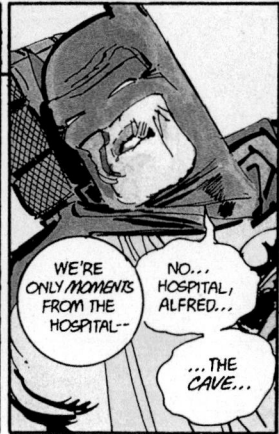

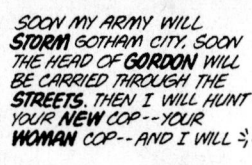

THE REST OF THE MUTANT LEADER'S STATEMENT IS UNFIT FOR BROADCAST.

I DON'T THINK YOU REALIZE WHAT YOU'RE SUGGESTING, DR. WOLPER.

HARVEY DENT DIDN'T EXACTLY BRING US POSITIVE PUBLICITY. AND *THIS* ONE...

I KNOW, GLEN. I *KNOW*--

ARKHAM HOME
FOR THE EMOTIONALLY TROUBLED

--BUT I'M NOT TALKING ABOUT A *RELEASE*. THIS WILL BE A *CONTROLLED ENVIRONMENT*-- AND IT WOULD BE SO GOOD FOR HIM.

HIM I'M NOT WORRIED ABOUT.

DR. GLEN F
CHIEF ADMI

PUSH

COME NOW, GLEN! HE'S BEEN NEARLY *COMATOSE* FOR MORE THAN A DECADE. IF YOU'D JUST *TALK* WITH HIM... FOR *FIVE MINUTES*, GLEN...

I DON'T KNOW, THERE'S SOMETHING ...WELL... SOMETHING *SUPERNATURAL* ABOUT THAT ONE.

HIEF ADMINIS

NOW THAT'S A *FINE* WAY TO SPEAK IN A HOUSE OF *MEDICINE*, ISN'T IT? LISTEN-- PUT ALL THE GUARDS YOU *WANT* IN THE STUDIO, IF IT WILL MAKE YOU FEEL BETTER.

FIVE MINUTES, GLEN. HE *IS* A PATIENT.

LEN FORB
ADMINISTRATOR

OKAY. ALL RIGHT. FIVE MINUTES.

'SCUSE ME, WE'RE HEADING STRAIGHT FOR A BRICK WALL.

DON'T... WORRY, ROBIN...

...IT'S JUST ...A HOLOGRAM...

SIR-- I URGE YOU TO *REJECT* DR. WOLPER'S SUGGESTION. I DON'T *DESERVE* THIS CHARITY... MY CRIMES...WERE *HORRIBLE* BEYOND ALL WORDS... I AM BEYOND REDEMPTION.

PLEASE-- JUST LOCK ME *AWAY*-- FROM HUMAN MEMORY...

SOB

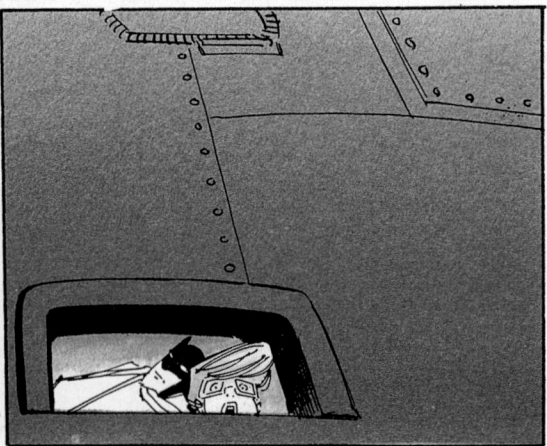

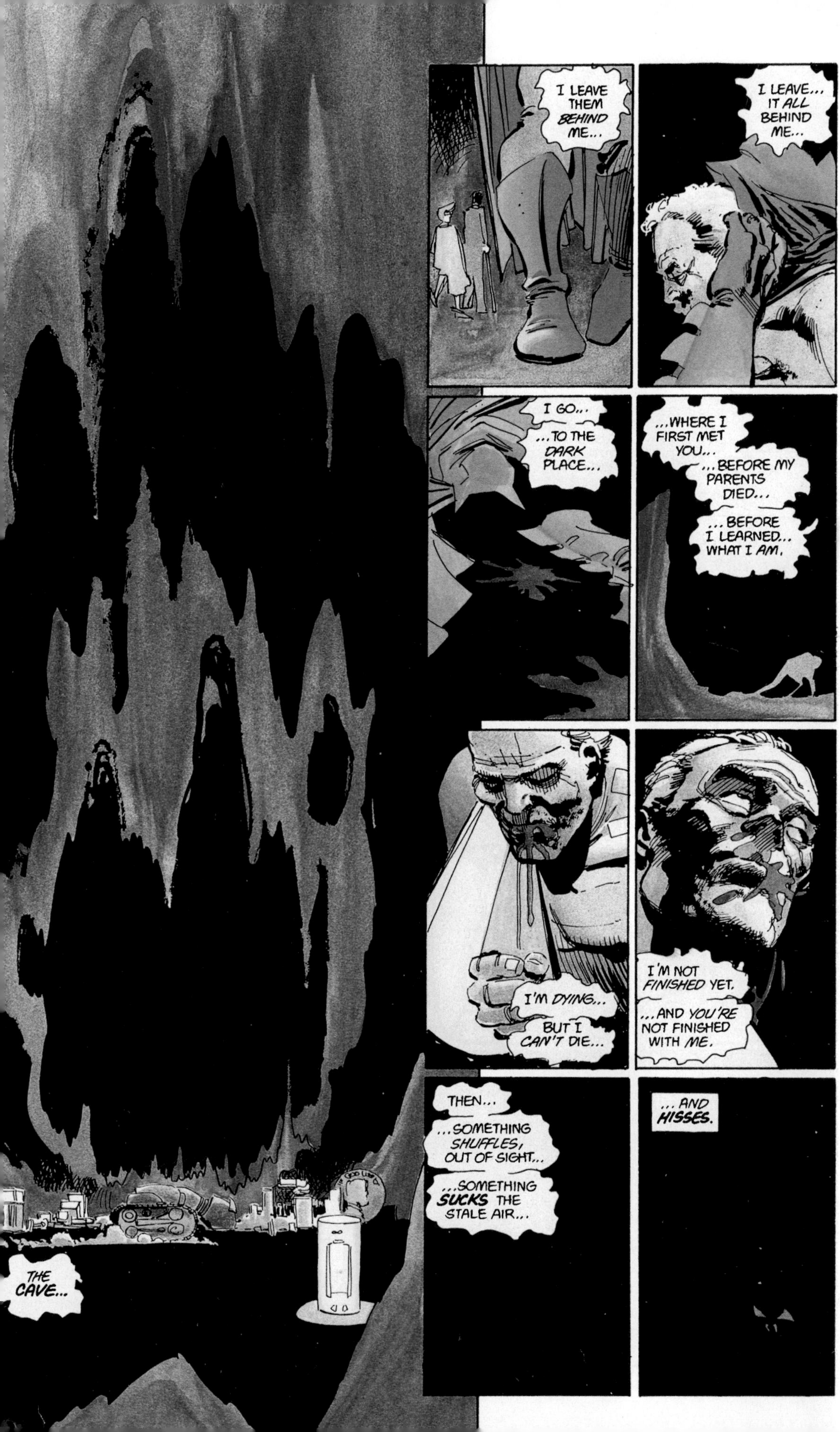

THE CAVE...
I LEAVE THEM *BEHIND* ME...
I LEAVE... IT *ALL* BEHIND ME...
I GO...
...TO THE *DARK* PLACE...
...WHERE I FIRST MET YOU...
...BEFORE MY PARENTS DIED...
...BEFORE I LEARNED... WHAT I *AM*.
I'M *DYING*...
BUT I *CAN'T* DIE...
I'M NOT *FINISHED* YET.
...AND *YOU'RE* NOT FINISHED WITH *ME*.
THEN...
...SOMETHING *SHUFFLES*, OUT OF SIGHT...
...SOMETHING ***SUCKS*** THE STALE AIR...
...AND ***HISSES***.

GLIDING WITH *ANCIENT* GRACE...

EYES *GLEAMING*, UNTOUCHED BY LOVE OR JOY OR SORROW...

BREATH HOT WITH THE TASTE OF FALLEN FOES... THE STENCH OF DEAD THINGS, *DAMNED* THINGS...

SURELY THE FIERCEST SURVIVOR ...THE *PUREST* WARRIOR...

GLARING, *HATING*...

...CLAIMING ME AS YOUR *OWN*.

WE WILL COME FOR OUR LEADER. WE WILL *RAZE* GOTHAM. WE WILL *RAPE* GOTHAM. WE WILL TASTE GOTHAM'S *BLOOD*.

ON HEARING THIS MESSAGE FROM THE MUTANTS, COMMISSIONER GORDON PUT HIMSELF AND HIS MEN ON TWENTY-FOUR HOUR ALERT--WHILE THE MAYOR WAS QUICK TO SPEAK OUT...

THIS WHOLE SITUATION IS THE RESULT OF GORDON'S *INCOMPETENCE*--AND OF THE TERRORIST ACTIONS OF THE *BATMAN*. I WISH TO SIT DOWN WITH THE MUTANT LEADER...TO NEGOTIATE A *SETTLEMENT*...

WHAT DO YOU THINK, TRISH? HIS HONOR GONE *NUTS*?

NOT AT ALL, BILL. FRANKLY I EXPECT THE MAYOR'S CREDIBILITY RATING TO GO THROUGH THE *ROOF*, *ESPECIALLY* IF HE'S *SUCCESSFUL* IN THE NEGOTIATIONS.

THIS, COMBINED WITH HIS STRONG STAND ON *BATMAN*-- AND MAKING A WOMAN THE NEXT POLICE COMMISSIONER-- WELL, I THINK WE'VE GOT A WHOLE NEW *MAYOR* ON OUR HANDS--

--PUBLIC PERCEPTION-WISE, THAT IS.

ALL THIS AND BRAINS TOO

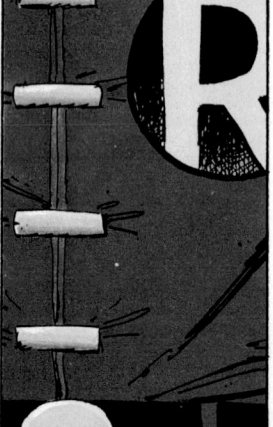

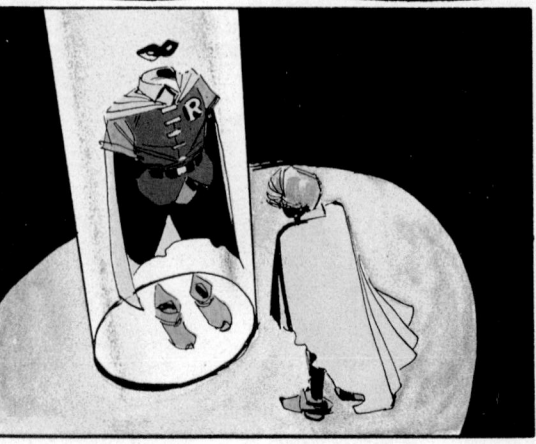

ARNOLD CRIMP FINGERS THE COLD STEEL THING IN HIS POCKET AND STARES AT THE MOVIE MARQUEE AND DOES NOT THROW UP.

HE THINKS ABOUT LED ZEPPELIN AND HOW THEY ARE TRYING TO KILL HIM.

HE HAD NOT KNOWN ABOUT LED ZEPPELIN UNTIL FATHER DON ON TV HAD EXPLAINED IT LAST NIGHT.

FATHER DON SAID THAT LED ZEPPELIN HID A PRAYER TO SATAN IN THEIR SONG "STAIRWAY TO HEAVEN."

THEY HID IT VERY WELL. THEY RECORDED IT BACKWARDS.

ARNOLD CRIMP TOOK THE ALBUM FROM THE RECORD STORE WHERE HE WORKED UNTIL THEY FIRED HIM THIS AFTERNOON AND TRANSFERRED "STAIRWAY TO HEAVEN" TO TAPE.

THEN HE PLAYED THE TAPE BACKWARDS.

HE PLAYED IT FORTY-SEVEN TIMES UNTIL HE WAS ABSOLUTELY CERTAIN THAT FATHER DON WAS RIGHT.

BUT THE YOUNG GIRL WHO WAS PAINTED LIKE A WHORE DIDN'T BELIEVE HIM.

THAT WAS THIS AFTERNOON, IN THE STORE. HE EXPLAINED IT TO HER VERY CAREFULLY. SHE SAID AWFUL WORDS.

HE LOST HIS TEMPER AND BROKE THE RECORD INTO FOUR PIECES THAT WERE EXACTLY THE SAME SIZE.

THE YOUNG GIRL WHO WAS PAINTED JUST LIKE A WHORE SCREAMED FOR THE MANAGER AND THE MANAGER WALKED OUT FROM THE BACK ROOM AND WOULDN'T EVEN LISTEN AND FIRED ARNOLD CRIMP.

THAT WAS THIS AFTERNOON, IN THE STORE.

EVERY MORNING AND EVENING UNTIL TONIGHT OF COURSE HE HAD WALKED SIX BLOCKS OUT OF HIS WAY TO AVOID THIS NEIGHBORHOOD.

IT'S WORSE THAN HE IMAGINED.

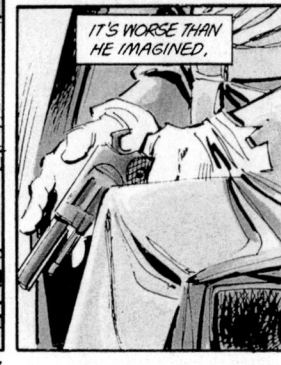

ROW ON ROW ON ROW ON ROW OF PICTURES OF WOMEN AND WORDS AND WORDS AND WORDS. HE STOPPED AT THIS ONE THE ONE HE IS IN RIGHT NOW AND READ THE TITLE THAT DID NOT MAKE HIM THROW UP.

THE TITLE IS "MY SWEET SATAN," WHICH IS WHAT ARNOLD CRIMP IS ABSOLUTELY CERTAIN HE HEARD WHEN HE PLAYED "STAIRWAY TO HEAVEN" BACKWARDS.

ON THE SCREEN A NUN A NUN IS DOING SOMETHING AND SHE'S PAINTED EXACTLY LIKE A WHORE--

THREE SLAIN IN BATMAN-INSPIRED PORN THEATER SHOOT-OUT. DETAILS TO FOLLOW...

IRON MAN VASQUEZ CAN'T TASTE HIS SNICKERS BAR.
HE KNOWS HE SHOULD BE OUT OF HERE, OUT AND HOME, WAITING FOR BIGGERS TO SEND THE SIXTY DOLLARS. THIRTY FOR EACH LEG, HE THINKS, FEELING NOTHING.
FEELING NOTHING AND NOT TASTING HIS SNICKERS BAR.
HE PUSHES THROUGH THE COTTON IN HIS HEAD AND REMEMBERS THE LAST TIME HE FELT SOMETHING.
IT WAS IN THE FIRST AND ONLY ROUND OF HIS LAST FIGHT. HIS LAST FIGHT WHEN CAPTAIN WARRIOR HIT HIM ACROSS THE NOSE.
BROKEN NOSE VASQUEZ, BIGGERS HAD CALLED HIM. JUST LAUGHED WHEN IRON MAN CRIED LIKE A BABY AND BEGGED FOR ANOTHER FIGHT.
THEN BIGGERS PUT HIS FAT ARM AROUND IRON MAN'S SHOULDER AND TOLD HIM THE ONLY WAY HE COULD MAKE MONEY NOW.
SUDDENLY HIS EYES STING AND IRON MAN HURTS ALL OVER AND REALIZES HE'S READING ABOUT A MAN.
THE BATMAN CONTROVERSY
A MAN WHO DRESSES UP LIKE A MONSTER AND MAKES THINGS RIGHT.
THE NEXT TIME IRON MAN VASQUEZ FEELS SOMETHING, HE'S STANDING IN A RESTAURANT WITH SOMETHING ON HIS FACE AND A GUN IN HIS HAND.
HE HEARS A TRUCK BACKFIRE--
CRAZED WOULD-BE KILLER DRESSES AS BATMAN-- AFTER THIS...
A DEVOUT CATHOLIC, PEPPI SPANDECK CAN'T SAY HE APPROVES OF THIS BATMAN.
AND WHEN HE HEARS THE WOMAN SCREAM DOWN THE STREET, HE KNOWS HE SHOULD BE AFRAID.
INSTEAD HE'S LOOKING AT THE ALARM SYSTEM THAT COST HIM TWO MONTHS' PROFITS AND THE IRON BARS OVER HIS WINDOWS THAT MAKE HIS BEAUTIFUL SHOP LOOK LIKE A PRISON...
HE CAN FEEL HIS PULSE, JUST BELOW HIS EARS. HE KNOWS HE'S GONE CRAZY. BUT THE MUGGER IS RUNNING, AFRAID. AFRAID OF PEPPI.
NOBODY IS HURT BADLY ENOUGH FOR THIS TO MAKE THE NEWS.

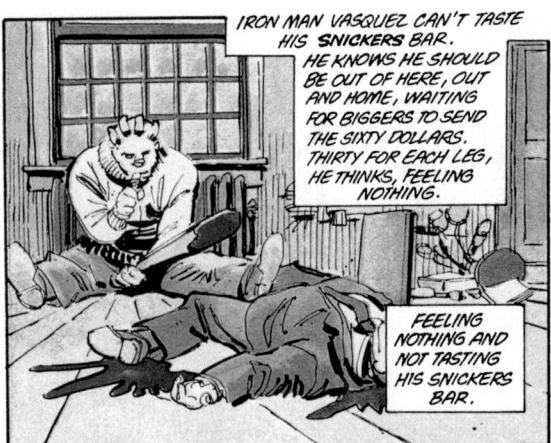

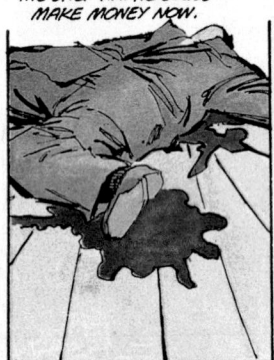

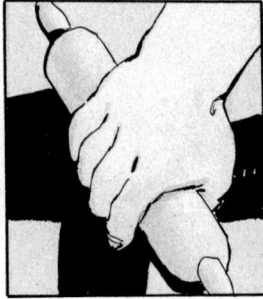

...AN *UPDATE*--THE *MAYOR* IS THIS MINUTE *IN CONSULTATION* WITH THE MUTANT *LEADER*, WHO HAS AGREED TO MEET HIM *ALONE.* MEANWHILE, THE MAYOR'S *LEADERSHIP QUOTIENT* HAS *SOARED*-- EXCUSE ME...

I'D EXPECTED THEM TO BE *SCREAMING* AND *FIGHTING.* BUT THEY STAND LIKE A CAPTIVE ARMY. I'D LIKE TO THINK THEY'RE *CRAZY*-- BUT HERE I AM, WALKING THE *MAYOR* TO MEET THEIR *LEADER*--

-- WITH ALL THE *CEREMONY* OF A *MILITARY CONFERENCE.*

THE CELL DOOR *OPENS.* THE AIR GOES *THICK.* I FEEL THE MAYOR *SHUDDER,* IN TIME WITH ME.

I ASK HIM ONE MORE TIME IF HE IS SURE HE WANTS TO GO IT ALONE. HE GURGLES, AND NODS.

I DON'T KNOW IF I'D CALL IT *COURAGE.*

I HEAR A NERVOUS GIGGLE AND AN ANIMAL *GROWL.* I HEAR HANDCUFF LINKS *SNAP.*

I SEE SOMETHING I'LL TAKE TO MY *GRAVE.*

SOME IDIOT STOPS ME FROM DOING THE *OBVIOUS* THING.

...THE MAYOR IS DEAD.

THE MUTANT LEADER RIPPED THE MAYOR'S THROAT OUT WITH HIS TEETH. THE MUTANT HAS BEEN RETURNED TO HIS CELL. MORE ON THIS AS WE GET IT.

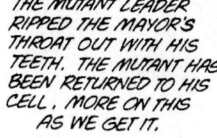

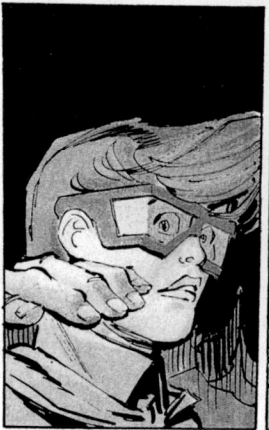

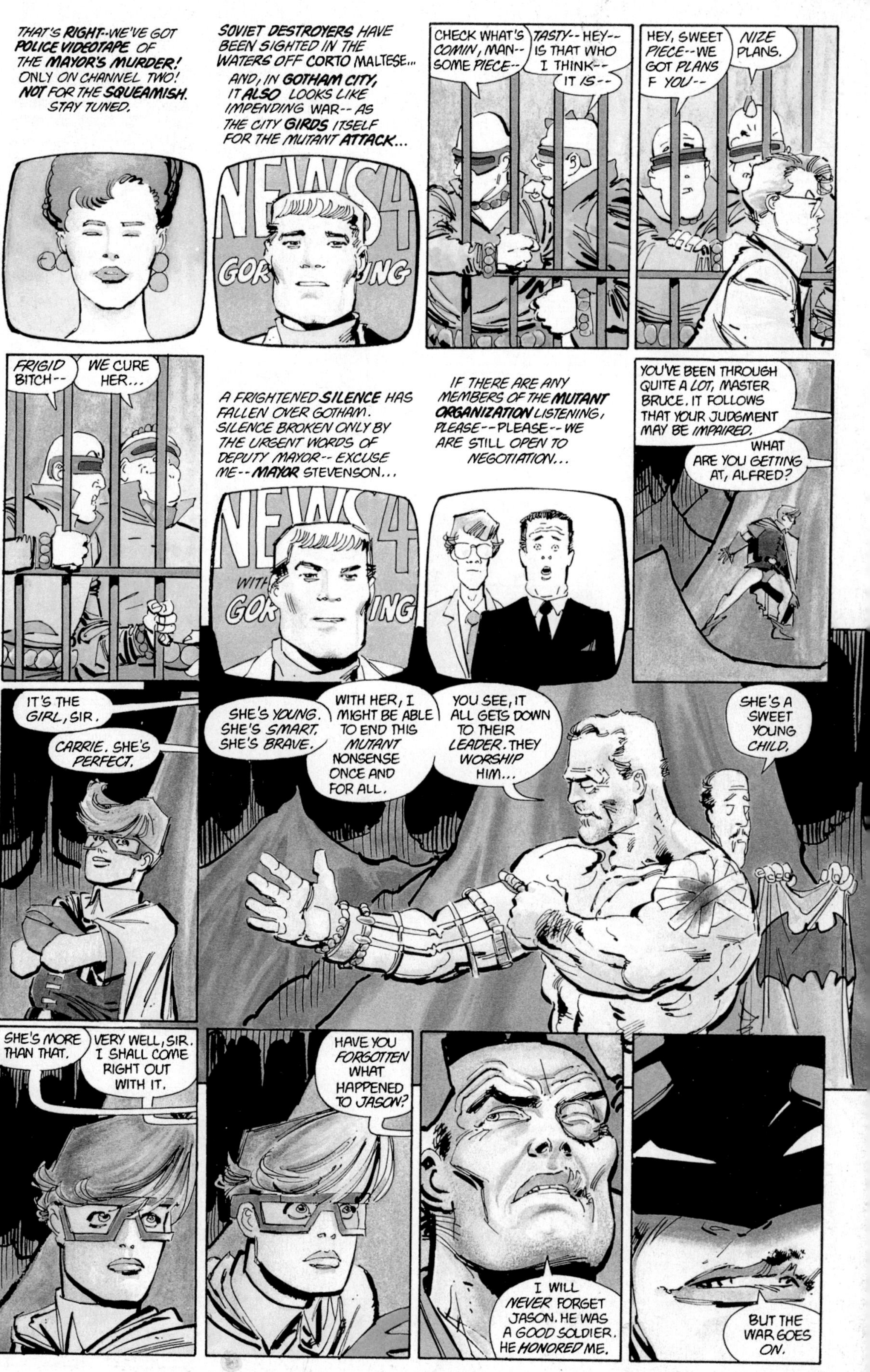
THAT'S RIGHT--WE'VE GOT POLICE VIDEOTAPE OF THE MAYOR'S MURDER! ONLY ON CHANNEL TWO! NOT FOR THE SQUEAMISH. STAY TUNED.
SOVIET DESTROYERS HAVE BEEN SIGHTED IN THE WATERS OFF CORTO MALTESE...
AND, IN GOTHAM CITY, IT ALSO LOOKS LIKE IMPENDING WAR--AS THE CITY GIRDS ITSELF FOR THE MUTANT ATTACK...
CHECK WHAT'S COMIN, MAN--SOME PIECE--
TASTY--HEY--IS THAT WHO I THINK--IT IS--
HEY, SWEET PIECE--WE GOT PLANS F YOU--
NIZE PLANS.
FRIGID BITCH--
WE CURE HER...
A FRIGHTENED SILENCE HAS FALLEN OVER GOTHAM. SILENCE BROKEN ONLY BY THE URGENT WORDS OF DEPUTY MAYOR--EXCUSE ME--MAYOR STEVENSON...
IF THERE ARE ANY MEMBERS OF THE MUTANT ORGANIZATION LISTENING, PLEASE--PLEASE--WE ARE STILL OPEN TO NEGOTIATION...
YOU'VE BEEN THROUGH QUITE A LOT, MASTER BRUCE. IT FOLLOWS THAT YOUR JUDGMENT MAY BE IMPAIRED.
WHAT ARE YOU GETTING AT, ALFRED?
IT'S THE GIRL, SIR.
CARRIE. SHE'S PERFECT.
SHE'S YOUNG. SHE'S SMART. SHE'S BRAVE.
WITH HER, I MIGHT BE ABLE TO END THIS MUTANT NONSENSE ONCE AND FOR ALL.
YOU SEE, IT ALL GETS DOWN TO THEIR LEADER. THEY WORSHIP HIM...
SHE'S A SWEET YOUNG CHILD.
SHE'S MORE THAN THAT.
VERY WELL, SIR. I SHALL COME RIGHT OUT WITH IT.
HAVE YOU FORGOTTEN WHAT HAPPENED TO JASON?
I WILL NEVER FORGET JASON. HE WAS A GOOD SOLDIER. HE HONORED ME.
BUT THE WAR GOES ON.

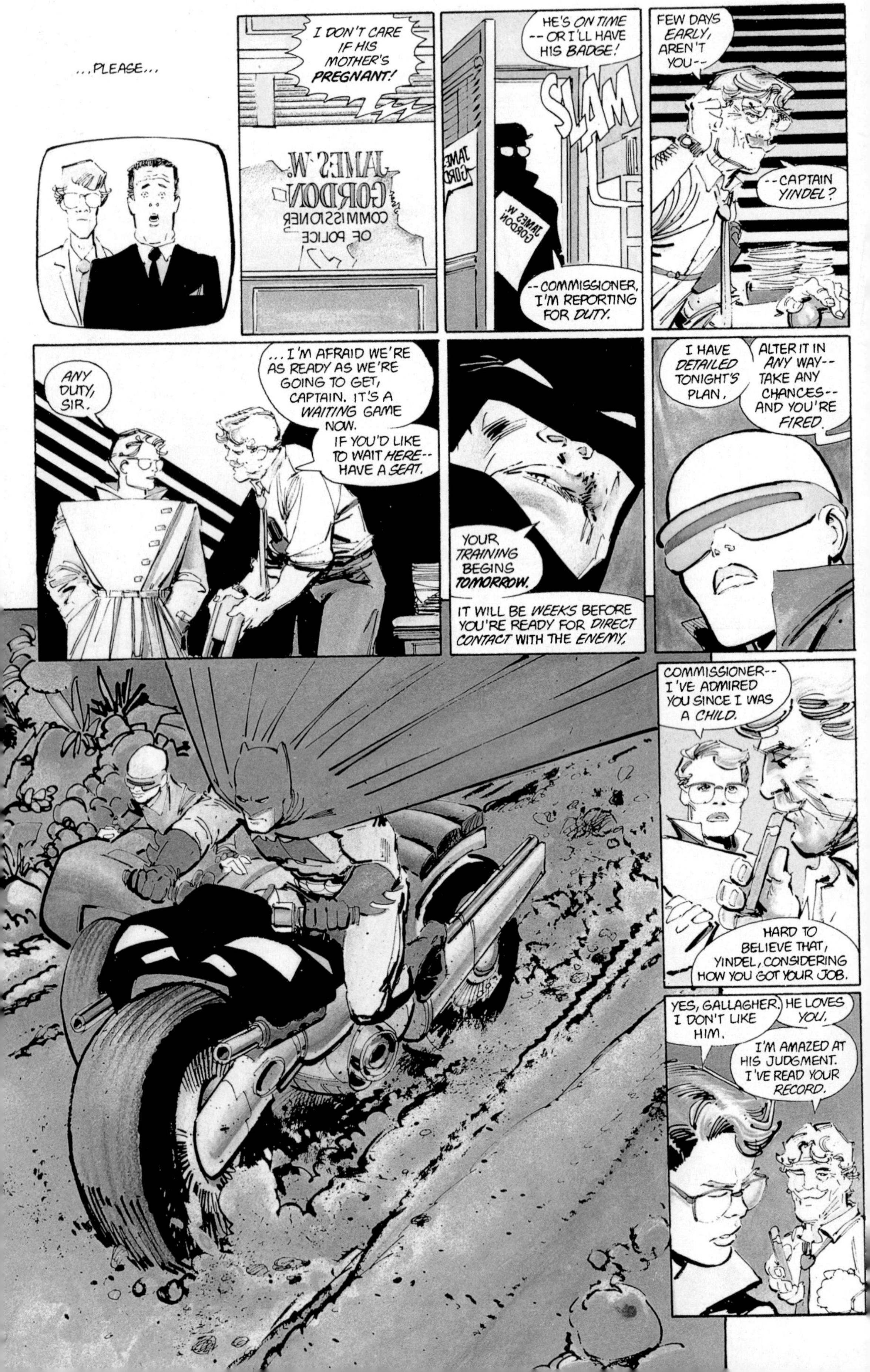
...PLEASE...
I DON'T CARE IF HIS MOTHER'S PREGNANT!
JAMES W. GORDON COMMISSIONER OF POLICE
HE'S ON TIME --OR I'LL HAVE HIS BADGE!
SLAM
--COMMISSIONER, I'M REPORTING FOR DUTY.
FEW DAYS EARLY, AREN'T YOU--
--CAPTAIN YINDEL?
ANY DUTY, SIR.
...I'M AFRAID WE'RE AS READY AS WE'RE GOING TO GET, CAPTAIN. IT'S A WAITING GAME NOW.
IF YOU'D LIKE TO WAIT HERE-- HAVE A SEAT.
YOUR TRAINING BEGINS TOMORROW.
IT WILL BE WEEKS BEFORE YOU'RE READY FOR DIRECT CONTACT WITH THE ENEMY.
I HAVE DETAILED TONIGHT'S PLAN.
ALTER IT IN ANY WAY-- TAKE ANY CHANCES-- AND YOU'RE FIRED.
COMMISSIONER-- I'VE ADMIRED YOU SINCE I WAS A CHILD.
HARD TO BELIEVE THAT, YINDEL, CONSIDERING HOW YOU GOT YOUR JOB.
YES, GALLAGHER. I DON'T LIKE HIM.
HE LOVES YOU.
I'M AMAZED AT HIS JUDGMENT. I'VE READ YOUR RECORD.

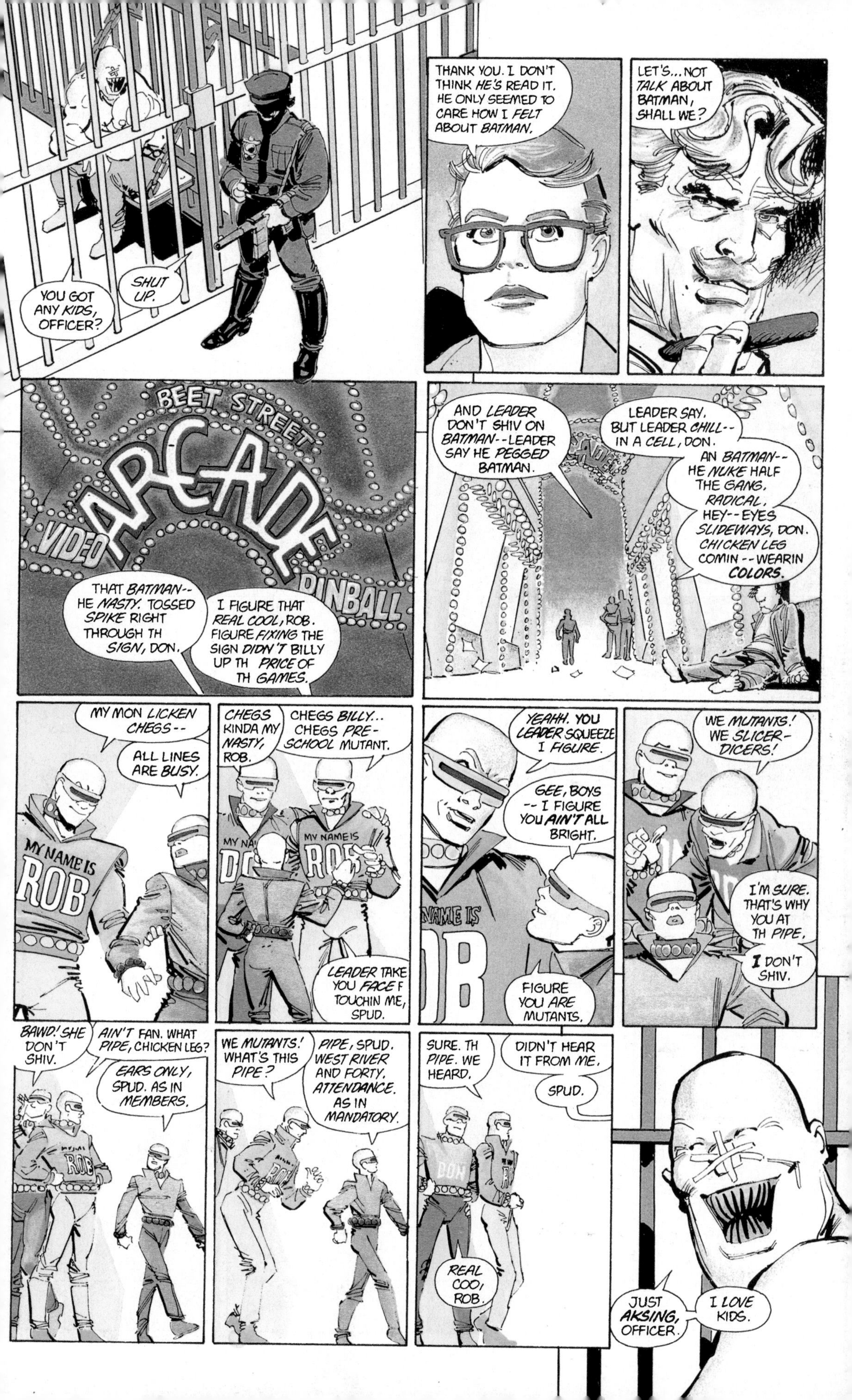

YOU GOT ANY KIDS, OFFICER?
SHUT UP.
THANK YOU. I DON'T THINK HE'S READ IT. HE ONLY SEEMED TO CARE HOW I FELT ABOUT BATMAN.
LET'S... NOT TALK ABOUT BATMAN, SHALL WE?
BEET STREET
VIDEO
ARCADE
PINBALL
THAT BATMAN-- HE NASTY. TOSSED SPIKE RIGHT THROUGH TH SIGN, DON.
I FIGURE THAT REAL COOL, ROB. FIGURE FIXING THE SIGN DIDN'T BILLY UP TH PRICE OF TH GAMES.
AND LEADER DON'T SHIV ON BATMAN--LEADER SAY HE PEGGED BATMAN.
LEADER SAY. BUT LEADER CHILL-- IN A CELL, DON.
AN BATMAN-- HE NUKE HALF THE GANG. RADICAL. HEY--EYES SLIDEWAYS, DON. CHICKEN LEG COMIN--WEARIN COLORS.
MY MON LICKEN CHEGS--
ALL LINES ARE BUSY.
MY NAME IS ROB
CHEGS KINDA MY NASTY, ROB.
CHEGS BILLY... CHEGS PRE-SCHOOL MUTANT.
LEADER TAKE YOU FACE F TOUCHIN ME, SPUD.
YEAHH. YOU LEADER SQUEEZE I FIGURE.
GEE, BOYS --I FIGURE YOU AIN'T ALL BRIGHT.
FIGURE YOU ARE MUTANTS.
WE MUTANTS! WE SLICER-DICERS!
I'M SURE. THAT'S WHY YOU AT TH PIPE.
I DON'T SHIV.
BAWD! SHE DON'T SHIV.
AIN'T FAN. WHAT PIPE, CHICKEN LEG?
EARS ONLY, SPUD. AS IN MEMBERS.
WE MUTANTS! WHAT'S THIS PIPE?
PIPE, SPUD. WEST RIVER AND FORTY. ATTENDANCE. AS IN MANDATORY.
SURE. TH PIPE. WE HEARD.
DIDN'T HEAR IT FROM ME.
SPUD.
REAL COO, ROB.
JUST AKSING, OFFICER.
I LOVE KIDS.

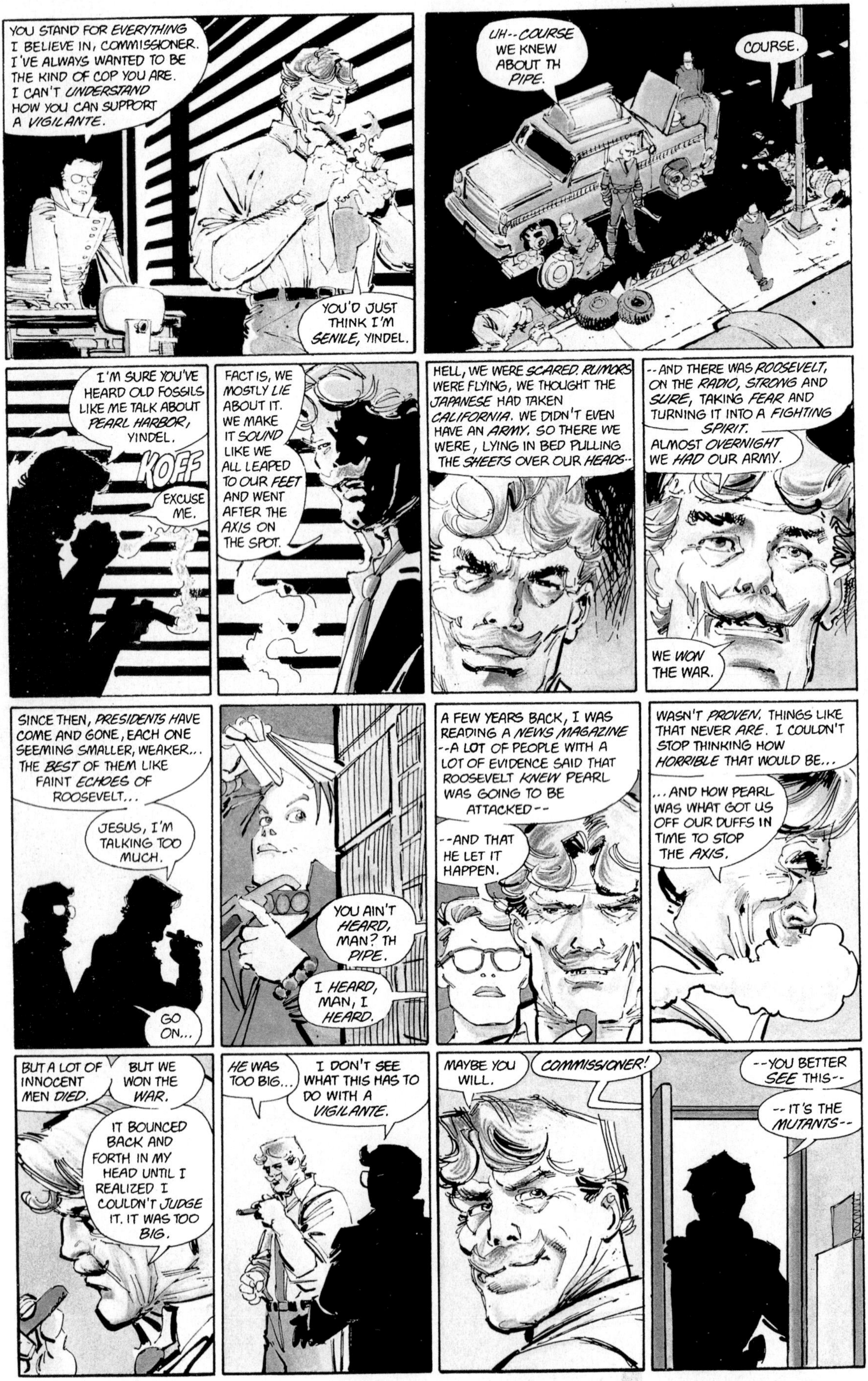
YOU STAND FOR EVERYTHING I BELIEVE IN, COMMISSIONER. I'VE ALWAYS WANTED TO BE THE KIND OF COP YOU ARE. I CAN'T UNDERSTAND HOW YOU CAN SUPPORT A VIGILANTE.
YOU'D JUST THINK I'M SENILE, YINDEL.
UH--COURSE WE KNEW ABOUT TH PIPE.
COURSE.
I'M SURE YOU'VE HEARD OLD FOSSILS LIKE ME TALK ABOUT PEARL HARBOR, YINDEL.
KOFF
EXCUSE ME.
FACT IS, WE MOSTLY LIE ABOUT IT. WE MAKE IT SOUND LIKE WE ALL LEAPED TO OUR FEET AND WENT AFTER THE AXIS ON THE SPOT.
HELL, WE WERE SCARED. RUMORS WERE FLYING, WE THOUGHT THE JAPANESE HAD TAKEN CALIFORNIA. WE DIDN'T EVEN HAVE AN ARMY. SO THERE WE WERE, LYING IN BED PULLING THE SHEETS OVER OUR HEADS--
--AND THERE WAS ROOSEVELT, ON THE RADIO, STRONG AND SURE, TAKING FEAR AND TURNING IT INTO A FIGHTING SPIRIT. ALMOST OVERNIGHT WE HAD OUR ARMY.
WE WON THE WAR.
SINCE THEN, PRESIDENTS HAVE COME AND GONE, EACH ONE SEEMING SMALLER, WEAKER... THE BEST OF THEM LIKE FAINT ECHOES OF ROOSEVELT...
JESUS, I'M TALKING TOO MUCH.
GO ON...
YOU AIN'T HEARD, MAN? TH PIPE.
I HEARD, MAN, I HEARD.
A FEW YEARS BACK, I WAS READING A NEWS MAGAZINE --A LOT OF PEOPLE WITH A LOT OF EVIDENCE SAID THAT ROOSEVELT KNEW PEARL WAS GOING TO BE ATTACKED--
--AND THAT HE LET IT HAPPEN.
WASN'T PROVEN. THINGS LIKE THAT NEVER ARE. I COULDN'T STOP THINKING HOW HORRIBLE THAT WOULD BE...
...AND HOW PEARL WAS WHAT GOT US OFF OUR DUFFS IN TIME TO STOP THE AXIS.
BUT A LOT OF INNOCENT MEN DIED.
BUT WE WON THE WAR.
IT BOUNCED BACK AND FORTH IN MY HEAD UNTIL I REALIZED I COULDN'T JUDGE IT. IT WAS TOO BIG.
HE WAS TOO BIG...
I DON'T SEE WHAT THIS HAS TO DO WITH A VIGILANTE.
MAYBE YOU WILL.
COMMISSIONER!
--YOU BETTER SEE THIS--
--IT'S THE MUTANTS--

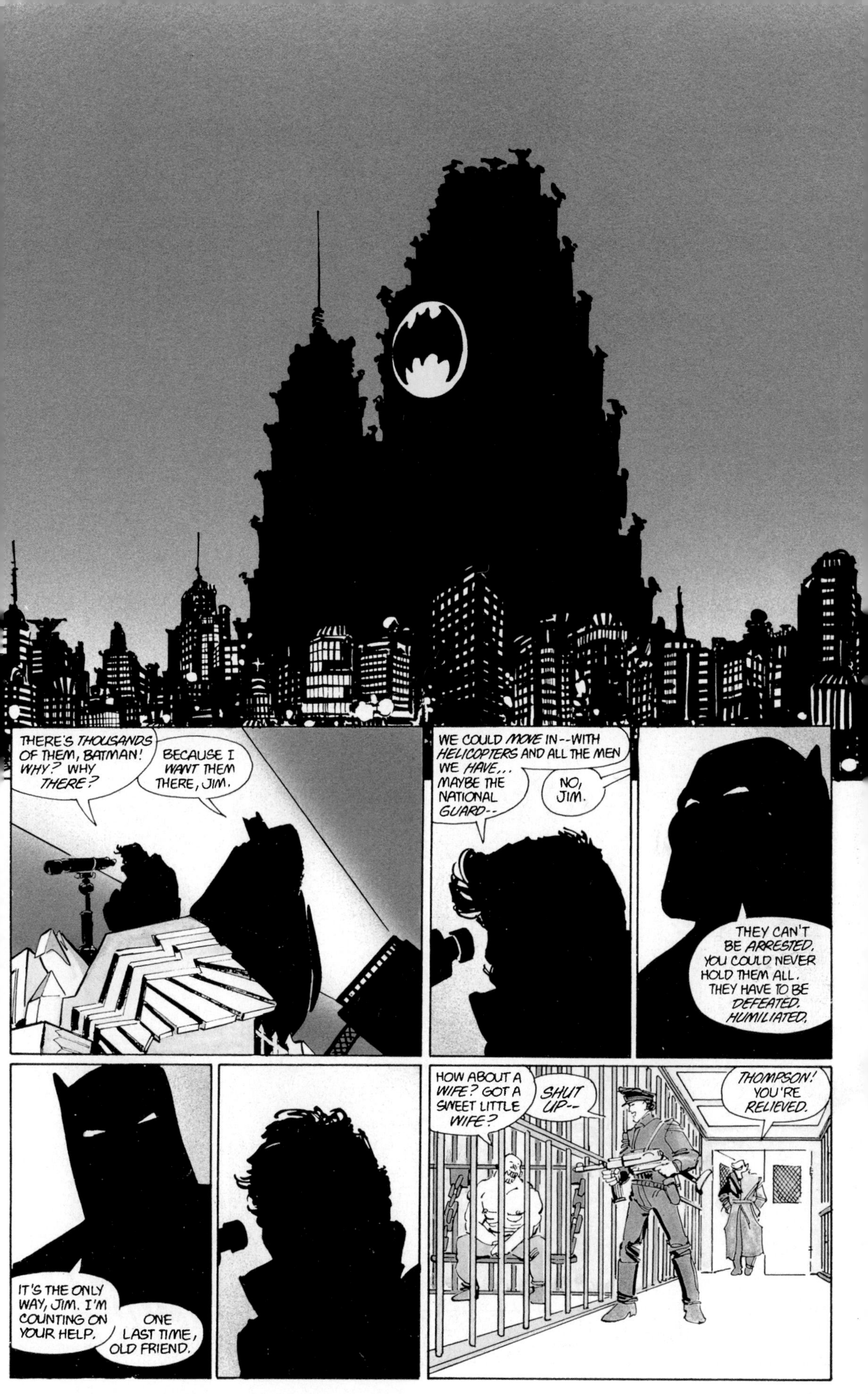

THERE'S THOUSANDS OF THEM, BATMAN! WHY? WHY THERE?
BECAUSE I WANT THEM THERE, JIM.
WE COULD MOVE IN--WITH HELICOPTERS AND ALL THE MEN WE HAVE... MAYBE THE NATIONAL GUARD--
NO, JIM.
THEY CAN'T BE ARRESTED. YOU COULD NEVER HOLD THEM ALL. THEY HAVE TO BE DEFEATED. HUMILIATED.
IT'S THE ONLY WAY, JIM. I'M COUNTING ON YOUR HELP.
ONE LAST TIME, OLD FRIEND.
HOW ABOUT A WIFE? GOT A SWEET LITTLE WIFE?
SHUT UP--
THOMPSON! YOU'RE RELIEVED.

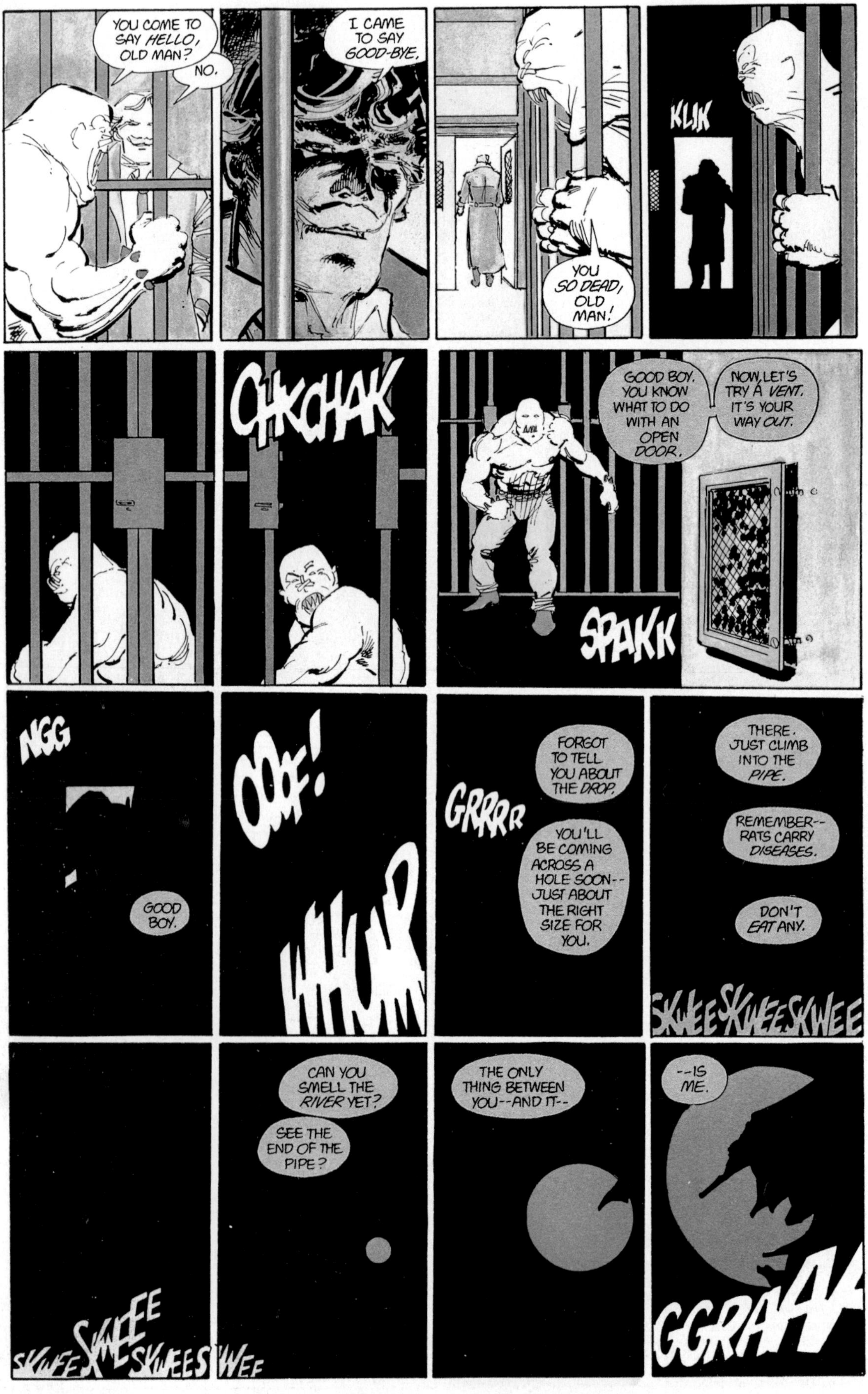
YOU COME TO SAY HELLO, OLD MAN?
NO.
I CAME TO SAY GOOD-BYE.
YOU SO DEAD, OLD MAN!
KLIK
CHKCHAK
GOOD BOY. YOU KNOW WHAT TO DO WITH AN OPEN DOOR.
NOW, LET'S TRY A VENT. IT'S YOUR WAY OUT.
SPAKK
NGG
GOOD BOY.
OOOF!
WHUMP
GRRRR
FORGOT TO TELL YOU ABOUT THE DROP.
YOU'LL BE COMING ACROSS A HOLE SOON-- JUST ABOUT THE RIGHT SIZE FOR YOU.
THERE. JUST CLIMB INTO THE PIPE.
REMEMBER-- RATS CARRY DISEASES.
DON'T EAT ANY.
SKWEESKWEESKWEE
SKWEESKWEESKWEESKWEE
CAN YOU SMELL THE RIVER YET?
SEE THE END OF THE PIPE?
THE ONLY THING BETWEEN YOU--AND IT--
--IS ME.
GGRAAA

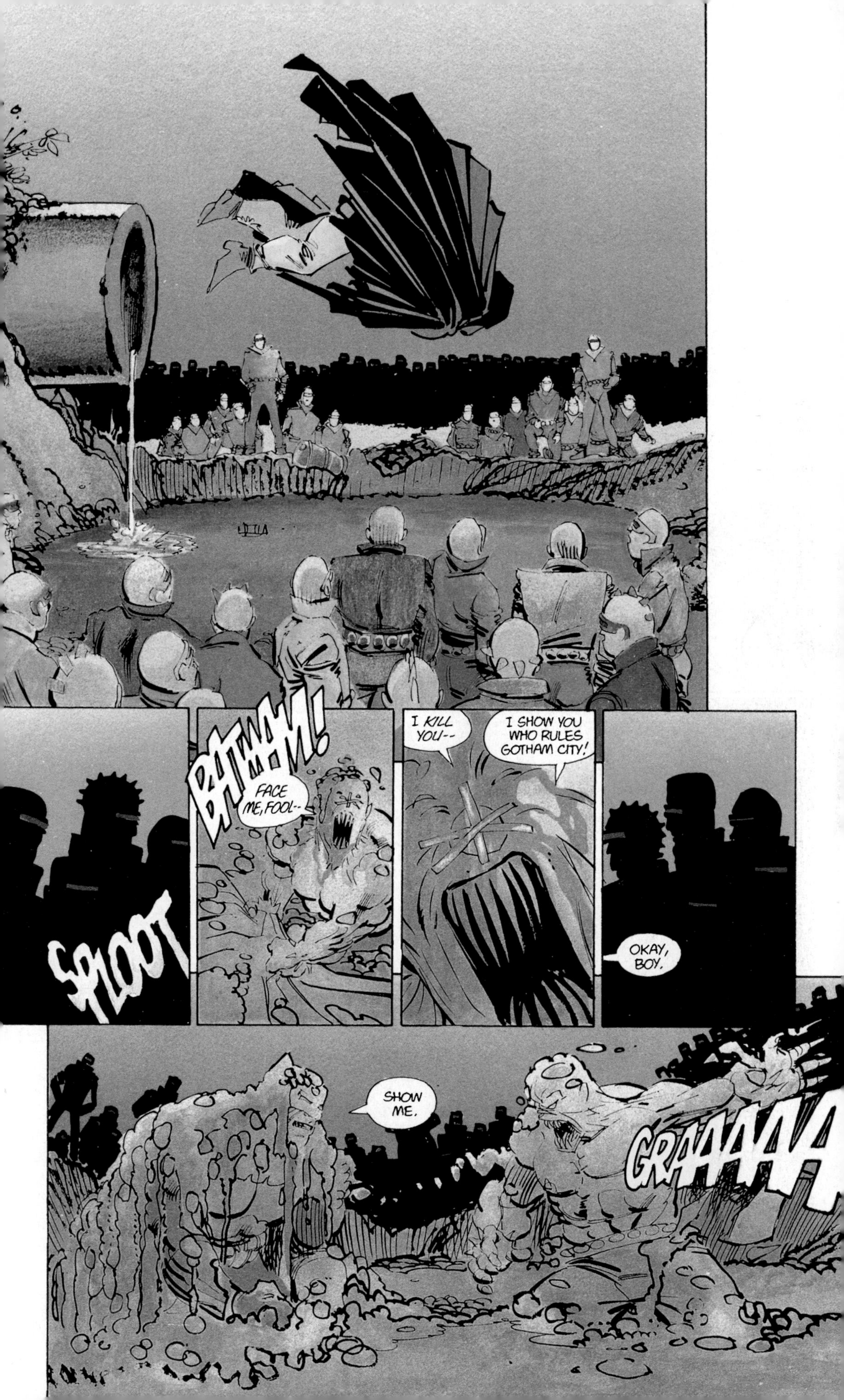
SPLOOT
BATMAN!
FACE ME, FOOL--
I KILL YOU--
I SHOW YOU WHO RULES GOTHAM CITY!
OKAY, BOY.
SHOW ME.
GRAAAAA

YOU SEE, DON. BATMAN --HE *NASTY*.

HOPE ROB DON'T SAY *BALLS* NASTY.

BALLS NASTY.

SHH!

HE'S FAST -- FASTER THAN I AM. AND STRONGER--

--AND SEEMINGLY IMPERVIOUS TO PAIN.

BUT THEY DO COME SMARTER.

--AND NOBODY'S VERY FAST WHEN HE'S THIGH-DEEP IN MUD.

I WAIT FOR HIM TO TRY A KICK--

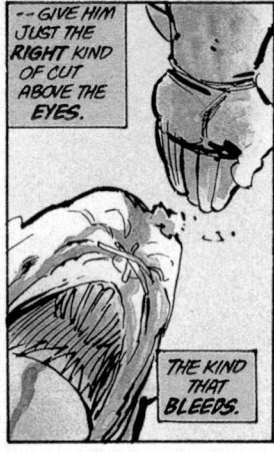

--GIVE HIM JUST THE *RIGHT* KIND OF CUT ABOVE THE EYES.

THE KIND THAT BLEEDS.

MY MISTAKE WAS TO TRY TO MATCH HIS SAVAGERY.

TO FIGHT LIKE A YOUNG MAN.

RIGHT ON SCHEDULE THE BLOOD HITS HIS EYES.

I GRAB A CLUMP OF MUD.

SPLOOT

LEADER'S *BOGGIN!*

LEADER BILLY BERSERK, SPUD. LEADER PEG BATMAN. YOU SEE.

SHH!

HE CHARGES, BLIND --

--A QUICK ONE TO THE NERVE CLUSTER IN HIS DELTOID. IT DOESN'T HURT HIM --

-- BUT NO FORCE ON EARTH COULD HELP HIM MOVE HIS *LEFT ARM* NOW.

HIS RIGHT--

--IT'S FAST--

--TOO FAST--

HE DUSTED! HE DUSTED!

MY MON *BATS* DON'T SHIV.

YOU SEE.

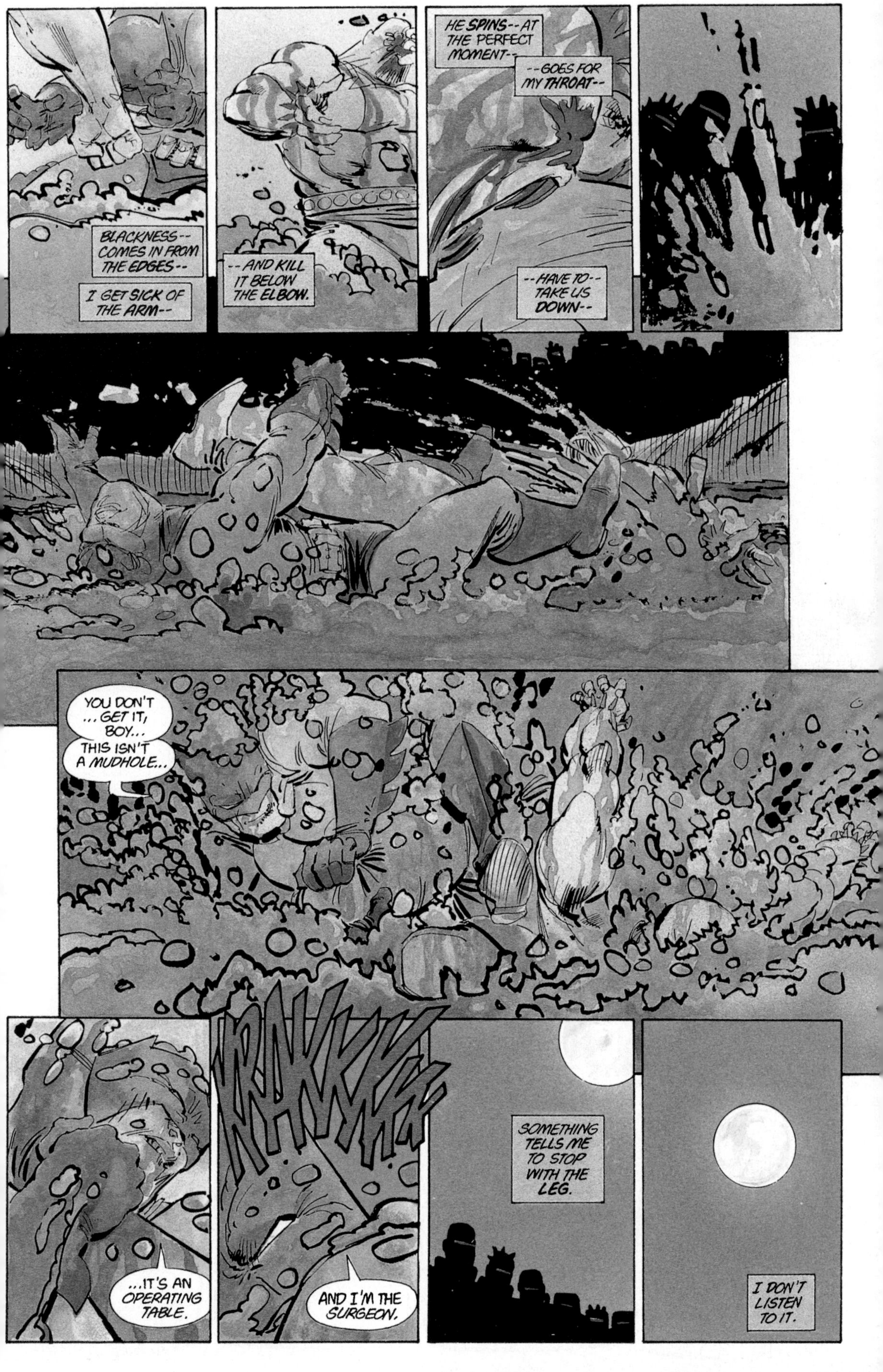
BLACKNESS-- COMES IN FROM THE EDGES--
I GET SICK OF THE ARM--
--AND KILL IT BELOW THE ELBOW.
HE SPINS--AT THE PERFECT MOMENT--
--GOES FOR MY THROAT--
--HAVE TO--TAKE US DOWN--
YOU DON'T ...GET IT, BOY... THIS ISN'T A MUDHOLE...
...IT'S AN OPERATING TABLE.
KRAKKK
AND I'M THE SURGEON.
SOMETHING TELLS ME TO STOP WITH THE LEG.
I DON'T LISTEN TO IT.

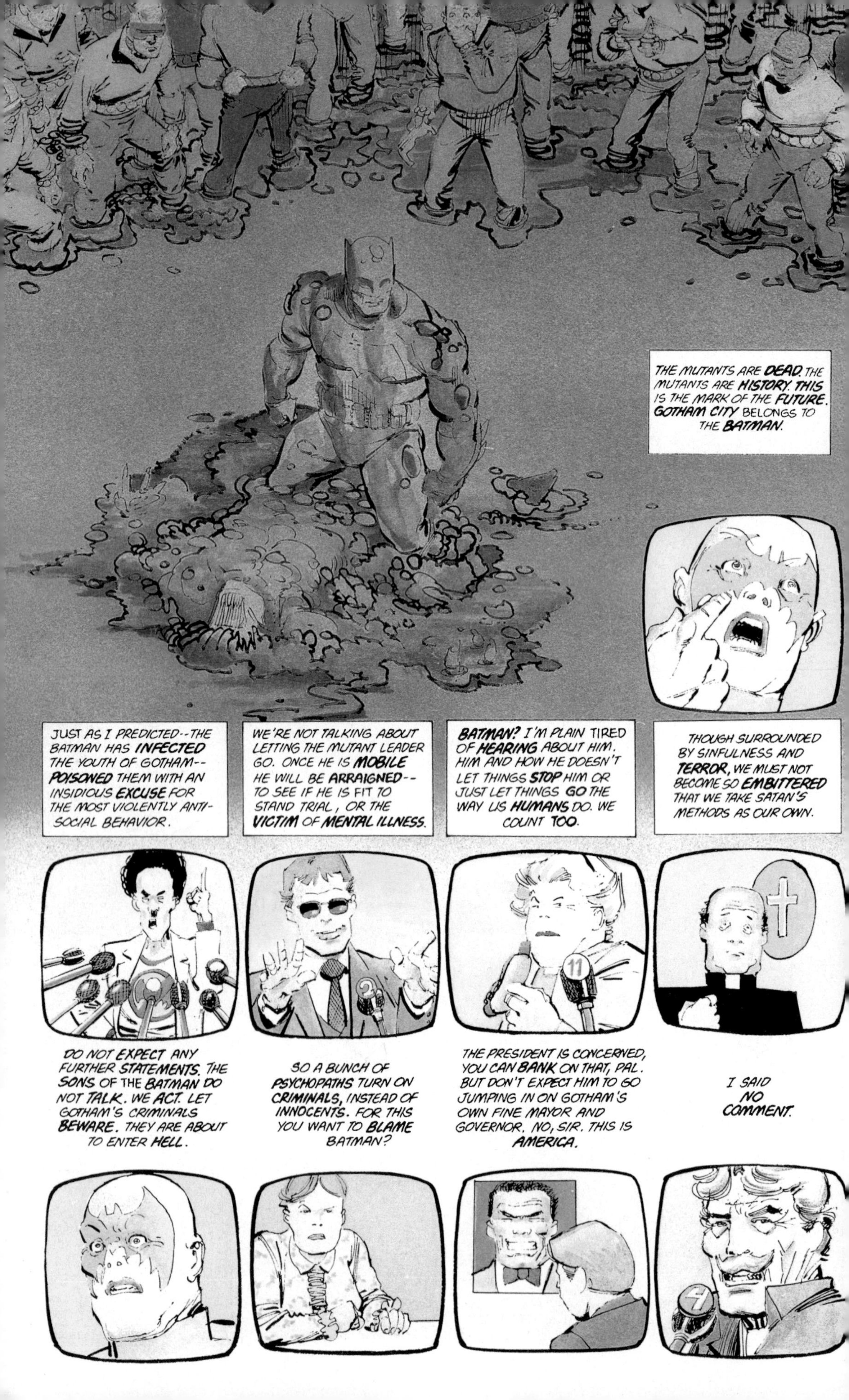
THE MUTANTS ARE DEAD. THE MUTANTS ARE HISTORY. THIS IS THE MARK OF THE FUTURE. GOTHAM CITY BELONGS TO THE BATMAN.
JUST AS I PREDICTED--THE BATMAN HAS INFECTED THE YOUTH OF GOTHAM--POISONED THEM WITH AN INSIDIOUS EXCUSE FOR THE MOST VIOLENTLY ANTI-SOCIAL BEHAVIOR.
WE'RE NOT TALKING ABOUT LETTING THE MUTANT LEADER GO. ONCE HE IS MOBILE HE WILL BE ARRAIGNED--TO SEE IF HE IS FIT TO STAND TRIAL, OR THE VICTIM OF MENTAL ILLNESS.
BATMAN? I'M PLAIN TIRED OF HEARING ABOUT HIM. HIM AND HOW HE DOESN'T LET THINGS STOP HIM OR JUST LET THINGS GO THE WAY US HUMANS DO. WE COUNT TOO.
THOUGH SURROUNDED BY SINFULNESS AND TERROR, WE MUST NOT BECOME SO EMBITTERED THAT WE TAKE SATAN'S METHODS AS OUR OWN.
11
DO NOT EXPECT ANY FURTHER STATEMENTS. THE SONS OF THE BATMAN DO NOT TALK. WE ACT. LET GOTHAM'S CRIMINALS BEWARE. THEY ARE ABOUT TO ENTER HELL.
SO A BUNCH OF PSYCHOPATHS TURN ON CRIMINALS, INSTEAD OF INNOCENTS. FOR THIS YOU WANT TO BLAME BATMAN?
THE PRESIDENT IS CONCERNED, YOU CAN BANK ON THAT, PAL. BUT DON'T EXPECT HIM TO GO JUMPING IN ON GOTHAM'S OWN FINE MAYOR AND GOVERNOR. NO, SIR. THIS IS AMERICA.
I SAID NO COMMENT.

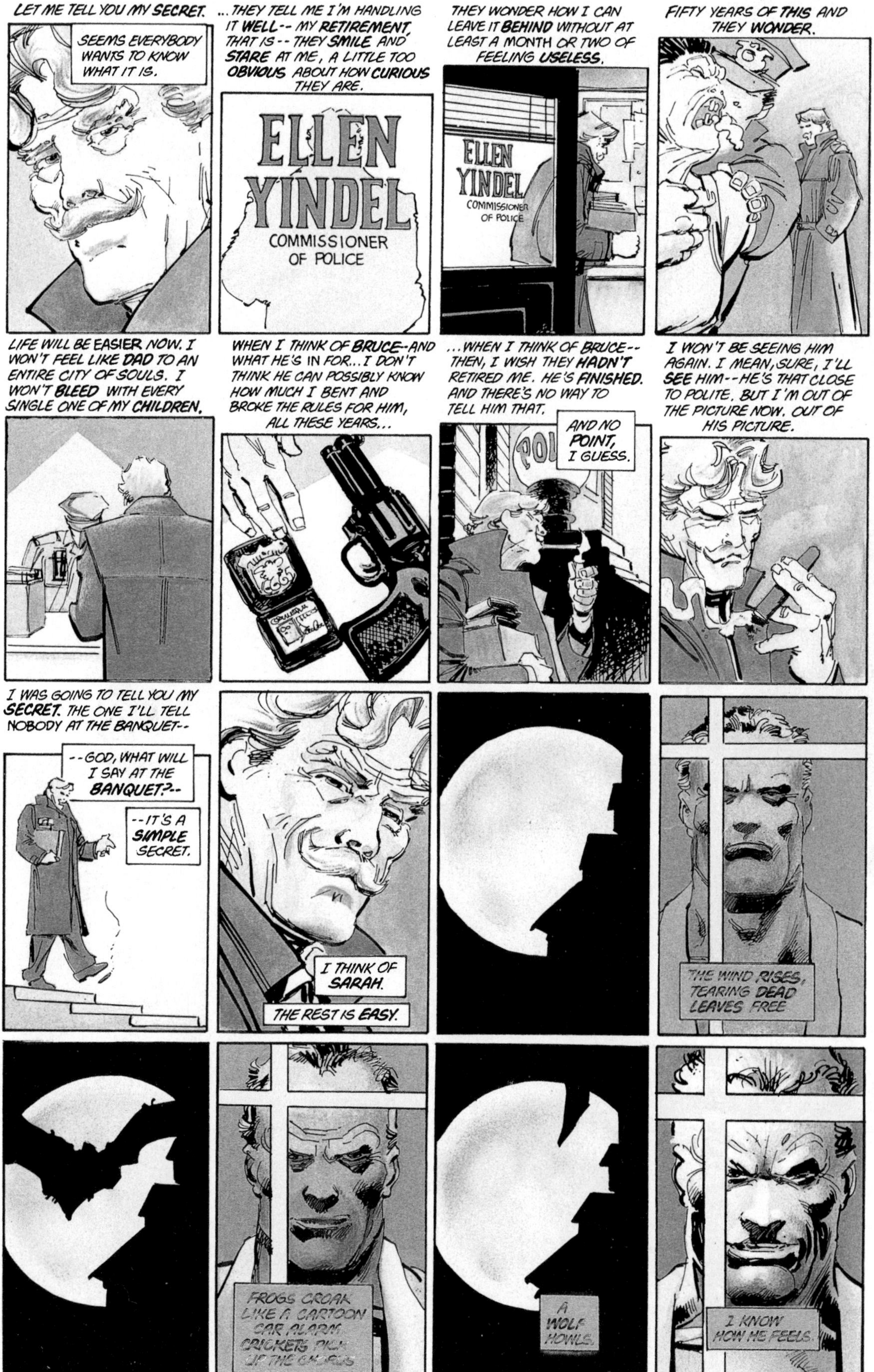
LET ME TELL YOU MY SECRET.
SEEMS EVERYBODY WANTS TO KNOW WHAT IT IS.
...THEY TELL ME I'M HANDLING IT WELL -- MY RETIREMENT, THAT IS -- THEY SMILE AND STARE AT ME, A LITTLE TOO OBVIOUS ABOUT HOW CURIOUS THEY ARE.
ELLEN YINDEL
COMMISSIONER OF POLICE
THEY WONDER HOW I CAN LEAVE IT BEHIND WITHOUT AT LEAST A MONTH OR TWO OF FEELING USELESS.
ELLEN YINDEL
COMMISSIONER OF POLICE
FIFTY YEARS OF THIS AND THEY WONDER.
LIFE WILL BE EASIER NOW. I WON'T FEEL LIKE DAD TO AN ENTIRE CITY OF SOULS. I WON'T BLEED WITH EVERY SINGLE ONE OF MY CHILDREN.
WHEN I THINK OF BRUCE--AND WHAT HE'S IN FOR... I DON'T THINK HE CAN POSSIBLY KNOW HOW MUCH I BENT AND BROKE THE RULES FOR HIM, ALL THESE YEARS...
...WHEN I THINK OF BRUCE-- THEN, I WISH THEY HADN'T RETIRED ME. HE'S FINISHED. AND THERE'S NO WAY TO TELL HIM THAT.
AND NO POINT, I GUESS.
I WON'T BE SEEING HIM AGAIN. I MEAN, SURE, I'LL SEE HIM--HE'S THAT CLOSE TO POLITE. BUT I'M OUT OF THE PICTURE NOW. OUT OF HIS PICTURE.
I WAS GOING TO TELL YOU MY SECRET. THE ONE I'LL TELL NOBODY AT THE BANQUET--
--GOD, WHAT WILL I SAY AT THE BANQUET?--
--IT'S A SIMPLE SECRET.
I THINK OF SARAH.
THE REST IS EASY.
THE WIND RISES, TEARING DEAD LEAVES FREE
FROGS CROAK LIKE A CARTOON CAR ALARM. CRICKETS PICK UP THE CHORUS.
A WOLF HOWLS.
I KNOW HOW HE FEELS.

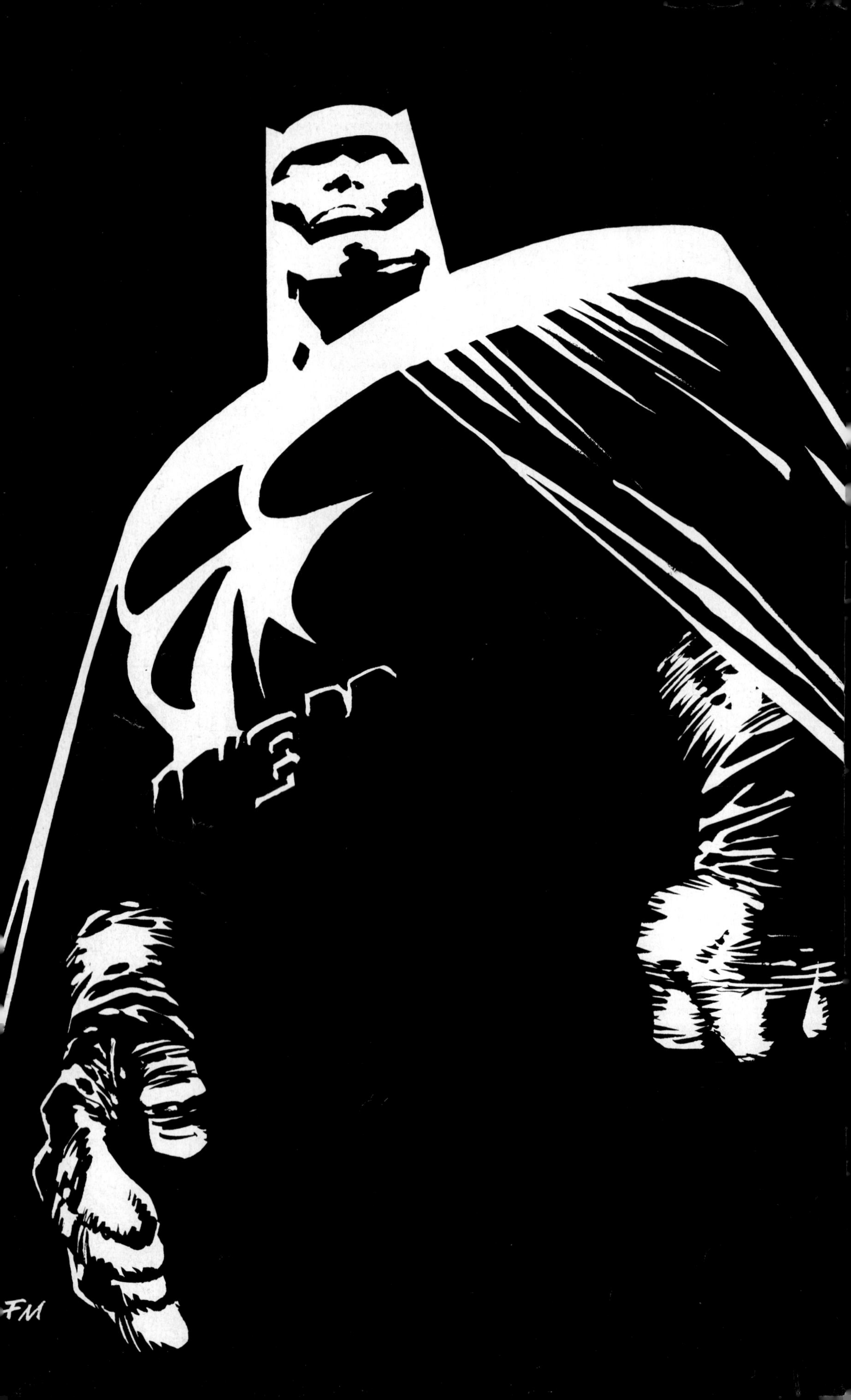
FM

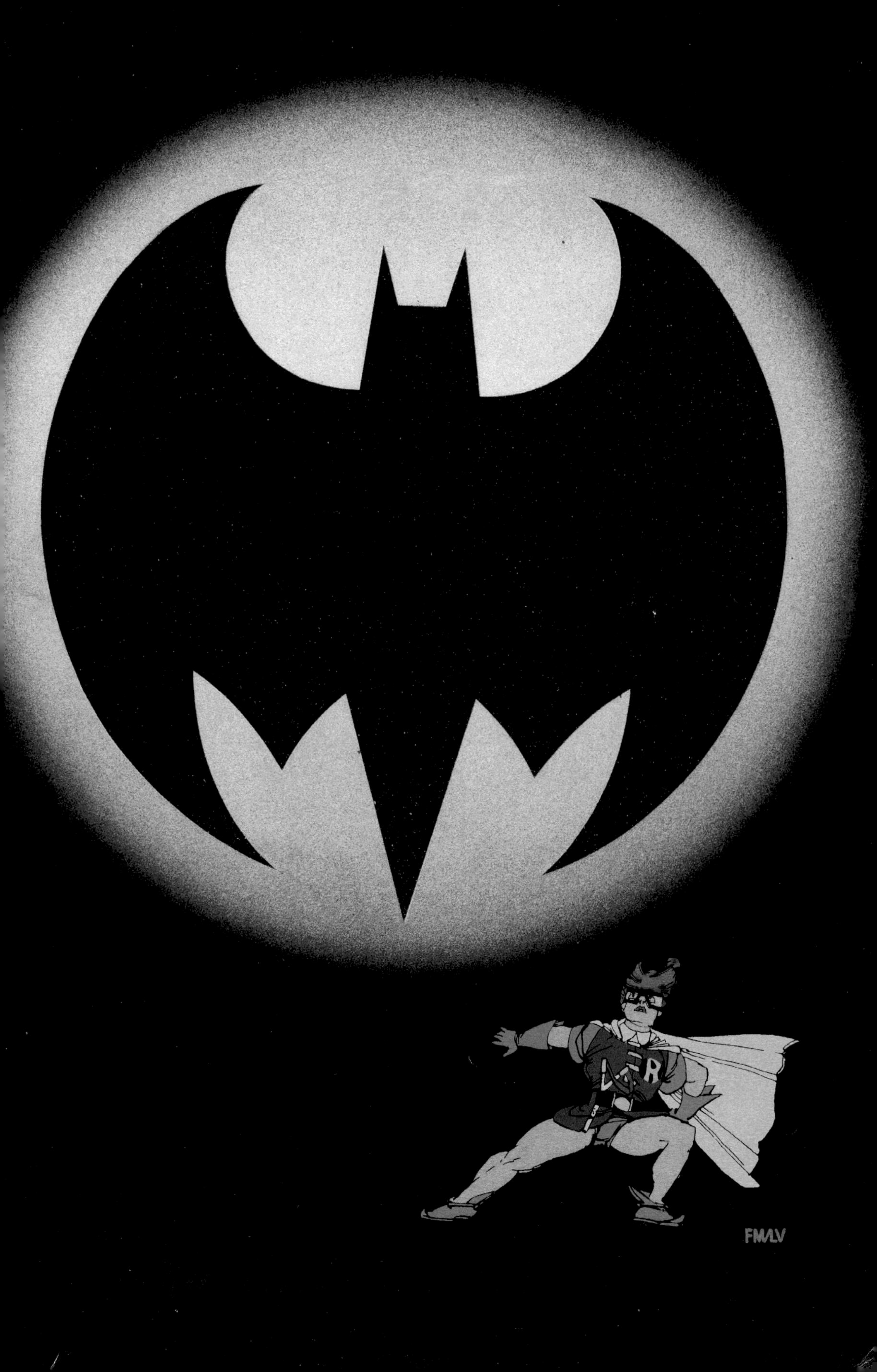
FM/LV

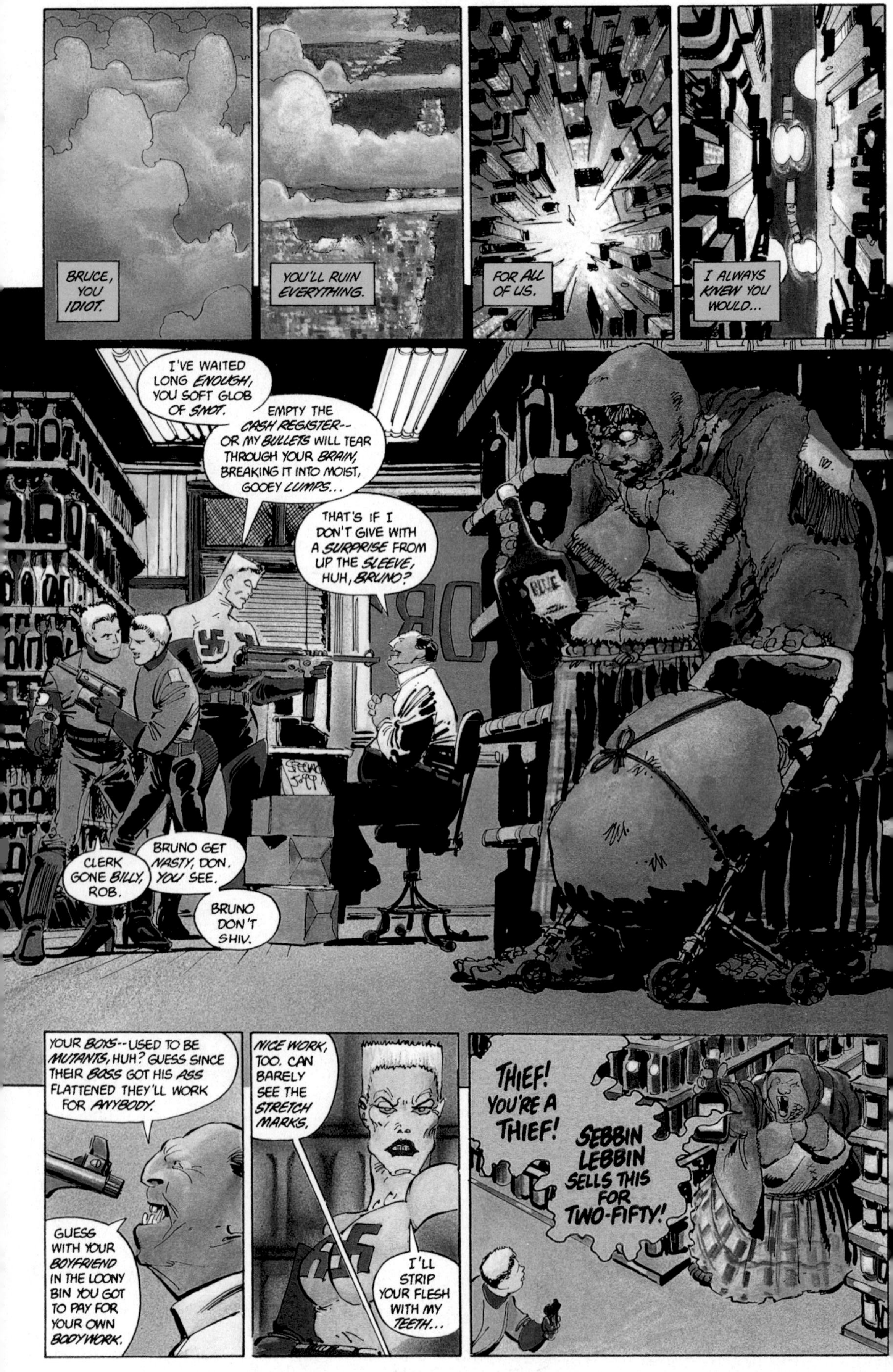
BRUCE, YOU IDIOT.
YOU'LL RUIN EVERYTHING.
FOR ALL OF US.
I ALWAYS KNEW YOU WOULD...
I'VE WAITED LONG ENOUGH, YOU SOFT GLOB OF SNOT.
EMPTY THE CASH REGISTER-- OR MY BULLETS WILL TEAR THROUGH YOUR BRAIN, BREAKING IT INTO MOIST, GOOEY LUMPS...
THAT'S IF I DON'T GIVE WITH A SURPRISE FROM UP THE SLEEVE, HUH, BRUNO?
CLERK GONE BILLY, ROB.
BRUNO GET NASTY, DON. YOU SEE.
BRUNO DON'T SHIV.
YOUR BOYS--USED TO BE MUTANTS, HUH? GUESS SINCE THEIR BOSS GOT HIS ASS FLATTENED THEY'LL WORK FOR ANYBODY.
GUESS WITH YOUR BOYFRIEND IN THE LOONY BIN YOU GOT TO PAY FOR YOUR OWN BODYWORK.
NICE WORK, TOO. CAN BARELY SEE THE STRETCH MARKS.
I'LL STRIP YOUR FLESH WITH MY TEETH...
THIEF! YOU'RE A THIEF!
SEBBIN LEBBIN SELLS THIS FOR TWO-FIFTY!

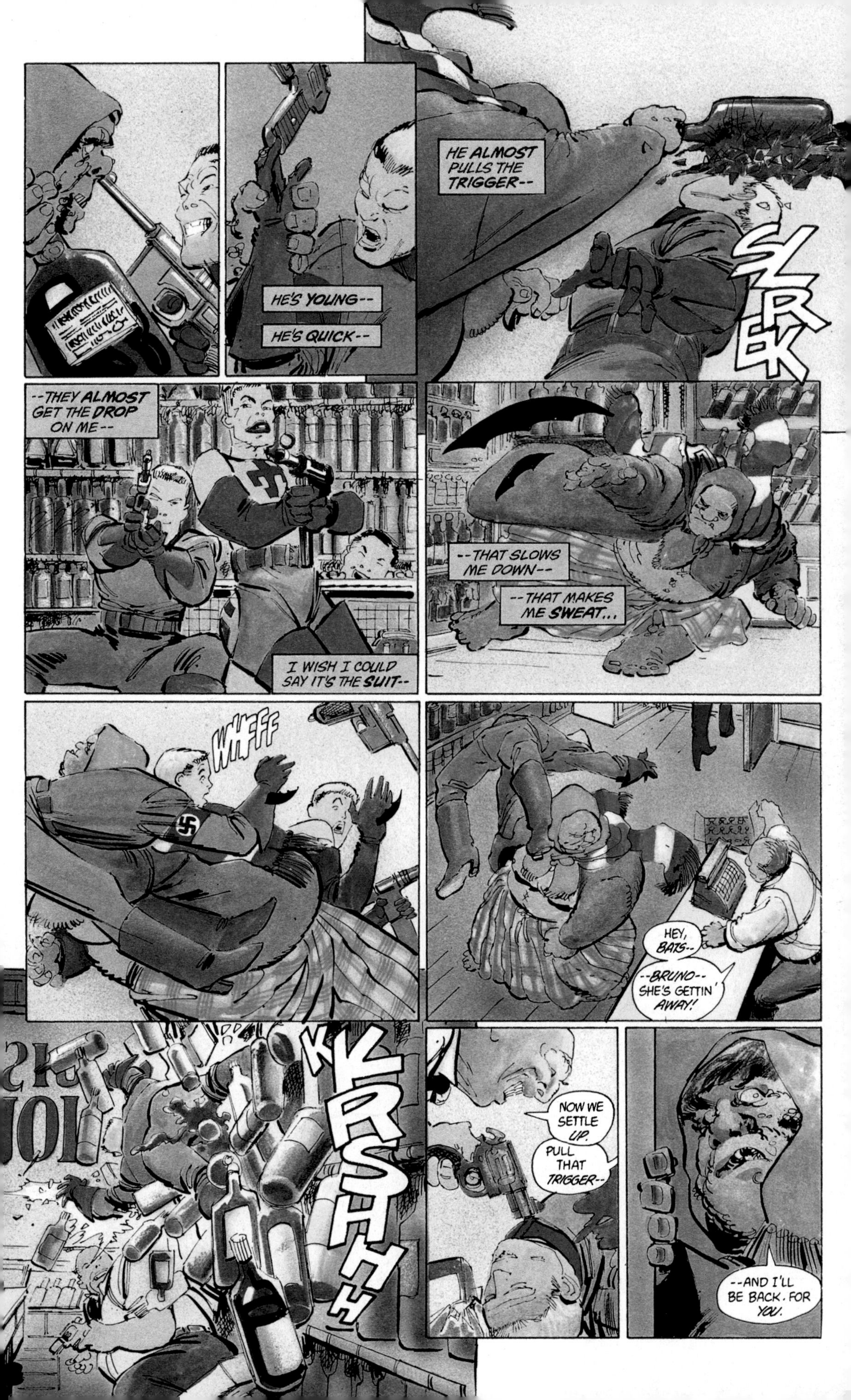
HE'S YOUNG--
HE'S QUICK--
HE ALMOST PULLS THE TRIGGER--
SLREK
--THEY ALMOST GET THE DROP ON ME--
I WISH I COULD SAY IT'S THE SUIT--
--THAT SLOWS ME DOWN--
--THAT MAKES ME SWEAT...
WHFFF
HEY, BATS--
--BRUNO-- SHE'S GETTIN' AWAY!
KKRSHHH
NOW WE SETTLE UP.
PULL THAT TRIGGER--
--AND I'LL BE BACK. FOR YOU.

BRUNO IS COMING YOUR WAY, ROBIN.

GET HER INTO THE ALLEY. DO NOT LET HER SEE YOU.

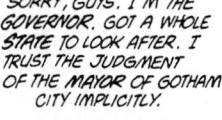

BOYS, BOYS, BOYS... ONE AT A TIME NOW... NOW HOW ABOUT THAT SMARTLY DRESSED YOUNGSTER IN THE FRONT ROW THERE...

MR. PRESIDENT-- WE'RE ALL ANXIOUS TO HEAR YOUR PLANS FOR THE CORTO MALTESE CRISIS. BUT FIRST, ANOTHER QUESTION MUCH ON THE MINDS OF AMERICA. WHAT IS YOUR POSITION ON THE BATMAN CONTROVERSY?

WELL, I DON'T THINK THAT'S MY BULL TO -- MY ROW TO HOE, BOYS... HEH... YOU SEE. THAT'S A RIGHT BIG STATE, ALL ITS OWN... AND IT'S GOT ITS OWN SOLID, CLEAR-HEADED GOVERNOR, YES, IT DOES...

SORRY, GUYS. I'M THE GOVERNOR. GOT A WHOLE STATE TO LOOK AFTER. I TRUST THE JUDGMENT OF THE MAYOR OF GOTHAM CITY IMPLICITLY.

AS MAYOR, IT IS MY DUTY TO ADMINISTRATE-- NOT TO RENDER MORAL JUDGMENTS. DON'T ASK ME TO INTERFERE WITH THE DECISION-MAKING POWER OF OUR NEW POLICE COMMISSIONER.

AND SO THE BATMAN BUCK IS PASSED-- TO ELLEN YINDEL, WHO REPLACES JAMES GORDON AS POLICE COMMISSIONER TONIGHT. WILL SHE FULFILL HER PROMISE TO ISSUE AN ARREST WARRANT FOR THE BATMAN?

CHANNEL TWO WILL BROADCAST THE BANQUET LIVE. GORDON IS SCHEDULED TO INTRODUCE YINDEL-- A GRACEFUL GESTURE, CONSIDERING THEIR DIFFERENCES. WE MAY SEE SOME SPARKS FLY. TOM?

THAT WE MAY, LOLA. WE'LL BE RIGHT BACK, AS JULIE PARKS BRINGS US A STORY WE DON'T KNOW WHETHER TO CLASSIFY AS AN ATMO-SPHERE ANOMALY-- OR A UFO SIGHTING.

I REPEAT, DO NOT LET BRUNO SEE YOU. THIS IS AN ORDER.

SPANG

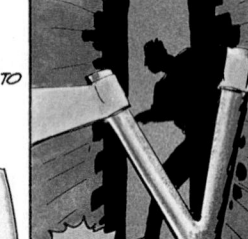

SPUD

BRAP

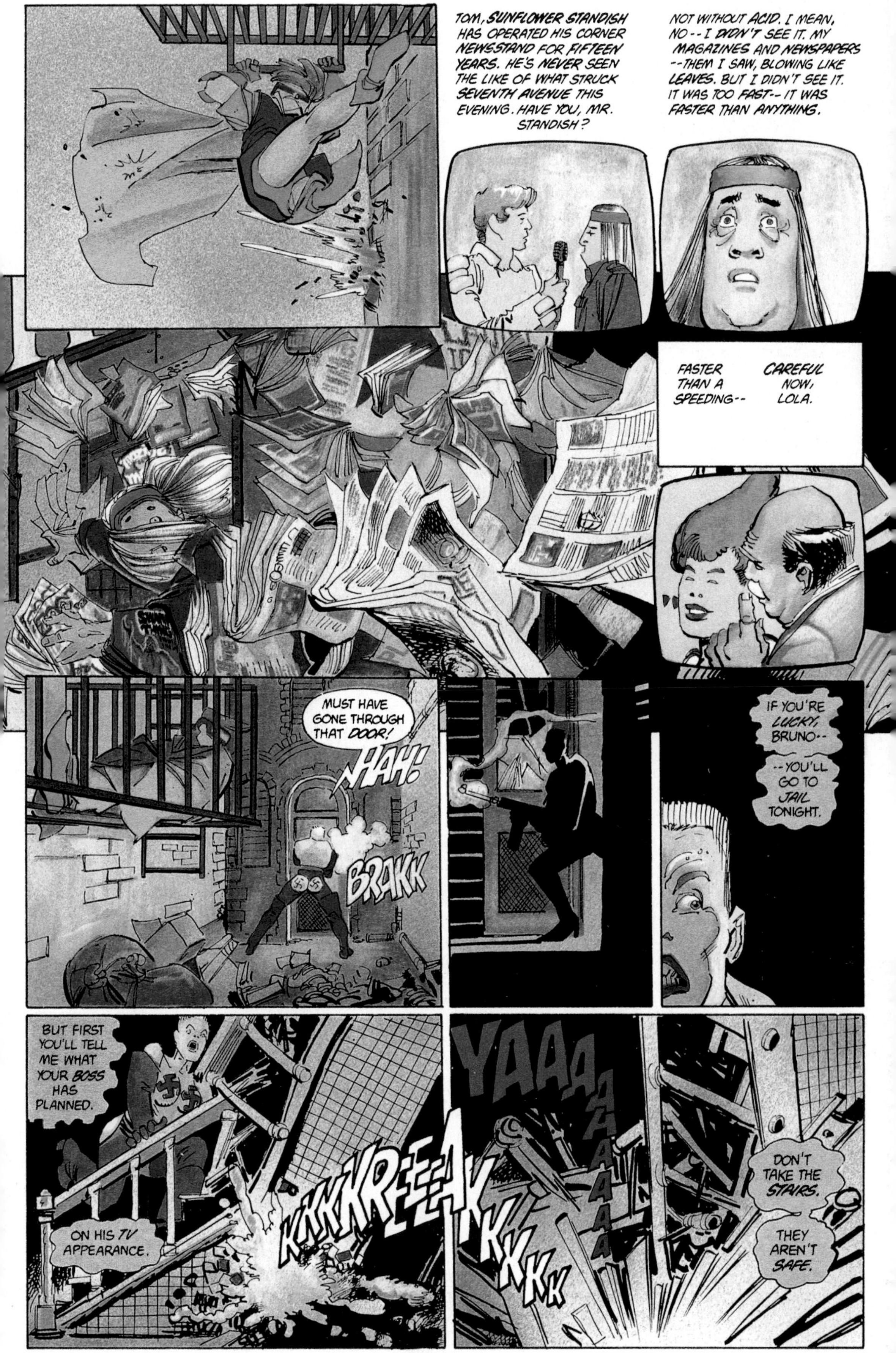
TOM, SUNFLOWER STANDISH HAS OPERATED HIS CORNER NEWSSTAND FOR FIFTEEN YEARS. HE'S NEVER SEEN THE LIKE OF WHAT STRUCK SEVENTH AVENUE THIS EVENING. HAVE YOU, MR. STANDISH?
NOT WITHOUT ACID. I MEAN, NO -- I DIDN'T SEE IT. MY MAGAZINES AND NEWSPAPERS --THEM I SAW, BLOWING LIKE LEAVES. BUT I DIDN'T SEE IT. IT WAS TOO FAST-- IT WAS FASTER THAN ANYTHING.
FASTER THAN A SPEEDING--
CAREFUL NOW, LOLA.
MUST HAVE GONE THROUGH THAT DOOR!
HAH!
BRAKK
IF YOU'RE LUCKY, BRUNO--
--YOU'LL GO TO JAIL TONIGHT.
BUT FIRST YOU'LL TELL ME WHAT YOUR BOSS HAS PLANNED.
ON HIS TV APPEARANCE.
YAAAAAAAAAAA
KKKKREEEAKKKKK
DON'T TAKE THE STAIRS.
THEY AREN'T SAFE.

NEVER MEANT-- TO GIVE HER TIME--

CHKCHAKK

"TO COCK THAT THING..."

BRAPP

THIS WOULD BE A STUPID DEATH...

MISSED.

LUCKY

LUCKY OLD MAN...

ANOTHER *BIZARRE* INCIDENT--THIS ONE IN THE SOUTH STREET *SUBWAY STATION.* ADVERTISING AGENT *BYRON BRASSBALLS* TOLD REPORTERS...

I DIDN'T DO ANYTHING *WRONG.* I WAS JUST TRYING TO *PROTECT* MYSELF. THE SUBWAYS ARE *DANGEROUS.* YOU DON'T NEED *ME* TO TELL YOU THAT. SO THERE I WAS, ALONE IN THE STATION EXCEPT FOR THIS "BEGGAR"-- I WANT THAT IN *QUOTES*--

--WHAT?...HOW WAS I TO KNOW HE DIDN'T HAVE A GUN? THEY NEVER *SHOW* YOU THAT UNTIL THEY'RE READY TO KILL YOU-- WHAT?...OH, SURE. THE *CRUTCHES.* A LOT OF THEM USE *CRUTCHES.* YOU KNOW WHAT I MEAN.

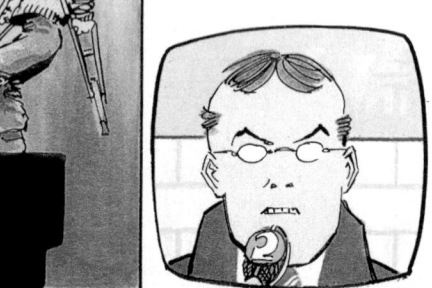

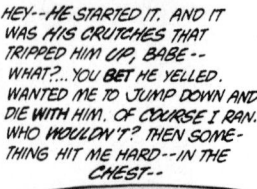

HEY--*HE* STARTED IT. AND IT WAS *HIS CRUTCHES* THAT TRIPPED HIM *UP,* BABE-- WHAT?...YOU *BET* HE YELLED. WANTED ME TO JUMP DOWN AND DIE *WITH* HIM. OF COURSE I RAN. WHO *WOULDN'T?* THEN SOME- THING HIT ME HARD--IN THE *CHEST*--

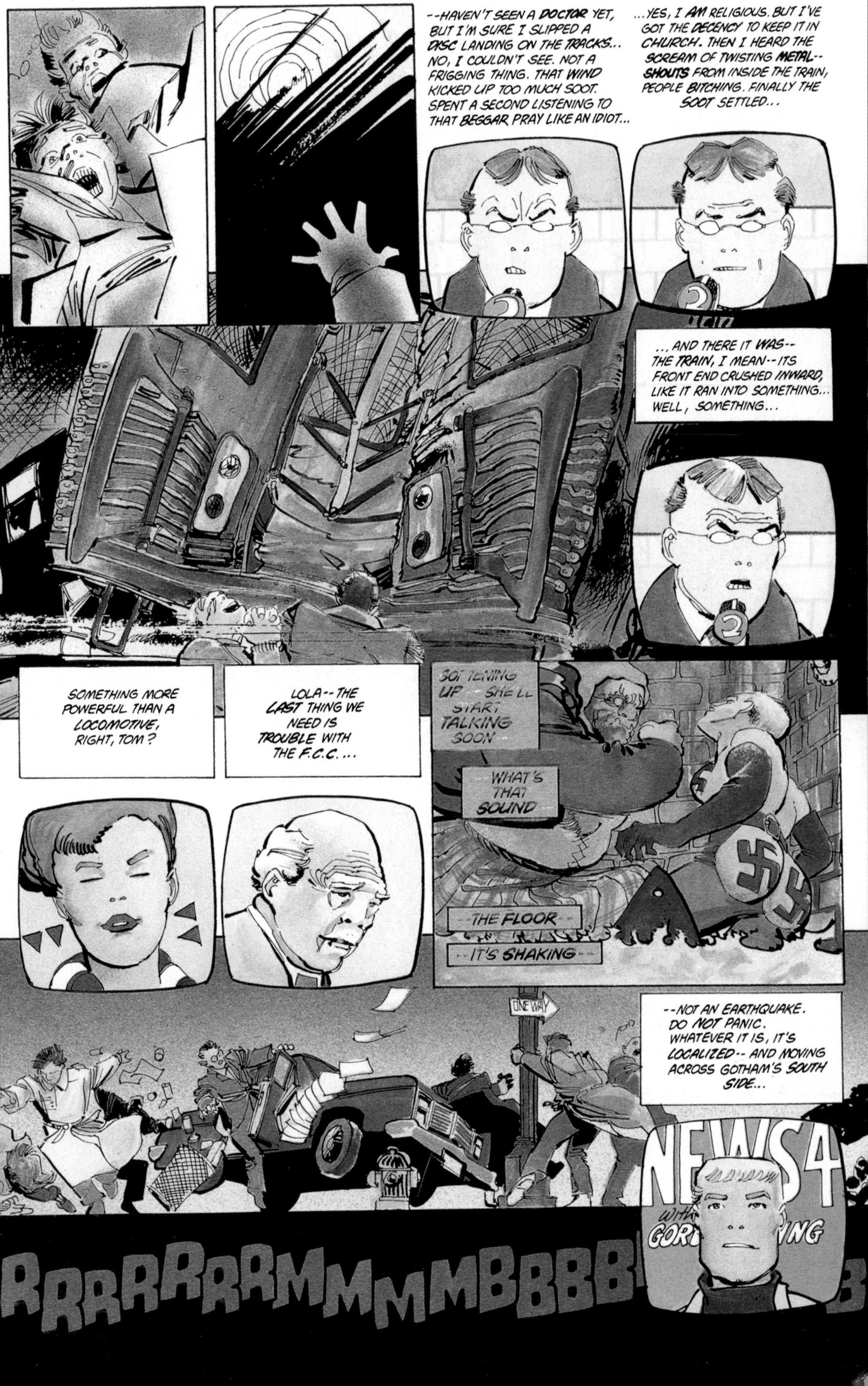
--HAVEN'T SEEN A DOCTOR YET, BUT I'M SURE I SLIPPED A DISC LANDING ON THE TRACKS... NO, I COULDN'T SEE. NOT A FRIGGING THING. THAT WIND KICKED UP TOO MUCH SOOT. SPENT A SECOND LISTENING TO THAT BEGGAR PRAY LIKE AN IDIOT...
...YES, I AM RELIGIOUS. BUT I'VE GOT THE DECENCY TO KEEP IT IN CHURCH. THEN I HEARD THE SCREAM OF TWISTING METAL--SHOUTS FROM INSIDE THE TRAIN, PEOPLE BITCHING. FINALLY THE SOOT SETTLED...
...AND THERE IT WAS--THE TRAIN, I MEAN--ITS FRONT END CRUSHED INWARD, LIKE IT RAN INTO SOMETHING... WELL, SOMETHING...
SOMETHING MORE POWERFUL THAN A LOCOMOTIVE, RIGHT, TOM?
LOLA--THE LAST THING WE NEED IS TROUBLE WITH THE F.C.C. ...
SOFTENING UP -- SHE'LL START TALKING SOON --
WHAT'S THAT SOUND
THE FLOOR
IT'S SHAKING
ONE WAY
--NOT AN EARTHQUAKE. DO NOT PANIC. WHATEVER IT IS, IT'S LOCALIZED-- AND MOVING ACROSS GOTHAM'S SOUTH SIDE...
NEWS4
RRRRRRRMMMMBBBBB

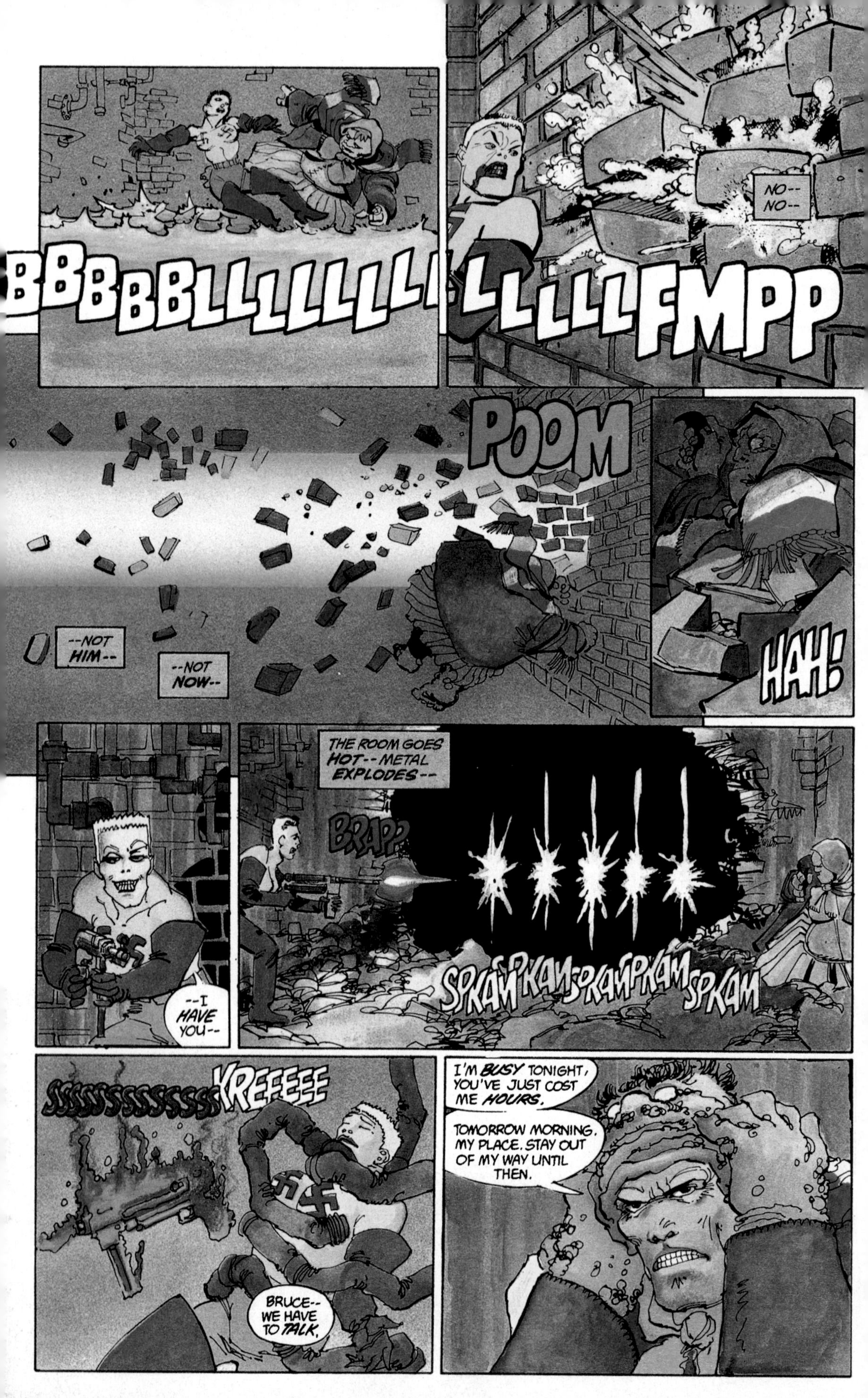

BBBBBLLLLLLLLLLLLLFMPP
NO--
NO--
POOM
--NOT
HIM--
--NOT
NOW--
HAH!
--I
HAVE
YOU--
THE ROOM GOES
HOT--METAL
EXPLODES--
BRAPP
SPKAM SPKAM SPKAM SPKAM SPKAM
SSSSSSSSSSSSSKREEEEE
BRUCE--
WE HAVE
TO TALK,
I'M BUSY TONIGHT,
YOU'VE JUST COST
ME HOURS.
TOMORROW MORNING.
MY PLACE. STAY OUT
OF MY WAY UNTIL
THEN.

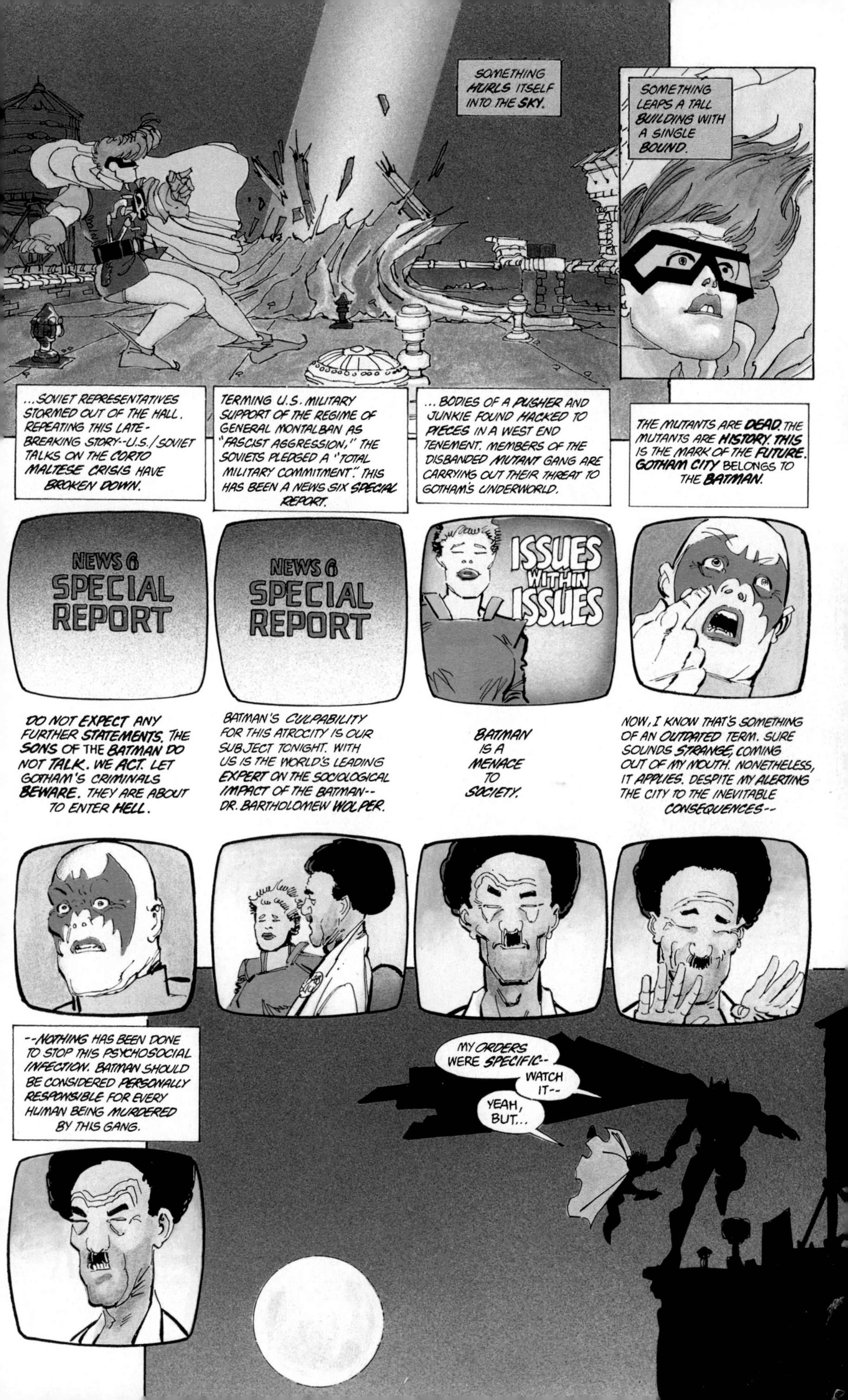

SOMETHING HURLS ITSELF INTO THE SKY.
SOMETHING LEAPS A TALL BUILDING WITH A SINGLE BOUND.
...SOVIET REPRESENTATIVES STORMED OUT OF THE HALL. REPEATING THIS LATE-BREAKING STORY--U.S./SOVIET TALKS ON THE CORTO MALTESE CRISIS HAVE BROKEN DOWN.
TERMING U.S. MILITARY SUPPORT OF THE REGIME OF GENERAL MONTALBAN AS "FASCIST AGGRESSION," THE SOVIETS PLEDGED A "TOTAL MILITARY COMMITMENT." THIS HAS BEEN A NEWS SIX SPECIAL REPORT.
...BODIES OF A PUSHER AND JUNKIE FOUND HACKED TO PIECES IN A WEST END TENEMENT. MEMBERS OF THE DISBANDED MUTANT GANG ARE CARRYING OUT THEIR THREAT TO GOTHAM'S UNDERWORLD.
THE MUTANTS ARE DEAD. THE MUTANTS ARE HISTORY. THIS IS THE MARK OF THE FUTURE. GOTHAM CITY BELONGS TO THE BATMAN.
NEWS 6 SPECIAL REPORT
NEWS 6 SPECIAL REPORT
ISSUES WITHIN ISSUES
DO NOT EXPECT ANY FURTHER STATEMENTS. THE SONS OF THE BATMAN DO NOT TALK. WE ACT. LET GOTHAM'S CRIMINALS BEWARE. THEY ARE ABOUT TO ENTER HELL.
BATMAN'S CULPABILITY FOR THIS ATROCITY IS OUR SUBJECT TONIGHT. WITH US IS THE WORLD'S LEADING EXPERT ON THE SOCIOLOGICAL IMPACT OF THE BATMAN-- DR. BARTHOLOMEW WOLPER.
BATMAN IS A MENACE TO SOCIETY.
NOW, I KNOW THAT'S SOMETHING OF AN OUTDATED TERM. SURE SOUNDS STRANGE, COMING OUT OF MY MOUTH. NONETHELESS, IT APPLIES. DESPITE MY ALERTING THE CITY TO THE INEVITABLE CONSEQUENCES--
--NOTHING HAS BEEN DONE TO STOP THIS PSYCHOSOCIAL INFECTION. BATMAN SHOULD BE CONSIDERED PERSONALLY RESPONSIBLE FOR EVERY HUMAN BEING MURDERED BY THIS GANG.
MY ORDERS WERE SPECIFIC--
WATCH IT--
YEAH, BUT...

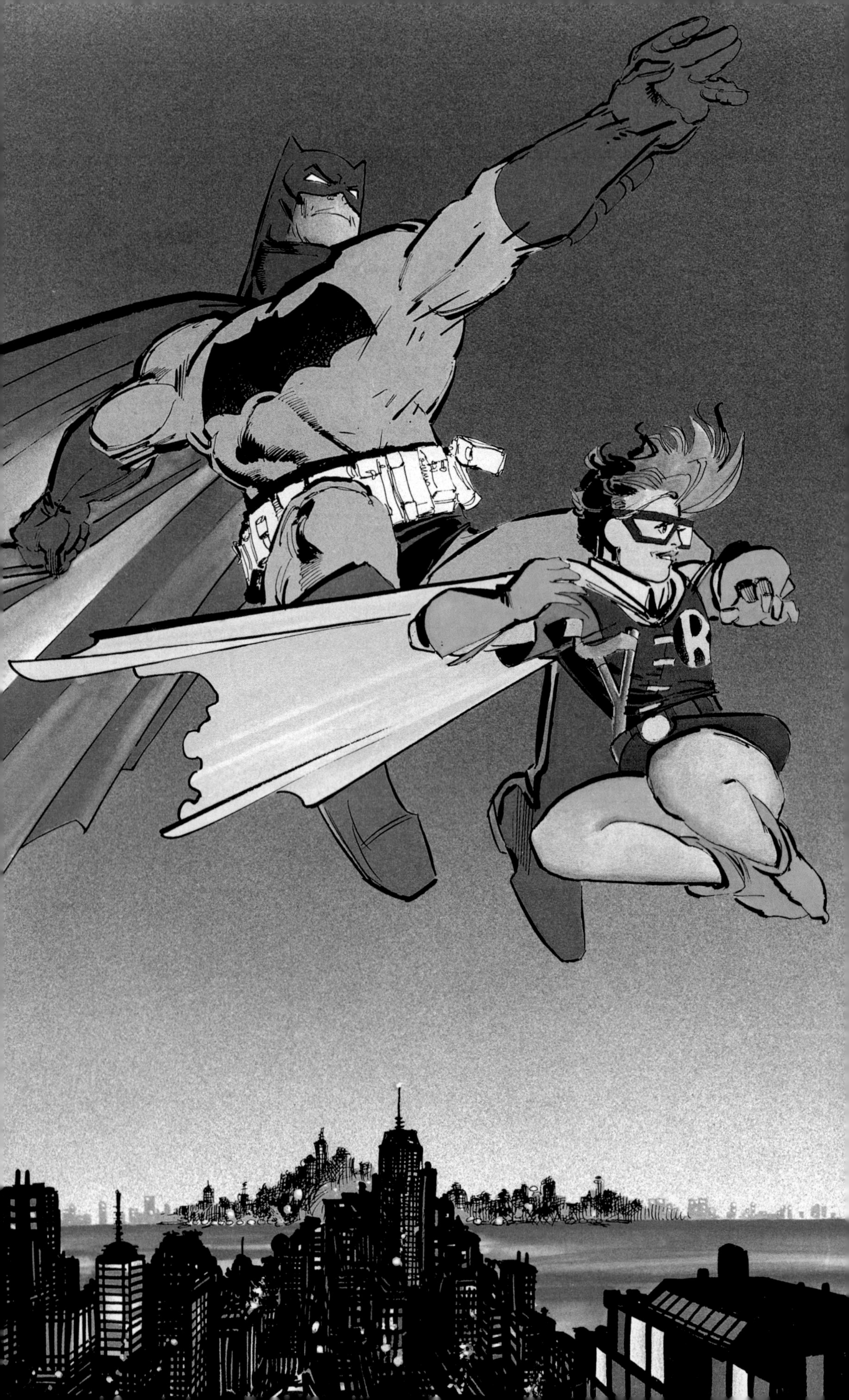

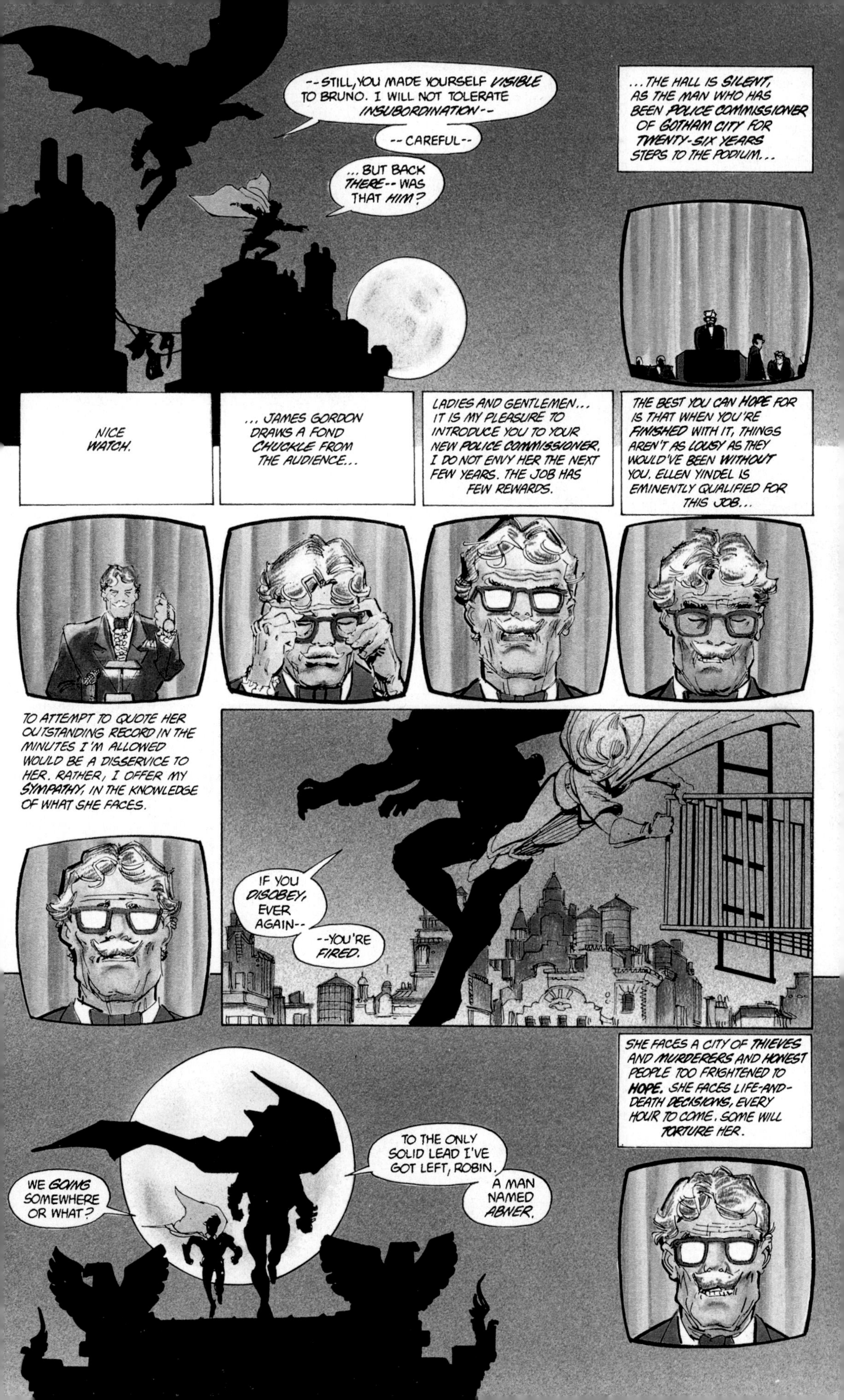
--STILL, YOU MADE YOURSELF VISIBLE TO BRUNO. I WILL NOT TOLERATE INSUBORDINATION--
--CAREFUL--
...BUT BACK THERE--WAS THAT HIM?
...THE HALL IS SILENT, AS THE MAN WHO HAS BEEN POLICE COMMISSIONER OF GOTHAM CITY FOR TWENTY-SIX YEARS STEPS TO THE PODIUM...
NICE WATCH.
...JAMES GORDON DRAWS A FOND CHUCKLE FROM THE AUDIENCE...
LADIES AND GENTLEMEN... IT IS MY PLEASURE TO INTRODUCE YOU TO YOUR NEW POLICE COMMISSIONER. I DO NOT ENVY HER THE NEXT FEW YEARS. THE JOB HAS FEW REWARDS.
THE BEST YOU CAN HOPE FOR IS THAT WHEN YOU'RE FINISHED WITH IT, THINGS AREN'T AS LOUSY AS THEY WOULD'VE BEEN WITHOUT YOU. ELLEN YINDEL IS EMINENTLY QUALIFIED FOR THIS JOB...
TO ATTEMPT TO QUOTE HER OUTSTANDING RECORD IN THE MINUTES I'M ALLOWED WOULD BE A DISSERVICE TO HER. RATHER, I OFFER MY SYMPATHY, IN THE KNOWLEDGE OF WHAT SHE FACES.
IF YOU DISOBEY, EVER AGAIN--
--YOU'RE FIRED.
SHE FACES A CITY OF THIEVES AND MURDERERS AND HONEST PEOPLE TOO FRIGHTENED TO HOPE. SHE FACES LIFE-AND-DEATH DECISIONS, EVERY HOUR TO COME. SOME WILL TORTURE HER.
WE GOING SOMEWHERE OR WHAT?
TO THE ONLY SOLID LEAD I'VE GOT LEFT, ROBIN.
A MAN NAMED ABNER.

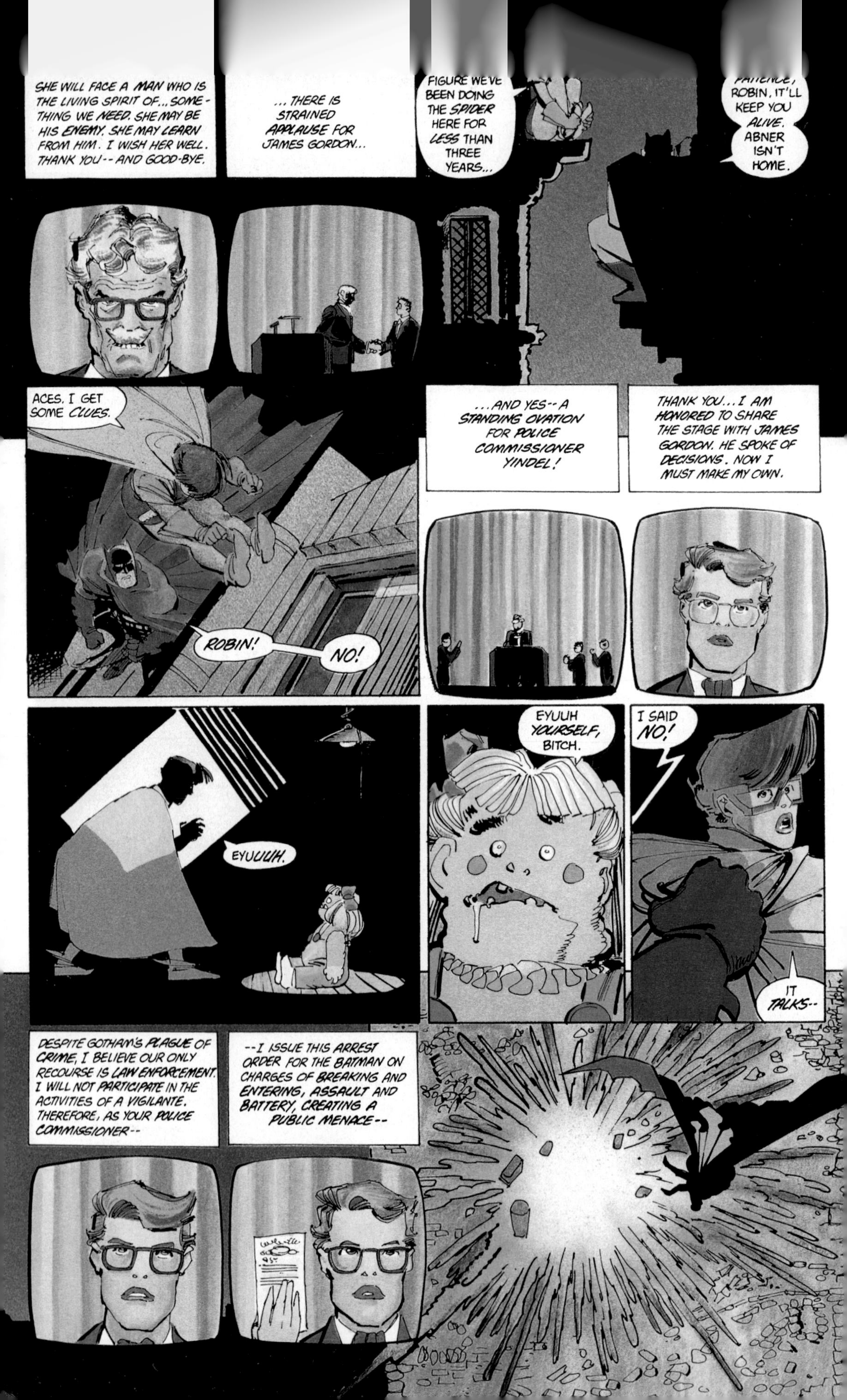
SHE WILL FACE A MAN WHO IS THE LIVING SPIRIT OF... SOME-THING WE NEED. SHE MAY BE HIS ENEMY. SHE MAY LEARN FROM HIM. I WISH HER WELL. THANK YOU-- AND GOOD-BYE.
...THERE IS STRAINED APPLAUSE FOR JAMES GORDON...
FIGURE WE'VE BEEN DOING THE SPIDER HERE FOR LESS THAN THREE YEARS...
PATIENCE, ROBIN. IT'LL KEEP YOU ALIVE. ABNER ISN'T HOME.
ACES. I GET SOME CLUES.
ROBIN!
NO!
...AND YES-- A STANDING OVATION FOR POLICE COMMISSIONER YINDEL!
THANK YOU... I AM HONORED TO SHARE THE STAGE WITH JAMES GORDON. HE SPOKE OF DECISIONS. NOW I MUST MAKE MY OWN.
EYUUUH.
EYUUH YOURSELF, BITCH.
I SAID NO!
IT TALKS--
DESPITE GOTHAM'S PLAGUE OF CRIME, I BELIEVE OUR ONLY RECOURSE IS LAW ENFORCEMENT. I WILL NOT PARTICIPATE IN THE ACTIVITIES OF A VIGILANTE. THEREFORE, AS YOUR POLICE COMMISSIONER--
--I ISSUE THIS ARREST ORDER FOR THE BATMAN ON CHARGES OF BREAKING AND ENTERING, ASSAULT AND BATTERY, CREATING A PUBLIC MENACE--

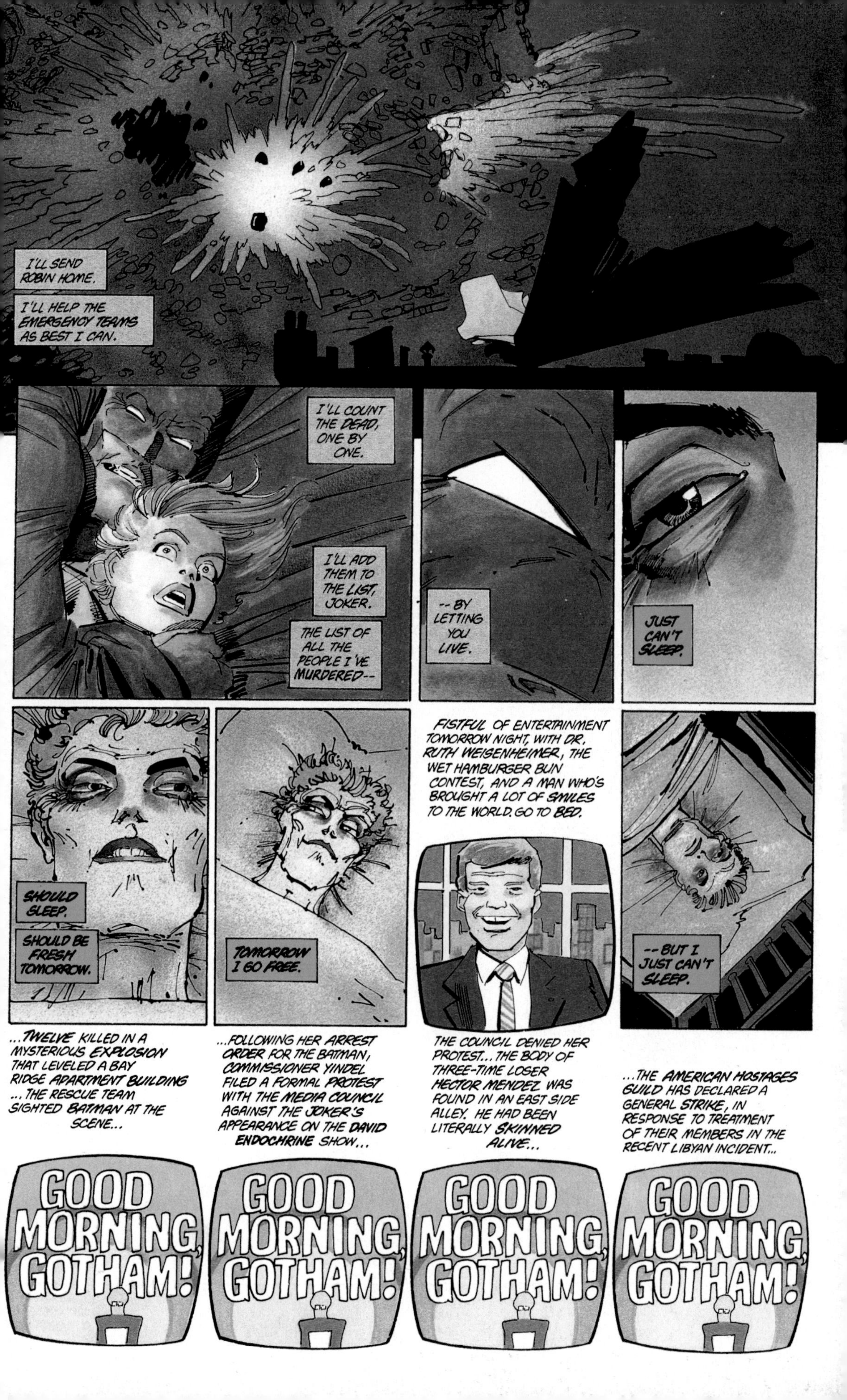
I'LL SEND ROBIN HOME.
I'LL HELP THE EMERGENCY TEAMS AS BEST I CAN.
I'LL COUNT THE DEAD, ONE BY ONE.
I'LL ADD THEM TO THE LIST, JOKER.
THE LIST OF ALL THE PEOPLE I'VE MURDERED--
--BY LETTING YOU LIVE.
JUST CAN'T SLEEP.
SHOULD SLEEP.
SHOULD BE FRESH TOMORROW.
TOMORROW I GO FREE.
FISTFUL OF ENTERTAINMENT TOMORROW NIGHT, WITH DR. RUTH WEISENHEIMER, THE WET HAMBURGER BUN CONTEST, AND A MAN WHO'S BROUGHT A LOT OF SMILES TO THE WORLD. GO TO BED.
--BUT I JUST CAN'T SLEEP.
...TWELVE KILLED IN A MYSTERIOUS EXPLOSION THAT LEVELED A BAY RIDGE APARTMENT BUILDING ... THE RESCUE TEAM SIGHTED BATMAN AT THE SCENE...
...FOLLOWING HER ARREST ORDER FOR THE BATMAN, COMMISSIONER YINDEL FILED A FORMAL PROTEST WITH THE MEDIA COUNCIL AGAINST THE JOKER'S APPEARANCE ON THE DAVID ENDOCHRINE SHOW...
THE COUNCIL DENIED HER PROTEST... THE BODY OF THREE-TIME LOSER HECTOR MENDEZ WAS FOUND IN AN EAST SIDE ALLEY. HE HAD BEEN LITERALLY SKINNED ALIVE...
...THE AMERICAN HOSTAGES GUILD HAS DECLARED A GENERAL STRIKE, IN RESPONSE TO TREATMENT OF THEIR MEMBERS IN THE RECENT LIBYAN INCIDENT...
GOOD MORNING, GOTHAM!
GOOD MORNING, GOTHAM!
GOOD MORNING, GOTHAM!
GOOD MORNING, GOTHAM!

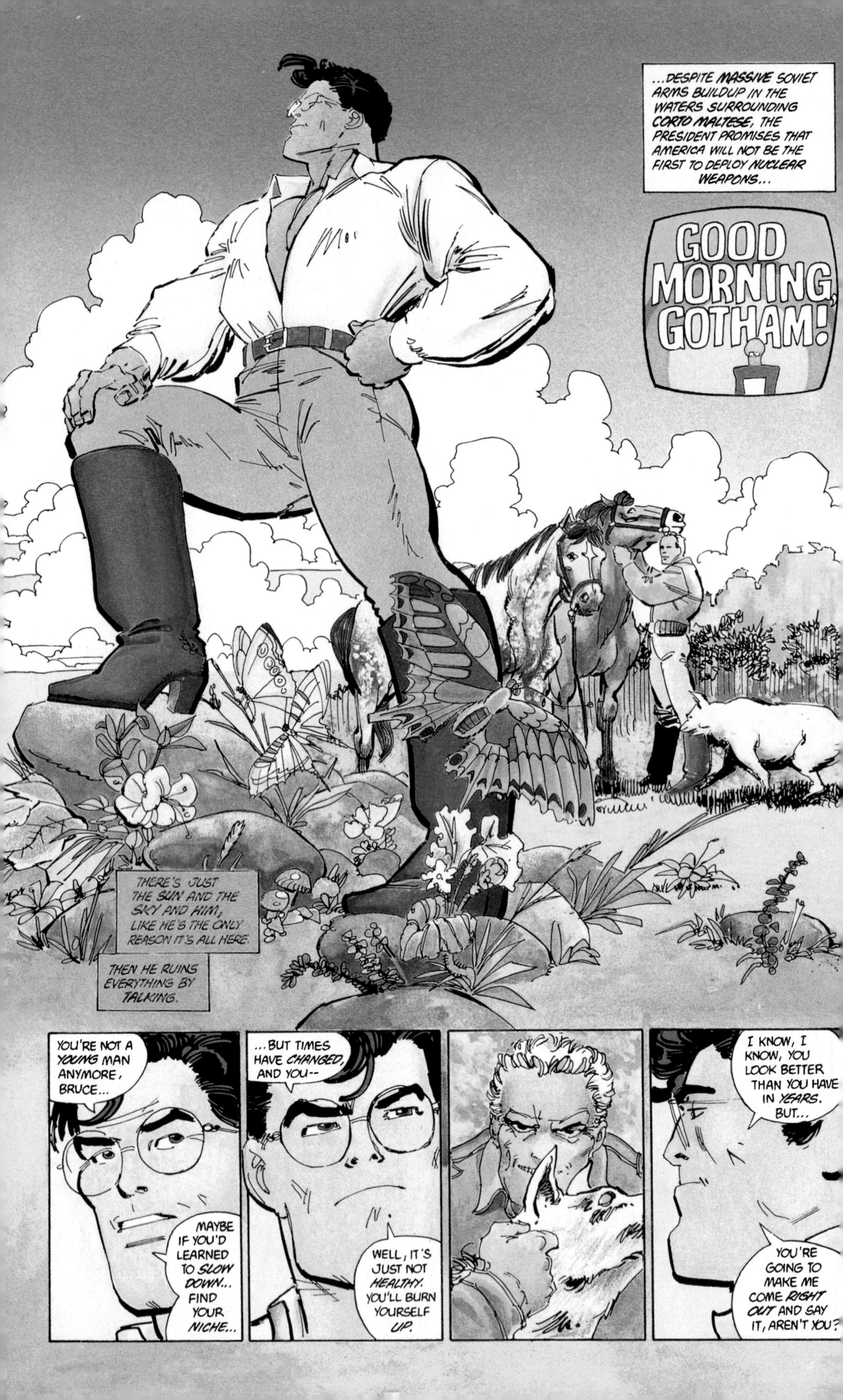
...DESPITE MASSIVE SOVIET ARMS BUILDUP IN THE WATERS SURROUNDING CORTO MALTESE, THE PRESIDENT PROMISES THAT AMERICA WILL NOT BE THE FIRST TO DEPLOY NUCLEAR WEAPONS...
GOOD MORNING, GOTHAM!
THERE'S JUST THE SUN AND THE SKY AND HIM, LIKE HE'S THE ONLY REASON IT'S ALL HERE.
THEN HE RUINS EVERYTHING BY TALKING.
YOU'RE NOT A YOUNG MAN ANYMORE, BRUCE...
MAYBE IF YOU'D LEARNED TO SLOW DOWN... FIND YOUR NICHE...
...BUT TIMES HAVE CHANGED, AND YOU--
WELL, IT'S JUST NOT HEALTHY. YOU'LL BURN YOURSELF UP.
I KNOW, I KNOW, YOU LOOK BETTER THAN YOU HAVE IN YEARS. BUT...
YOU'RE GOING TO MAKE ME COME RIGHT OUT AND SAY IT, AREN'T YOU?

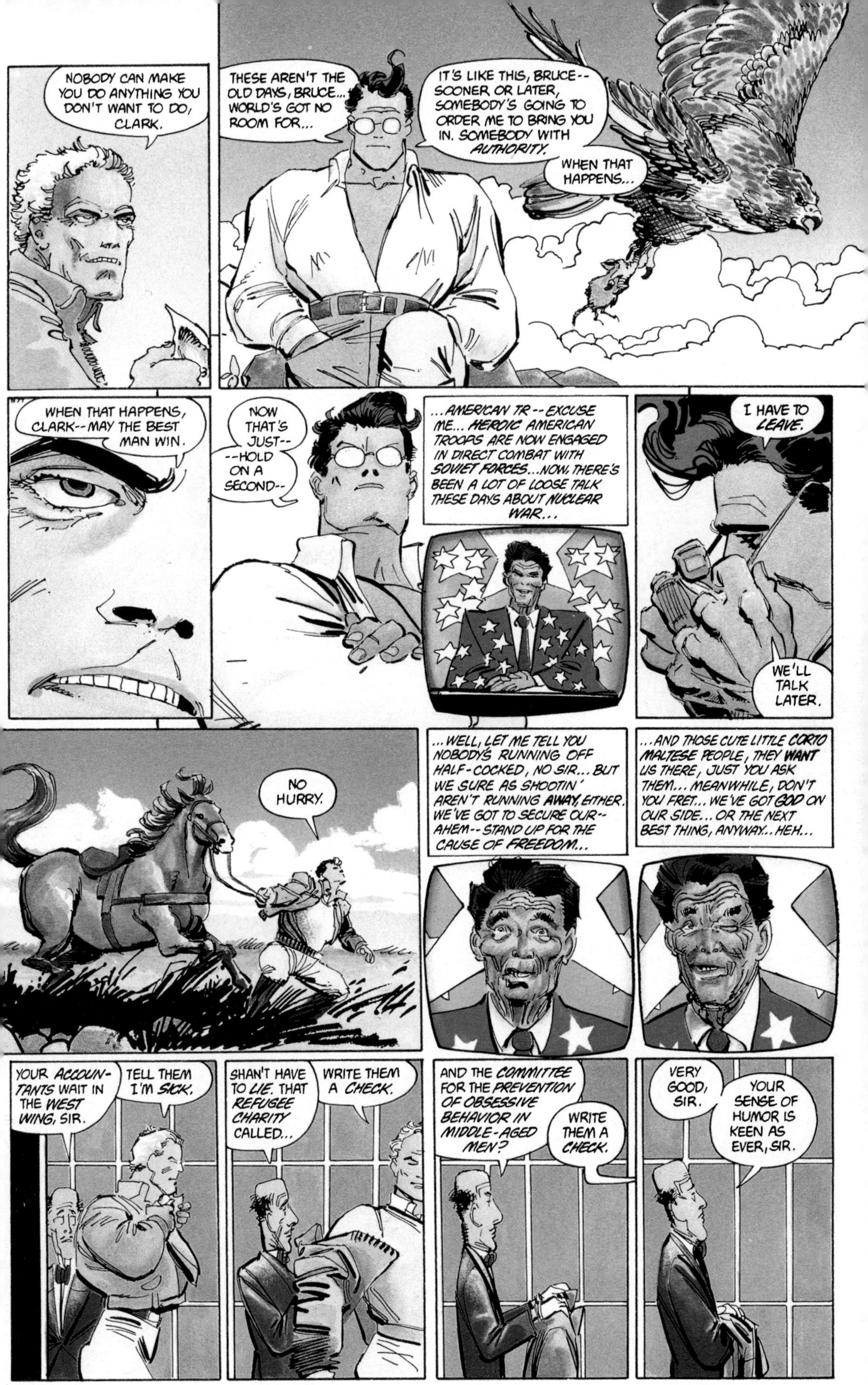

NOBODY CAN MAKE YOU DO ANYTHING YOU DON'T WANT TO DO, CLARK.
THESE AREN'T THE OLD DAYS, BRUCE... WORLD'S GOT NO ROOM FOR...
IT'S LIKE THIS, BRUCE-- SOONER OR LATER, SOMEBODY'S GOING TO ORDER ME TO BRING YOU IN. SOMEBODY WITH AUTHORITY.
WHEN THAT HAPPENS...
WHEN THAT HAPPENS, CLARK--MAY THE BEST MAN WIN.
NOW THAT'S JUST--
--HOLD ON A SECOND--
...AMERICAN TR--EXCUSE ME... HEROIC AMERICAN TROOPS ARE NOW ENGAGED IN DIRECT COMBAT WITH SOVIET FORCES...NOW, THERE'S BEEN A LOT OF LOOSE TALK THESE DAYS ABOUT NUCLEAR WAR...
I HAVE TO LEAVE.
WE'LL TALK LATER.
NO HURRY.
...WELL, LET ME TELL YOU NOBODY'S RUNNING OFF HALF-COCKED, NO SIR... BUT WE SURE AS SHOOTIN' AREN'T RUNNING AWAY, EITHER. WE'VE GOT TO SECURE OUR-- AHEM--STAND UP FOR THE CAUSE OF FREEDOM...
...AND THOSE CUTE LITTLE CORTO MALTESE PEOPLE, THEY WANT US THERE, JUST YOU ASK THEM... MEANWHILE, DON'T YOU FRET... WE'VE GOT GOD ON OUR SIDE... OR THE NEXT BEST THING, ANYWAY... HEH...
YOUR ACCOUNTANTS WAIT IN THE WEST WING, SIR.
TELL THEM I'M SICK.
SHAN'T HAVE TO LIE. THAT REFUGEE CHARITY CALLED...
WRITE THEM A CHECK.
AND THE COMMITTEE FOR THE PREVENTION OF OBSESSIVE BEHAVIOR IN MIDDLE-AGED MEN?
WRITE THEM A CHECK.
VERY GOOD, SIR.
YOUR SENSE OF HUMOR IS KEEN AS EVER, SIR.

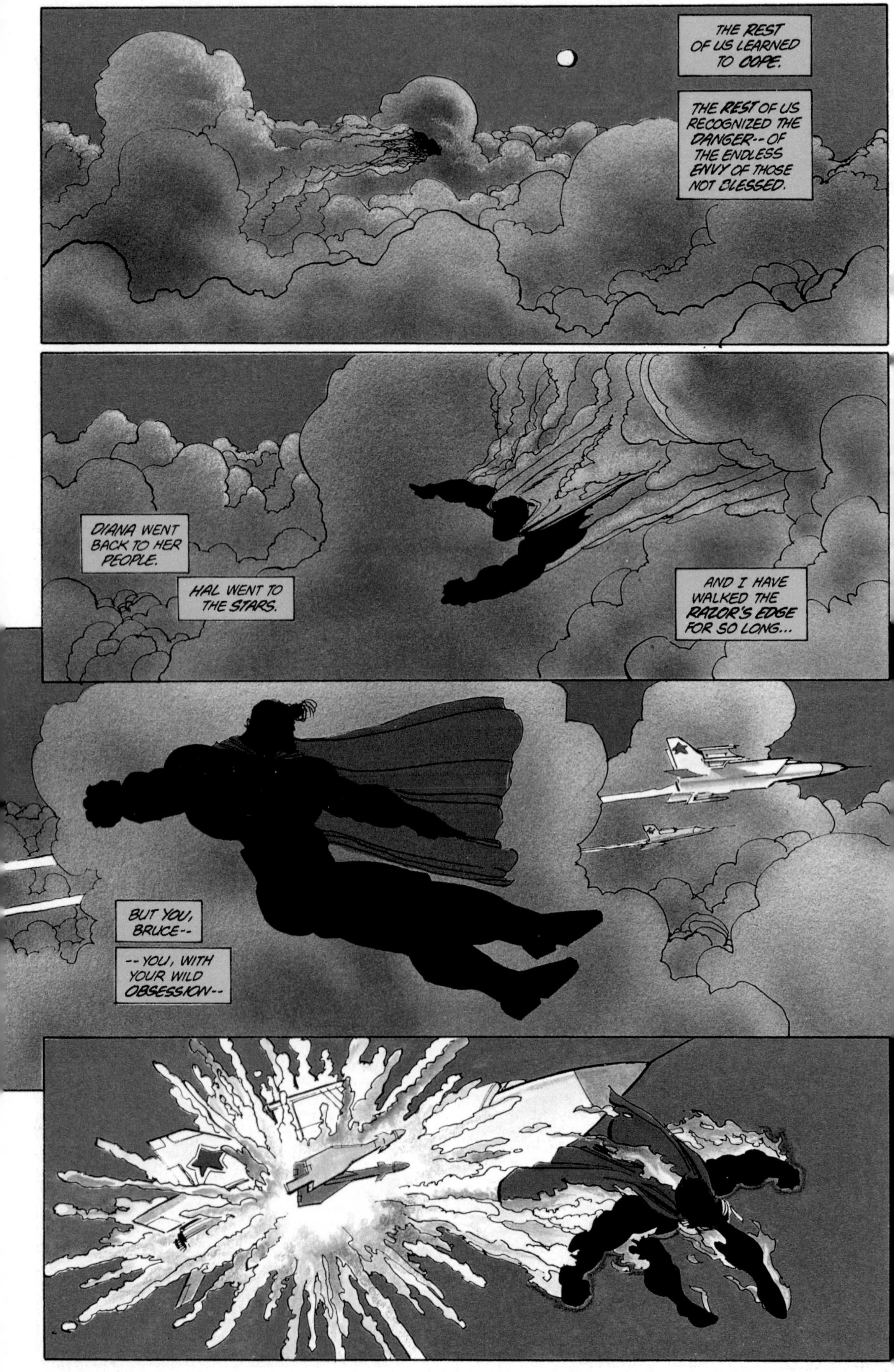
THE REST OF US LEARNED TO COPE.
THE REST OF US RECOGNIZED THE DANGER--OF THE ENDLESS ENVY OF THOSE NOT BLESSED.
DIANA WENT BACK TO HER PEOPLE.
HAL WENT TO THE STARS.
AND I HAVE WALKED THE RAZOR'S EDGE FOR SO LONG...
BUT YOU, BRUCE--
--YOU, WITH YOUR WILD OBSESSION--

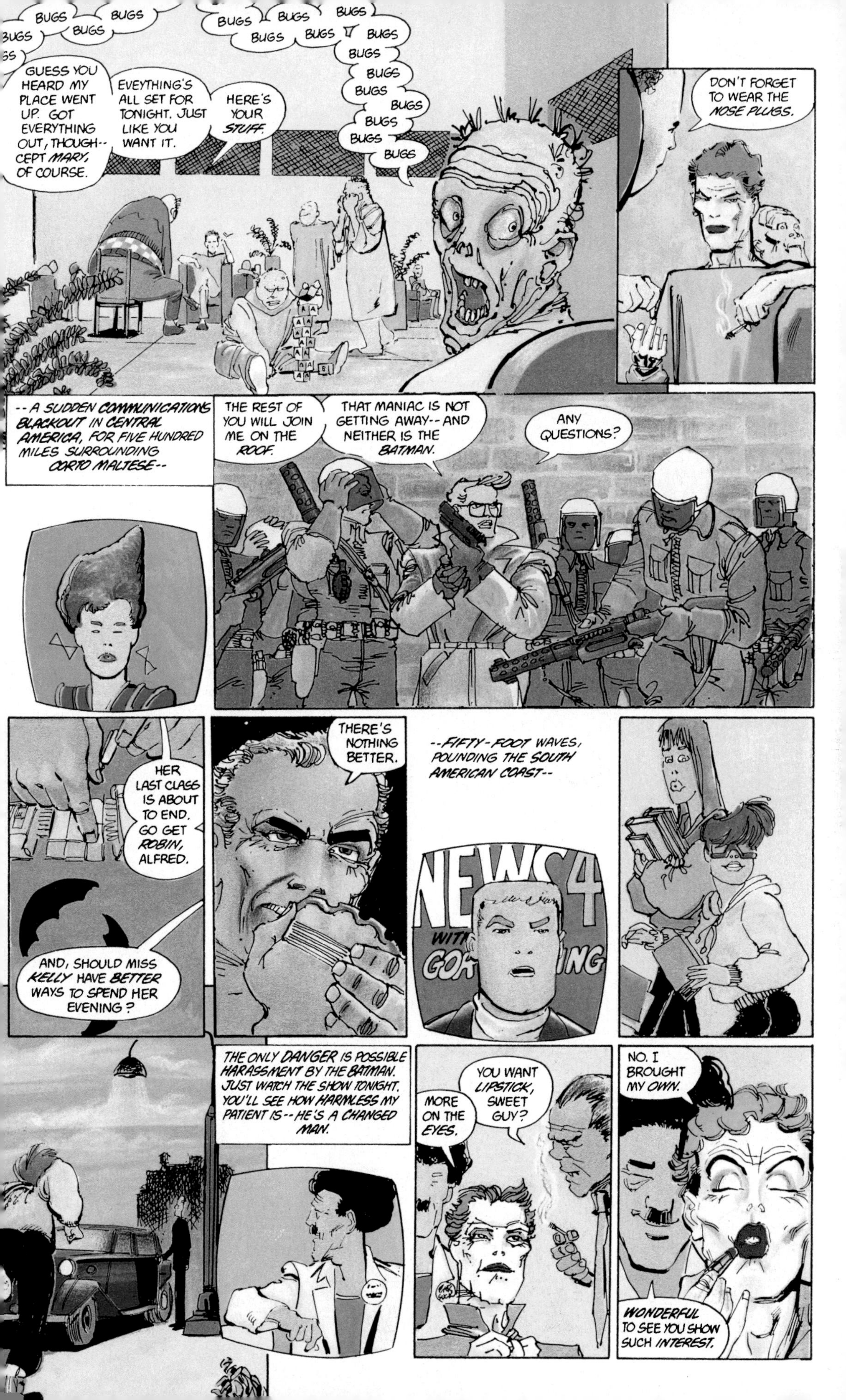
BUGS BUGS BUGS BUGS BUGS BUGS BUGS BUGS BUGS BUGS BUGS BUGS BUGS BUGS BUGS BUGS
GUESS YOU HEARD MY PLACE WENT UP. GOT EVERYTHING OUT, THOUGH--CEPT MARY, OF COURSE.
EVEYTHING'S ALL SET FOR TONIGHT. JUST LIKE YOU WANT IT.
HERE'S YOUR STUFF.
DON'T FORGET TO WEAR THE NOSE PLUGS.
--A SUDDEN COMMUNICATIONS BLACKOUT IN CENTRAL AMERICA, FOR FIVE HUNDRED MILES SURROUNDING CORTO MALTESE--
THE REST OF YOU WILL JOIN ME ON THE ROOF.
THAT MANIAC IS NOT GETTING AWAY--AND NEITHER IS THE BATMAN.
ANY QUESTIONS?
HER LAST CLASS IS ABOUT TO END. GO GET ROBIN, ALFRED.
AND, SHOULD MISS KELLY HAVE BETTER WAYS TO SPEND HER EVENING?
THERE'S NOTHING BETTER.
--FIFTY-FOOT WAVES, POUNDING THE SOUTH AMERICAN COAST--
NEWS 4
THE ONLY DANGER IS POSSIBLE HARASSMENT BY THE BATMAN. JUST WATCH THE SHOW TONIGHT. YOU'LL SEE HOW HARMLESS MY PATIENT IS--HE'S A CHANGED MAN.
MORE ON THE EYES.
YOU WANT LIPSTICK, SWEET GUY?
NO. I BROUGHT MY OWN.
WONDERFUL TO SEE YOU SHOW SUCH INTEREST.

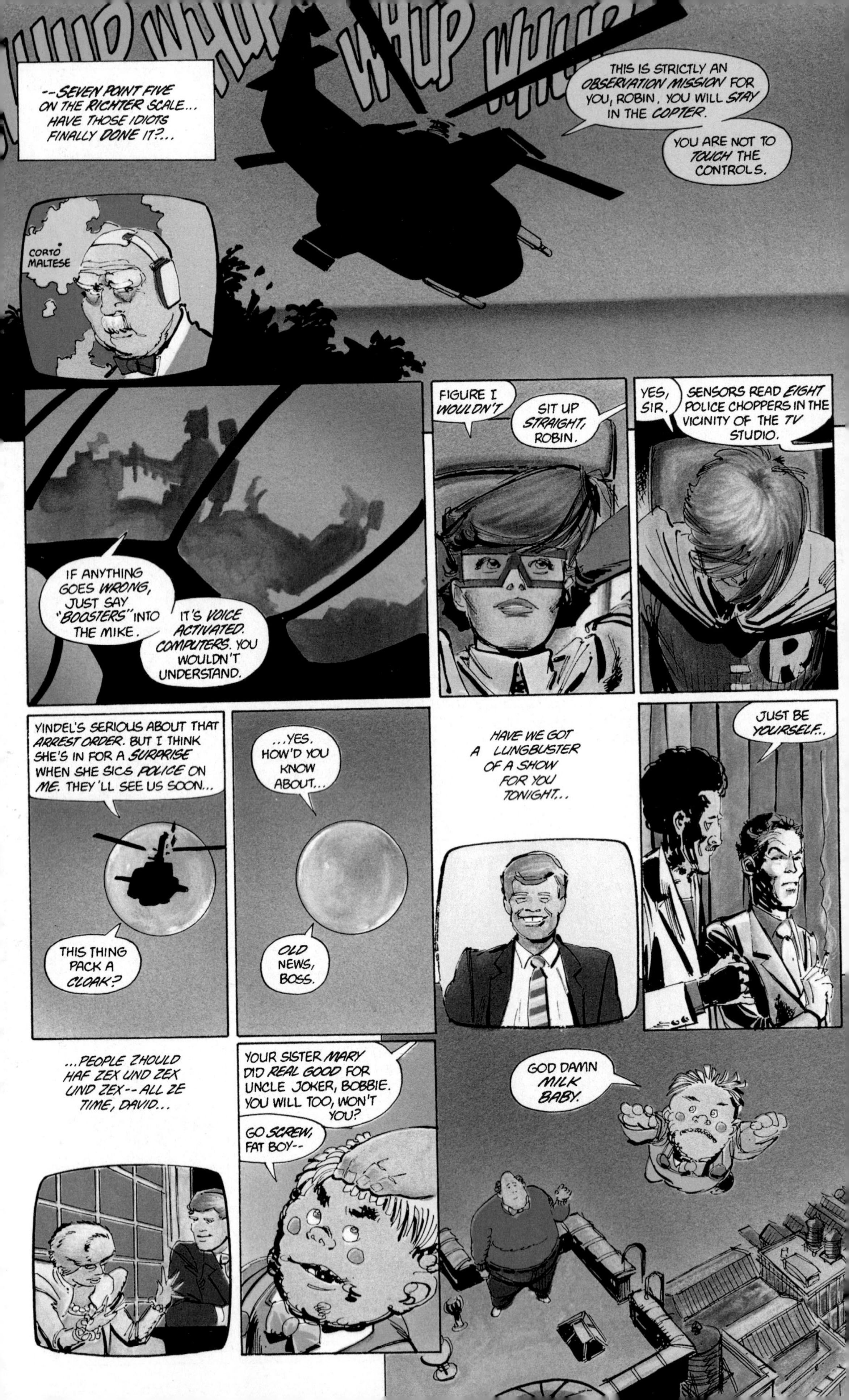

WHUP WHUP WHUP WHUP
--SEVEN POINT FIVE ON THE RICHTER SCALE... HAVE THOSE IDIOTS FINALLY DONE IT?...
THIS IS STRICTLY AN OBSERVATION MISSION FOR YOU, ROBIN. YOU WILL STAY IN THE COPTER.
YOU ARE NOT TO TOUCH THE CONTROLS.
CORTO MALTESE
IF ANYTHING GOES WRONG, JUST SAY "BOOSTERS" INTO THE MIKE.
IT'S VOICE ACTIVATED. COMPUTERS. YOU WOULDN'T UNDERSTAND.
FIGURE I WOULDN'T.
SIT UP STRAIGHT, ROBIN.
YES, SIR.
SENSORS READ EIGHT POLICE CHOPPERS IN THE VICINITY OF THE TV STUDIO.
YINDEL'S SERIOUS ABOUT THAT ARREST ORDER. BUT I THINK SHE'S IN FOR A SURPRISE WHEN SHE SICS POLICE ON ME. THEY'LL SEE US SOON...
THIS THING PACK A CLOAK?
...YES. HOW'D YOU KNOW ABOUT...
OLD NEWS, BOSS.
HAVE WE GOT A LUNGBUSTER OF A SHOW FOR YOU TONIGHT...
JUST BE YOURSELF...
...PEOPLE ZHOULD HAF ZEX UND ZEX UND ZEX--ALL ZE TIME, DAVID...
YOUR SISTER MARY DID REAL GOOD FOR UNCLE JOKER, BOBBIE. YOU WILL TOO, WON'T YOU?
GO SCREW, FAT BOY--
GOD DAMN MILK BABY.

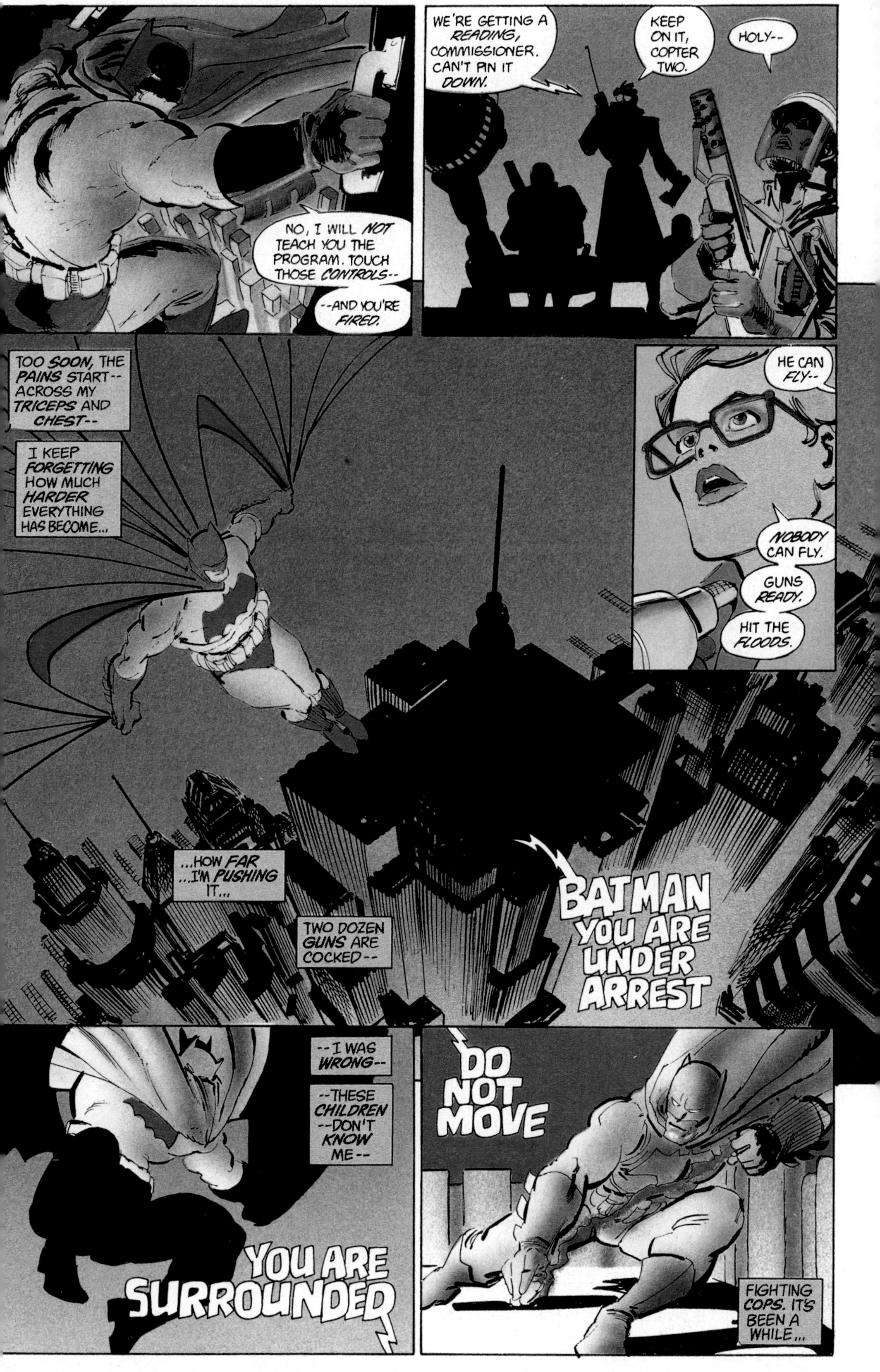
NO, I WILL NOT TEACH YOU THE PROGRAM. TOUCH THOSE CONTROLS--
--AND YOU'RE FIRED.
WE'RE GETTING A READING, COMMISSIONER. CAN'T PIN IT DOWN.
KEEP ON IT, COPTER TWO.
HOLY--
TOO SOON, THE PAINS START-- ACROSS MY TRICEPS AND CHEST--
I KEEP FORGETTING HOW MUCH HARDER EVERYTHING HAS BECOME...
HE CAN FLY--
NOBODY CAN FLY.
GUNS READY.
HIT THE FLOODS.
...HOW FAR ...I'M PUSHING IT...
TWO DOZEN GUNS ARE COCKED--
BATMAN YOU ARE UNDER ARREST
--I WAS WRONG--
--THESE CHILDREN --DON'T KNOW ME--
YOU ARE SURROUNDED
DO NOT MOVE
FIGHTING COPS. IT'S BEEN A WHILE...

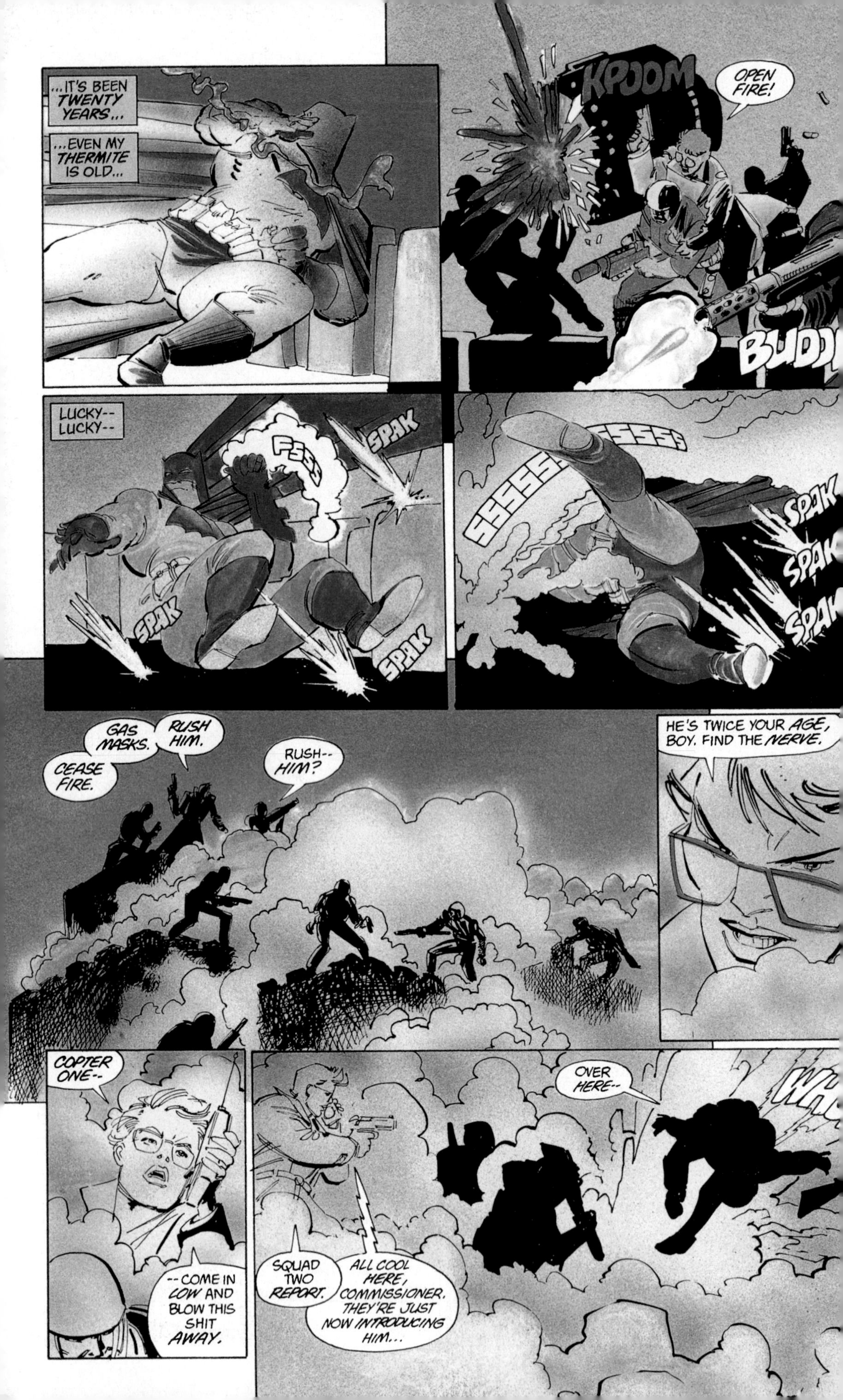
...IT'S BEEN TWENTY YEARS...
...EVEN MY THERMITE IS OLD...
KPJOOM
OPEN FIRE!
BUDD
LUCKY-- LUCKY--
F555
SPAK
SPAK
SPAK
555555555555
SPAK
SPAK
SPAK
GAS MASKS.
RUSH HIM.
CEASE FIRE.
RUSH-- HIM?
HE'S TWICE YOUR AGE, BOY. FIND THE NERVE.
COPTER ONE--
--COME IN LOW AND BLOW THIS SHIT AWAY.
OVER HERE--
SQUAD TWO REPORT.
ALL COOL HERE, COMMISSIONER. THEY'RE JUST NOW INTRODUCING HIM...

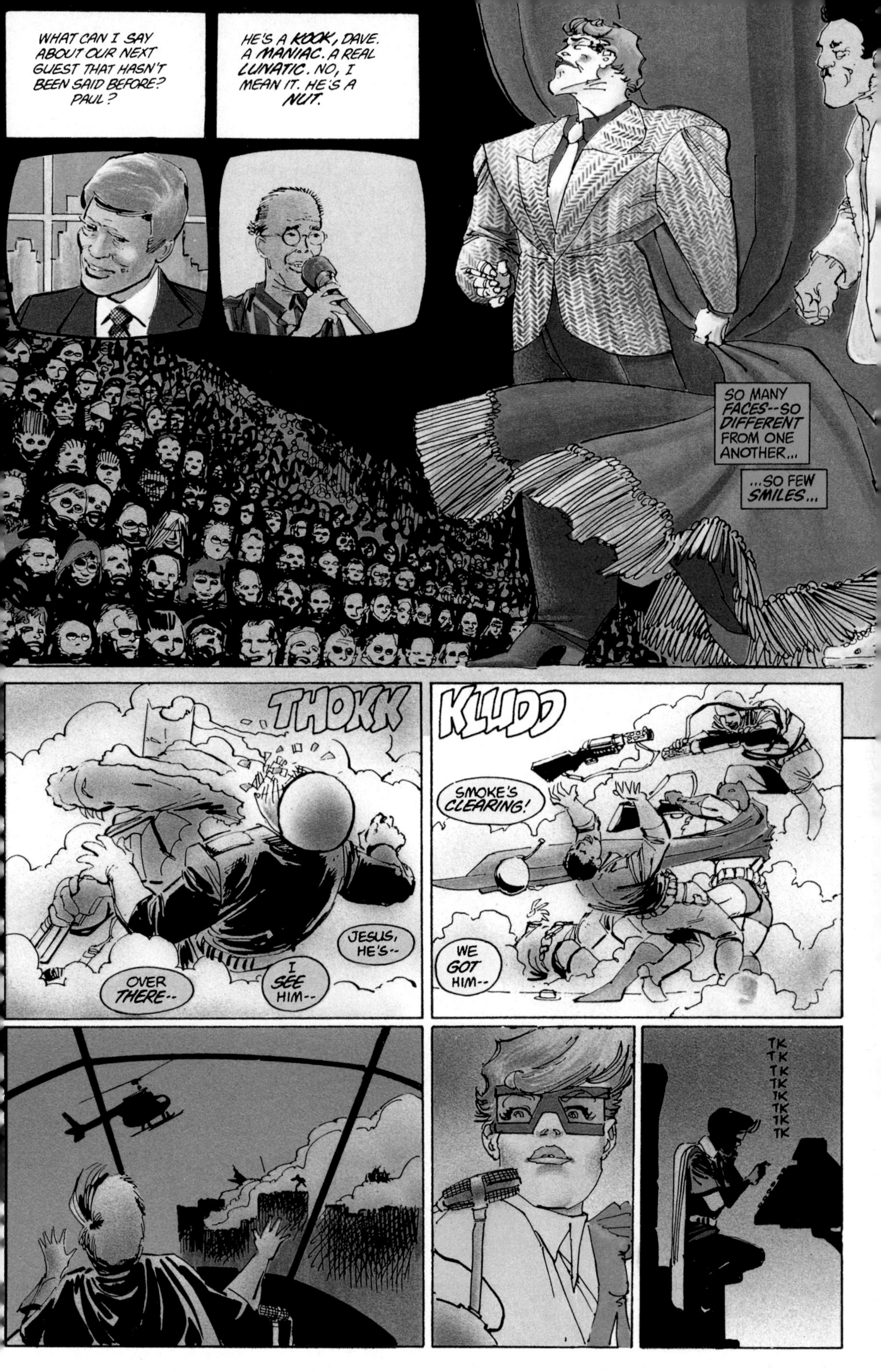
WHAT CAN I SAY ABOUT OUR NEXT GUEST THAT HASN'T BEEN SAID BEFORE? PAUL?
HE'S A KOOK, DAVE. A MANIAC. A REAL LUNATIC. NO, I MEAN IT. HE'S A NUT.
SO MANY FACES--SO DIFFERENT FROM ONE ANOTHER...
...SO FEW SMILES...
THOKK
JESUS, HE'S--
I SEE HIM--
OVER THERE--
KLUDD
SMOKE'S CLEARING!
WE GOT HIM--
TK T TK T TK TK TK TK TK TK TK TK TK

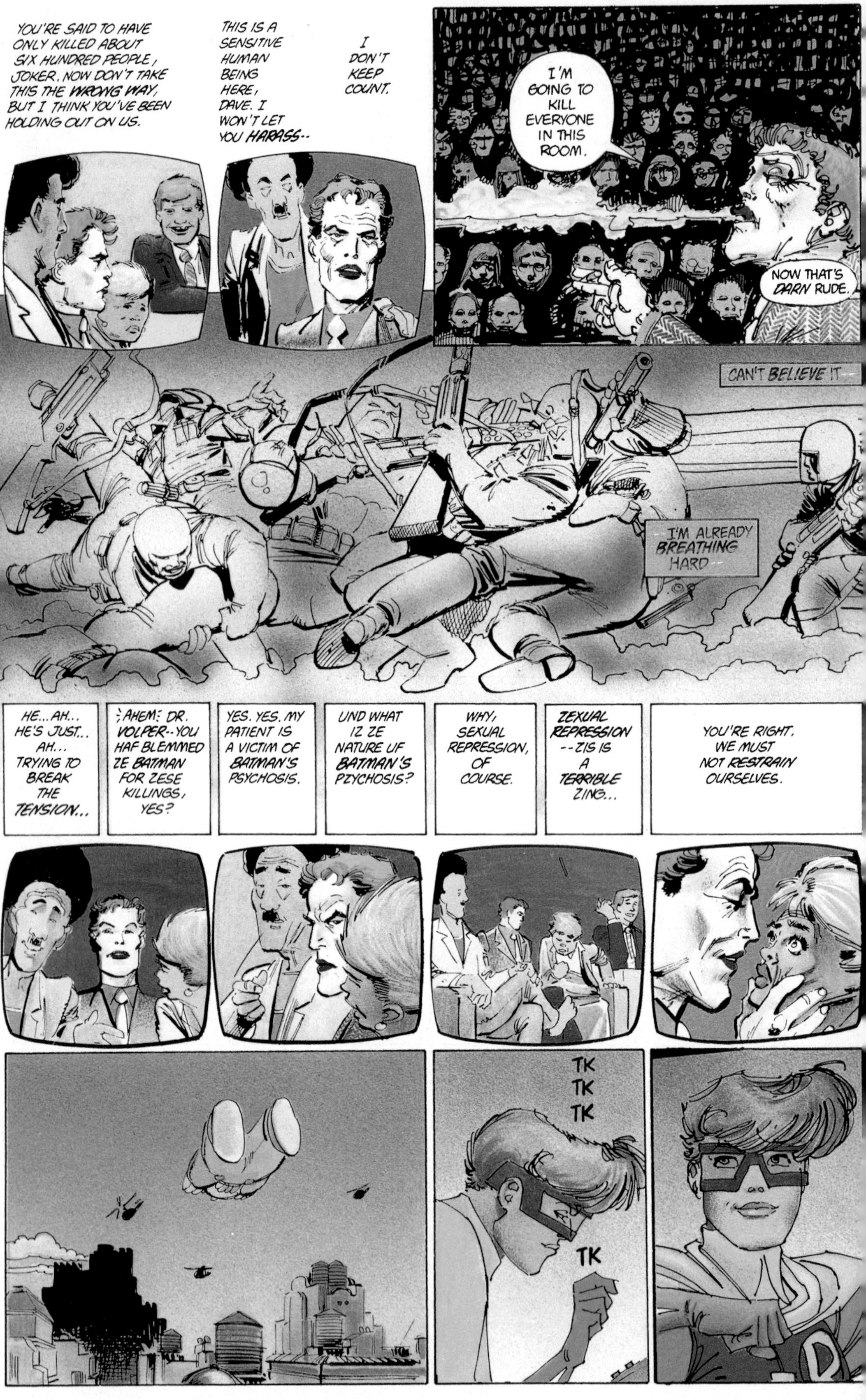

YOU'RE SAID TO HAVE ONLY KILLED ABOUT SIX HUNDRED PEOPLE, JOKER. NOW DON'T TAKE THIS THE *WRONG WAY*, BUT I THINK YOU'VE BEEN HOLDING OUT ON US.

THIS IS A SENSITIVE HUMAN BEING HERE, DAVE. I WON'T LET YOU *HARASS*--

I DON'T KEEP COUNT.

I'M GOING TO KILL EVERYONE IN THIS ROOM.

NOW THAT'S *DARN* RUDE.

CAN'T *BELIEVE* IT

I'M ALREADY *BREATHING* HARD--

HE...AH... HE'S JUST... AH... TRYING TO BREAK THE TENSION...

¿AHEM¿ DR. VOLPER--YOU HAF BLEMMED ZE BATMAN FOR ZESE KILLINGS, YES?

YES. YES. MY PATIENT IS A VICTIM OF *BATMAN'S* PSYCHOSIS.

UND WHAT IZ ZE NATURE UF *BATMAN'S* PZYCHOSIS?

WHY, SEXUAL REPRESSION, OF COURSE.

ZEXUAL REPRESSION --ZIS IS A TERRIBLE ZING...

YOU'RE RIGHT. WE MUST NOT RESTRAIN OURSELVES.

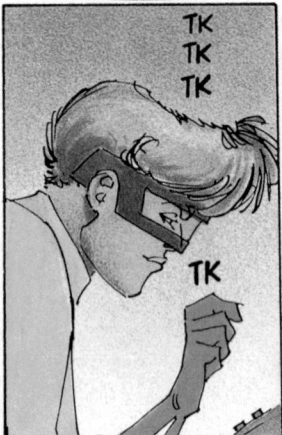

TK
TK
TK

TK

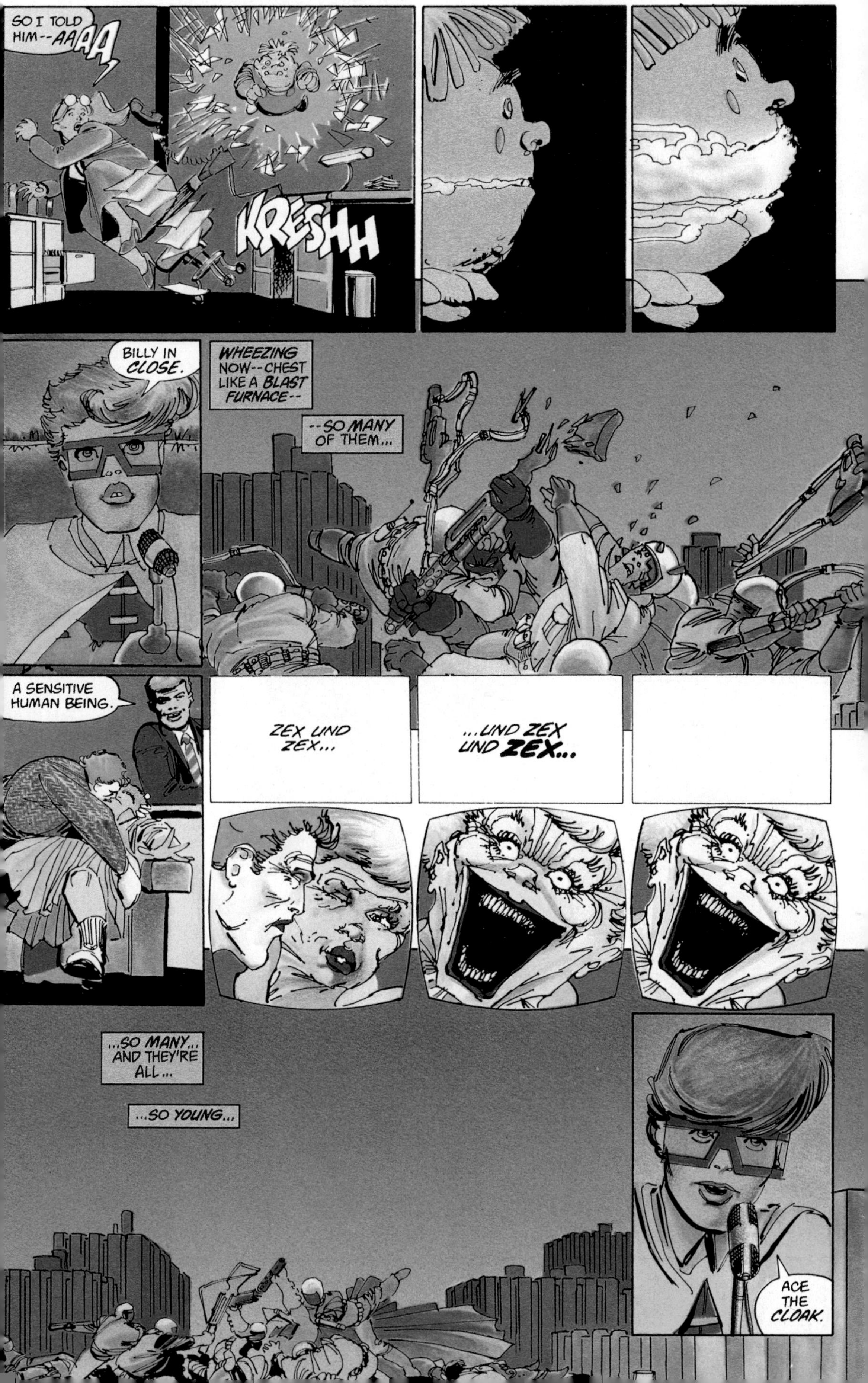
SO I TOLD HIM--AAAA
KRESHH
BILLY IN CLOSE.
WHEEZING NOW--CHEST LIKE A BLAST FURNACE--
--SO MANY OF THEM...
A SENSITIVE HUMAN BEING.
ZEX UND ZEX...
...UND ZEX UND ZEX...
...SO MANY... AND THEY'RE ALL...
...SO YOUNG...
ACE THE CLOAK.

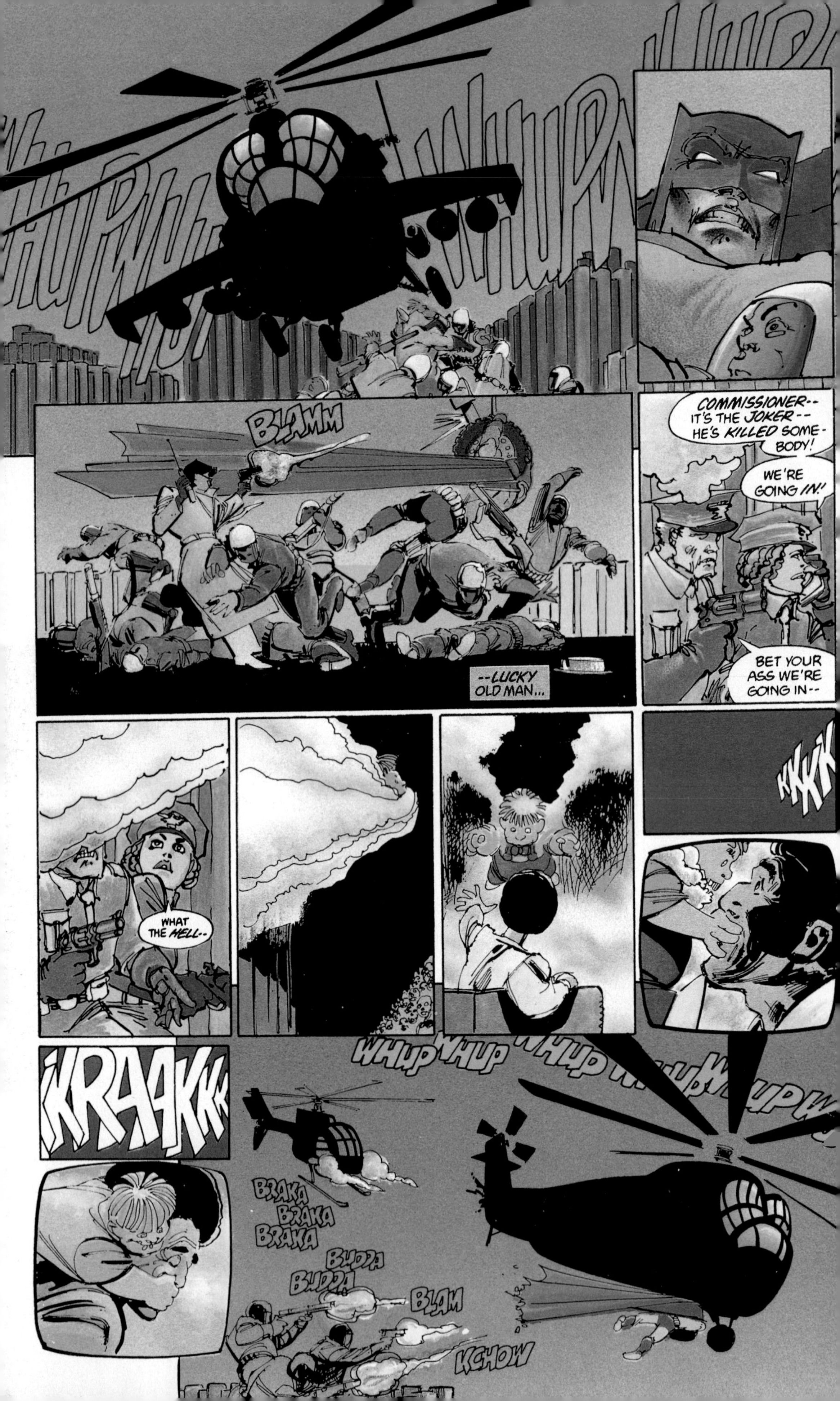

WHUPWHUP
BLAMM
--LUCKY
OLD MAN...
COMMISSIONER--
IT'S THE JOKER--
HE'S KILLED SOMEBODY!
WE'RE
GOING IN!
BET YOUR
ASS WE'RE
GOING IN--
WHAT
THE HELL--
KKKK
KRAAKKK
WHUP WHUP WHUP
BRAKA
BRAKA
BRAKA
BUDDA
BUDDA
BLAM
KCHOW

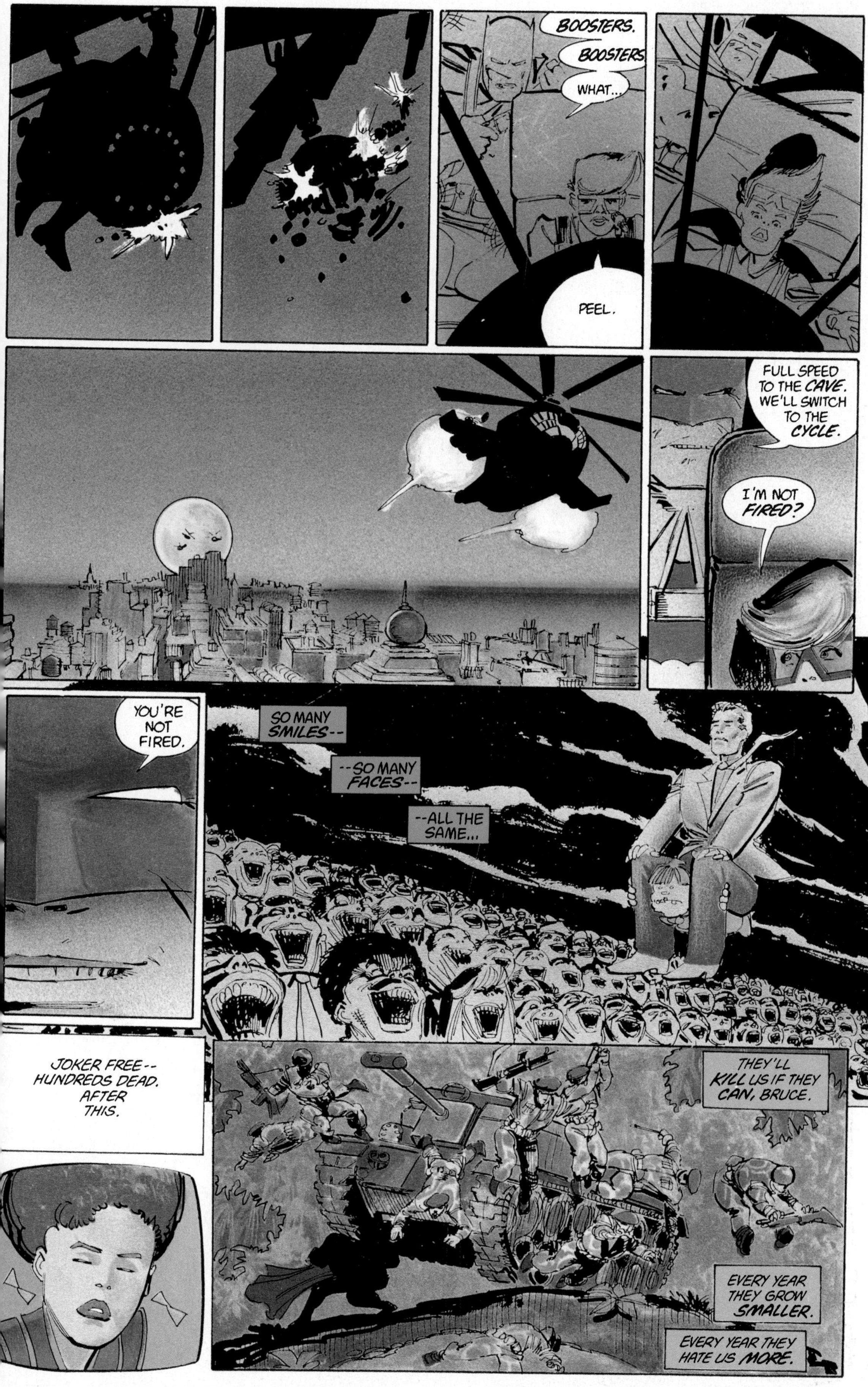

BOOSTERS.
BOOSTERS.
WHAT...
PEEL.
FULL SPEED TO THE CAVE. WE'LL SWITCH TO THE CYCLE.
I'M NOT FIRED?
YOU'RE NOT FIRED.
SO MANY SMILES--
--SO MANY FACES--
--ALL THE SAME...
JOKER FREE-- HUNDREDS DEAD. AFTER THIS.
THEY'LL KILL US IF THEY CAN, BRUCE.
EVERY YEAR THEY GROW SMALLER.
EVERY YEAR THEY HATE US MORE.

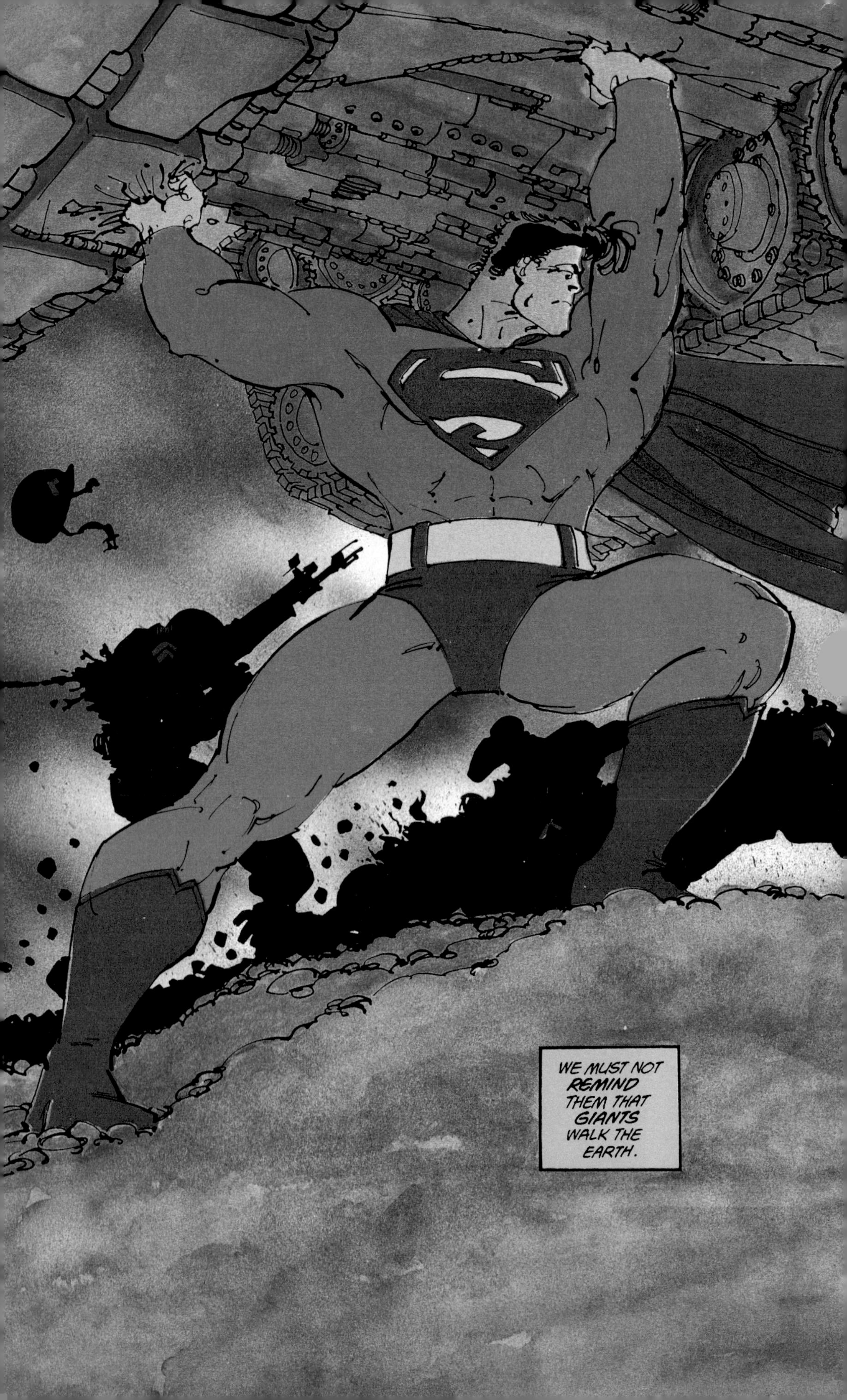
WE MUST NOT REMIND THEM THAT GIANTS WALK THE EARTH.

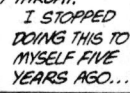

...URGING THE PUBLIC NOT TO WORRY, THE PRESIDENT HAS PLACED STRATEGIC AIR COMMANDS ON *RED ALERT*. "WE WON'T MAKE THE *FIRST* MOVE", SAID THE PRESIDENT, "BUT WE'RE READY TO MAKE THE *LAST*."

THE POPE TODAY DECLARED THAT THE CHURCH'S STAND ON CONTRACEPTION WILL *NOT* CHANGE, DESPITE YESTERDAY'S FIREBOMBING OF ST. PETER'S SQUARE... AND, IN *LOCAL* NEWS...

MY HEAD GOES *LIGHT* AND THE *SMOKE* COATS THE INSIDE OF MY *MOUTH* AND LEAVES A PATCH OF RED-HOT GRAVEL AT THE BASE OF MY *THROAT*.

I STOPPED DOING THIS TO MYSELF FIVE YEARS AGO...

CORTO MALTESE

COMMISSIONER --WHITTAKER'S GONE ALL *SICK*.

HE'S JUST A *ROOKIE*...

SEND HIM HOME, MERKEL. TELL HIM IT'S ALL RIGHT.

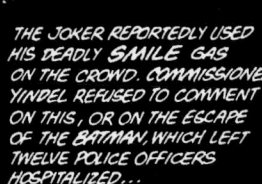

...*TWO HUNDRED AND SIX* WERE SLAIN DURING THE JOKER'S ESCAPE FROM THE *DAVID ENDOCHRINE SHOW* INCLUDING HOST ENDOCHRINE AND DR. BARTHOLOMEW WOLPER.

THE JOKER REPORTEDLY USED HIS DEADLY *SMILE* GAS ON THE CROWD. *COMMISSIONER YINDEL* REFUSED TO COMMENT ON THIS, OR ON THE ESCAPE OF THE *BATMAN*, WHICH LEFT TWELVE POLICE OFFICERS HOSPITALIZED...

KYLE ESCORT SERVICE, INC.

YOU SHOULDN'T HAVE COME *BACK*, BRUCE.

AMERICAN EXPRESS CARDS WELCOME

THEY'VE *CHANGED*. YOU DON'T *KNOW* HOW THEY'VE CHANGED.

THEY'LL *KILL* YOU...

SELINA--

I NEED YOUR *HELP*.

IT'S VERY IMPORTANT.

OH, JESUS.

KLIK CHAK

YOU GET THE HELL OUT OF *HEG*

THE YEARS HAVE NOT BEEN *KIND*, SELINA...

MMFF

AH, SELINA--YOU SHOULD BE *GRATEFUL* I CHANGED MY LIPSTICK. YOU *ARE* GRATEFUL?...

YES... GRATEFUL...

NOW...YOUR GIRL *ELSIE* IS ESCORTING A *CONGRESSMAN* TONIGHT. MEETING HIM AT HIS *HOTEL*.

WHY DON'T YOU CALL ELSIE IN HERE?

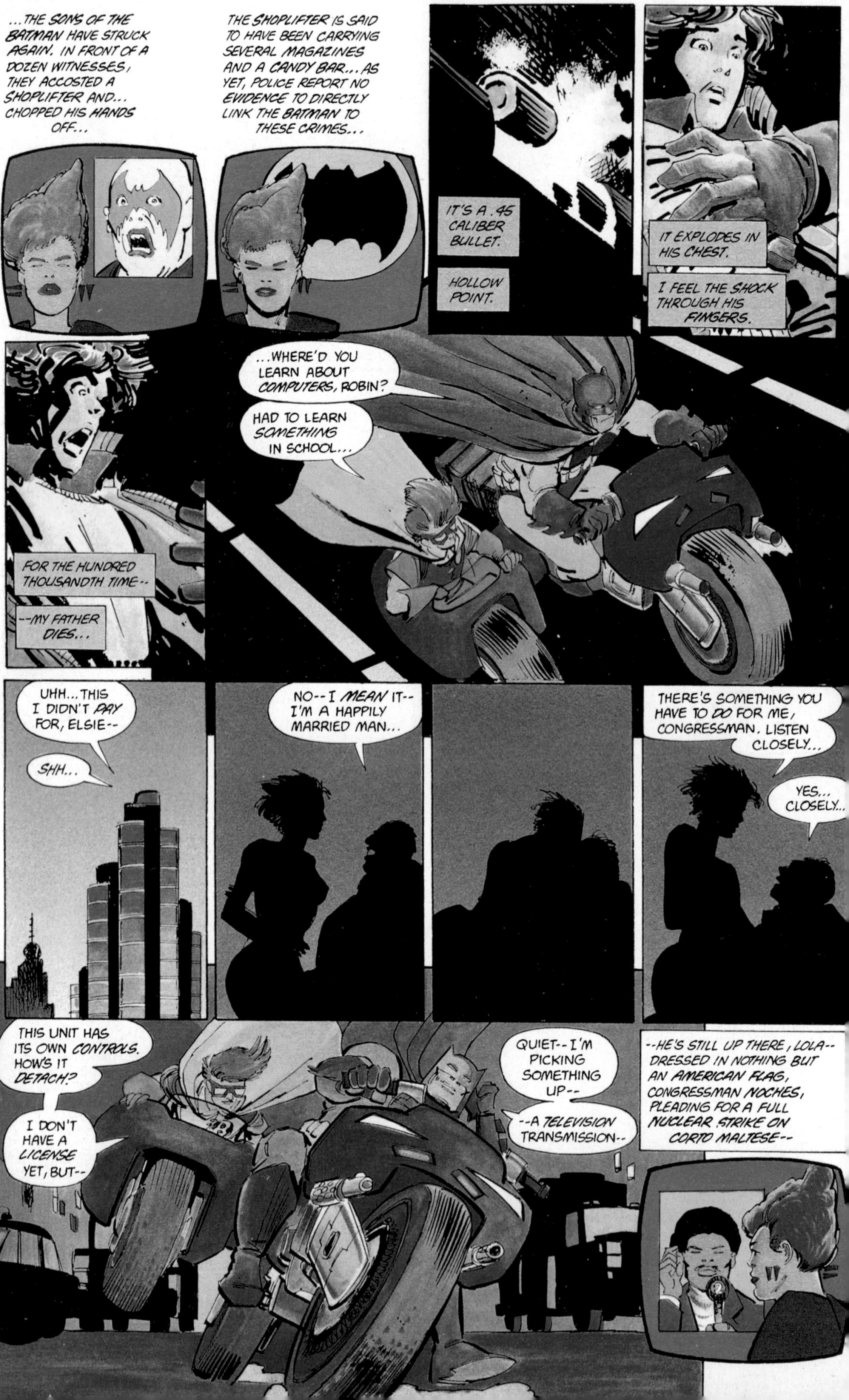
...THE SONS OF THE BATMAN HAVE STRUCK AGAIN. IN FRONT OF A DOZEN WITNESSES, THEY ACCOSTED A SHOPLIFTER AND... CHOPPED HIS HANDS OFF...
THE SHOPLIFTER IS SAID TO HAVE BEEN CARRYING SEVERAL MAGAZINES AND A CANDY BAR... AS YET, POLICE REPORT NO EVIDENCE TO DIRECTLY LINK THE BATMAN TO THESE CRIMES...
IT'S A .45 CALIBER BULLET.
HOLLOW POINT.
IT EXPLODES IN HIS CHEST.
I FEEL THE SHOCK THROUGH HIS FINGERS.
FOR THE HUNDRED THOUSANDTH TIME--
--MY FATHER DIES...
...WHERE'D YOU LEARN ABOUT COMPUTERS, ROBIN?
HAD TO LEARN SOMETHING IN SCHOOL...
UHH... THIS I DIDN'T PAY FOR, ELSIE--
SHH...
NO-- I MEAN IT-- I'M A HAPPILY MARRIED MAN...
THERE'S SOMETHING YOU HAVE TO DO FOR ME, CONGRESSMAN. LISTEN CLOSELY...
YES... CLOSELY...
THIS UNIT HAS ITS OWN CONTROLS. HOW'S IT DETACH?
I DON'T HAVE A LICENSE YET, BUT--
QUIET-- I'M PICKING SOMETHING UP--
--A TELEVISION TRANSMISSION--
--HE'S STILL UP THERE, LOLA-- DRESSED IN NOTHING BUT AN AMERICAN FLAG, CONGRESSMAN NOCHES, PLEADING FOR A FULL NUCLEAR STRIKE ON CORTO MALTESE--

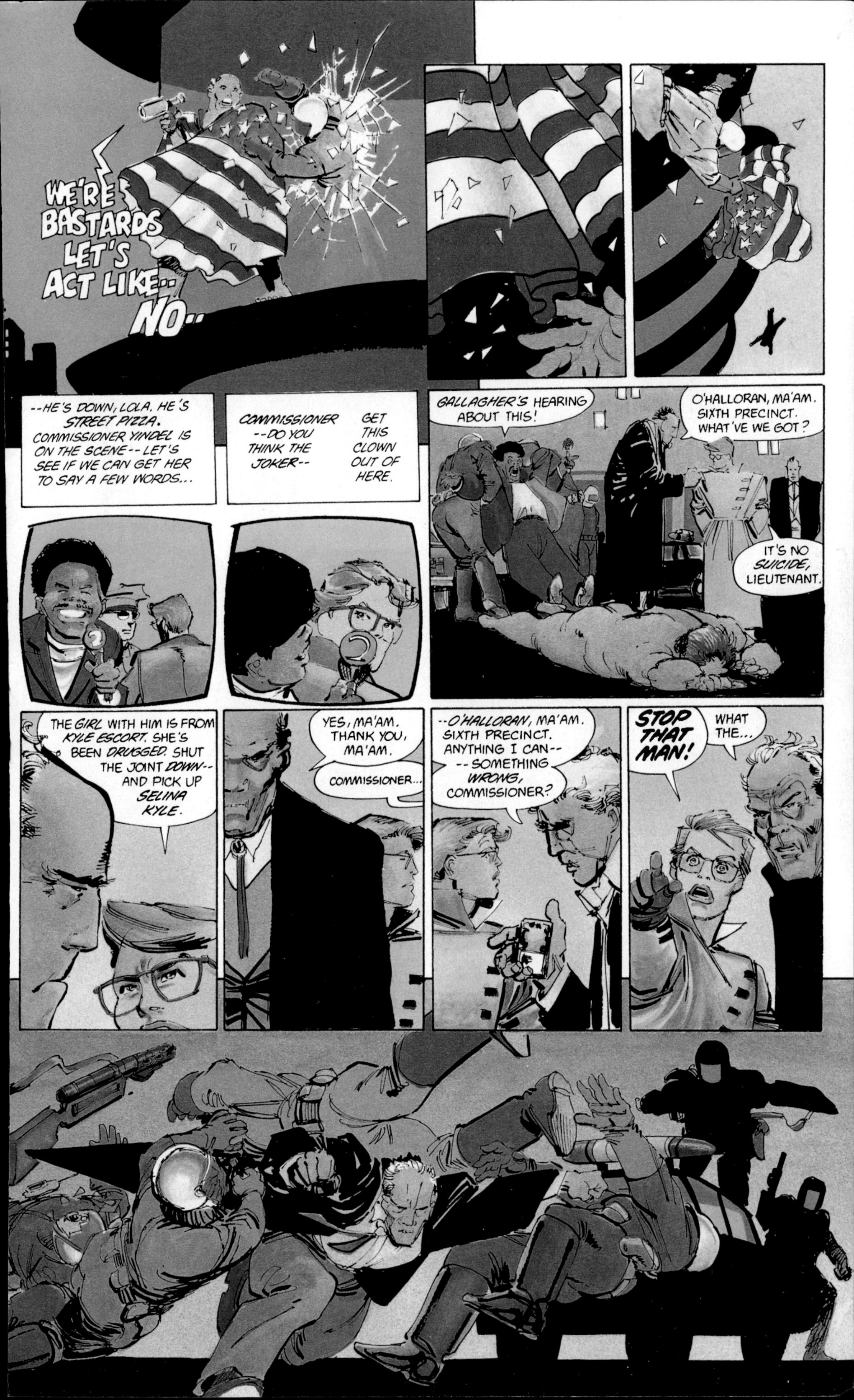
WE'RE BASTARDS LET'S ACT LIKE.. NO..
--HE'S DOWN, LOLA. HE'S STREET PIZZA. COMMISSIONER YINDEL IS ON THE SCENE--LET'S SEE IF WE CAN GET HER TO SAY A FEW WORDS...
COMMISSIONER --DO YOU THINK THE JOKER--
GET THIS CLOWN OUT OF HERE.
GALLAGHER'S HEARING ABOUT THIS!
O'HALLORAN, MA'AM. SIXTH PRECINCT. WHAT'VE WE GOT?
IT'S NO SUICIDE, LIEUTENANT.
THE GIRL WITH HIM IS FROM KYLE ESCORT. SHE'S BEEN DRUGGED. SHUT THE JOINT DOWN--AND PICK UP SELINA KYLE.
YES, MA'AM. THANK YOU, MA'AM.
COMMISSIONER...
--O'HALLORAN, MA'AM. SIXTH PRECINCT. ANYTHING I CAN--
--SOMETHING WRONG, COMMISSIONER?
STOP THAT MAN!
WHAT THE...

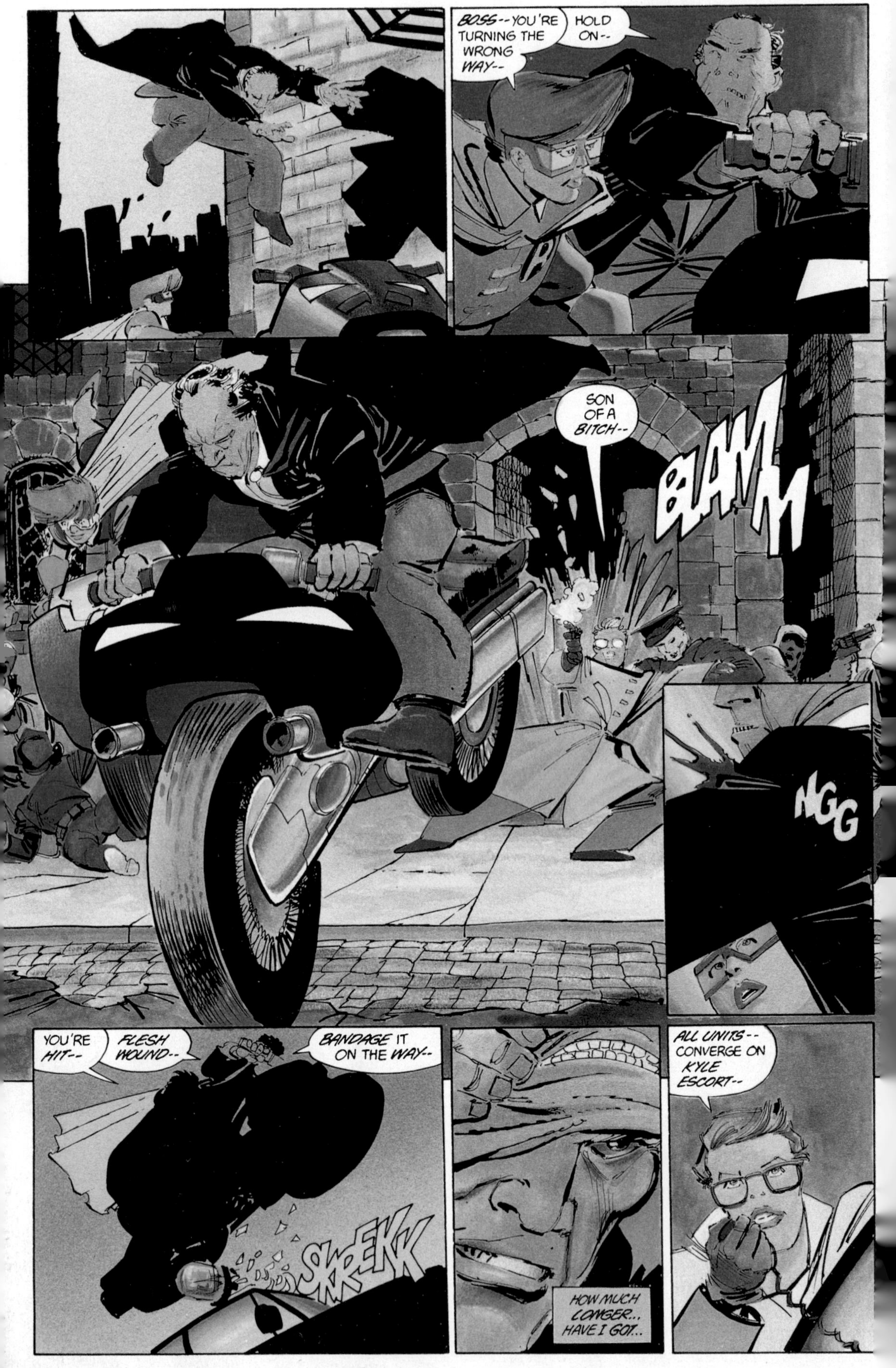

BOSS--YOU'RE TURNING THE WRONG WAY--
HOLD ON--
SON OF A BITCH--
BLAMM
NGG
YOU'RE HIT--
FLESH WOUND--
BANDAGE IT ON THE WAY--
SKREEKK
HOW MUCH LONGER... HAVE I GOT...
ALL UNITS--CONVERGE ON KYLE ESCORT--

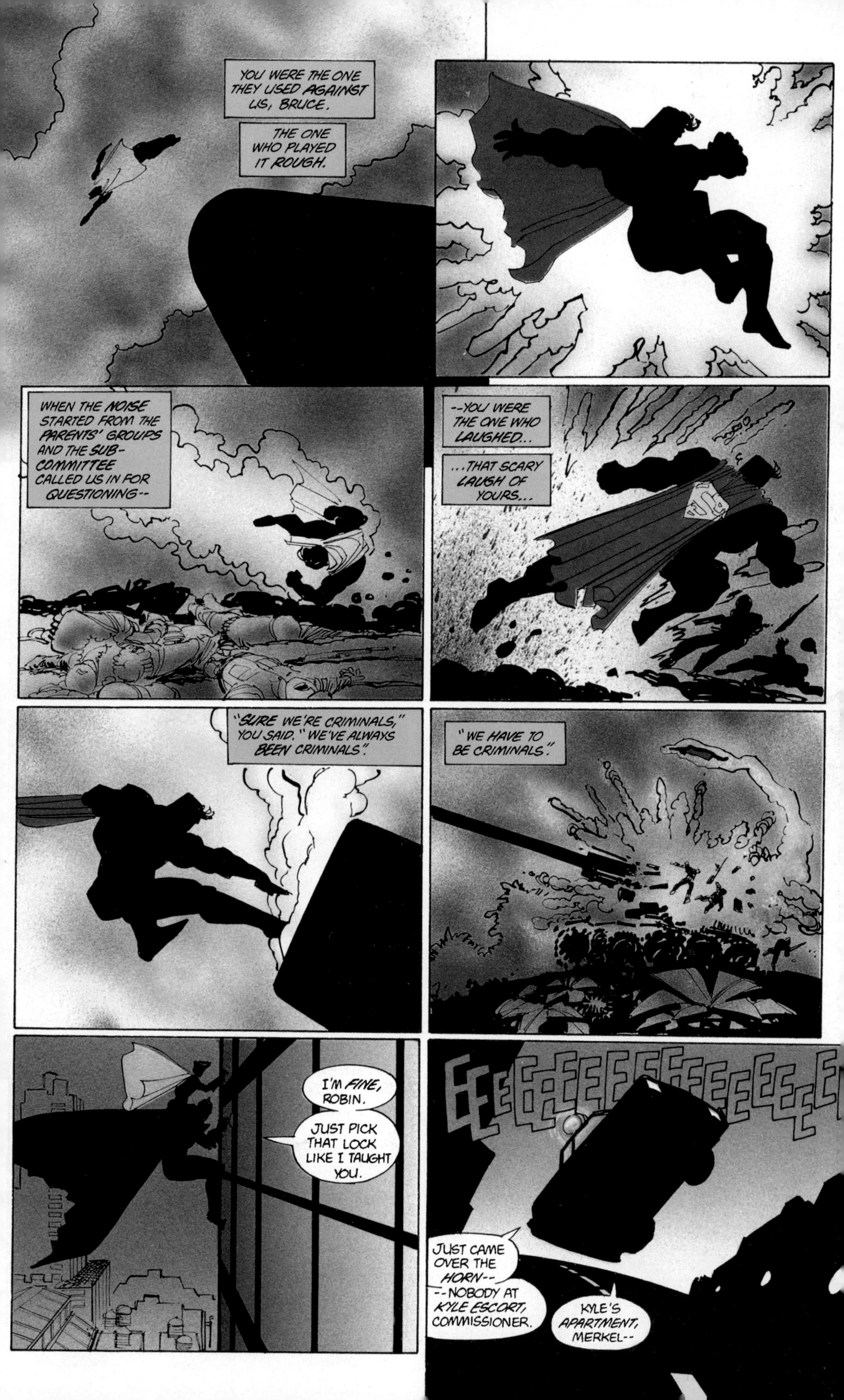
YOU WERE THE ONE THEY USED AGAINST US, BRUCE.
THE ONE WHO PLAYED IT ROUGH.
WHEN THE NOISE STARTED FROM THE PARENTS' GROUPS AND THE SUB-COMMITTEE CALLED US IN FOR QUESTIONING--
--YOU WERE THE ONE WHO LAUGHED...
...THAT SCARY LAUGH OF YOURS...
"SURE WE'RE CRIMINALS," YOU SAID. "WE'VE ALWAYS BEEN CRIMINALS".
"WE HAVE TO BE CRIMINALS".
I'M FINE, ROBIN.
JUST PICK THAT LOCK LIKE I TAUGHT YOU.
EEEEEEEEEEEEEEEEEEEEEEEN
JUST CAME OVER THE HORN--
--NOBODY AT KYLE ESCORT, COMMISSIONER.
KYLE'S APARTMENT, MERKEL--

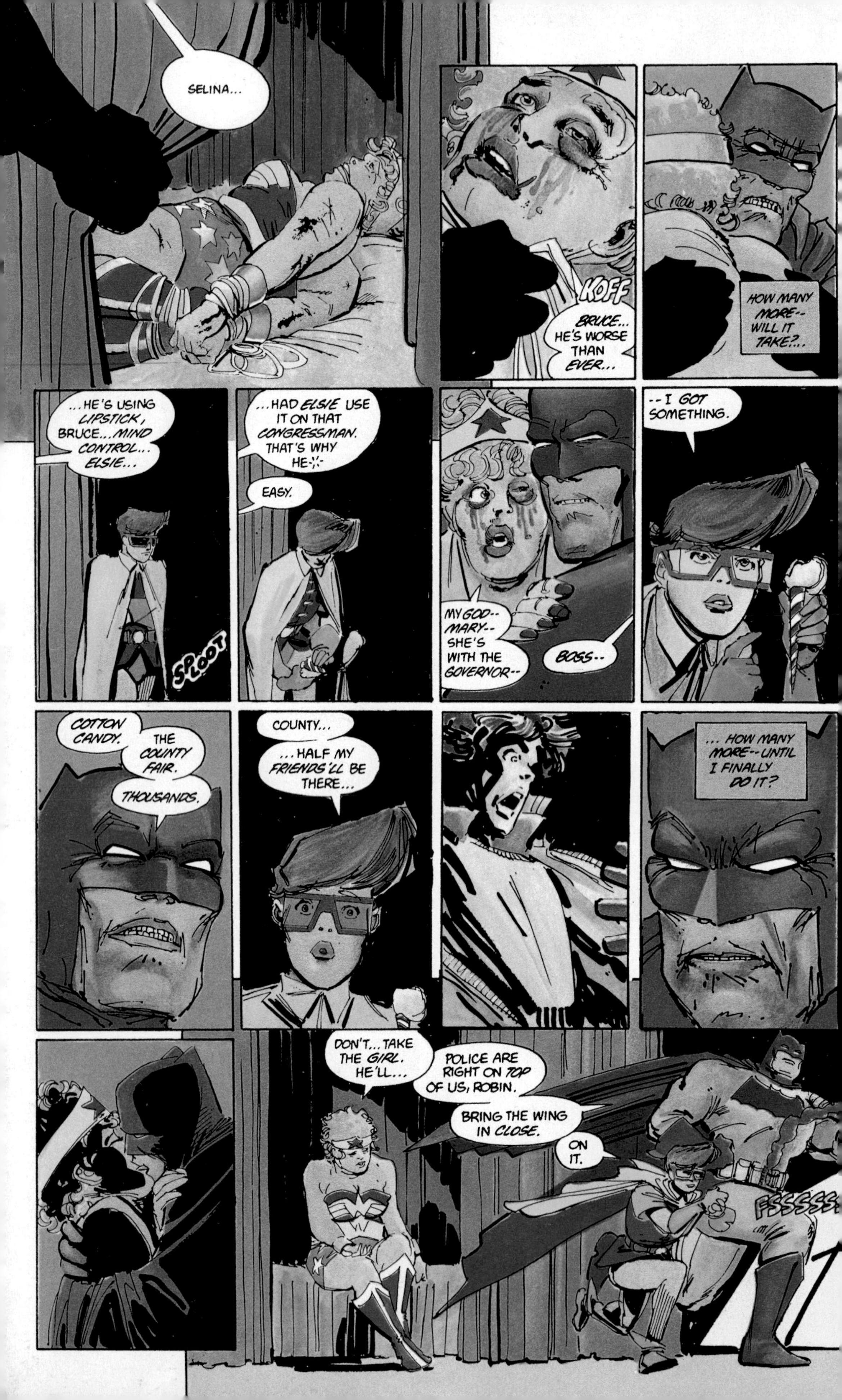
SELINA...
KOFF
BRUCE... HE'S WORSE THAN EVER...
HOW MANY MORE-- WILL IT TAKE?...
...HE'S USING LIPSTICK, BRUCE...MIND CONTROL... ELSIE...
SPLOOT
...HAD ELSIE USE IT ON THAT CONGRESSMAN. THAT'S WHY HE--
EASY.
MY GOD-- MARY-- SHE'S WITH THE GOVERNOR--
BOSS--
--I GOT SOMETHING.
COTTON CANDY.
THE COUNTY FAIR.
THOUSANDS.
COUNTY...
...HALF MY FRIENDS'LL BE THERE...
... HOW MANY MORE-- UNTIL I FINALLY DO IT?
DON'T... TAKE THE GIRL. HE'LL...
POLICE ARE RIGHT ON TOP OF US, ROBIN.
BRING THE WING IN CLOSE.
ON IT.
FSSSSS

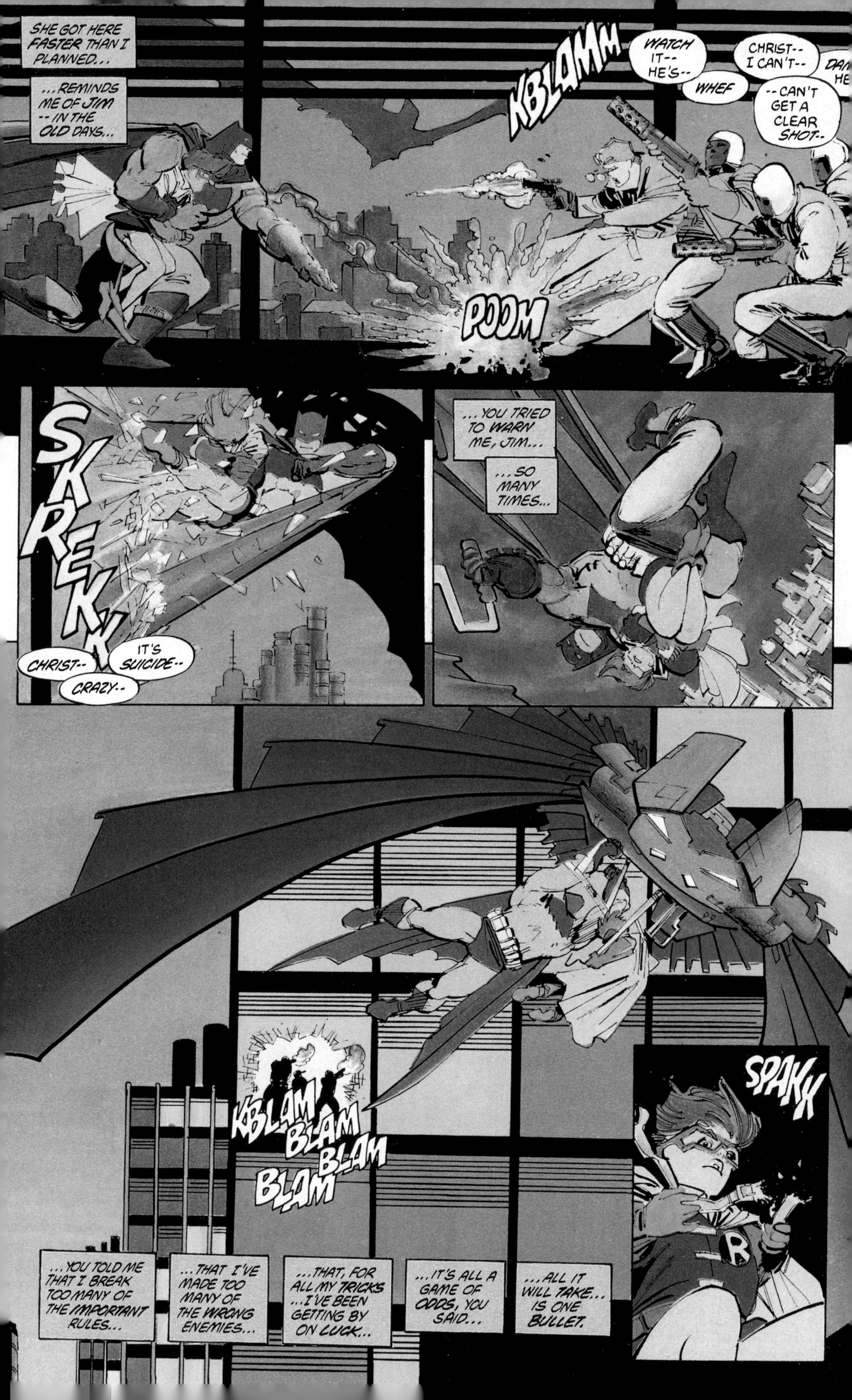

SHE GOT HERE FASTER THAN I PLANNED...
...REMINDS ME OF JIM -- IN THE OLD DAYS...
KBLAMM
WATCH IT-- HE'S--
WHEF
CHRIST-- I CAN'T--
--CAN'T GET A CLEAR SHOT--
POOM
SKREKK
CHRIST--
CRAZY--
IT'S SUICIDE--
...YOU TRIED TO WARN ME, JIM...
...SO MANY TIMES...
KBLAM BLAM BLAM BLAM
SPAKK
...YOU TOLD ME THAT I BREAK TOO MANY OF THE IMPORTANT RULES...
...THAT I'VE MADE TOO MANY OF THE WRONG ENEMIES...
...THAT, FOR ALL MY TRICKS ...I'VE BEEN GETTING BY ON LUCK...
...IT'S ALL A GAME OF ODDS, YOU SAID...
...ALL IT WILL TAKE... IS ONE BULLET.

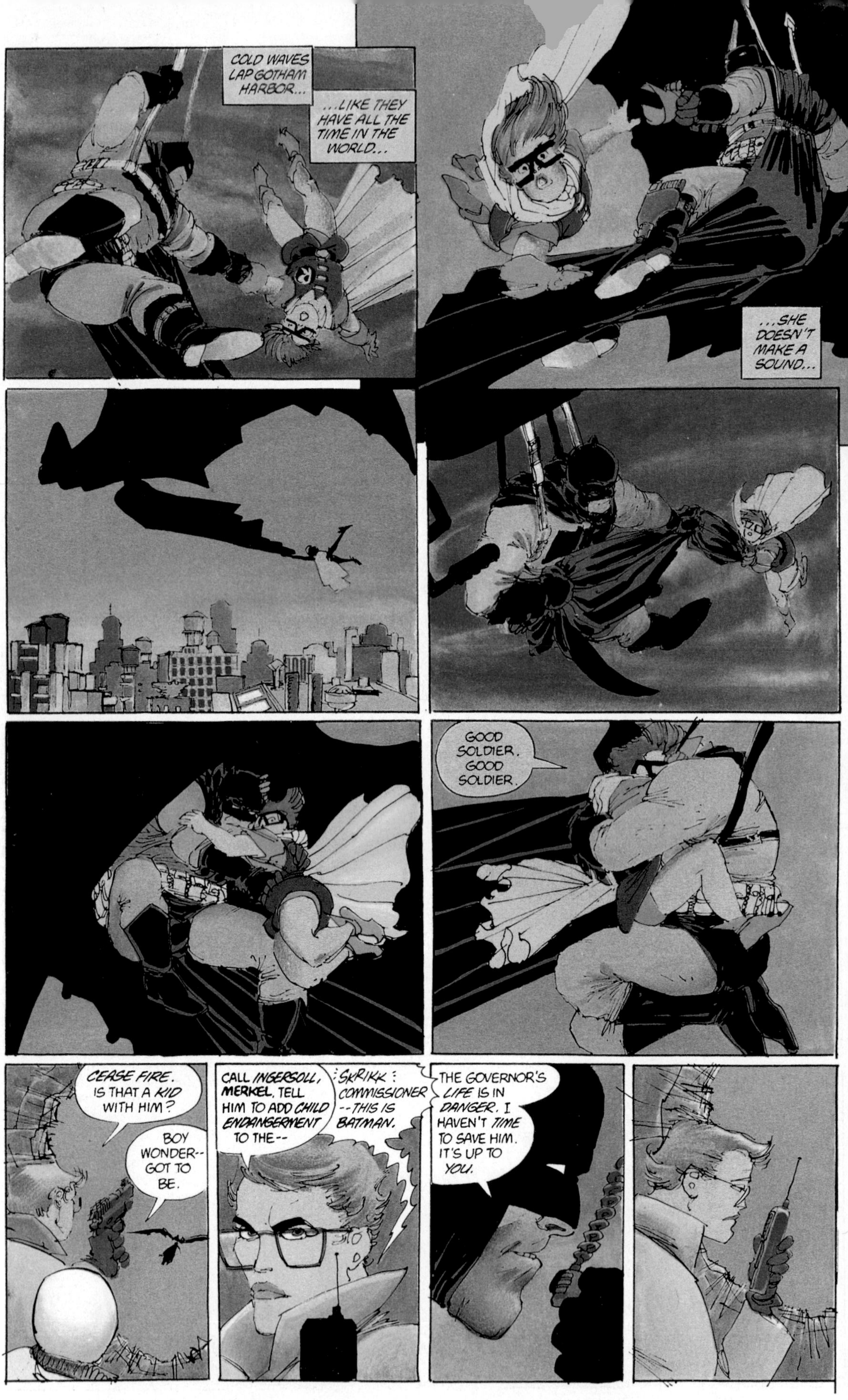
COLD WAVES LAP GOTHAM HARBOR...
...LIKE THEY HAVE ALL THE TIME IN THE WORLD...
...SHE DOESN'T MAKE A SOUND...
GOOD SOLDIER. GOOD SOLDIER.
CEASE FIRE. IS THAT A KID WITH HIM?
BOY WONDER--GOT TO BE.
CALL INGERSOLL, MERKEL. TELL HIM TO ADD CHILD ENDANGERMENT TO THE--
SKRIKK
COMMISSIONER --THIS IS BATMAN.
THE GOVERNOR'S LIFE IS IN DANGER. I HAVEN'T TIME TO SAVE HIM. IT'S UP TO YOU.

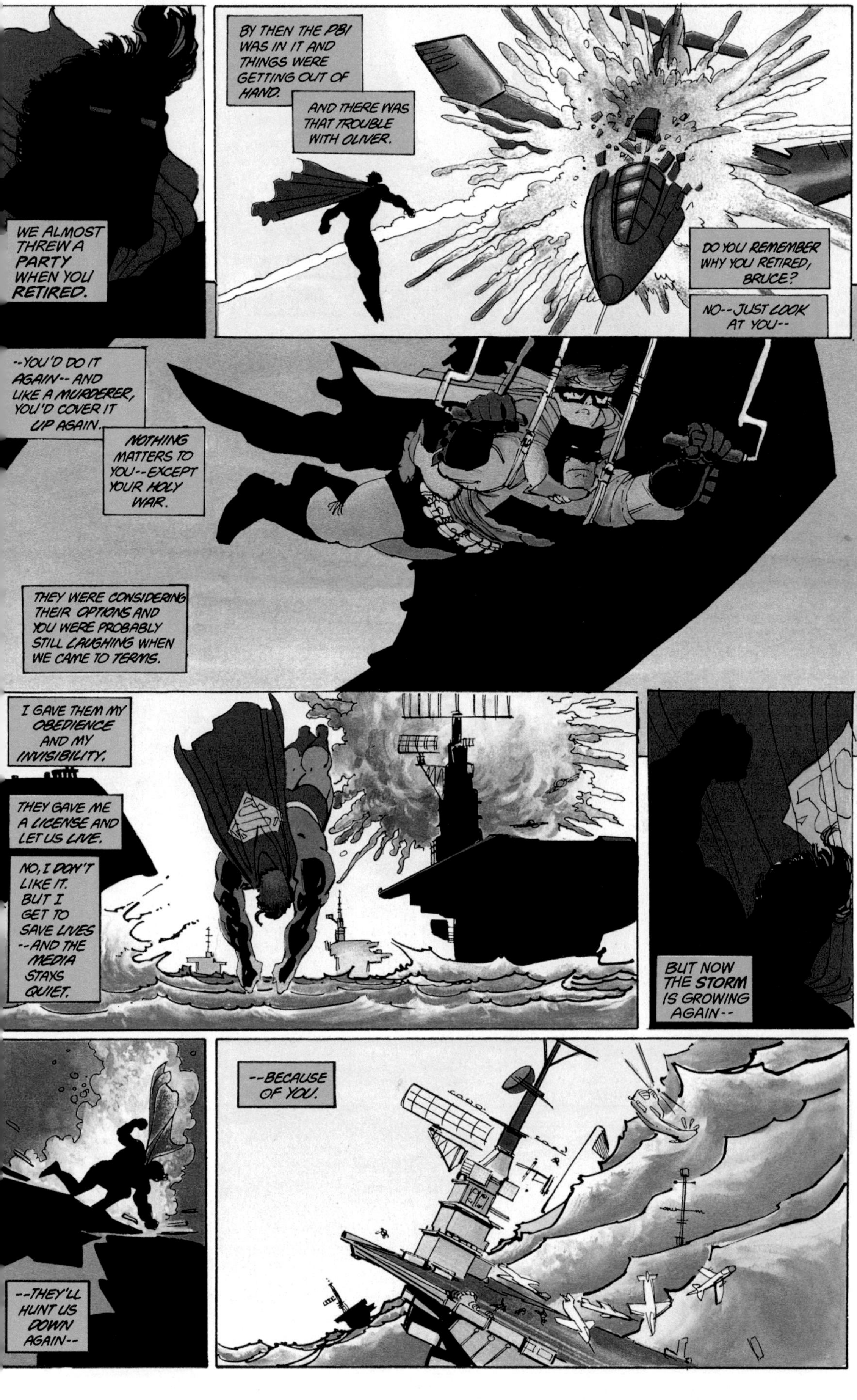
WE ALMOST THREW A PARTY WHEN YOU RETIRED.
BY THEN THE PBI WAS IN IT AND THINGS WERE GETTING OUT OF HAND.
AND THERE WAS THAT TROUBLE WITH OLIVER.
DO YOU REMEMBER WHY YOU RETIRED, BRUCE?
NO--JUST LOOK AT YOU--
--YOU'D DO IT AGAIN--AND LIKE A MURDERER, YOU'D COVER IT UP AGAIN.
NOTHING MATTERS TO YOU--EXCEPT YOUR HOLY WAR.
THEY WERE CONSIDERING THEIR OPTIONS AND YOU WERE PROBABLY STILL LAUGHING WHEN WE CAME TO TERMS.
I GAVE THEM MY OBEDIENCE AND MY INVISIBILITY.
THEY GAVE ME A LICENSE AND LET US LIVE.
NO, I DON'T LIKE IT. BUT I GET TO SAVE LIVES --AND THE MEDIA STAYS QUIET.
BUT NOW THE STORM IS GROWING AGAIN--
--THEY'LL HUNT US DOWN AGAIN--
--BECAUSE OF YOU.

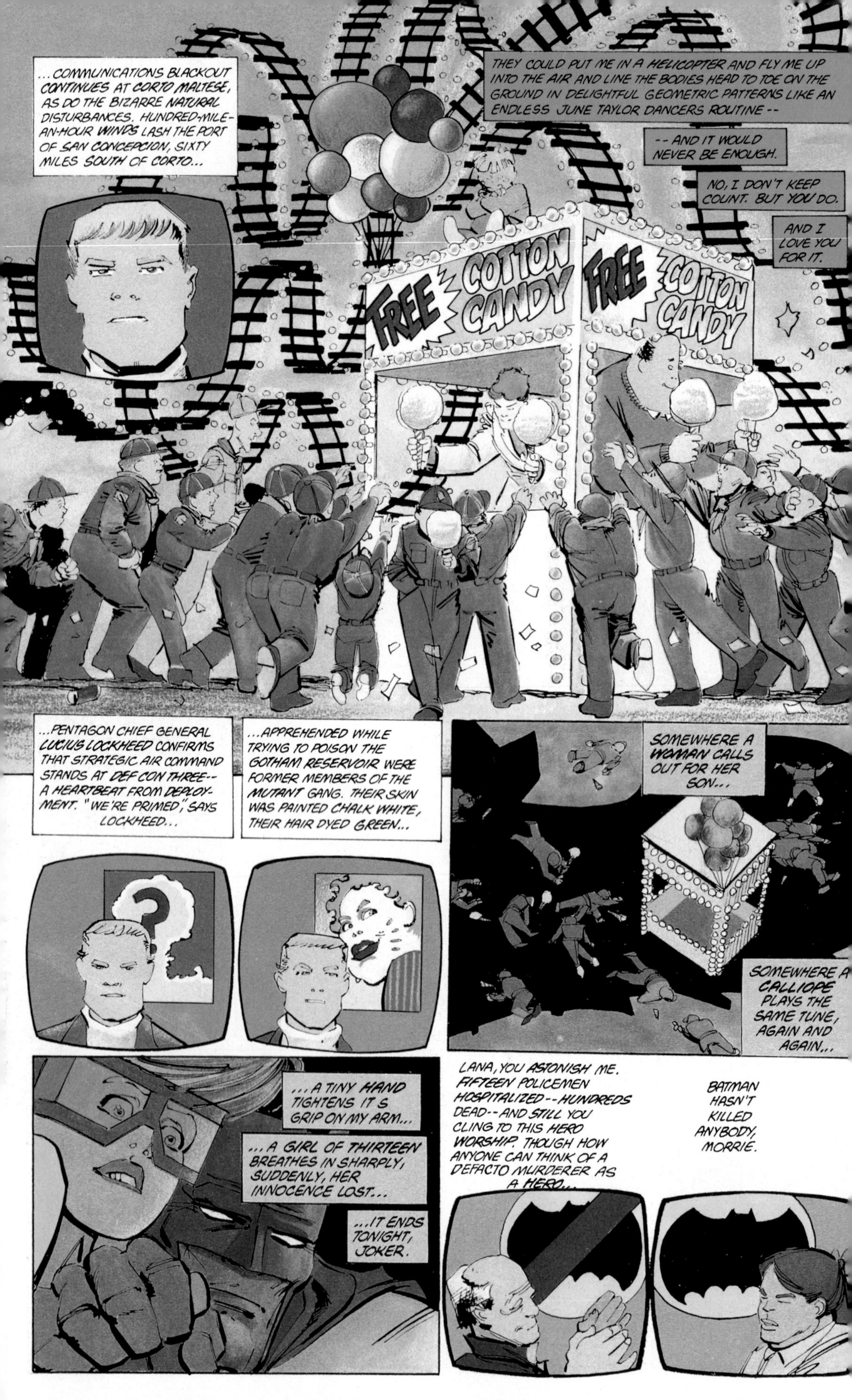

...COMMUNICATIONS BLACKOUT CONTINUES AT CORTO MALTESE, AS DO THE BIZARRE NATURAL DISTURBANCES. HUNDRED-MILE-AN-HOUR WINDS LASH THE PORT OF SAN CONCEPCION, SIXTY MILES SOUTH OF CORTO...
THEY COULD PUT ME IN A HELICOPTER AND FLY ME UP INTO THE AIR AND LINE THE BODIES HEAD TO TOE ON THE GROUND IN DELIGHTFUL GEOMETRIC PATTERNS LIKE AN ENDLESS JUNE TAYLOR DANCERS ROUTINE --
-- AND IT WOULD NEVER BE ENOUGH.
NO, I DON'T KEEP COUNT. BUT YOU DO.
AND I LOVE YOU FOR IT.
FREE COTTON CANDY
FREE COTTON CANDY
...PENTAGON CHIEF GENERAL LUCIUS LOCKHEED CONFIRMS THAT STRATEGIC AIR COMMAND STANDS AT DEF CON THREE-- A HEARTBEAT FROM DEPLOYMENT. "WE'RE PRIMED," SAYS LOCKHEED...
...APPREHENDED WHILE TRYING TO POISON THE GOTHAM RESERVOIR WERE FORMER MEMBERS OF THE MUTANT GANG. THEIR SKIN WAS PAINTED CHALK WHITE, THEIR HAIR DYED GREEN...
SOMEWHERE A WOMAN CALLS OUT FOR HER SON...
SOMEWHERE A CALLIOPE PLAYS THE SAME TUNE, AGAIN AND AGAIN...
...A TINY HAND TIGHTENS IT S GRIP ON MY ARM...
...A GIRL OF THIRTEEN BREATHES IN SHARPLY, SUDDENLY, HER INNOCENCE LOST...
...IT ENDS TONIGHT, JOKER.
LANA, YOU ASTONISH ME. FIFTEEN POLICEMEN HOSPITALIZED--HUNDREDS DEAD--AND STILL YOU CLING TO THIS HERO WORSHIP. THOUGH HOW ANYONE CAN THINK OF A DEFACTO MURDERER AS A HERO...
BATMAN HASN'T KILLED ANYBODY, MORRIE.

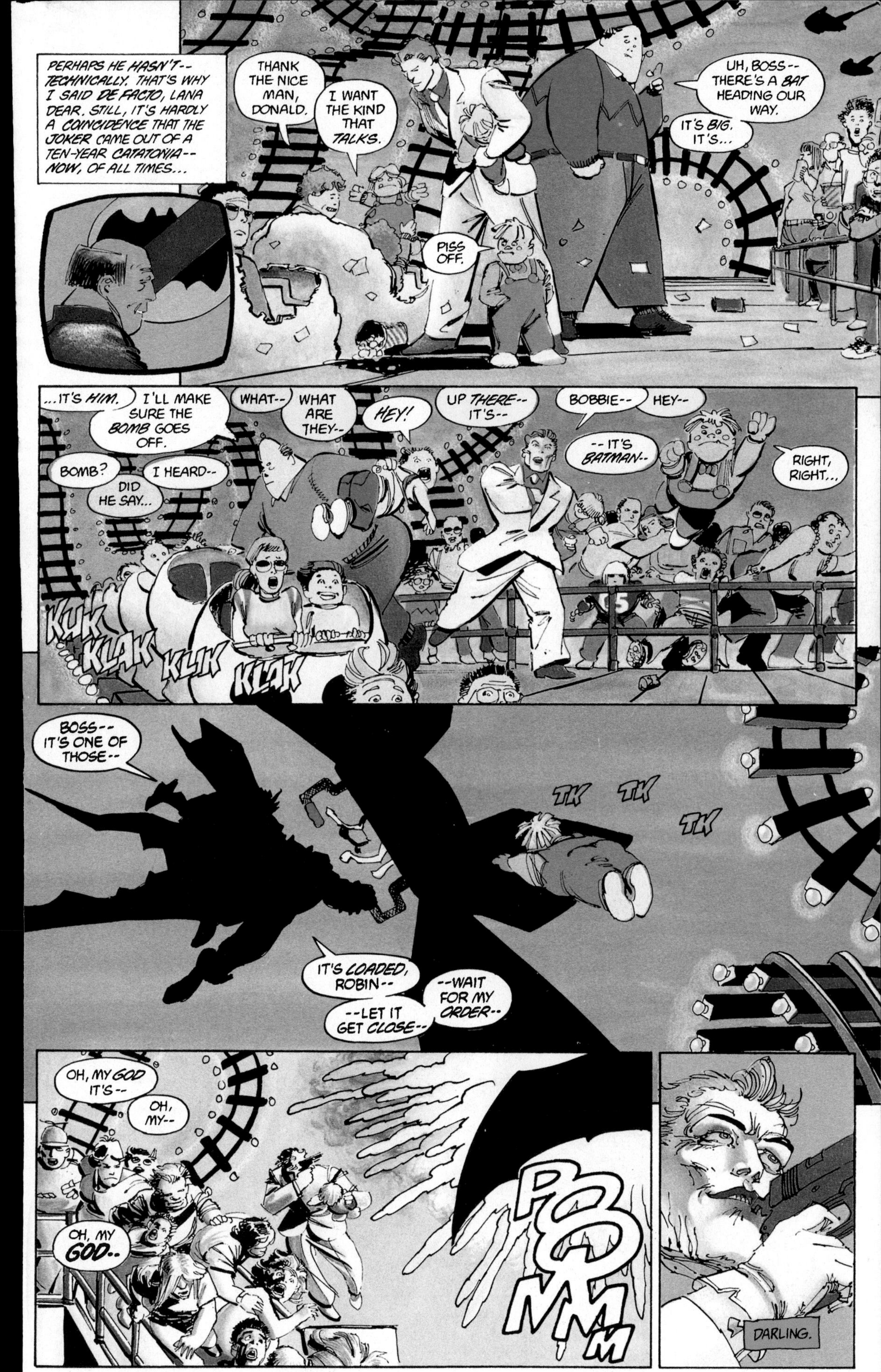

PERHAPS HE HASN'T-- TECHNICALLY. THAT'S WHY I SAID DE FACTO, LANA DEAR. STILL, IT'S HARDLY A COINCIDENCE THAT THE JOKER CAME OUT OF A TEN-YEAR CATATONIA-- NOW, OF ALL TIMES...
THANK THE NICE MAN, DONALD.
I WANT THE KIND THAT TALKS.
PISS OFF.
UH, BOSS-- THERE'S A BAT HEADING OUR WAY.
IT'S BIG. IT'S...
...IT'S HIM.
I'LL MAKE SURE THE BOMB GOES OFF.
BOMB?
DID HE SAY...
I HEARD--
WHAT--
WHAT ARE THEY--
HEY!
UP THERE-- IT'S--
BOBBIE--
HEY--
--IT'S BATMAN--
RIGHT, RIGHT...
KUK KLAK KLIK KLAK
BOSS-- IT'S ONE OF THOSE--
TK TK TK
IT'S LOADED, ROBIN--
--LET IT GET CLOSE--
--WAIT FOR MY ORDER--
OH, MY GOD IT'S--
OH, MY--
OH, MY GOD..
BOOMM
DARLING.

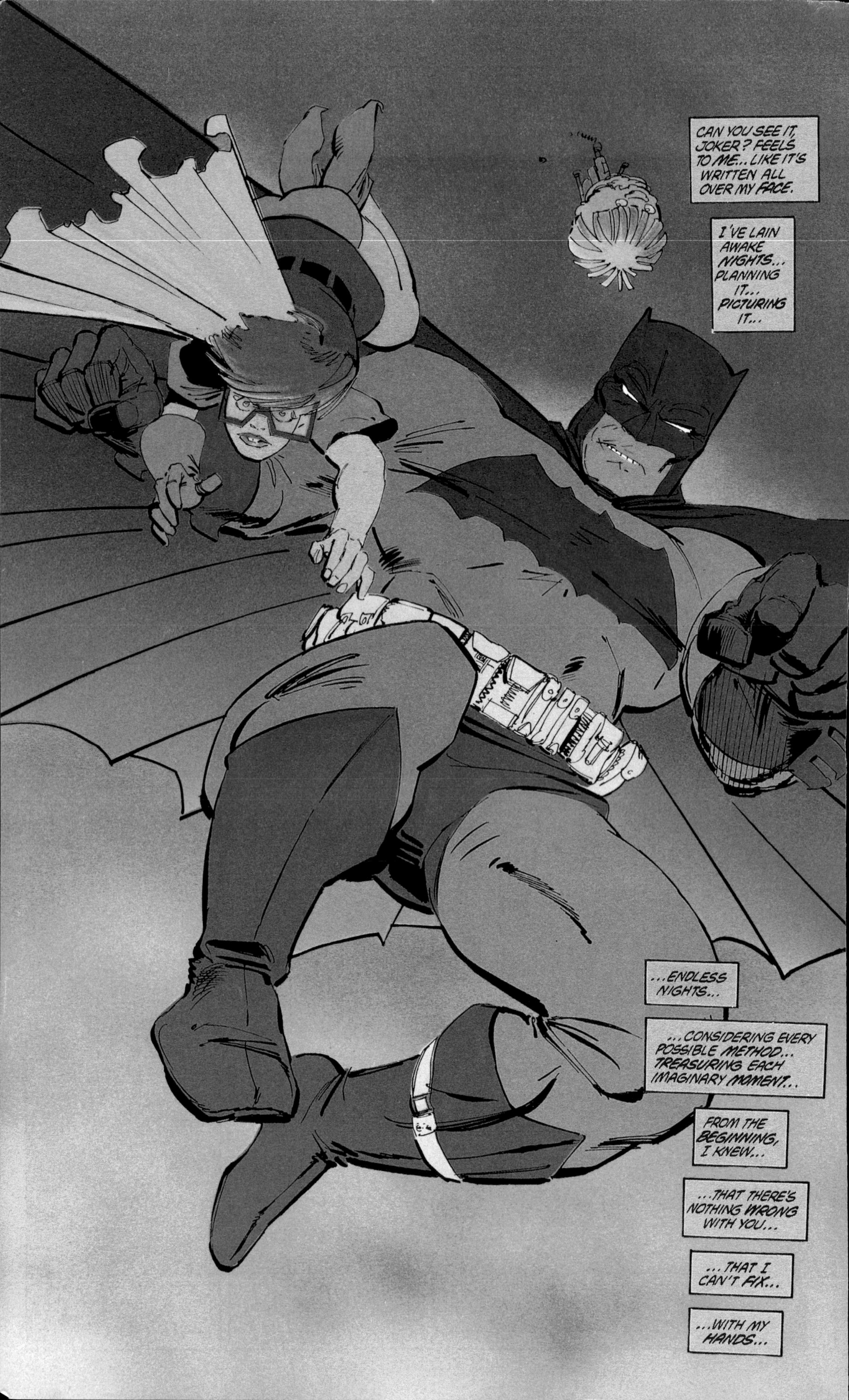
CAN YOU SEE IT, JOKER? FEELS TO ME... LIKE IT'S WRITTEN ALL OVER MY FACE.
I'VE LAIN AWAKE NIGHTS... PLANNING IT... PICTURING IT...
...ENDLESS NIGHTS...
...CONSIDERING EVERY POSSIBLE METHOD... TREASURING EACH IMAGINARY MOMENT...
FROM THE BEGINNING, I KNEW...
...THAT THERE'S NOTHING WRONG WITH YOU...
...THAT I CAN'T FIX...
...WITH MY HANDS...

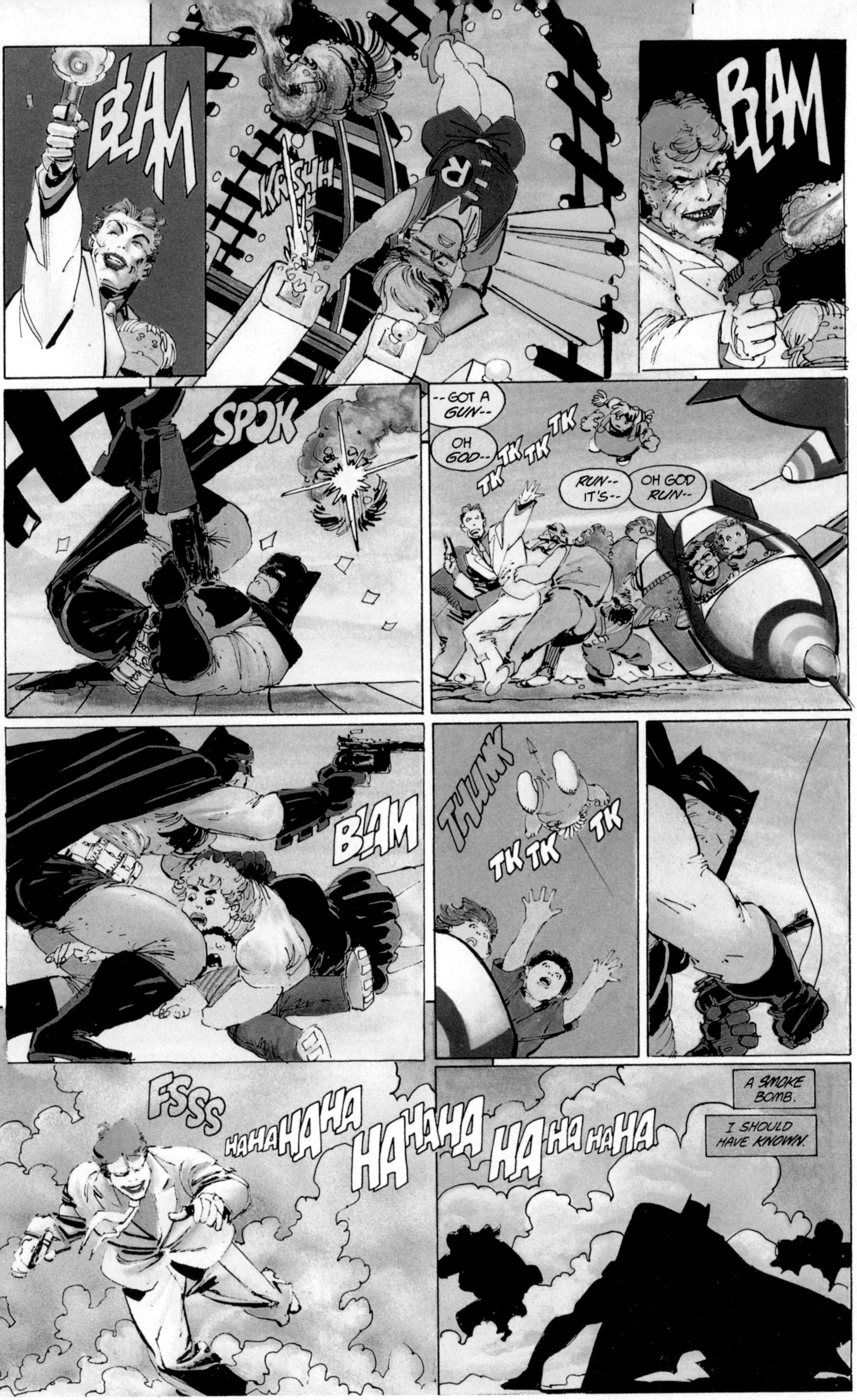
BLAM
KRSHH
BLAM
SPOK
--GOT A GUN--
OH GOD--
TK TK TK TK
RUN-- IT'S--
OH GOD RUN--
BLAM
THUNK
TK TK TK
FSSS
HAHAHAHA HAHAHAHA HAHAHAHA
A SMOKE BOMB.
I SHOULD HAVE KNOWN.

Panel 1: NO, JOKER.

YOU'RE PLAYING THE *WRONG* GAME. THE *OLD* GAME.

TONIGHT YOU'RE TAKING NO HOSTAGES.

Panel 2: *THUNK THUNK THUNK BLAM THUNK* AAAGG

TONIGHT I'M TAKING NO PRISONERS.

Panel 3: *BLAMM*

OUT OF YOUR *MIND*--

CHECK THE *STATISTICS*, LANA *DEAR*--HECK, IF YOU TOSS IN THE VICTIMS OF HIS *FAN CLUB*, THE *BATMAN*-RELATED *BODY COUNT* IS UP THERE WITH A MINOR *WAR*.

Panel 4: IT *IS* A WAR, MORRIE--THOUGH HE SEEMS TO BE THE ONLY ONE WITH *BALLS* ENOUGH TO *FIGHT* IT.

WHO GAVE THIS *THUG* THE RIGHT TO DECLARE *MARTIAL LAW*, HM? LAST I HEARD, THAT TAKES AN ACT OF *CONGRESS*.

BILLY GONE BILLY CAN'T

BELIEVE I'M DOING THIS--

Panel 5: OH, REAL COO--

--LIKE ALL FAN--

BLAM

KPWEE

KLIK KLAK KLIK KLAK KLIK KLAK

--LIKE GOODYEAR THERE--

--WON'T DUST ME--

--BEFORE THE DOLL--

--DOES THE MAXIMUM FLASH--

TK TK TK

KLIK KLAK

BLAM

KLIK KLAK

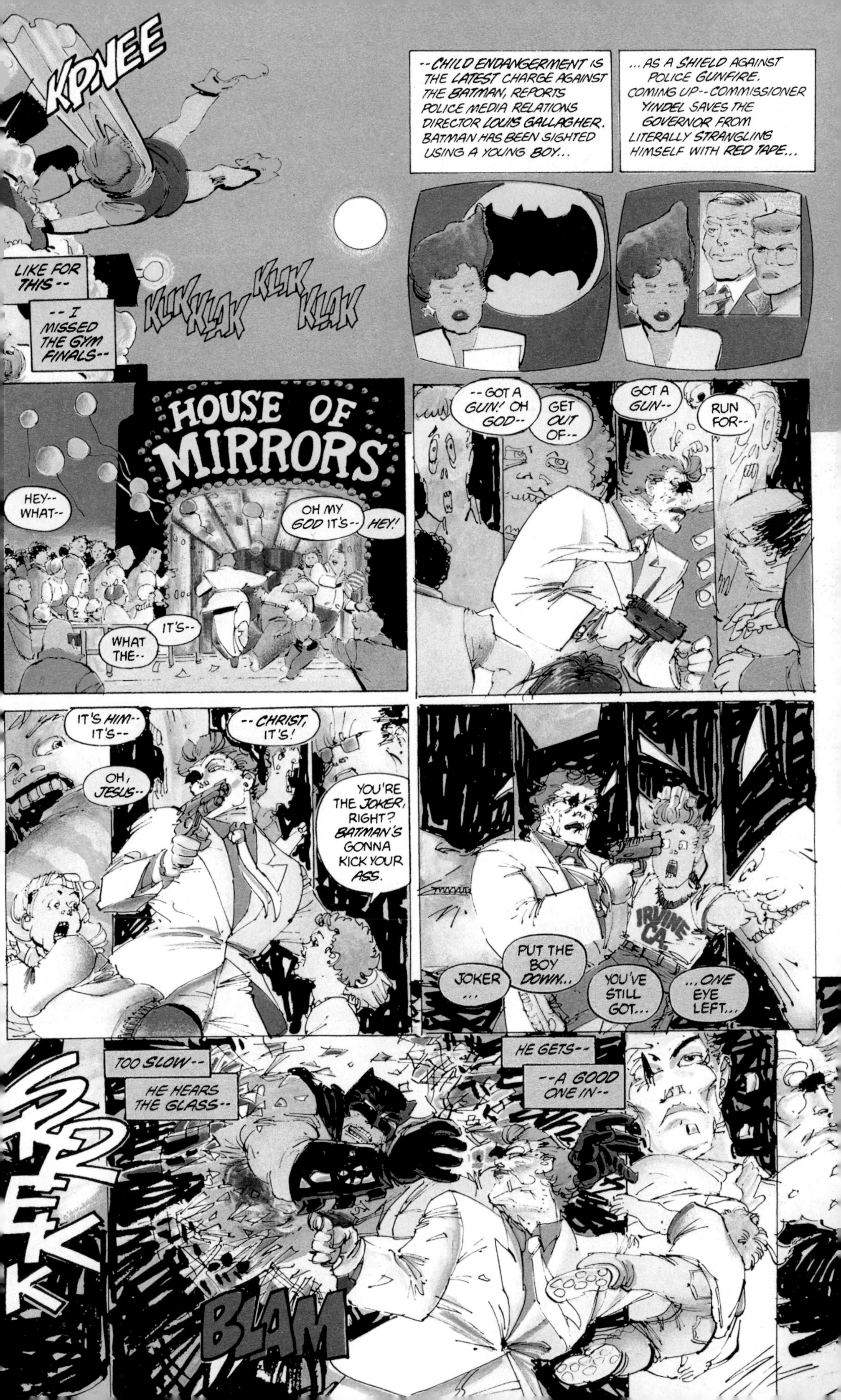

KPVEE
LIKE FOR THIS--
--I MISSED THE GYM FINALS--
KLIK KLAK KLIK KLAK
--CHILD ENDANGERMENT IS THE LATEST CHARGE AGAINST THE BATMAN, REPORTS POLICE MEDIA RELATIONS DIRECTOR LOUIS GALLAGHER. BATMAN HAS BEEN SIGHTED USING A YOUNG BOY...
...AS A SHIELD AGAINST POLICE GUNFIRE. COMING UP--COMMISSIONER YINDEL SAVES THE GOVERNOR FROM LITERALLY STRANGLING HIMSELF WITH RED TAPE...
HOUSE OF MIRRORS
HEY-- WHAT--
OH MY GOD IT'S--
HEY!
WHAT THE--
IT'S--
--GOT A GUN! OH GOD--
GET OUT OF--
GOT A GUN--
RUN FOR--
IT'S HIM-- IT'S--
--CHRIST, IT'S!
OH, JESUS--
YOU'RE THE JOKER, RIGHT? BATMAN'S GONNA KICK YOUR ASS.
IRVINE CA.
JOKER ...
PUT THE BOY DOWN...
YOU'VE STILL GOT...
...ONE EYE LEFT...
SPKZZEKK
TOO SLOW--
HE HEARS THE GLASS--
HE GETS--
--A GOOD ONE IN--
BLAM

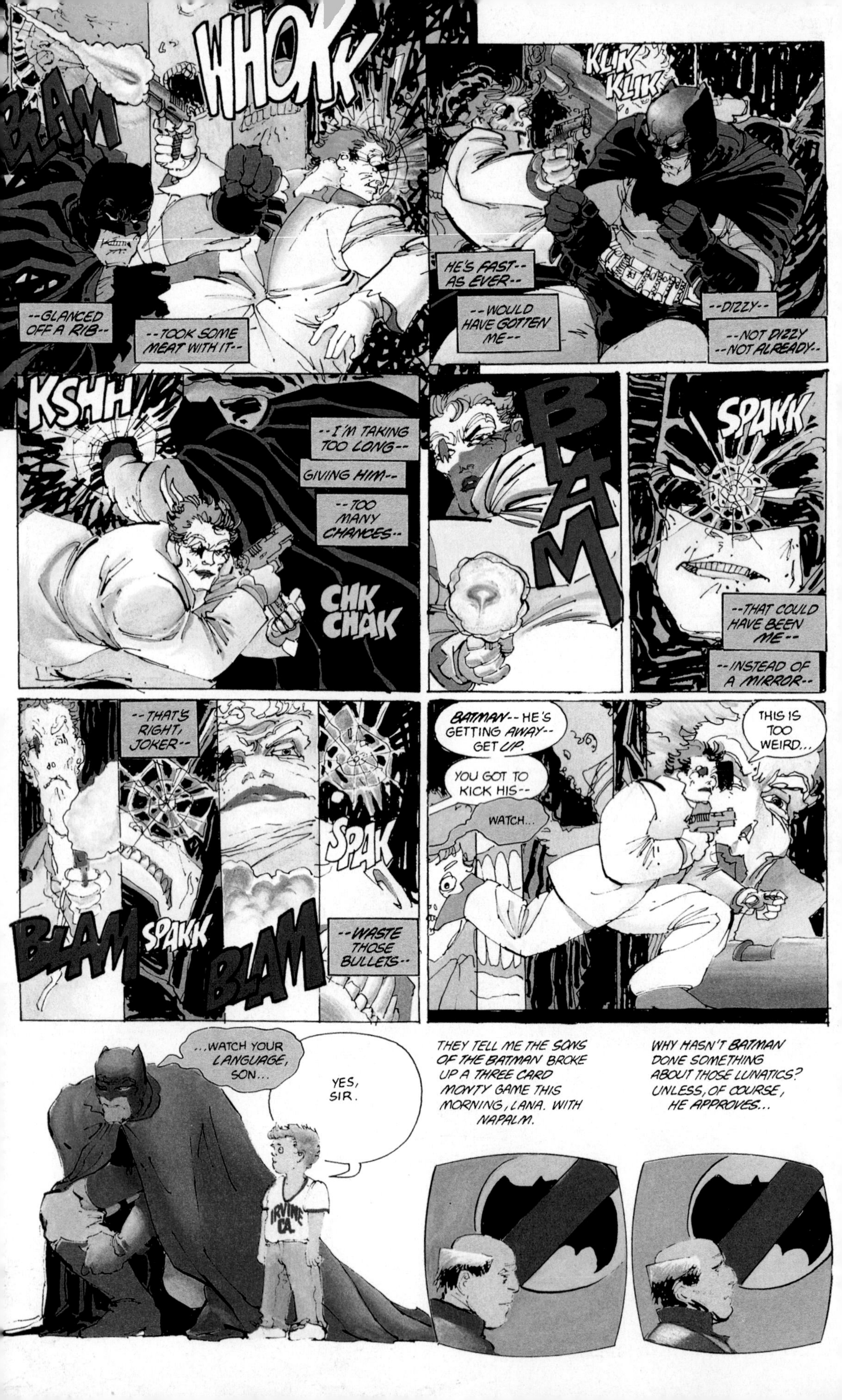

BLAM
WHOKK
--GLANCED OFF A RIB--
--TOOK SOME MEAT WITH IT--
KLIK KLIK
HE'S FAST-- AS EVER--
--WOULD HAVE GOTTEN ME--
--DIZZY--
--NOT DIZZY --NOT ALREADY--
KSHH
--I'M TAKING TOO LONG--
GIVING HIM--
--TOO MANY CHANCES--
CHK CHAK
BLAM
SPAKK
--THAT COULD HAVE BEEN ME--
--INSTEAD OF A MIRROR--
--THAT'S RIGHT, JOKER--
BLAM
SPAKK
BLAM
SPAK
--WASTE THOSE BULLETS--
BATMAN-- HE'S GETTING AWAY-- GET UP.
YOU GOT TO KICK HIS--
WATCH...
THIS IS TOO WEIRD...
...WATCH YOUR LANGUAGE, SON...
YES, SIR.
IRVINE CA.
THEY TELL ME THE SONS OF THE BATMAN BROKE UP A THREE CARD MONTY GAME THIS MORNING, LANA. WITH NAPALM.
WHY HASN'T BATMAN DONE SOMETHING ABOUT THOSE LUNATICS? UNLESS, OF COURSE, HE APPROVES...

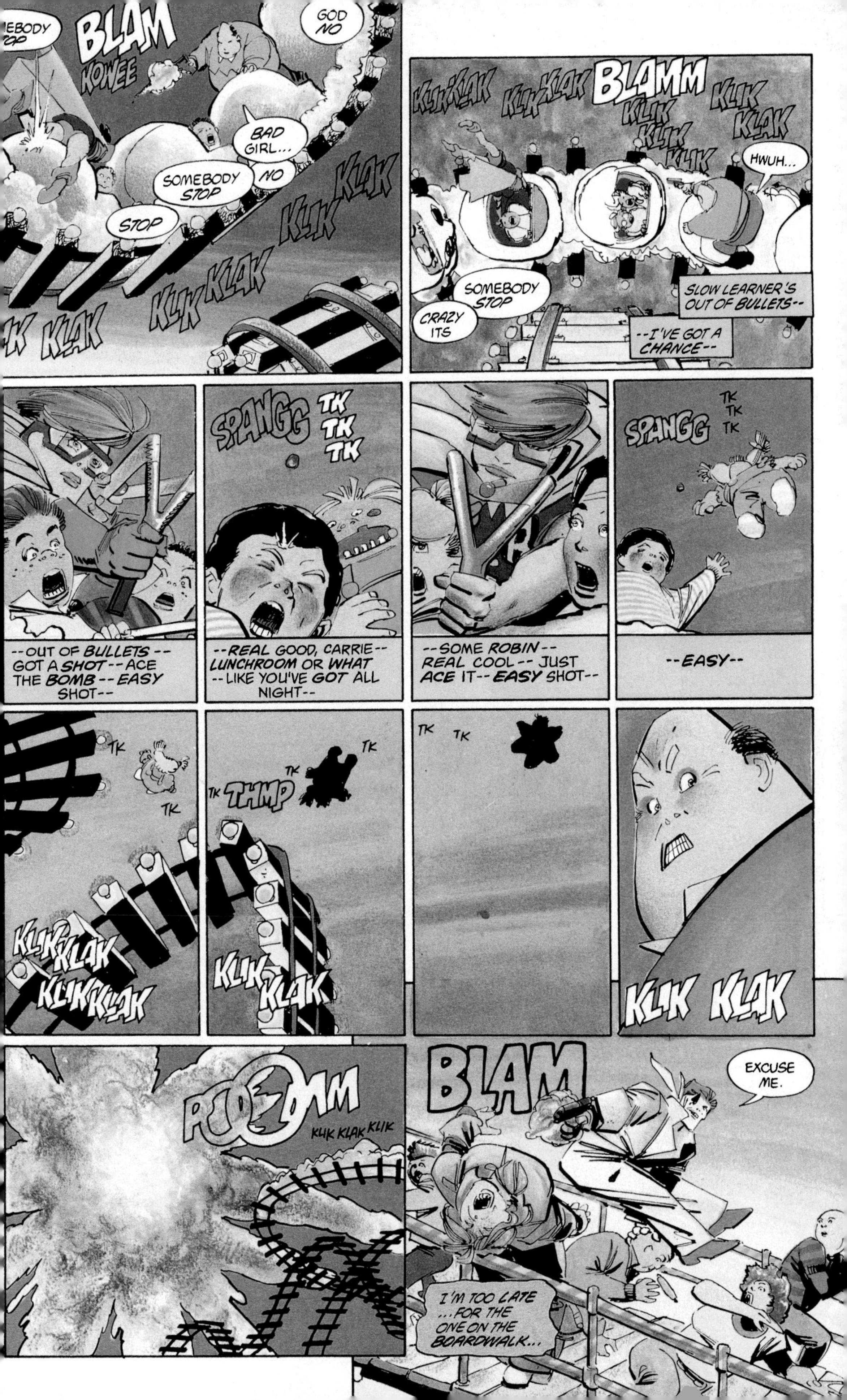

EBODY
TOP
BLAM
KOWEE
GOD
NO
BAD
GIRL...
SOMEBODY
STOP
NO
STOP
KLIK
KLAK
KLIK KLAK
K KLAK
KLIK KLAK KLIK KLAK BLAMM
KLIK KLIK KLIK
KLIK KLAK
HWUH...
SOMEBODY
STOP
CRAZY
ITS
SLOW LEARNER'S
OUT OF BULLETS--
--I'VE GOT A
CHANCE--
--OUT OF BULLETS --
GOT A SHOT -- ACE
THE BOMB -- EASY
SHOT--
SPANGG TK TK TK
--REAL GOOD, CARRIE--
LUNCHROOM OR WHAT
--LIKE YOU'VE GOT ALL
NIGHT--
--SOME ROBIN--
REAL COOL -- JUST
ACE IT-- EASY SHOT--
SPANGG TK TK TK
--EASY--
TK
TK
KLIK KLAK
KLIK KLAK
TK
TK THMP TK
KLIK
KLAK
TK TK
KLIK KLAK
POOOOM
KLIK KLAK KLIK
BLAM
EXCUSE
ME.
I'M TOO LATE
...FOR THE
ONE ON THE
BOARDWALK...

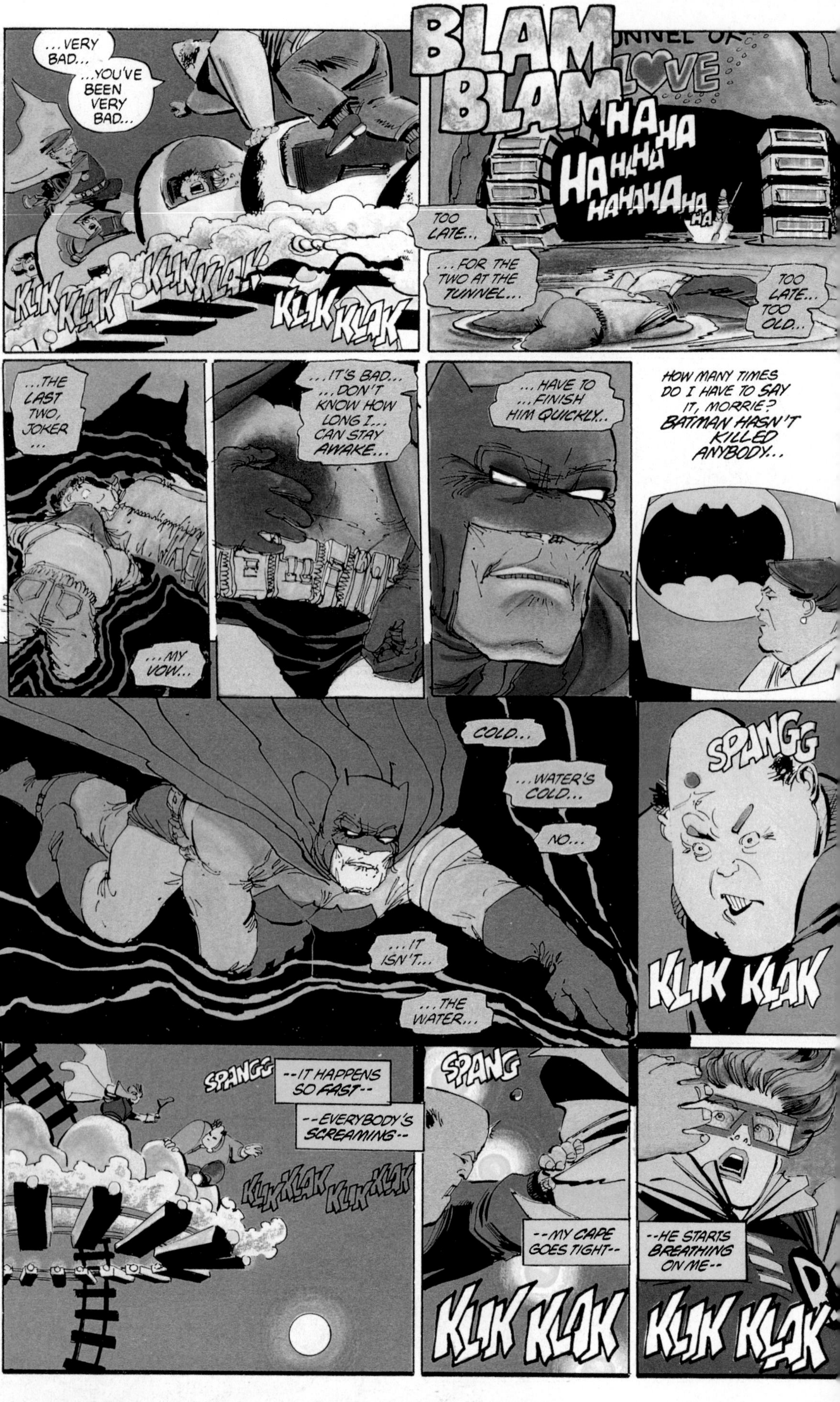

...VERY BAD...
...YOU'VE BEEN VERY BAD...
KLIK KLAK
KLIK KLAK
KLIK KLAK
BLAM
BLAM
TUNNEL OF LOVE
HA HA HA HA HA HAHAHAHA HA HA
TOO LATE...
...FOR THE TWO AT THE TUNNEL...
TOO LATE... TOO OLD...
...THE LAST TWO, JOKER...
...MY VOW...
...IT'S BAD... ...DON'T KNOW HOW LONG I... CAN STAY AWAKE...
...HAVE TO ...FINISH HIM QUICKLY...
HOW MANY TIMES DO I HAVE TO SAY IT, MORRIE? BATMAN HASN'T KILLED ANYBODY...
COLD...
...WATER'S COLD...
NO...
...IT ISN'T...
...THE WATER...
SPANGG
KLIK KLAK
SPANGG
--IT HAPPENS SO FAST--
--EVERYBODY'S SCREAMING--
KLIK KLAK KLIK KLAK
SPANG
--MY CAPE GOES TIGHT--
KLIK KLAK
--HE STARTS BREATHING ON ME--
KLIK KLAK

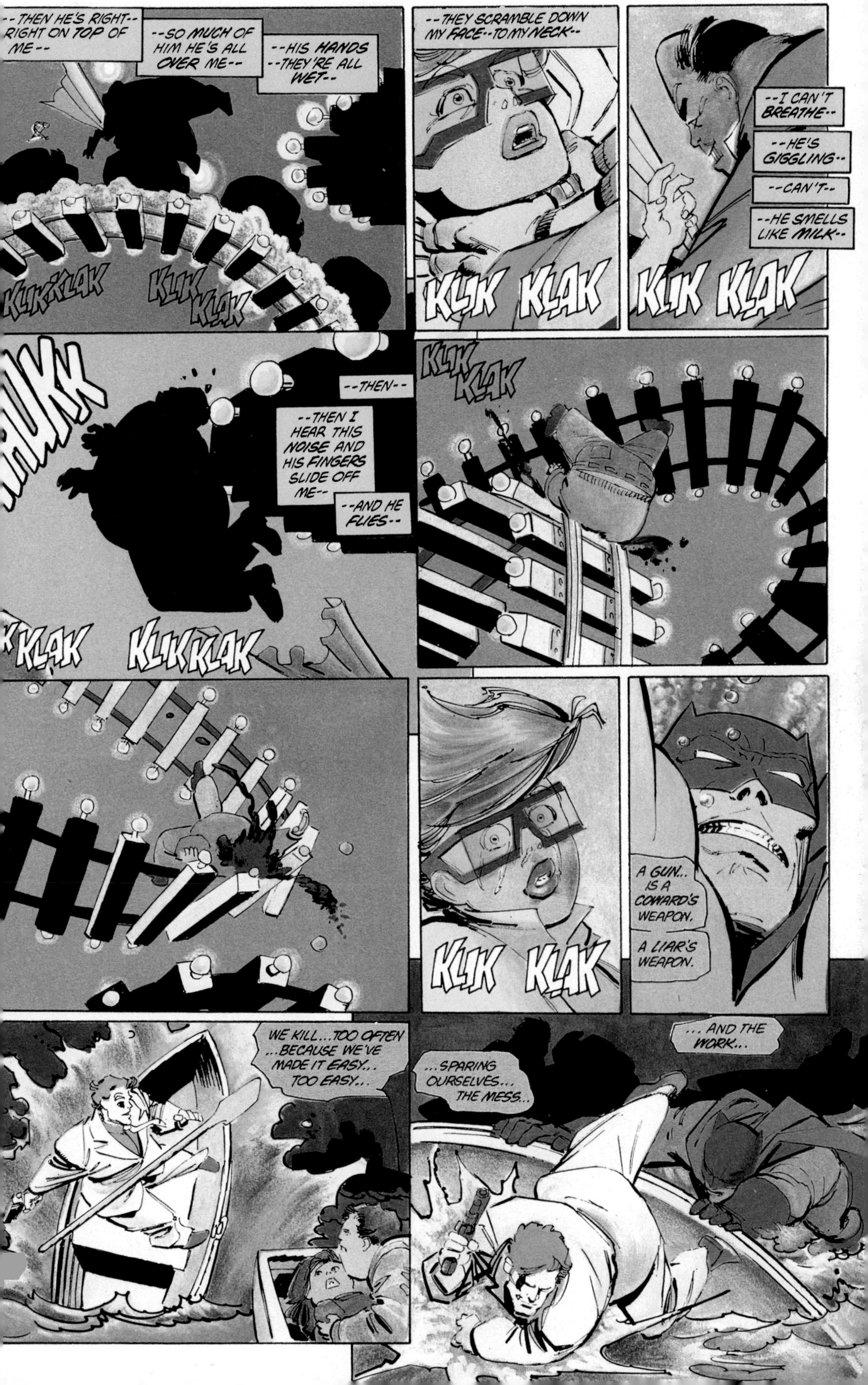

--THEN HE'S RIGHT-- RIGHT ON TOP OF ME--
--SO MUCH OF HIM HE'S ALL OVER ME--
--HIS HANDS --THEY'RE ALL WET--
KLIK KLAK
KLIK KLAK
--THEY SCRAMBLE DOWN MY FACE--TO MY NECK--
KLIK KLAK
--I CAN'T BREATHE--
--HE'S GIGGLING--
--CAN'T--
--HE SMELLS LIKE MILK--
KLIK KLAK
THUKK
--THEN--
--THEN I HEAR THIS NOISE AND HIS FINGERS SLIDE OFF ME--
--AND HE FLIES--
KLAK
KLIK KLAK
KLIK KLAK
KLIK KLAK
A GUN.. IS A COWARD'S WEAPON.
A LIAR'S WEAPON.
WE KILL...TOO OFTEN ...BECAUSE WE'VE MADE IT EASY.. TOO EASY...
...SPARING OURSELVES... THE MESS...
...AND THE WORK...

IT HAPPENS... SO SLOWLY...

...IT HAPPENS ...IN FIVE SECONDS...

...THE BLADE IS SHARP...

...I BARELY FELT IT ENTER MY STOMACH...

...HE'S TALKING... I CAN'T HEAR HIM...

...SOMETHING IS ROARING... I CAN'T...HEAR ANYTHING...

...HIS NECK... ...WILL HAVE TO DO...

...HE'S MOVING ...MORE QUICKLY THAN I AM...

...STABBING...

SHKK

THNK

SHKK

THNK

SHKK RAKK

...THE ROAR... IS FADING...I HEAR... VOICES...

--SHEER PANDEMONIUM HERE AT THE COUNTY FAIR, LOLA! THE JOKER HAS BEEN SIGHTED --SIXTEEN CUB SCOUTS HAVE BEEN FOUND DEAD --DOZENS HAVE BEEN WOUNDED BY EXPLOSIONS--

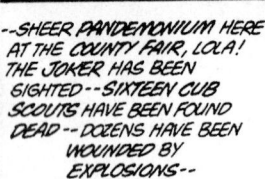

--AND BATMAN HAS BEEN SEEN --HE AND THE JOKER EXCHANGED GUNFIRE IN A CROWD-- HEY-- WHAT--LOLA-- THEY'RE EVACUATING THE COUNTY FAIR--

...VOICES CALLING ME... A KILLER...

...I WISH I WERE...

THEY'RE GONE..?

...THE WITNESSES, I MEAN...

I'M REALLY...VERY DISAPPOINTED WITH YOU, MY SWEET... THE MOMENT WAS... PERFECT...

...AND YOU... DIDN'T HAVE THE NERVE...

PARALYSIS... REALLY...

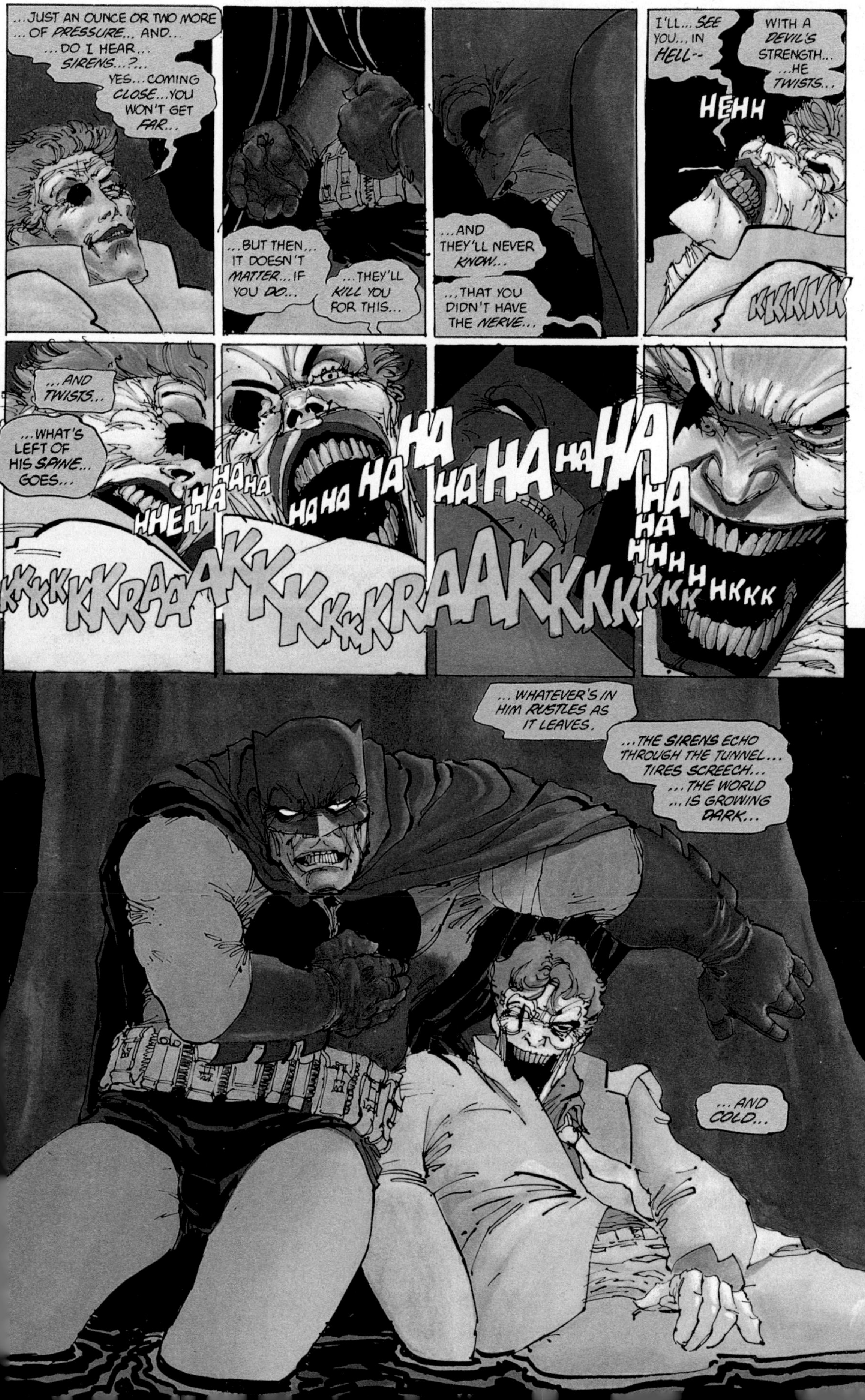
...JUST AN OUNCE OR TWO MORE ... OF PRESSURE... AND... ...DO I HEAR... SIRENS...?...
YES...COMING CLOSE...YOU WON'T GET FAR...
...BUT THEN... IT DOESN'T MATTER...IF YOU DO...
...THEY'LL KILL YOU FOR THIS...
...AND THEY'LL NEVER KNOW...
...THAT YOU DIDN'T HAVE THE NERVE...
I'LL... SEE YOU... IN HELL--
WITH A DEVIL'S STRENGTH... ...HE TWISTS...
HEHH
KKKKK
...AND TWISTS...
...WHAT'S LEFT OF HIS SPINE... GOES...
HHEHHAHAha
HAHA HA HA
HA HA HA ha HA
HA HA HHH HKKK HKKK
KKKKKRAAAKKKKKKRAAKKKKK
...WHATEVER'S IN HIM RUSTLES AS IT LEAVES.
...THE SIRENS ECHO THROUGH THE TUNNEL... TIRES SCREECH... ...THE WORLD ...IS GROWING DARK...
...AND COLD...

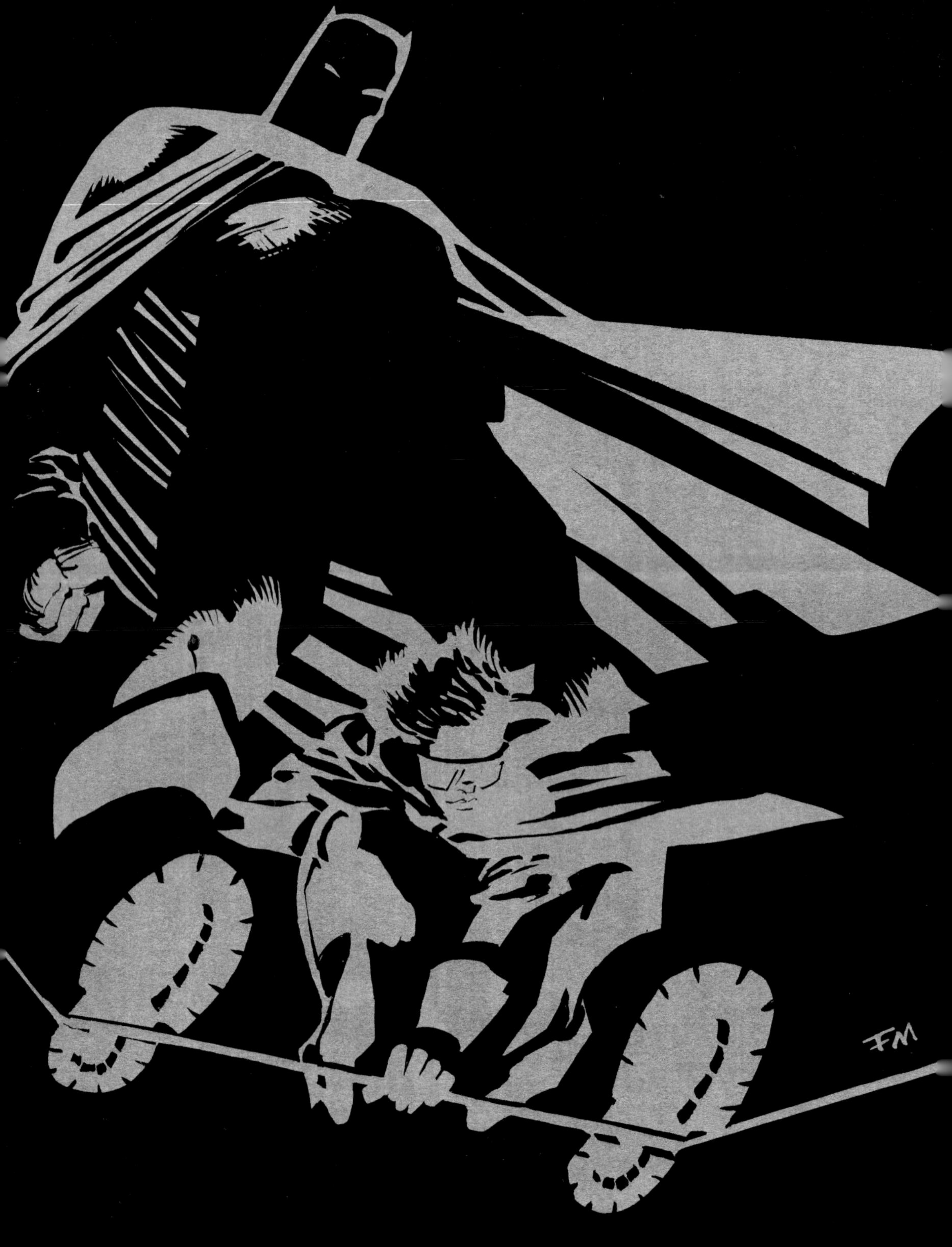
FM

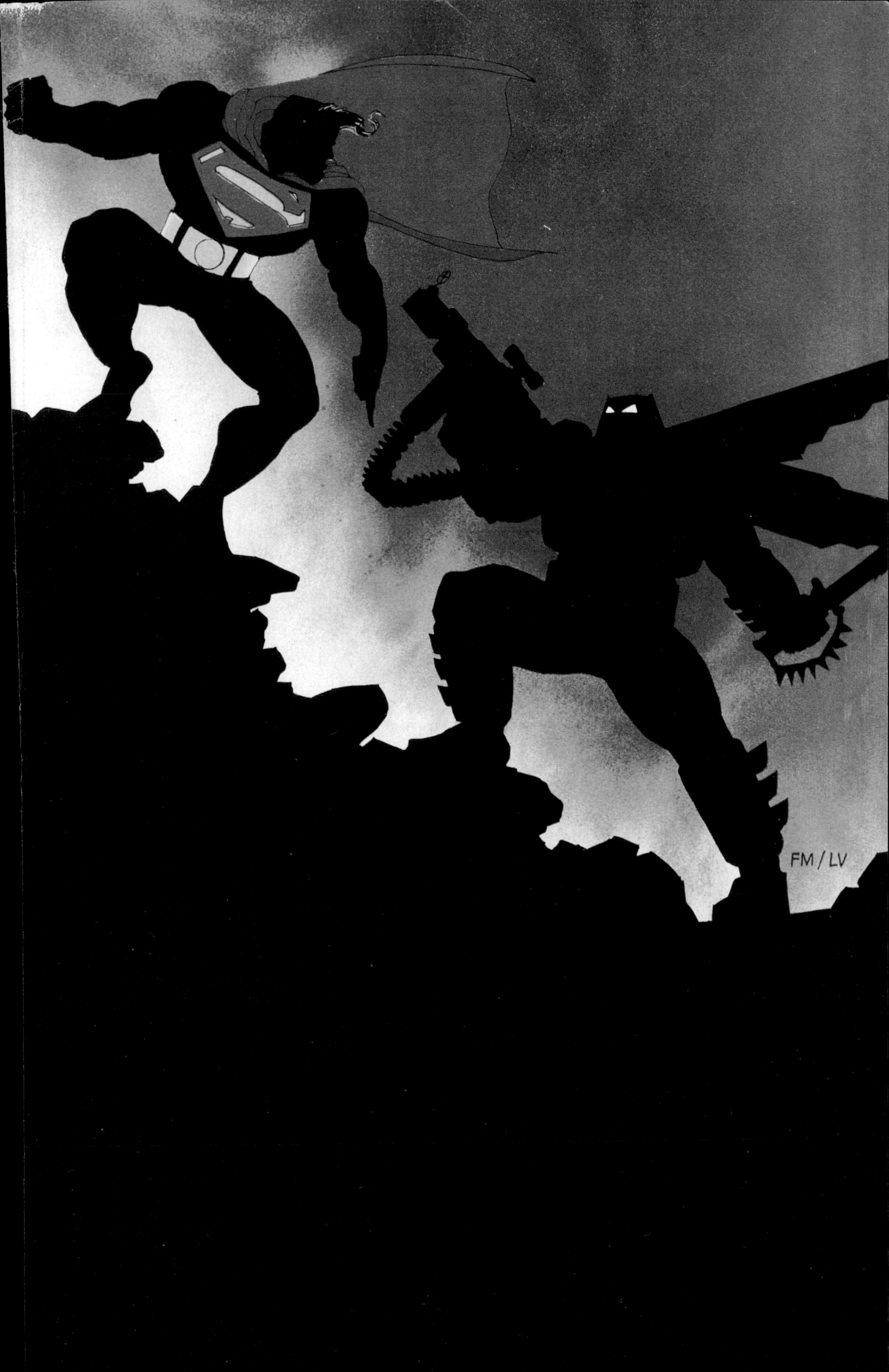
FM / LV

BOOK FOUR: THE DARK KNIGHT FALLS

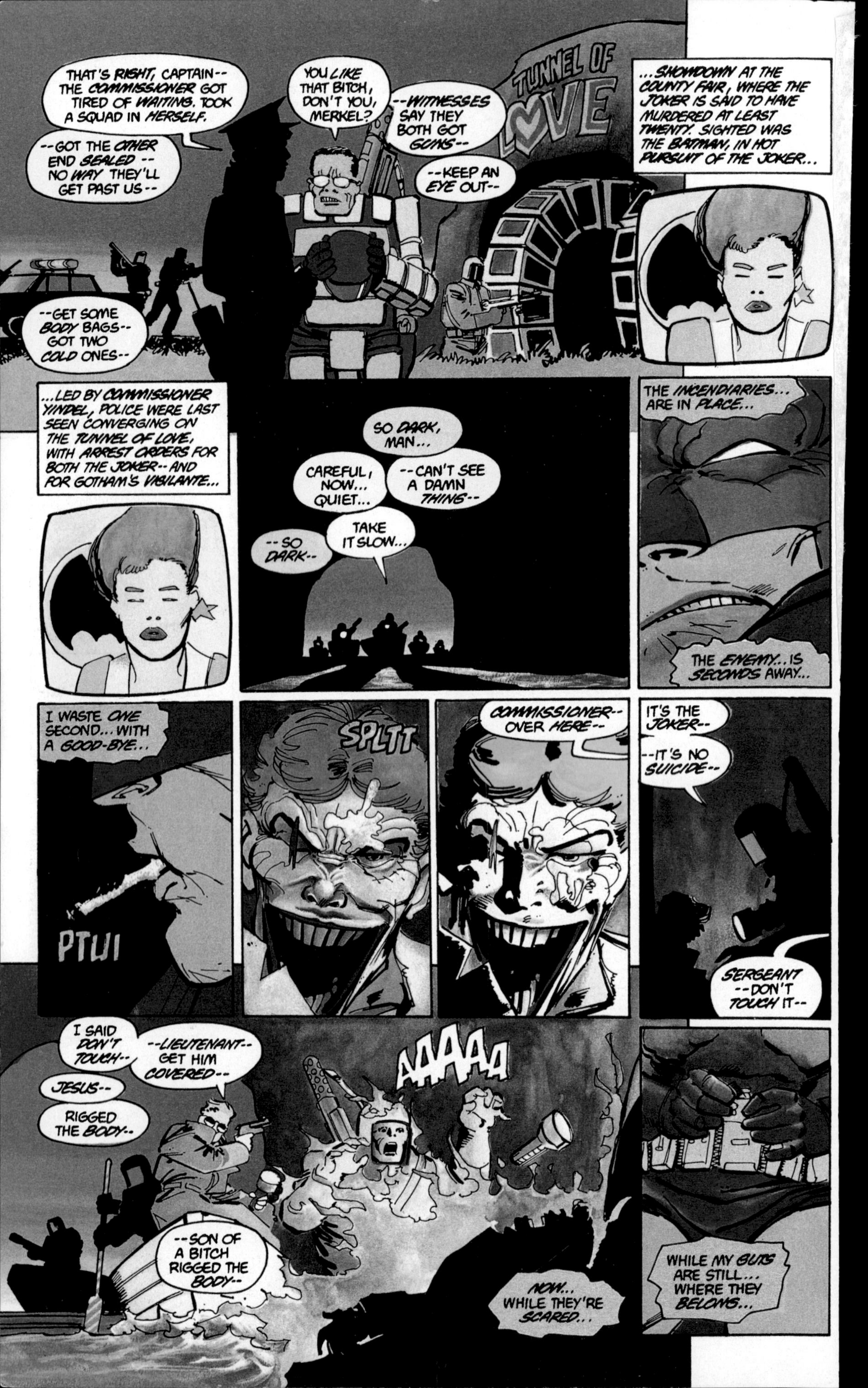
THAT'S RIGHT, CAPTAIN-- THE COMMISSIONER GOT TIRED OF WAITING. TOOK A SQUAD IN HERSELF.
--GOT THE OTHER END SEALED -- NO WAY THEY'LL GET PAST US--
YOU LIKE THAT BITCH, DON'T YOU, MERKEL?
--WITNESSES SAY THEY BOTH GOT GUNS--
--KEEP AN EYE OUT--
TUNNEL OF LOVE
--GET SOME BODY BAGS-- GOT TWO COLD ONES--
...SHOWDOWN AT THE COUNTY FAIR, WHERE THE JOKER IS SAID TO HAVE MURDERED AT LEAST TWENTY. SIGHTED WAS THE BATMAN, IN HOT PURSUIT OF THE JOKER...
...LED BY COMMISSIONER YINDEL, POLICE WERE LAST SEEN CONVERGING ON THE TUNNEL OF LOVE, WITH ARREST ORDERS FOR BOTH THE JOKER-- AND FOR GOTHAM'S VIGILANTE...
SO DARK, MAN...
CAREFUL, NOW... QUIET...
--CAN'T SEE A DAMN THING--
--SO DARK--
TAKE IT SLOW...
THE INCENDIARIES... ARE IN PLACE...
THE ENEMY... IS SECONDS AWAY...
I WASTE ONE SECOND... WITH A GOOD-BYE...
PTUI
SPLTT
COMMISSIONER-- OVER HERE--
IT'S THE JOKER--
--IT'S NO SUICIDE--
SERGEANT --DON'T TOUCH IT--
I SAID DON'T TOUCH--
--LIEUTENANT-- GET HIM COVERED--
JESUS--
RIGGED THE BODY--
AAAAA
--SON OF A BITCH RIGGED THE BODY--
NOW... WHILE THEY'RE SCARED...
WHILE MY GUTS ARE STILL... WHERE THEY BELONG...

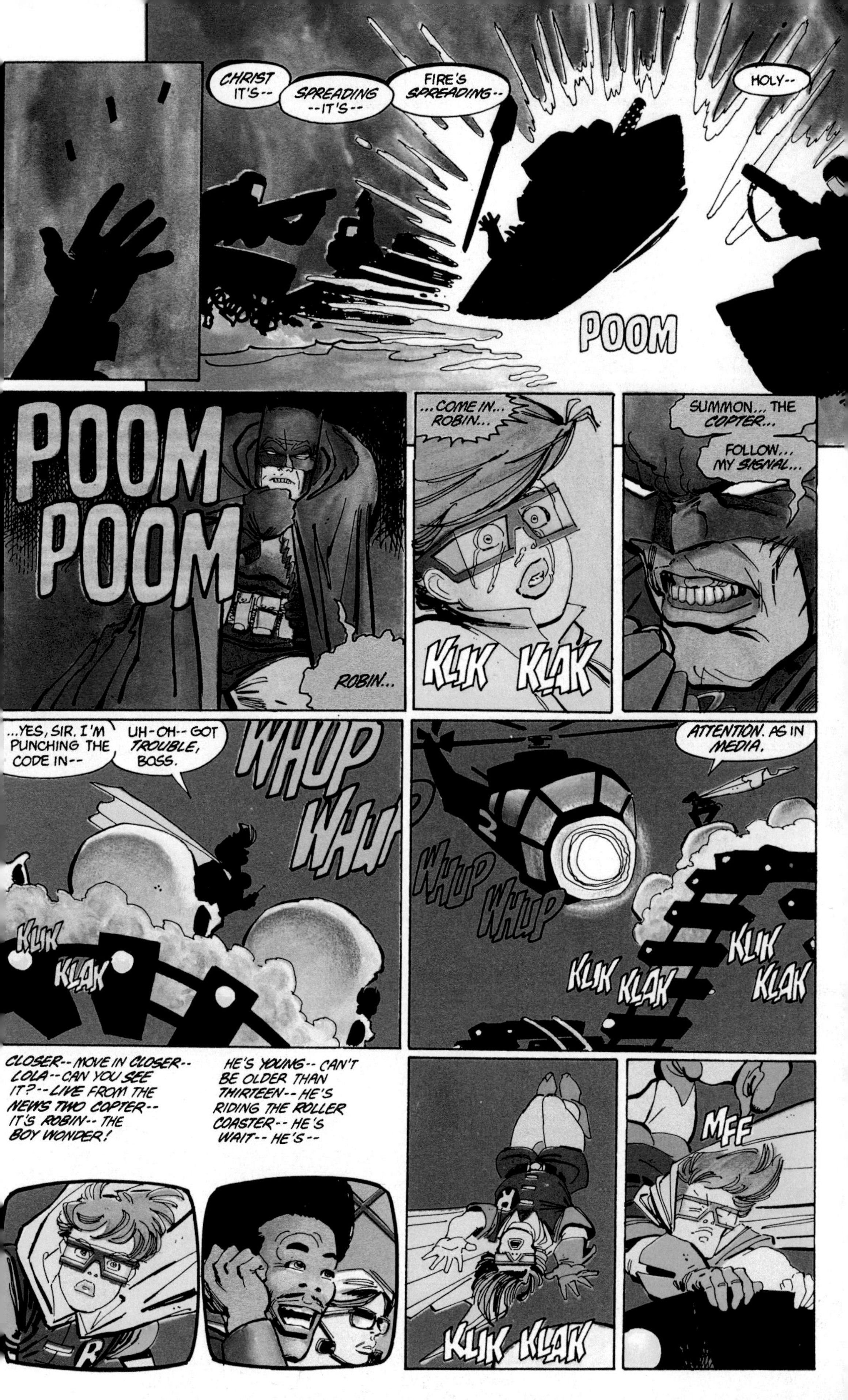
CHRIST IT'S--
SPREADING --IT'S--
FIRE'S SPREADING--
HOLY--
POOM
POOM POOM
ROBIN...
...COME IN... ROBIN...
KLIK KLAK
SUMMON... THE COPTER...
FOLLOW... MY SIGNAL...
...YES, SIR. I'M PUNCHING THE CODE IN--
UH-OH-- GOT TROUBLE, BOSS.
WHUP WHUP
KLIK KLAK
ATTENTION. AS IN MEDIA.
WHUP WHUP
KLIK KLAK
KLIK KLAK
CLOSER-- MOVE IN CLOSER-- LOLA-- CAN YOU SEE IT?-- LIVE FROM THE NEWS TWO COPTER-- IT'S ROBIN-- THE BOY WONDER!
HE'S YOUNG-- CAN'T BE OLDER THAN THIRTEEN-- HE'S RIDING THE ROLLER COASTER-- HE'S WAIT-- HE'S--
KLIK KLAK
MFF

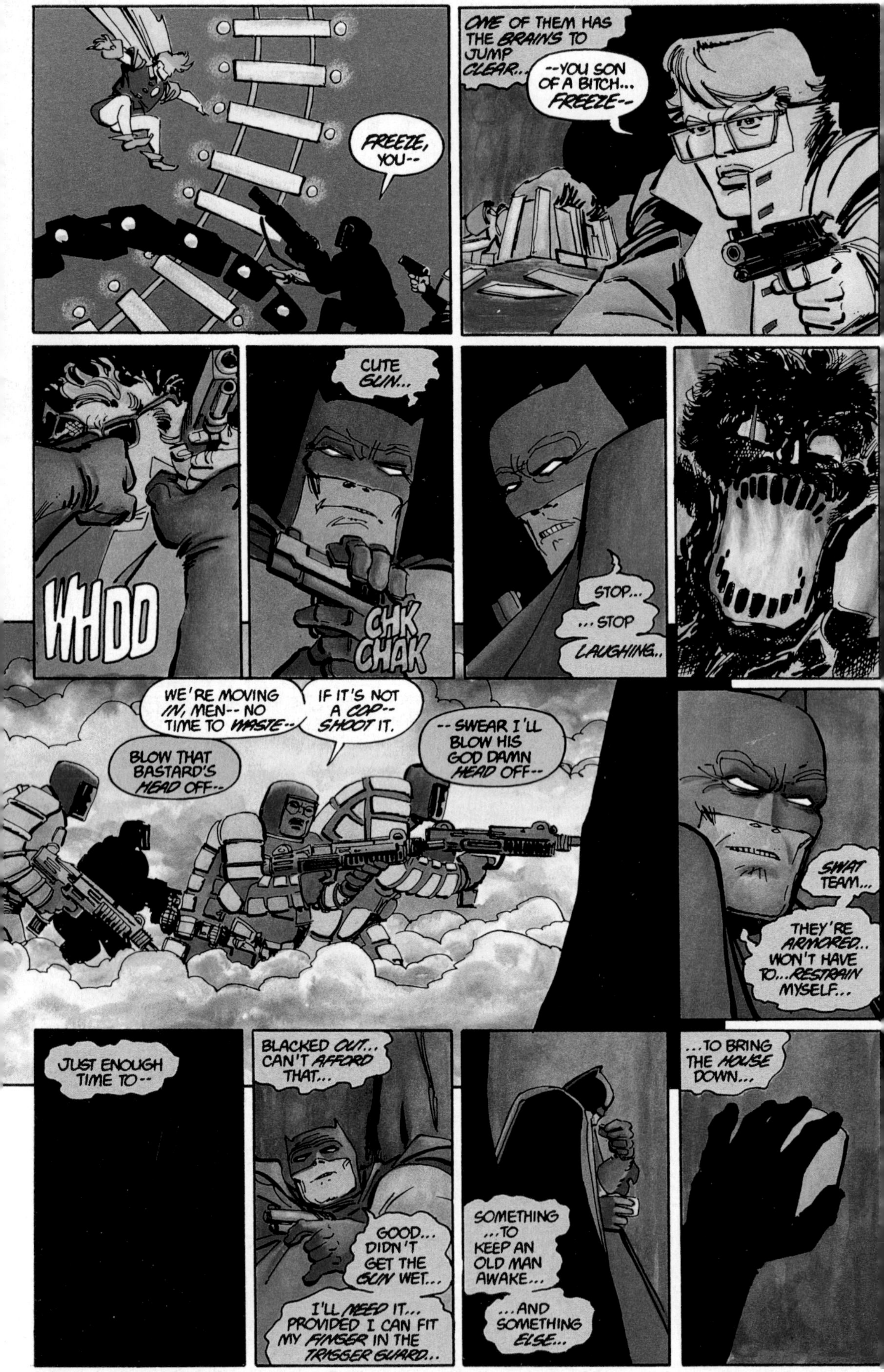
FREEZE, YOU--
ONE OF THEM HAS THE BRAINS TO JUMP CLEAR...
--YOU SON OF A BITCH... FREEZE--
WHDD
CUTE GUN...
CHK CHAK
STOP...
...STOP LAUGHING...
WE'RE MOVING IN, MEN-- NO TIME TO WASTE--
IF IT'S NOT A COP-- SHOOT IT.
BLOW THAT BASTARD'S HEAD OFF--
-- SWEAR I'LL BLOW HIS GOD DAMN HEAD OFF--
SWAT TEAM...
THEY'RE ARMORED... WON'T HAVE TO...RESTRAIN MYSELF...
JUST ENOUGH TIME TO--
BLACKED OUT... CAN'T AFFORD THAT...
GOOD... DIDN'T GET THE GUN WET...
I'LL NEED IT... PROVIDED I CAN FIT MY FINGER IN THE TRIGGER GUARD...
SOMETHING ...TO KEEP AN OLD MAN AWAKE...
...AND SOMETHING ELSE...
...TO BRING THE HOUSE DOWN...

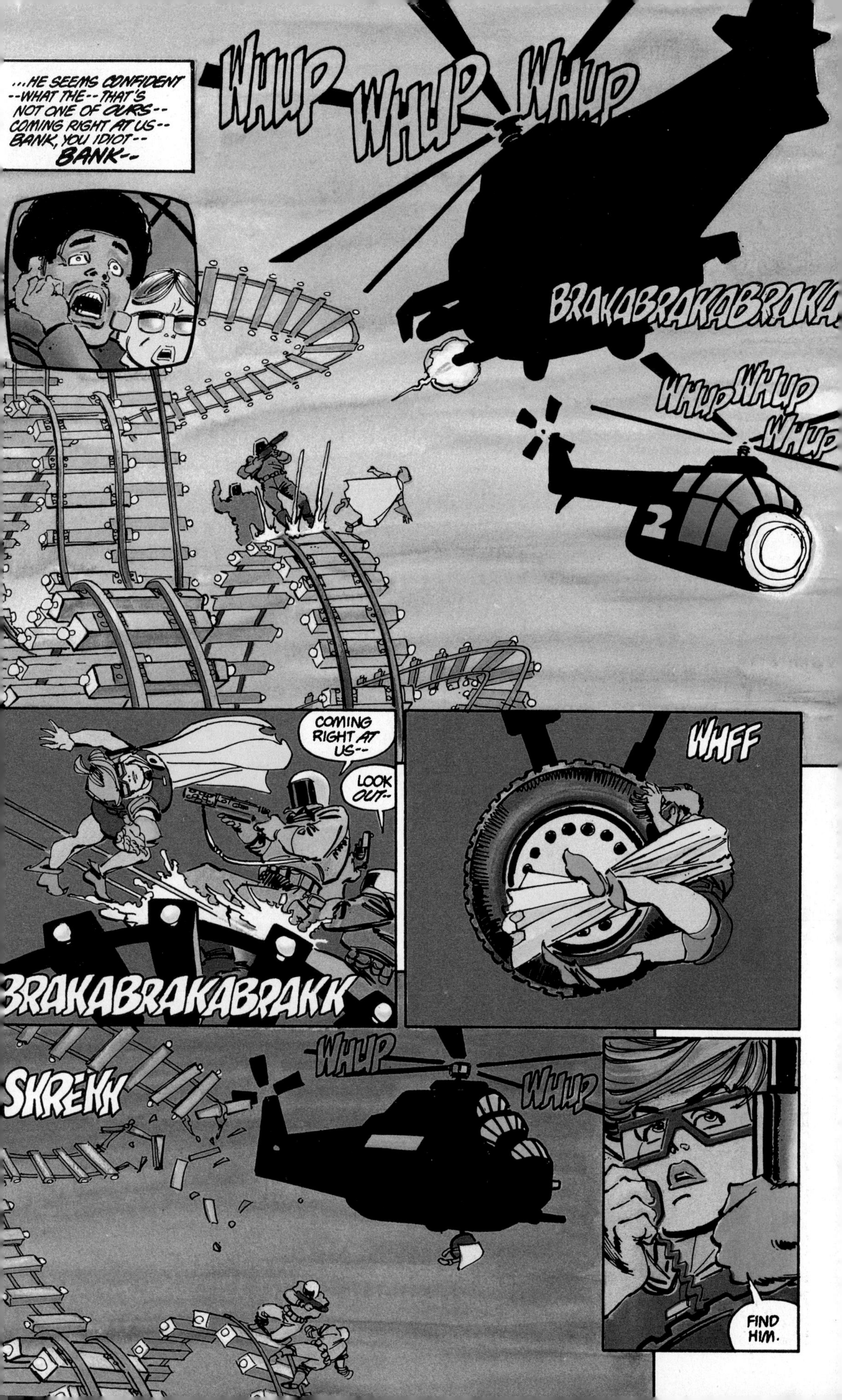
...HE SEEMS CONFIDENT --WHAT THE--THAT'S NOT ONE OF OURS-- COMING RIGHT AT US-- BANK, YOU IDIOT-- BANK--
WHUP WHUP WHUP
BRAKABRAKABRAKA
WHUP WHUP WHUP
2
COMING RIGHT AT US--
LOOK OUT--
BRAKABRAKABRAKK
WHFF
SHREKK
WHUP
WHUP
FIND HIM.

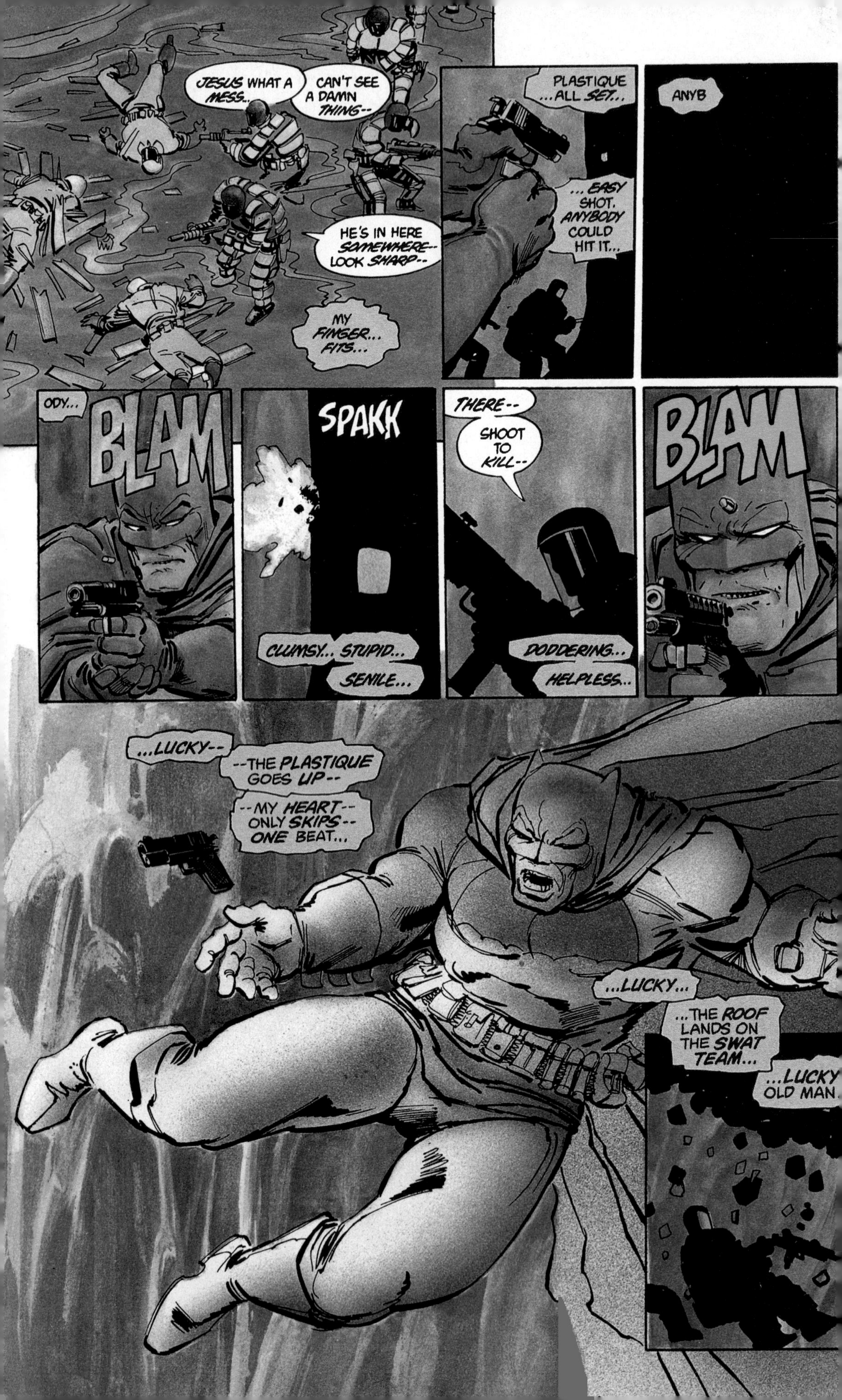
JESUS WHAT A MESS...
CAN'T SEE A DAMN THING--
HE'S IN HERE SOMEWHERE-- LOOK SHARP--
MY FINGER... FITS...
PLASTIQUE ...ALL SET...
...EASY SHOT. ANYBODY COULD HIT IT...
ANYB
ODY...
BLAM
SPAKK
CLUMSY... STUPID...
SENILE...
THERE--
SHOOT TO KILL--
DODDERING...
HELPLESS...
BLAM
...LUCKY--
--THE PLASTIQUE GOES UP--
--MY HEART-- ONLY SKIPS-- ONE BEAT...
...LUCKY...
...THE ROOF LANDS ON THE SWAT TEAM...
...LUCKY OLD MAN...

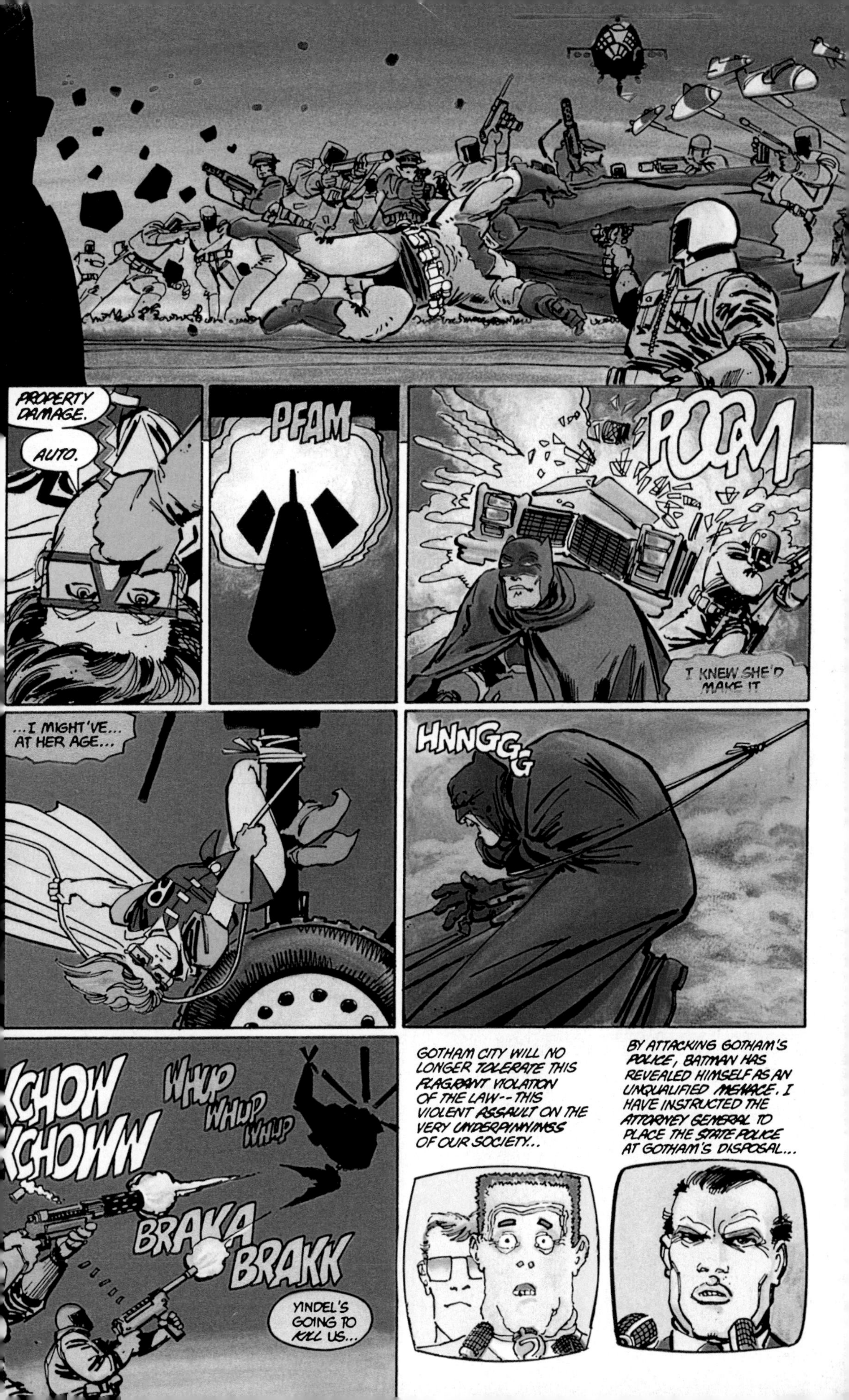
PROPERTY DAMAGE.
AUTO.
PFAM
POOM
I KNEW SHE'D MAKE IT
...I MIGHT'VE... AT HER AGE...
HNNGGG
KCHOW KCHOWN
WHUP WHUP WHUP
BRAKA BRAKK
YINDEL'S GOING TO KILL US...
GOTHAM CITY WILL NO LONGER TOLERATE THIS FLAGRANT VIOLATION OF THE LAW--THIS VIOLENT ASSAULT ON THE VERY UNDERPINNINGS OF OUR SOCIETY...
BY ATTACKING GOTHAM'S POLICE, BATMAN HAS REVEALED HIMSELF AS AN UNQUALIFIED MENACE. I HAVE INSTRUCTED THE ATTORNEY GENERAL TO PLACE THE STATE POLICE AT GOTHAM'S DISPOSAL...

...THE JOKER'S BODY FOUND MUTILATED AND BURNED... MURDER IS ADDED TO THE CHARGES AGAINST THE BATMAN...

BRUCE. IT'S OVER.

YOU LOOK TIRED, KENT.

WELL, YOU'VE EARNED A GOOD NIGHT'S SLEEP.

HECK OF A POLICE ACTION, IF YOU ASK ME...

I DIDN'T...

YOU CAN SAY WHAT YOU WANT. YOU CAN CALL HIM WHAT YOU WANT. YOU DON'T HAVE TO WALK DOWN AVENUE D AT NIGHT.

YOU DON'T HAVE TO HEAR THE SUCKING SOUNDS THEY MAKE EVERY TIME YOU WALK BY. THIS ONE. HE'D BEEN WORKING THE NERVE UP FOR WEEKS BEFORE HE WAS HORNY ENOUGH...

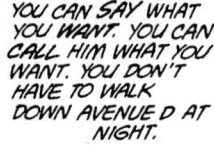

...NO, HORNY HE WASN'T. HE WAS JUST LOOKING TO HURT SOMEBODY AND HE'S THE KIND WHO HURTS WOMEN. I WISH THEY WERE RARE. HE GAVE HIMSELF AN EXCUSE...

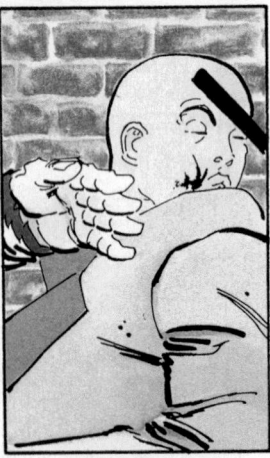

SO NOW HE'S GIGGLING LIKE HE'S TURNED ON! I FIGURE HE'S SERIOUS ENOUGH TO RUN AFTER ME. I GO FOR THE MACE.

THE CREEP'S PULLING OUT HIS WEAPON WHEN THERE'S THIS SHRIEK.

STRAIGHT OUT OF HELL THERE'S THIS SHRIEK...

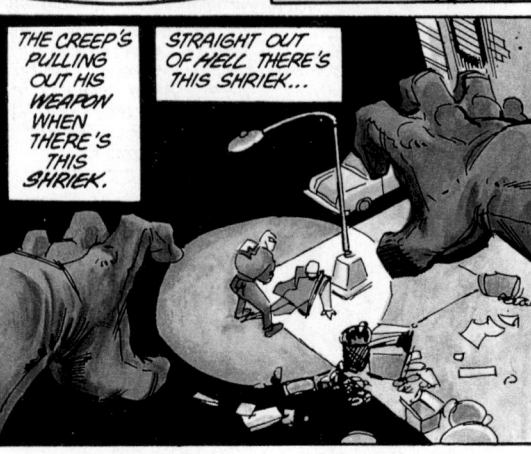

...IT TURNS INTO A GROWL-- FLAPPING OF WINGS--BIG WINGS--

-- SOMETHING WET HAPPENS TO THE CREEP--

--A SIDE OF *BEEF* SLAMS INTO THE *LAMPPOST*--

--A *SWITCHBLADE* SNAPS OPEN--

BONES START POPPING INSIDE THE *CREEP*-- HE'S *SCREAMING* AND *BEGGING*--

--WHAT *GRABBED* HIM IS *LAUGHING* AND SO AM *I*...

AND THE MAN WHO *ASSAULTED* YOU?

STILL IN THE *HOSPITAL*.

HE'S *OLD*, HE'S ALMOST *DEAD*...

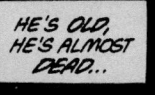

SUTURE.

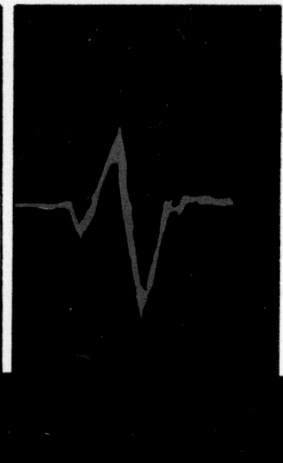

HE'S GOING TO BE *OKAY*, RIGHT?

HE'LL *LIVE*...

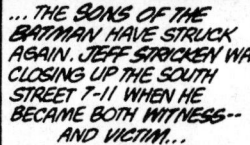

DO NOT EXPECT ANY FURTHER STATEMENTS. THE *SONS* OF THE *BATMAN* DO NOT *TALK*. WE *ACT*. LET *GOTHAM*'S CRIMINALS *BEWARE*. THEY ARE ABOUT TO ENTER *HELL*.

THE MUTANTS ARE *DEAD*. THE MUTANTS ARE *HISTORY*. THIS IS THE MARK OF THE *FUTURE*. *GOTHAM CITY* BELONGS TO THE *BATMAN*.

...THE *SONS* OF THE *BATMAN* HAVE STRUCK AGAIN. *JEFF STRICKEN* WAS CLOSING UP THE *SOUTH STREET 7-11* WHEN HE BECAME BOTH WITNESS-- AND VICTIM...

THEY'RE *YOUNGER* THAN YOU'D THINK--*THIS ONE* WAS, ANYWAY. COULDN'T HAVE BEEN OLDER THAN *SIXTEEN*...THAT'S RIGHT, THERE WAS JUST *ONE* OF THEM...

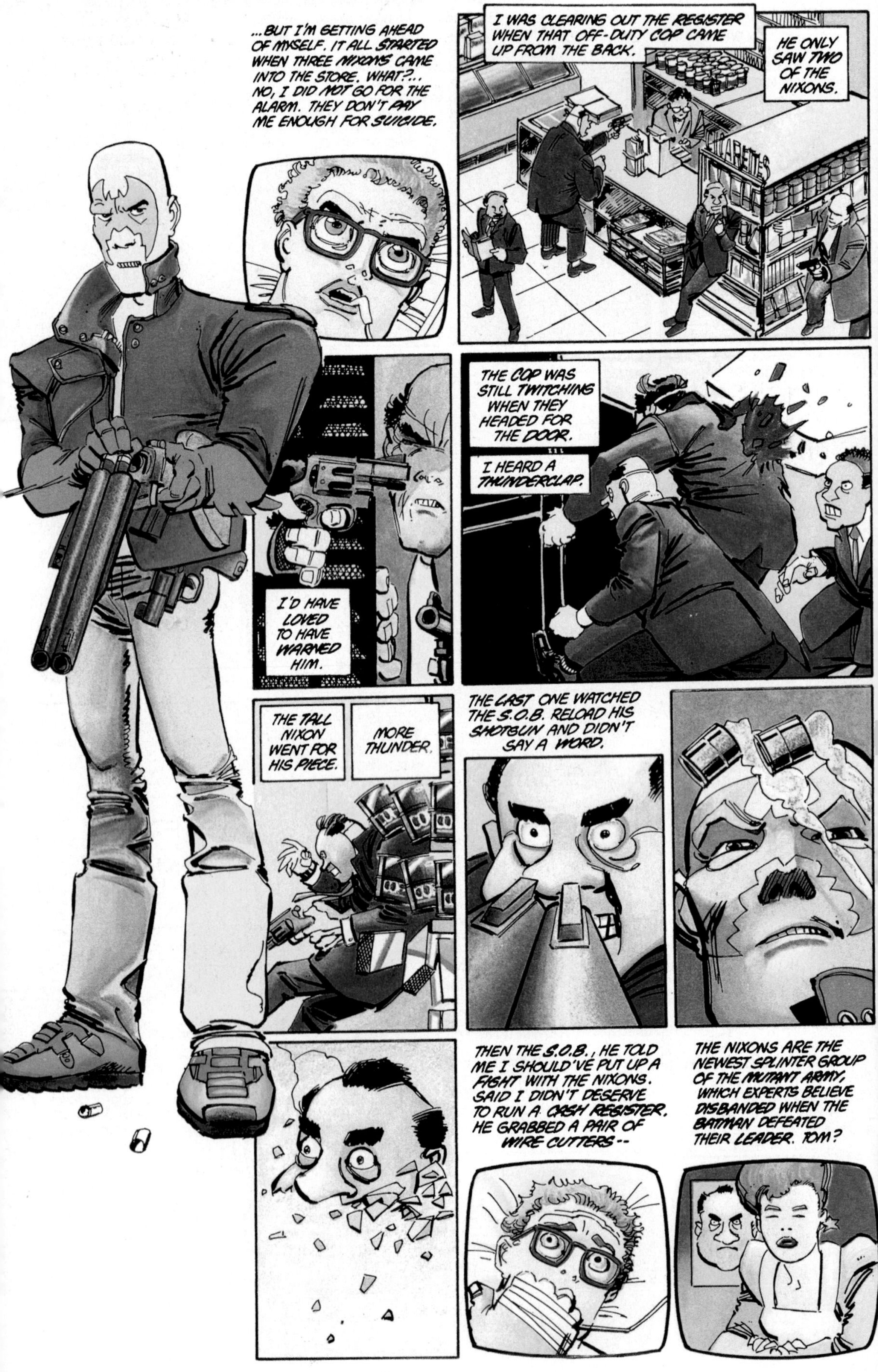
...BUT I'M GETTING AHEAD OF MYSELF. IT ALL STARTED WHEN THREE NIXONS CAME INTO THE STORE. WHAT?.. NO, I DID NOT GO FOR THE ALARM. THEY DON'T PAY ME ENOUGH FOR SUICIDE.
I WAS CLEARING OUT THE REGISTER WHEN THAT OFF-DUTY COP CAME UP FROM THE BACK.
HE ONLY SAW TWO OF THE NIXONS.
CIGARETTES
I'D HAVE LOVED TO HAVE WARNED HIM.
THE COP WAS STILL TWITCHING WHEN THEY HEADED FOR THE DOOR.
I HEARD A THUNDERCLAP.
THE TALL NIXON WENT FOR HIS PIECE.
MORE THUNDER.
THE LAST ONE WATCHED THE S.O.B. RELOAD HIS SHOTGUN AND DIDN'T SAY A WORD.
THEN THE S.O.B., HE TOLD ME I SHOULD'VE PUT UP A FIGHT WITH THE NIXONS. SAID I DIDN'T DESERVE TO RUN A CASH REGISTER. HE GRABBED A PAIR OF WIRE CUTTERS--
THE NIXONS ARE THE NEWEST SPLINTER GROUP OF THE MUTANT ARMY, WHICH EXPERTS BELIEVE DISBANDED WHEN THE BATMAN DEFEATED THEIR LEADER. TOM?

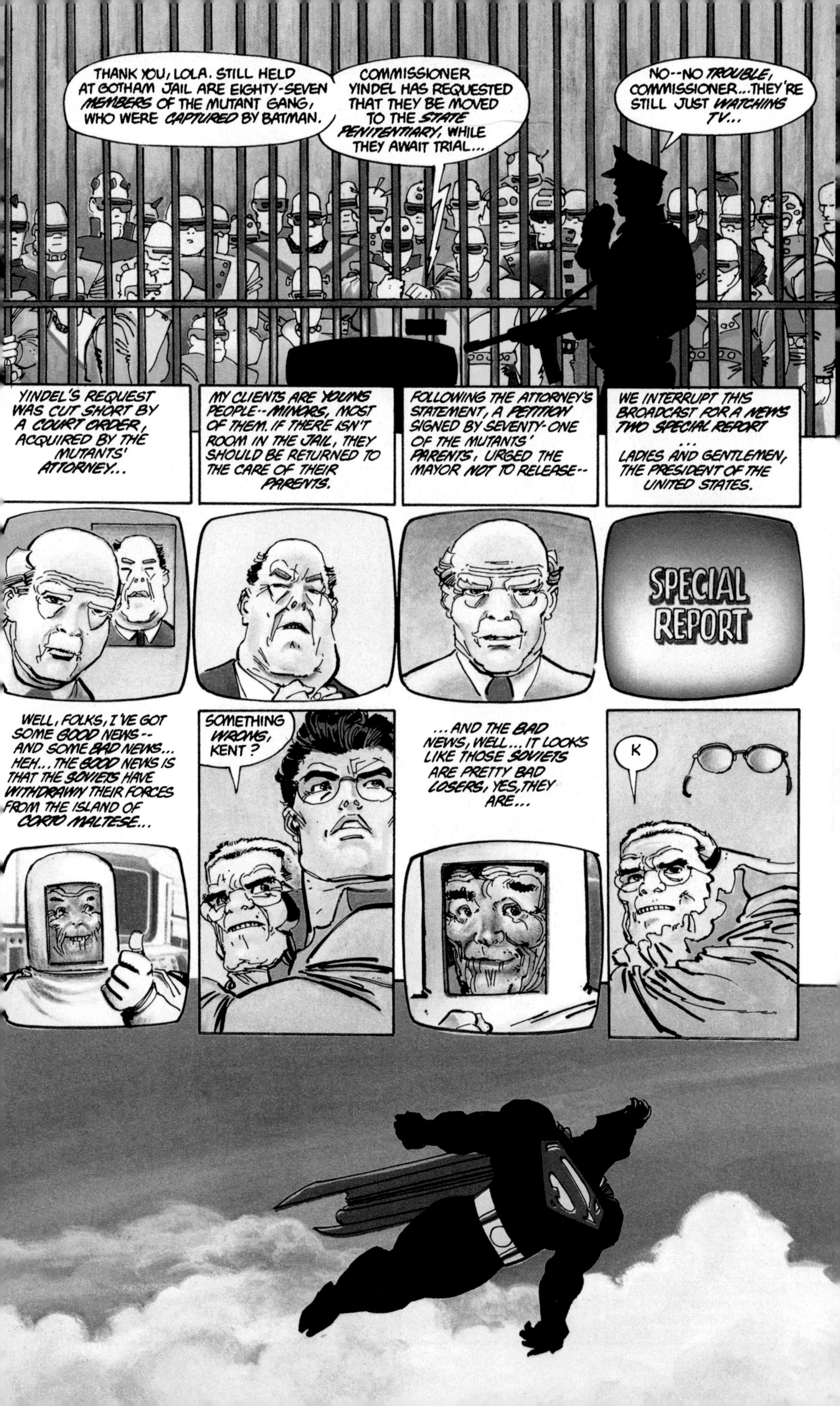

THANK YOU, LOLA. STILL HELD AT GOTHAM JAIL ARE EIGHTY-SEVEN MEMBERS OF THE MUTANT GANG, WHO WERE CAPTURED BY BATMAN.
COMMISSIONER YINDEL HAS REQUESTED THAT THEY BE MOVED TO THE STATE PENITENTIARY, WHILE THEY AWAIT TRIAL...
NO--NO TROUBLE, COMMISSIONER...THEY'RE STILL JUST WATCHING TV...
YINDEL'S REQUEST WAS CUT SHORT BY A COURT ORDER, ACQUIRED BY THE MUTANTS' ATTORNEY...
MY CLIENTS ARE YOUNG PEOPLE--MINORS, MOST OF THEM. IF THERE ISN'T ROOM IN THE JAIL, THEY SHOULD BE RETURNED TO THE CARE OF THEIR PARENTS.
FOLLOWING THE ATTORNEY'S STATEMENT, A PETITION SIGNED BY SEVENTY-ONE OF THE MUTANTS' PARENTS, URGED THE MAYOR NOT TO RELEASE--
WE INTERRUPT THIS BROADCAST FOR A NEWS TWO SPECIAL REPORT ... LADIES AND GENTLEMEN, THE PRESIDENT OF THE UNITED STATES.
SPECIAL REPORT
WELL, FOLKS, I'VE GOT SOME GOOD NEWS-- AND SOME BAD NEWS... HEH... THE GOOD NEWS IS THAT THE SOVIETS HAVE WITHDRAWN THEIR FORCES FROM THE ISLAND OF CORTO MALTESE...
SOMETHING WRONG, KENT?
...AND THE BAD NEWS, WELL... IT LOOKS LIKE THOSE SOVIETS ARE PRETTY BAD LOSERS, YES, THEY ARE...
K

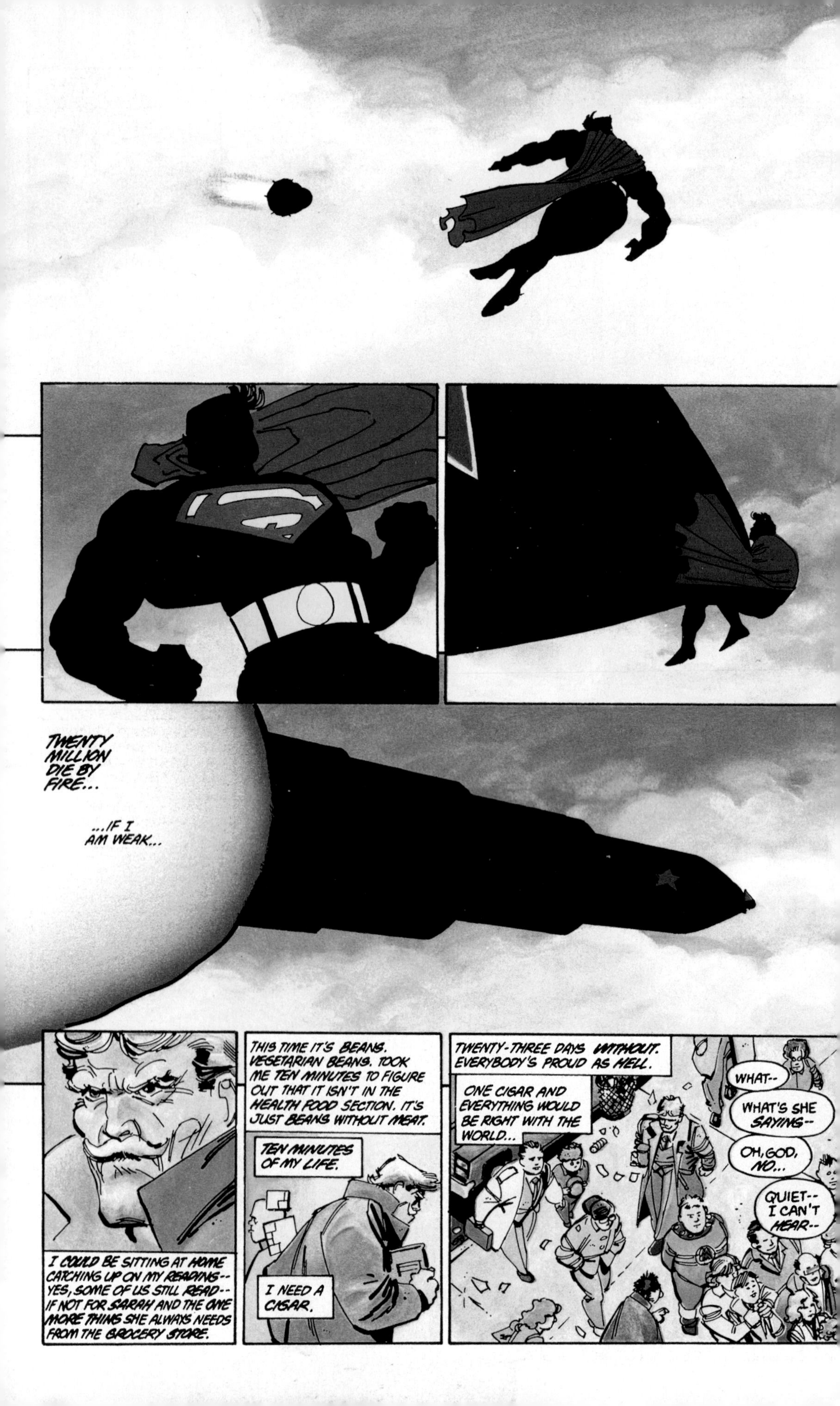
TWENTY MILLION DIE BY FIRE...
...IF I AM WEAK...
I COULD BE SITTING AT HOME CATCHING UP ON MY READING-- YES, SOME OF US STILL READ-- IF NOT FOR SARAH AND THE ONE MORE THING SHE ALWAYS NEEDS FROM THE GROCERY STORE.
THIS TIME IT'S BEANS. VEGETARIAN BEANS. TOOK ME TEN MINUTES TO FIGURE OUT THAT IT ISN'T IN THE HEALTH FOOD SECTION. IT'S JUST BEANS WITHOUT MEAT.
TEN MINUTES OF MY LIFE.
I NEED A CIGAR.
TWENTY-THREE DAYS WITHOUT. EVERYBODY'S PROUD AS HELL.
ONE CIGAR AND EVERYTHING WOULD BE RIGHT WITH THE WORLD...
WHAT--
WHAT'S SHE SAYING--
OH, GOD, NO...
QUIET-- I CAN'T HEAR--

A *SOVIET NUCLEAR WARHEAD*-- SECONDS FROM *DETONATION* OVER *CORTO MALTESE*-- THIS IS *IT,* FOLKS--*FIRST STRIKE!* TOM?

LOLA CHONG GIVES GOOD NEWS

NEWS 2 GOTHA

CAREFUL--BE *CAREFUL* HOW YOU *PUT* THINGS, LOLA. THIS IS *ONE MISSILE*-- THERE ARE NO INDICATIONS THAT THIS IS PART OF A *FULL-SCALE* ATTACK...

TELL THAT TO THE AMERICAN TROOPS *STATIONED* THERE, TOM.

HOLD IT... WE'VE JUST GOTTEN WORD THAT IT'S *NOT* A CONVENTIONAL NUCLEAR WARHEAD--WE *SWITCH* YOU NOW TO *DAN MUSK,* ABOARD THE *NEWS TWO SHUTTLE.* WHAT'S THE WORD, DAN?

STILL *COLLATING,* LOLA-- BUT IT'S A *BIG* ONE-- *HEAVY MEGATONNAGE*-- WITH *UNUSUAL COMPUTER* ACTIVITY-- WE CAN'T BE *CERTAIN* OF ITS CAPABIL-ITIES...

...AT THE VERY *LEAST, CORTO* WILL BE *LEVELED*-- THE FIRES MIGHT *SPREAD* TO MAINLAND *SOUTH AMERICA*-- SHOULD IT GENERATE A *SUFFICIENT MAGNETIC PULSE,* THERE MIGHT--

THANKS FOR THE *DATA,* DAN, BUT WE'LL ALL KNOW SOON *ENOUGH* WHAT IT CAN DO. RIGHT NOW, WE'VE GOT AUTHOR *HARLAN ELLISON* IN THE STUDIO...

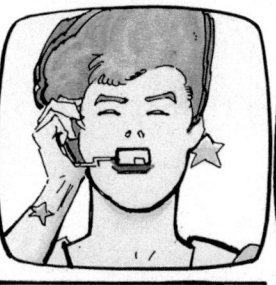

MR. *PRESIDENT* --GIVE THE *WORD*--

NOW YOU JUST KEEP YOUR SHIRT ON, LUCIUS...

MR. *PRESIDENT* --WE'LL LOOK LIKE *WIMPS* IF WE DON'T--

--LET'S SEE WHAT OUR OWN LITTLE DETERRENT CAN DO...

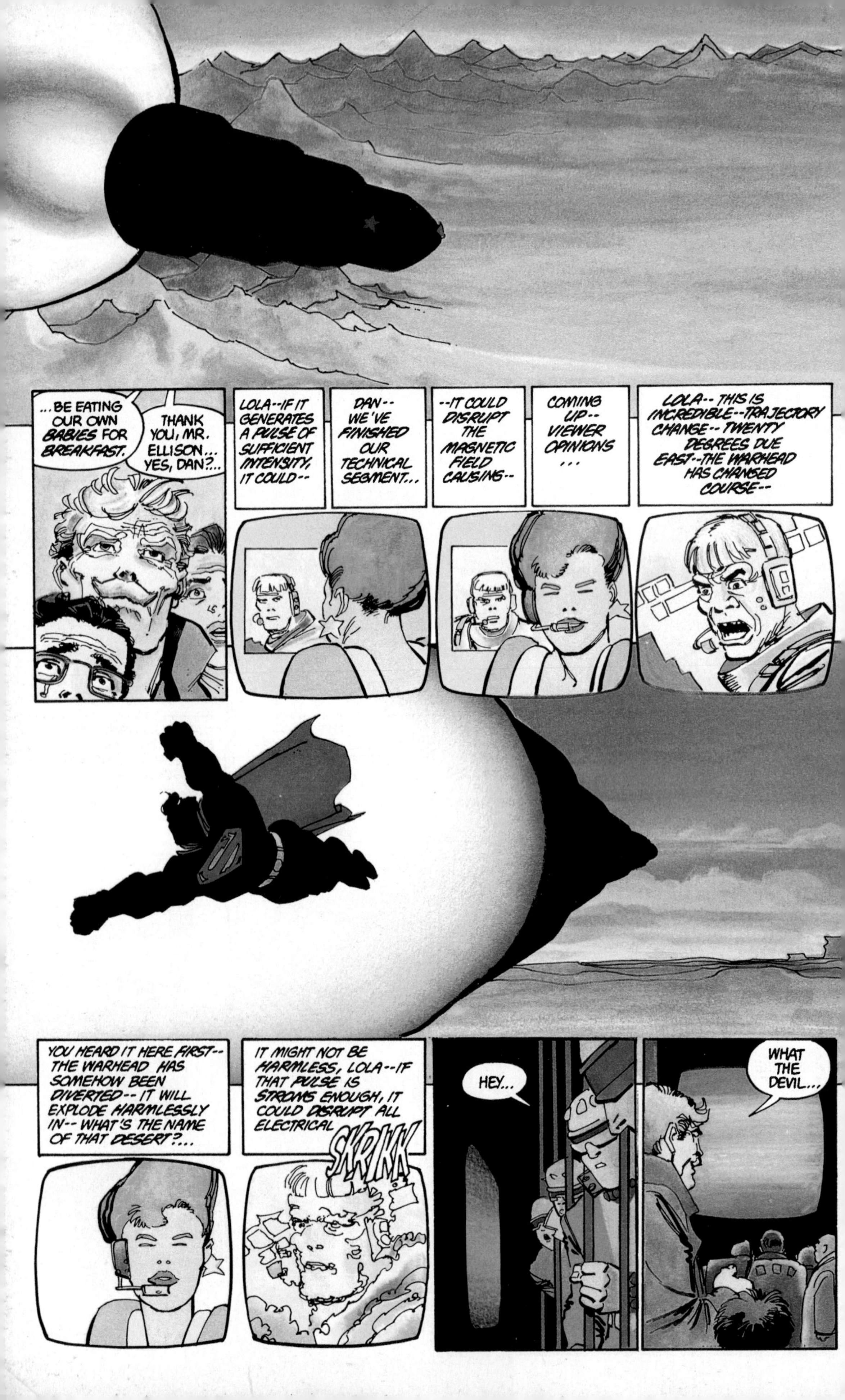
...BE EATING OUR OWN BABIES FOR BREAKFAST.
THANK YOU, MR. ELLISON... YES, DAN?...
LOLA--IF IT GENERATES A PULSE OF SUFFICIENT INTENSITY, IT COULD--
DAN-- WE'VE FINISHED OUR TECHNICAL SEGMENT...
--IT COULD DISRUPT THE MAGNETIC FIELD CAUSING--
COMING UP-- VIEWER OPINIONS ...
LOLA-- THIS IS INCREDIBLE--TRAJECTORY CHANGE-- TWENTY DEGREES DUE EAST--THE WARHEAD HAS CHANGED COURSE--
YOU HEARD IT HERE FIRST-- THE WARHEAD HAS SOMEHOW BEEN DIVERTED-- IT WILL EXPLODE HARMLESSLY IN-- WHAT'S THE NAME OF THAT DESERT?...
IT MIGHT NOT BE HARMLESS, LOLA--IF THAT PULSE IS STRONG ENOUGH, IT COULD DISRUPT ALL ELECTRICAL
SKRIKK
HEY...
WHAT THE DEVIL...

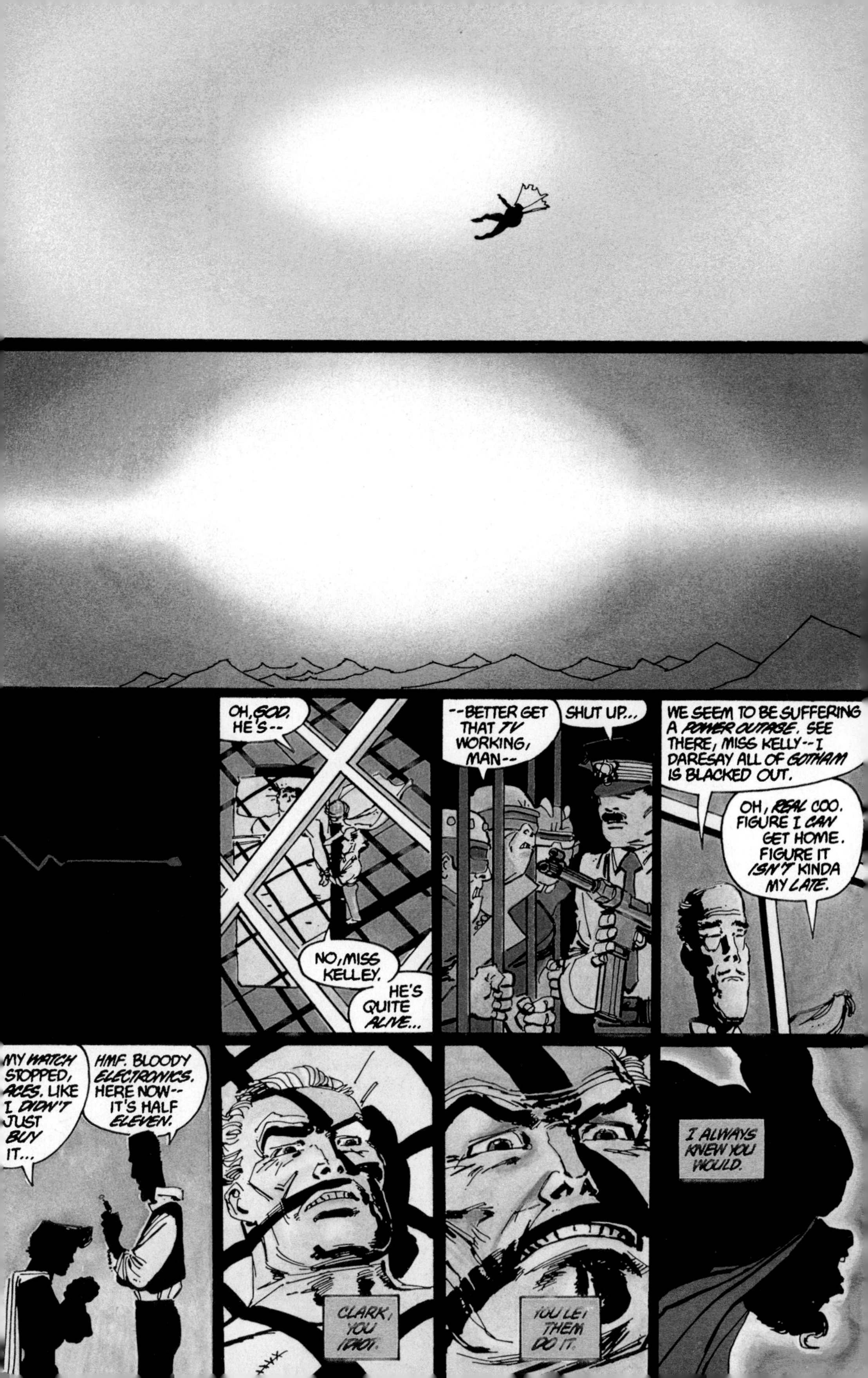
OH, GOD, HE'S--
NO, MISS KELLEY.
HE'S QUITE ALIVE...
--BETTER GET THAT TV WORKING, MAN--
SHUT UP...
WE SEEM TO BE SUFFERING A POWER OUTAGE. SEE THERE, MISS KELLY-- I DARESAY ALL OF GOTHAM IS BLACKED OUT.
OH, REAL COO. FIGURE I CAN GET HOME. FIGURE IT ISN'T KINDA MY LATE.
MY WATCH STOPPED, ACES. LIKE I DIDN'T JUST BUY IT...
HMF. BLOODY ELECTRONICS. HERE NOW-- IT'S HALF ELEVEN.
CLARK, YOU IDIOT.
YOU LET THEM DO IT.
I ALWAYS KNEW YOU WOULD.

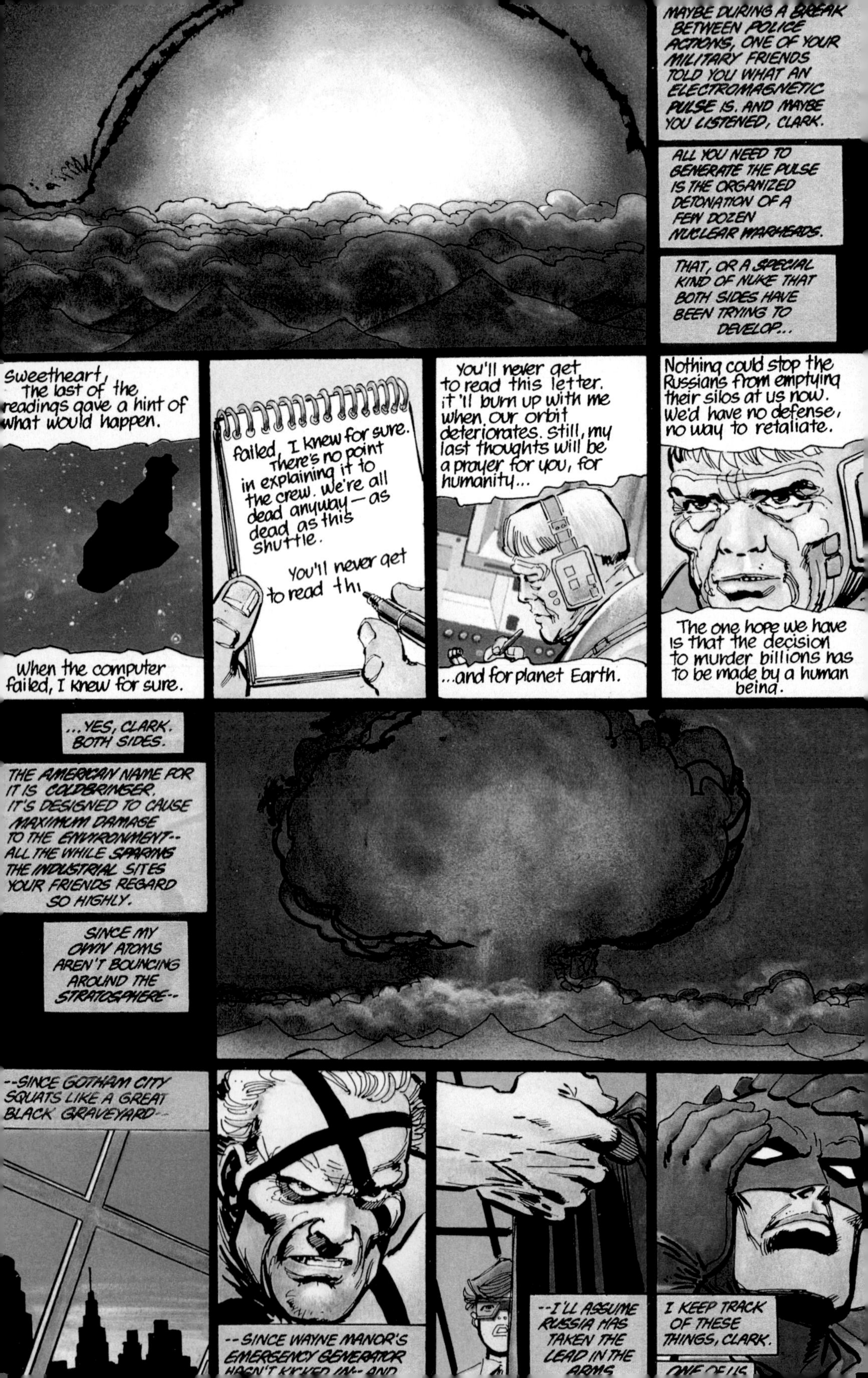
MAYBE DURING A BREAK BETWEEN POLICE ACTIONS, ONE OF YOUR MILITARY FRIENDS TOLD YOU WHAT AN ELECTROMAGNETIC PULSE IS. AND MAYBE YOU LISTENED, CLARK.
ALL YOU NEED TO GENERATE THE PULSE IS THE ORGANIZED DETONATION OF A FEW DOZEN NUCLEAR WARHEADS.
THAT, OR A SPECIAL KIND OF NUKE THAT BOTH SIDES HAVE BEEN TRYING TO DEVELOP...
Sweetheart, The last of the readings gave a hint of what would happen.
When the computer failed, I knew for sure.
failed, I knew for sure. There's no point in explaining it to the crew. We're all dead anyway—as dead as this shuttle.
You'll never get to read thi
You'll never get to read this letter. it'll burn up with me when our orbit deteriorates. Still, my last thoughts will be a prayer for you, for humanity...
...and for planet Earth.
Nothing could stop the Russians from emptying their silos at us now. We'd have no defense, no way to retaliate.
The one hope we have is that the decision to murder billions has to be made by a human being.
...YES, CLARK. BOTH SIDES.
THE AMERICAN NAME FOR IT IS COLDBRINGER. IT'S DESIGNED TO CAUSE MAXIMUM DAMAGE TO THE ENVIRONMENT-- ALL THE WHILE SPARING THE INDUSTRIAL SITES YOUR FRIENDS REGARD SO HIGHLY.
SINCE MY OWN ATOMS AREN'T BOUNCING AROUND THE STRATOSPHERE--
--SINCE GOTHAM CITY SQUATS LIKE A GREAT BLACK GRAVEYARD--
--SINCE WAYNE MANOR'S EMERGENCY GENERATOR
--I'LL ASSUME RUSSIA HAS TAKEN THE LEAD IN THE
I KEEP TRACK OF THESE THINGS, CLARK.

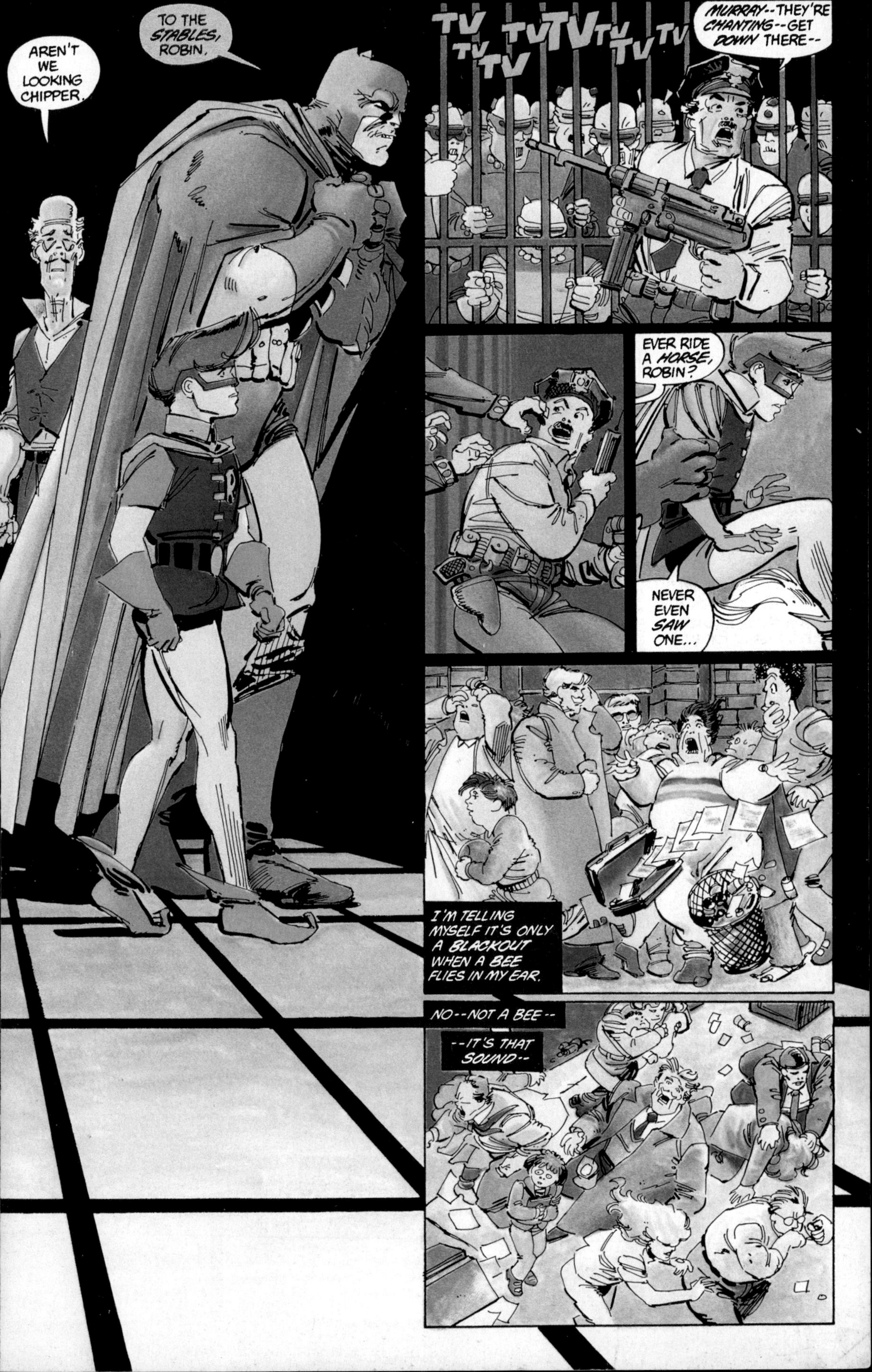
TO THE STABLES, ROBIN.
AREN'T WE LOOKING CHIPPER.
TV TV TV TV TV TV TV TV TV TV
MURRAY--THEY'RE CHANTING--GET DOWN THERE--
EVER RIDE A HORSE, ROBIN?
NEVER EVEN SAW ONE...
I'M TELLING MYSELF IT'S ONLY A BLACKOUT WHEN A BEE FLIES IN MY EAR.
NO--NOT A BEE--
--IT'S THAT SOUND--

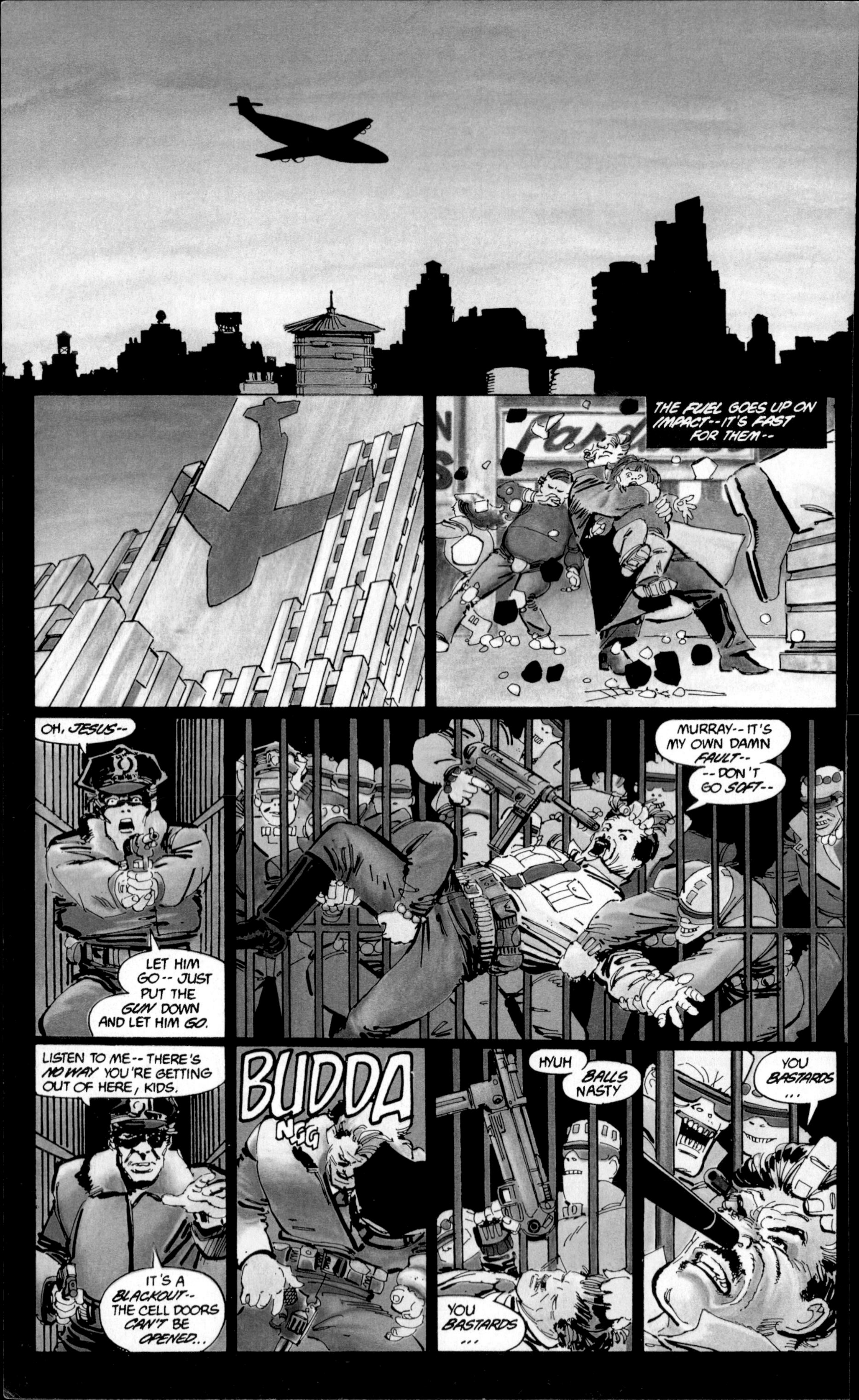
THE FUEL GOES UP ON IMPACT-- IT'S FAST FOR THEM--
OH, JESUS--
LET HIM GO-- JUST PUT THE GUN DOWN AND LET HIM GO.
MURRAY-- IT'S MY OWN DAMN FAULT--
--DON'T GO SOFT--
LISTEN TO ME-- THERE'S NO WAY YOU'RE GETTING OUT OF HERE, KIDS.
IT'S A BLACKOUT-- THE CELL DOORS CAN'T BE OPENED...
BUDDA
NGG
HYUH
BALLS NASTY
YOU BASTARDS ...
YOU BASTARDS ...

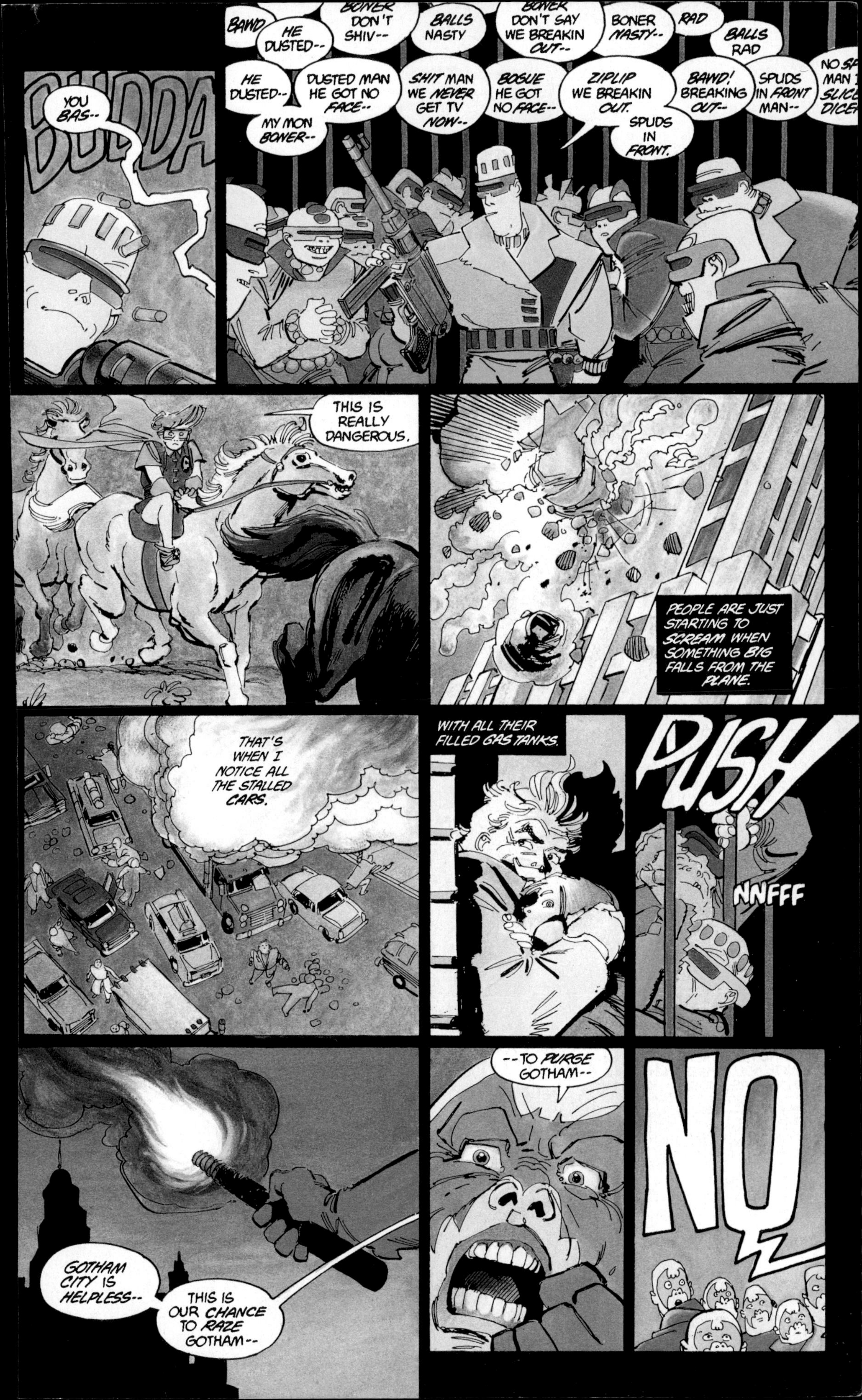
BUDDA
YOU BAS--
BAWD
HE DUSTED--
BONER DON'T SHIV--
BALLS NASTY
BONER DON'T SAY WE BREAKIN OUT--
BONER NASTY--
RAD
BALLS RAD
HE DUSTED--
DUSTED MAN HE GOT NO FACE--
MY MON BONER--
SHIT MAN WE NEVER GET TV NOW--
BOGUE HE GOT NO FACE--
ZIPLIP WE BREAKIN OUT.
SPUDS IN FRONT.
BAWD! BREAKING OUT--
SPUDS IN FRONT MAN--
THIS IS REALLY DANGEROUS.
PEOPLE ARE JUST STARTING TO SCREAM WHEN SOMETHING BIG FALLS FROM THE PLANE.
THAT'S WHEN I NOTICE ALL THE STALLED CARS.
WITH ALL THEIR FILLED GAS TANKS.
PUSH
NNFFF
GOTHAM CITY IS HELPLESS--
THIS IS OUR CHANCE TO RAZE GOTHAM--
--TO PURGE GOTHAM--
NO

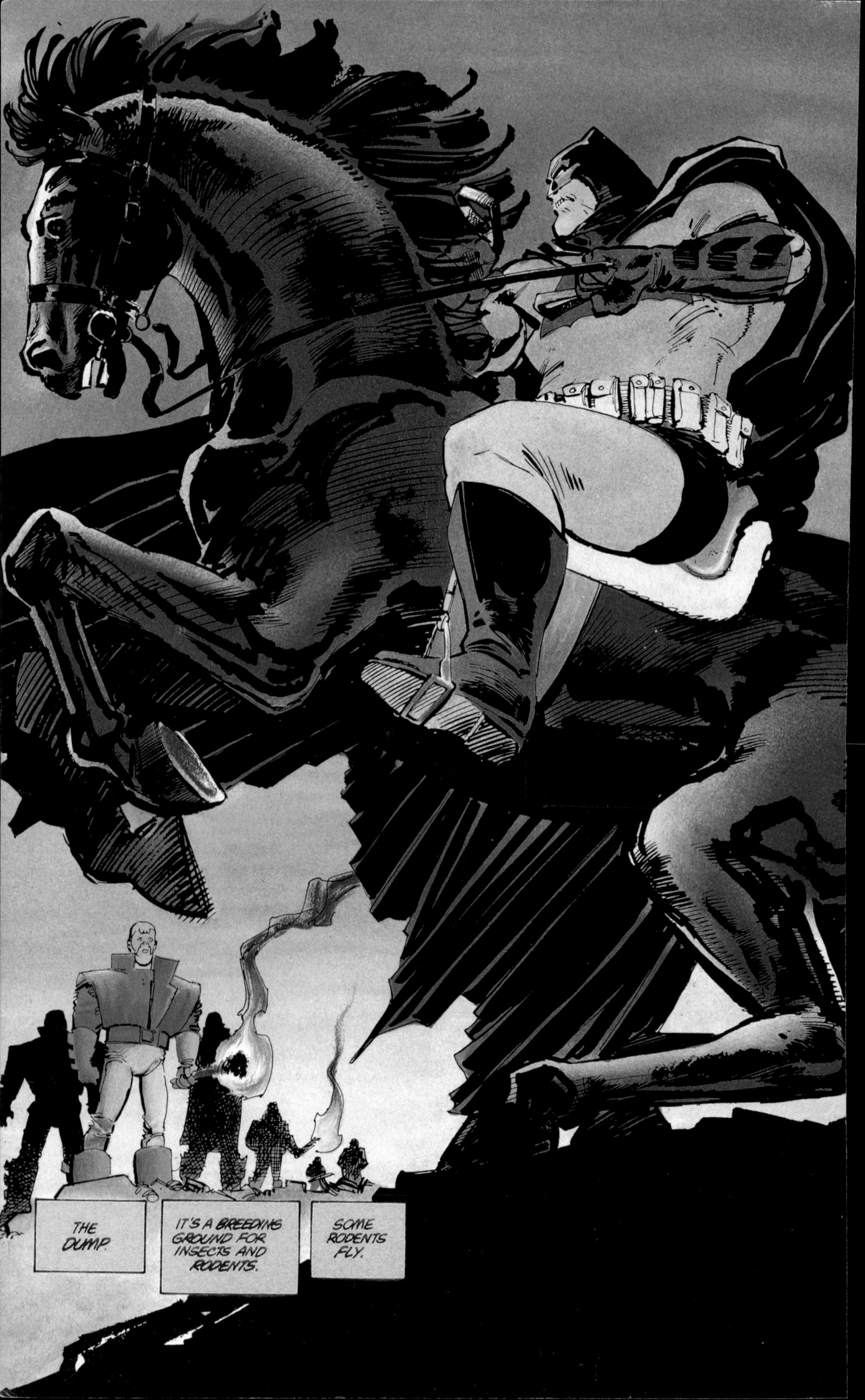
THE DUMP.
IT'S A BREEDING GROUND FOR INSECTS AND RODENTS.
SOME RODENTS FLY.

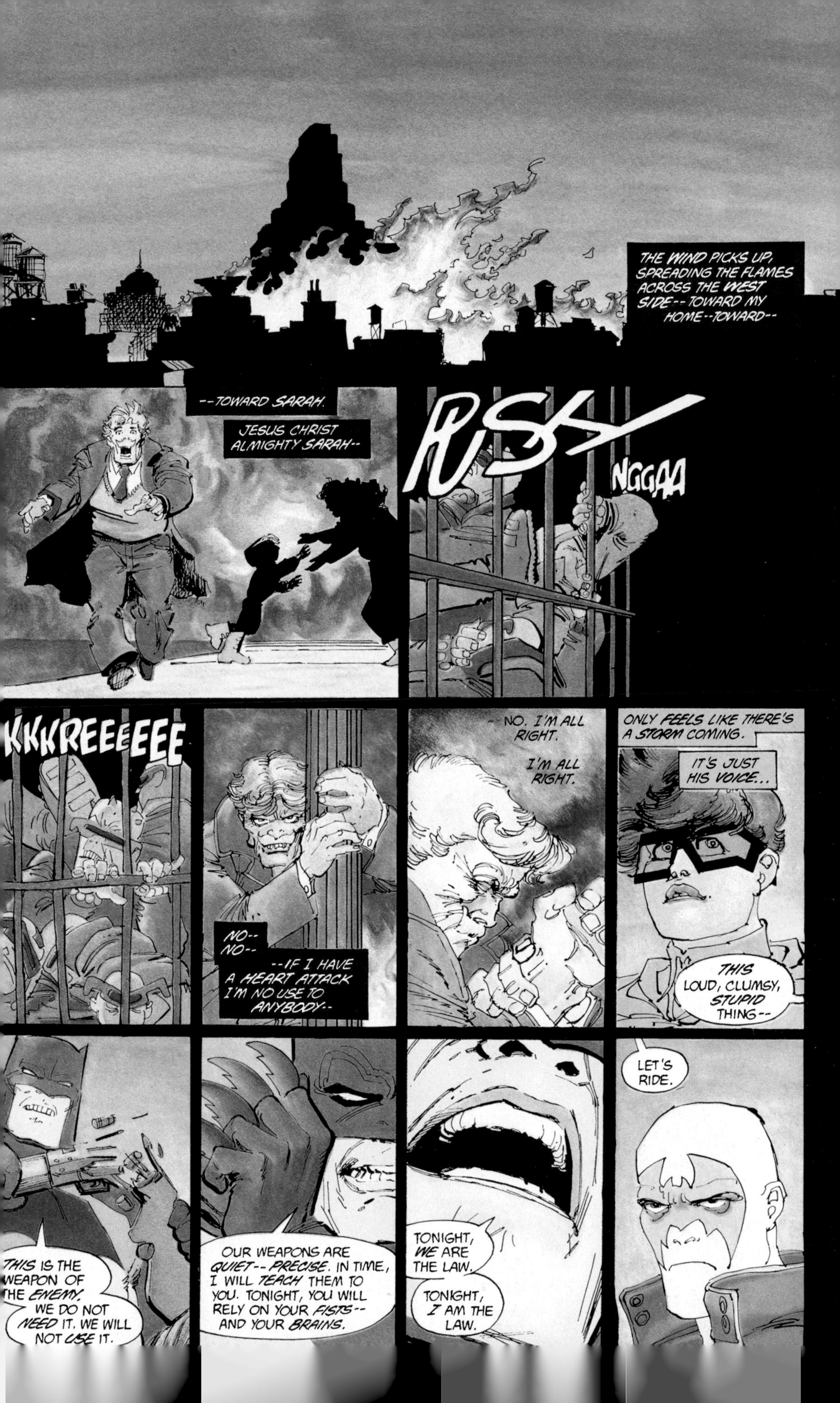

THE WIND PICKS UP, SPREADING THE FLAMES ACROSS THE WEST SIDE--TOWARD MY HOME--TOWARD--
--TOWARD SARAH.
JESUS CHRIST ALMIGHTY SARAH--
RUSKY
NGGAA
KKKREEEEEEE
NO--
NO--
--IF I HAVE A HEART ATTACK I'M NO USE TO ANYBODY--
NO. I'M ALL RIGHT.
I'M ALL RIGHT.
ONLY FEELS LIKE THERE'S A STORM COMING.
IT'S JUST HIS VOICE...
THIS LOUD, CLUMSY, STUPID THING--
THIS IS THE WEAPON OF THE ENEMY. WE DO NOT NEED IT. WE WILL NOT USE IT.
OUR WEAPONS ARE QUIET--PRECISE. IN TIME, I WILL TEACH THEM TO YOU. TONIGHT, YOU WILL RELY ON YOUR FISTS--AND YOUR BRAINS.
TONIGHT, WE ARE THE LAW.
TONIGHT, I AM THE LAW.
LET'S RIDE.

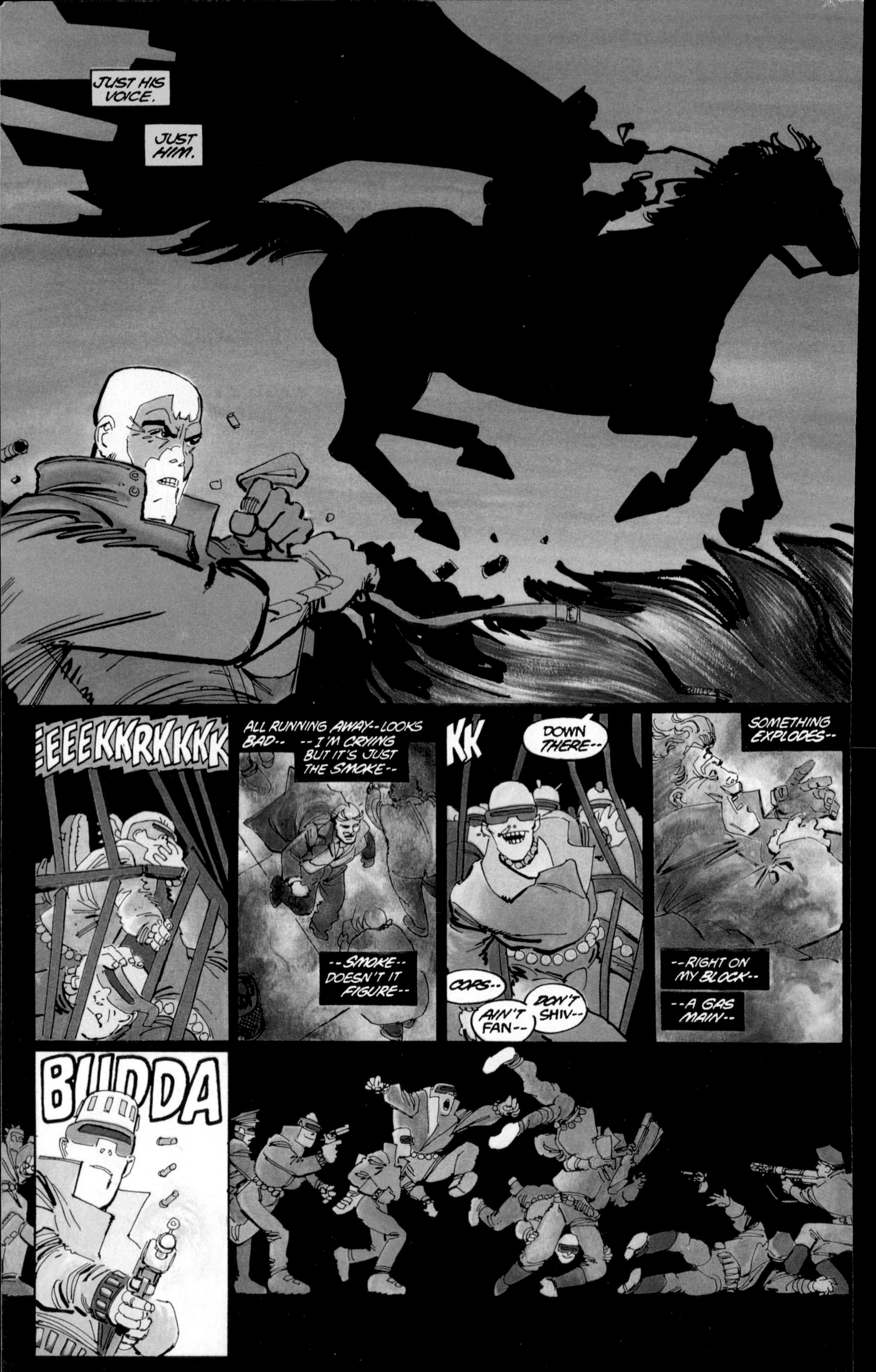
JUST HIS VOICE.
JUST HIM.
EEEEKKRKKKK
ALL RUNNING AWAY--LOOKS BAD-- --I'M CRYING BUT IT'S JUST THE SMOKE--
--SMOKE-- DOESN'T IT FIGURE--
KK
DOWN THERE--
COPS--
AIN'T FAN--
DON'T SHIV--
SOMETHING EXPLODES--
--RIGHT ON MY BLOCK--
--A GAS MAIN--
BUDDA

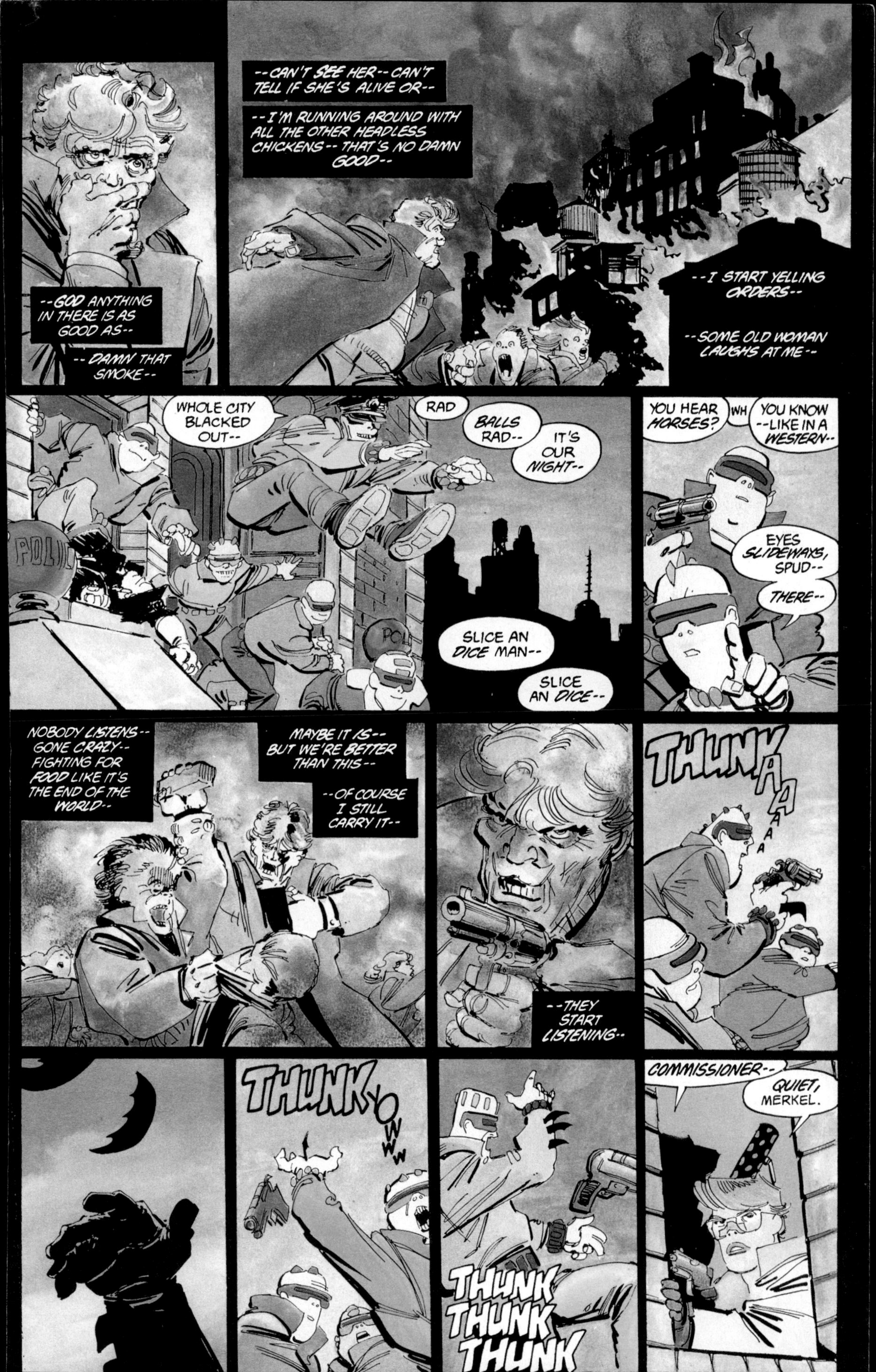
--GOD ANYTHING IN THERE IS AS GOOD AS--
--DAMN THAT SMOKE--
--CAN'T SEE HER--CAN'T TELL IF SHE'S ALIVE OR--
--I'M RUNNING AROUND WITH ALL THE OTHER HEADLESS CHICKENS--THAT'S NO DAMN GOOD--
--I START YELLING ORDERS--
--SOME OLD WOMAN LAUGHS AT ME--
WHOLE CITY BLACKED OUT--
RAD
BALLS RAD--
IT'S OUR NIGHT--
SLICE AN DICE MAN--
SLICE AN DICE--
YOU HEAR HORSES?
WH
YOU KNOW --LIKE IN A WESTERN--
EYES SLIDEWAYS, SPUD--
THERE--
NOBODY LISTENS--GONE CRAZY--FIGHTING FOR FOOD LIKE IT'S THE END OF THE WORLD--
MAYBE IT IS--BUT WE'RE BETTER THAN THIS--
--OF COURSE I STILL CARRY IT--
--THEY START LISTENING--
THUNK
AAAAA
THUNK
OWWW
THUNK THUNK THUNK
COMMISSIONER--
QUIET, MERKEL.

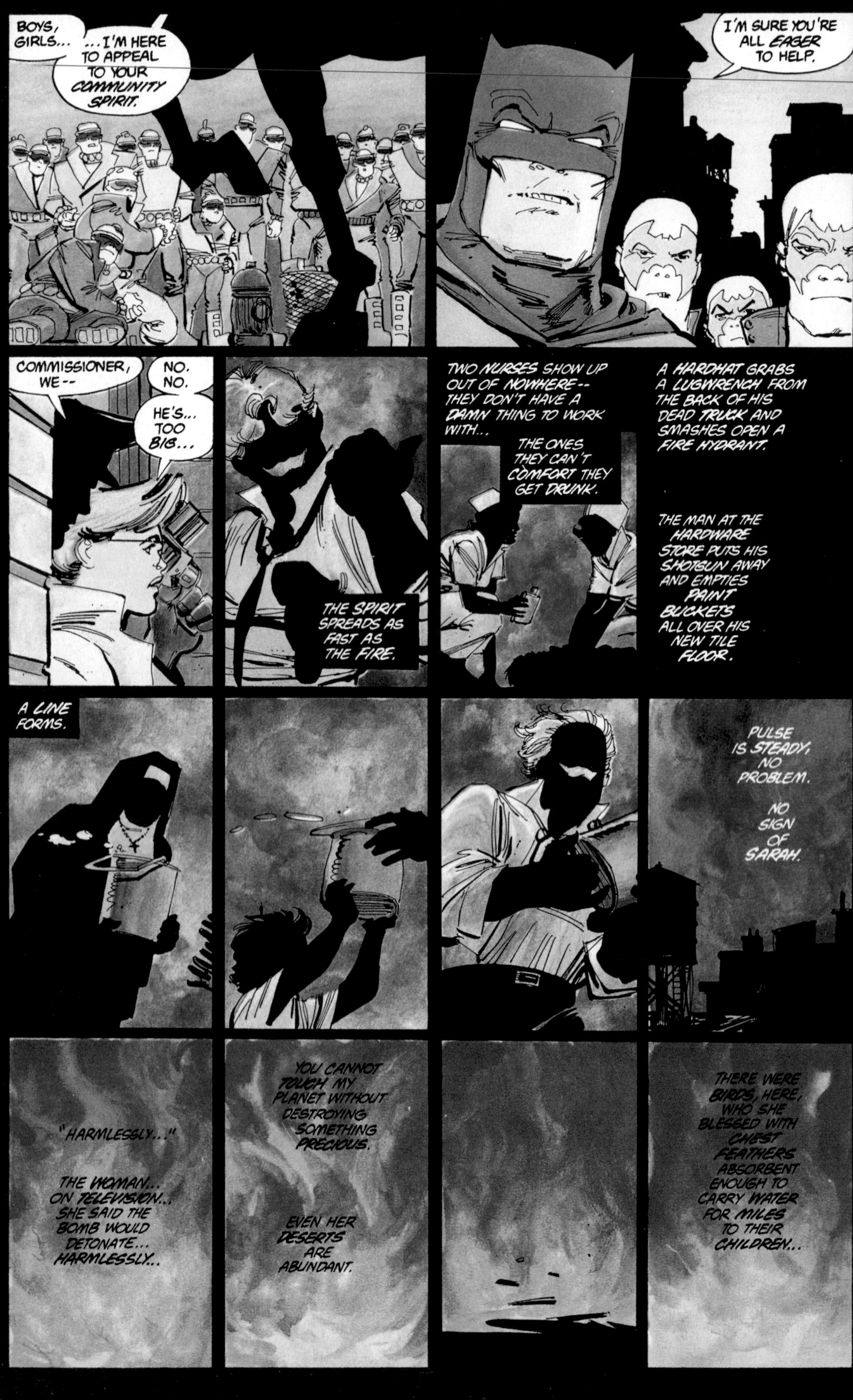
BOYS, GIRLS...
...I'M HERE TO APPEAL TO YOUR COMMUNITY SPIRIT.
I'M SURE YOU'RE ALL EAGER TO HELP.
COMMISSIONER, WE--
NO. NO.
HE'S... TOO BIG...
THE SPIRIT SPREADS AS FAST AS THE FIRE.
TWO NURSES SHOW UP OUT OF NOWHERE-- THEY DON'T HAVE A DAMN THING TO WORK WITH...
THE ONES THEY CAN'T COMFORT THEY GET DRUNK.
A HARDHAT GRABS A LUGWRENCH FROM THE BACK OF HIS DEAD TRUCK AND SMASHES OPEN A FIRE HYDRANT.
THE MAN AT THE HARDWARE STORE PUTS HIS SHOTGUN AWAY AND EMPTIES PAINT BUCKETS ALL OVER HIS NEW TILE FLOOR.
A LINE FORMS.
PULSE IS STEADY, NO PROBLEM.
NO SIGN OF SARAH.
"HARMLESSLY..."
THE WOMAN... ON TELEVISION... SHE SAID THE BOMB WOULD DETONATE... HARMLESSLY...
YOU CANNOT TOUCH MY PLANET WITHOUT DESTROYING SOMETHING PRECIOUS.
EVEN HER DESERTS ARE ABUNDANT.
THERE WERE BIRDS, HERE, WHO SHE BLESSED WITH CHEST FEATHERS ABSORBENT ENOUGH TO CARRY WATER FOR MILES TO THEIR CHILDREN...

...BULLFROGS, WHO SLEPT FOR YEARS IN DRIED-OUT RIVERBEDS... THEN DUG THEIR WAY TO THE SURFACE WHEN THE RAINS CAME...

NOW... THERE IS ONLY BLACKENED GLASS...

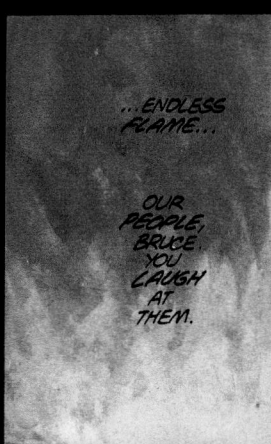

...ENDLESS FLAME...

OUR PEOPLE, BRUCE, YOU LAUGH AT THEM.

THEY CAN DO THIS... AND YOU LAUGH...

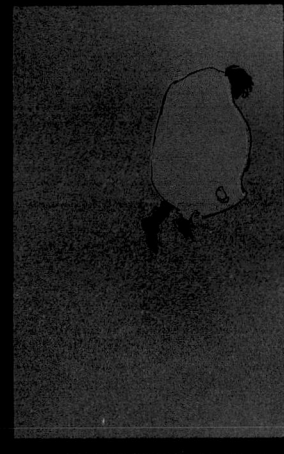

...THEY CAN SPLIT THE VERY FABRIC OF REALITY... BLAST A HUNDRED THOUSAND TONS OF SAND INTO THE SKY...

...BLOTTING OUT THE SOURCE OF ALL MY POWER... THE HOPE FOR SCREAMING MILLIONS...

MAGNETIC STORM ...YOU HAVE EVERY REASON TO BE OUTRAGED, MOTHER EARTH... YOU HAVE GIVEN THEM... EVERYTHING...

THEY ARE TINY AND STUPID AND VICIOUS ...BUT PLEASE... LISTEN TO THEM...

PLEASE...I AM SLOW AND DYING...

I NEED ONLY... REACH THE SUN...

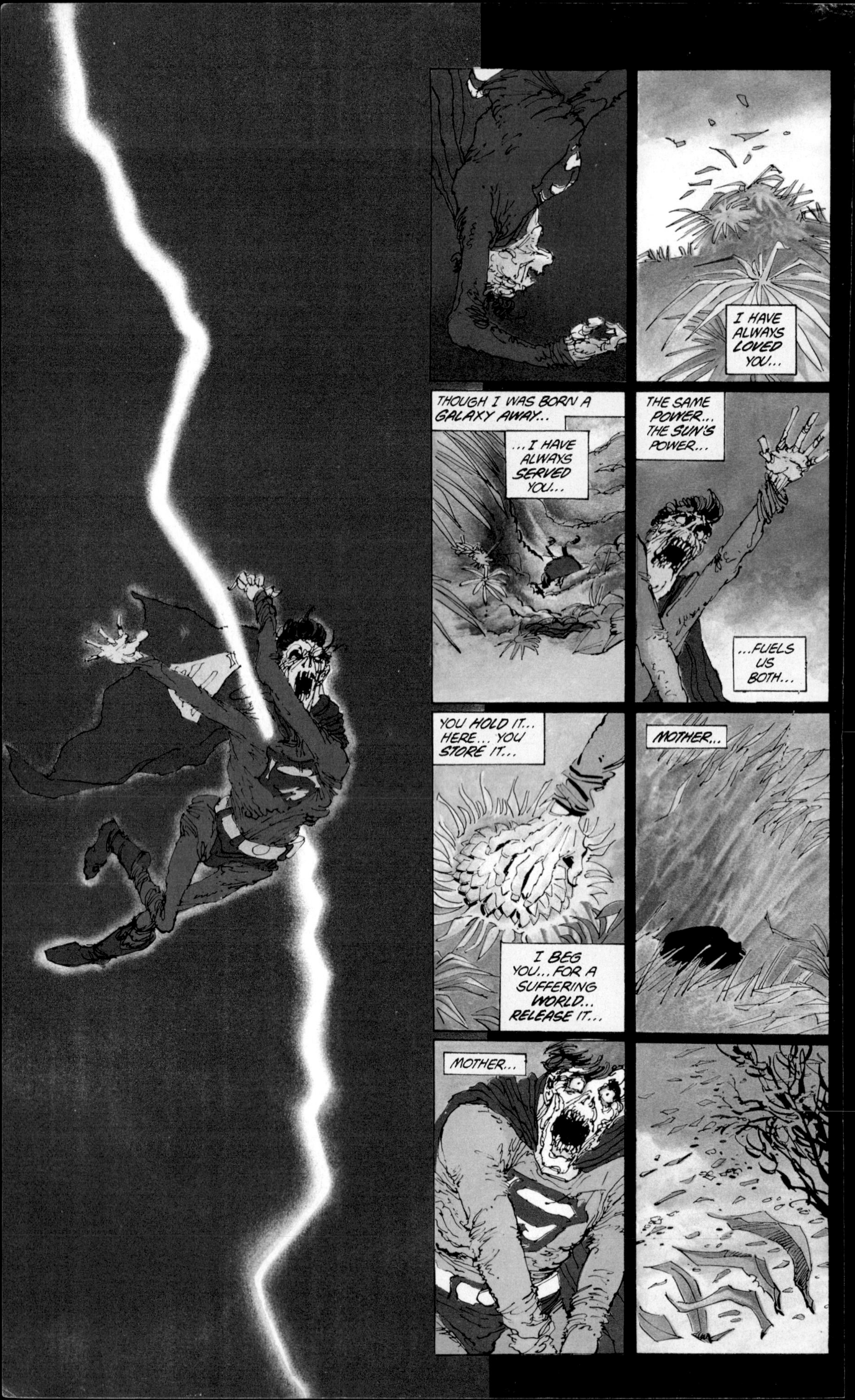
I HAVE ALWAYS LOVED YOU...
THOUGH I WAS BORN A GALAXY AWAY...
...I HAVE ALWAYS SERVED YOU...
THE SAME POWER... THE SUN'S POWER...
...FUELS US BOTH...
YOU HOLD IT... HERE... YOU STORE IT...
I BEG YOU... FOR A SUFFERING WORLD... RELEASE IT...
MOTHER...
MOTHER...

YOU ARE...SO GENEROUS...

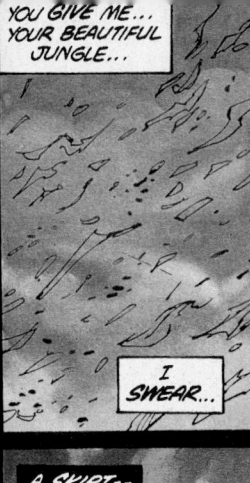

YOU GIVE ME... YOUR BEAUTIFUL JUNGLE...

I SWEAR...

...YOUR ADOPTED SON WILL HONOR YOU.

FROM MY BUILDING--

--SHE SCREAMS--

SARAH'S HEIGHT--

--SARAH'S HAIR--

A SKIRT--

--THAT COULD BE SARAH'S--

TRY NOT TO JUDGE THEM TOO HARSHLY. IT WAS A CRUEL TEST, FOR ALL OF US...

...AND, WE CAN HOPE, A LESSON...

NONE OF US CAN LOOK BACK ON THAT NIGHT WITHOUT SHAME. EVEN BEFORE IT ALL....I WAS WRAPPED IN MYSELF. YOU SEE, I HAVE ALWAYS BEEN RATHER SENSITIVE TO NOISE...

...AND THAT BOY-- HE SEEMED TO KEEP PACE WITH ME DELIBERATELY, TAKING THE JOY FROM MY EVENING WALK...

...WITH HIS HORRIBLY LOUD RADIO...

WHEN IT SHRIEKED, I BLAMED THE BOY. TRUTH TO TELL, I TURNED TO CONFRONT HIM...

...THEN I NOTICED HIS OWN CONFUSION -- AND THE DARKNESS THAT SEEMED TO FALL ACROSS THE ENTIRE CITY. I HEARD SHOUTS...

YES, I WAS SHOUTING. WHAT DO YOU EXPECT? I HAPPENED TO BE UP AGAINST A BITCH OF A DEADLINE. WHAT?... ...YES, OF COURSE I'D HEARD ABOUT THE BOMB. BUT I'VE GOT PROBLEMS OF MY OWN.

I'M NOT CRAZY ABOUT GETTING OUT OF MY CAR-- NOT IN THAT NEIGHBORHOOD--

--BUT I KNOW I BETTER CALL THE AGENCY AND MAKE SURE MY ASS IS COVERED.

SO I'M BARELY STANDING UP WHEN THERE'S THIS EXPLOSION KNOCKS ME FLAT--

MY ANKLE FEELS LIKE IT'S BROKEN-- SOMEBODY IS GOING TO GET SUED--

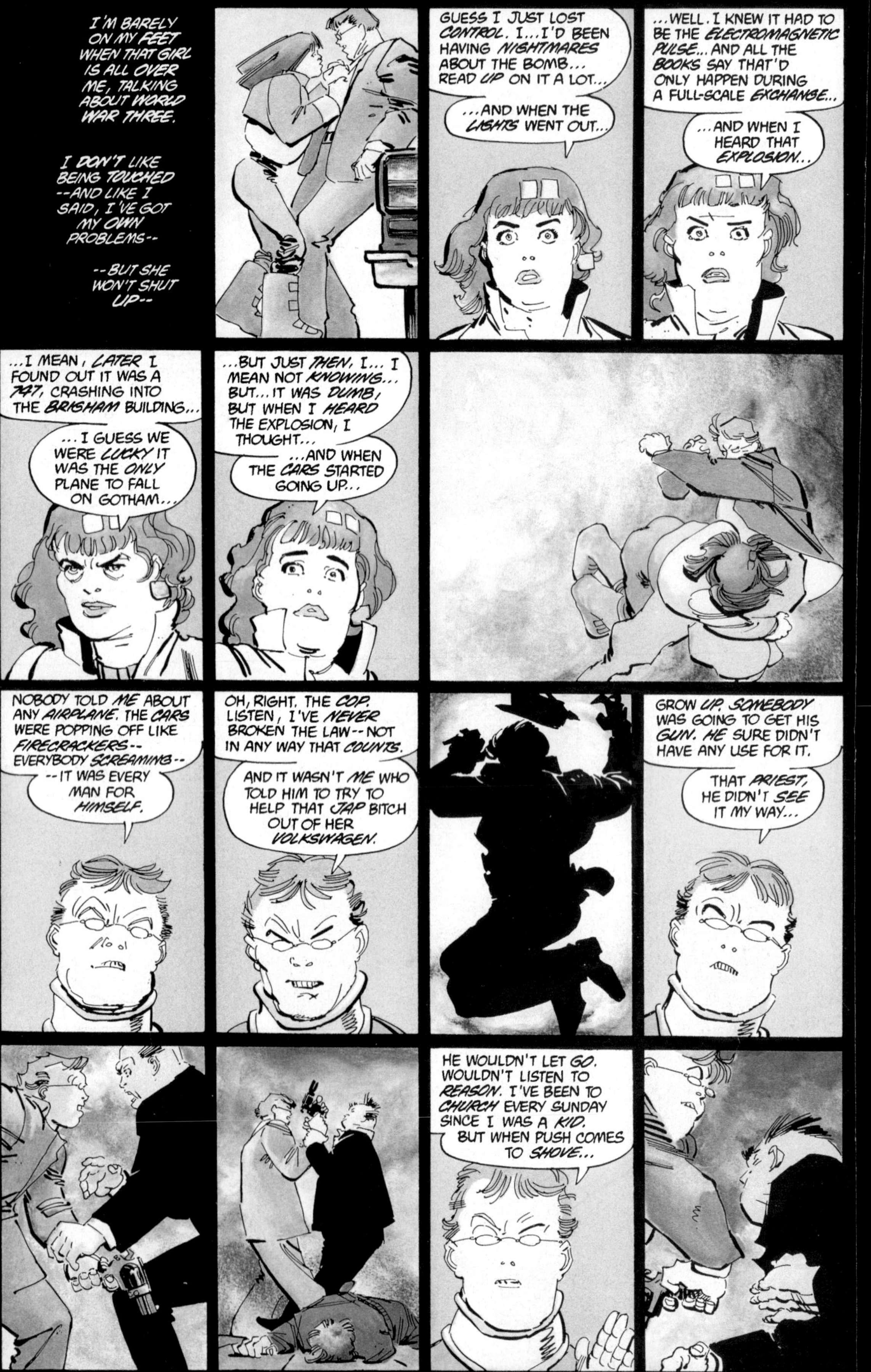
I'M BARELY ON MY FEET WHEN THAT GIRL IS ALL OVER ME, TALKING ABOUT WORLD WAR THREE.
I DON'T LIKE BEING TOUCHED --AND LIKE I SAID, I'VE GOT MY OWN PROBLEMS--
--BUT SHE WON'T SHUT UP--
GUESS I JUST LOST CONTROL. I...I'D BEEN HAVING NIGHTMARES ABOUT THE BOMB... READ UP ON IT A LOT...
...AND WHEN THE LIGHTS WENT OUT...
...WELL. I KNEW IT HAD TO BE THE ELECTROMAGNETIC PULSE... AND ALL THE BOOKS SAY THAT'D ONLY HAPPEN DURING A FULL-SCALE EXCHANGE...
...AND WHEN I HEARD THAT EXPLOSION...
...I MEAN, LATER I FOUND OUT IT WAS A 747, CRASHING INTO THE BRIGHAM BUILDING...
...I GUESS WE WERE LUCKY IT WAS THE ONLY PLANE TO FALL ON GOTHAM...
...BUT JUST THEN, I... I MEAN NOT KNOWING... BUT... IT WAS DUMB, BUT WHEN I HEARD THE EXPLOSION, I THOUGHT...
...AND WHEN THE CARS STARTED GOING UP...
NOBODY TOLD ME ABOUT ANY AIRPLANE. THE CARS WERE POPPING OFF LIKE FIRECRACKERS-- EVERYBODY SCREAMING--
--IT WAS EVERY MAN FOR HIMSELF.
OH, RIGHT. THE COP. LISTEN, I'VE NEVER BROKEN THE LAW--NOT IN ANY WAY THAT COUNTS.
AND IT WASN'T ME WHO TOLD HIM TO TRY TO HELP THAT JAP BITCH OUT OF HER VOLKSWAGEN.
GROW UP. SOMEBODY WAS GOING TO GET HIS GUN. HE SURE DIDN'T HAVE ANY USE FOR IT.
THAT PRIEST, HE DIDN'T SEE IT MY WAY...
HE WOULDN'T LET GO. WOULDN'T LISTEN TO REASON. I'VE BEEN TO CHURCH EVERY SUNDAY SINCE I WAS A KID.
BUT WHEN PUSH COMES TO SHOVE...

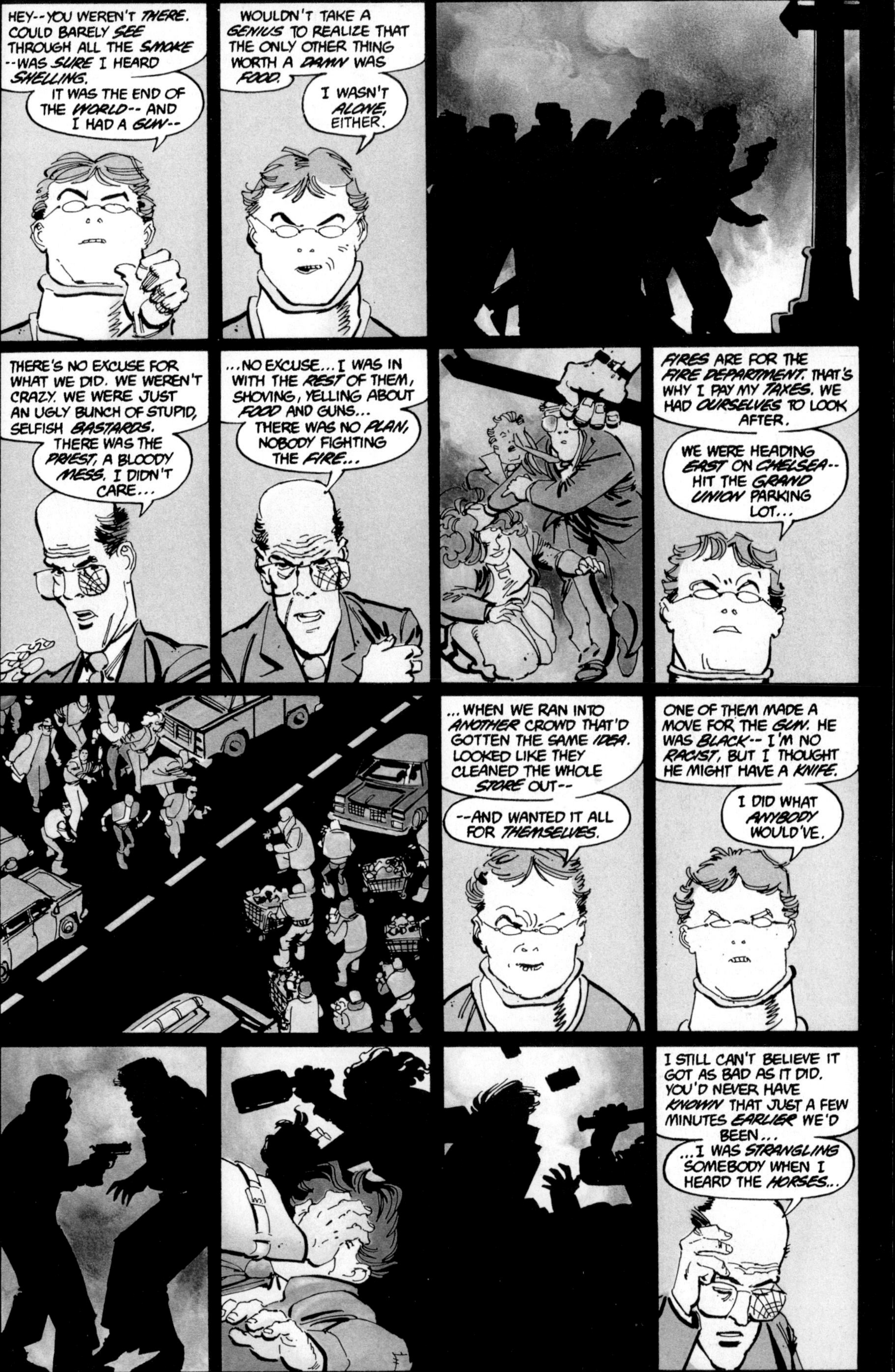
HEY--YOU WEREN'T THERE. COULD BARELY SEE THROUGH ALL THE SMOKE --WAS SURE I HEARD SHELLING.
IT WAS THE END OF THE WORLD-- AND I HAD A GUN--
WOULDN'T TAKE A GENIUS TO REALIZE THAT THE ONLY OTHER THING WORTH A DAMN WAS FOOD.
I WASN'T ALONE, EITHER.
THERE'S NO EXCUSE FOR WHAT WE DID. WE WEREN'T CRAZY. WE WERE JUST AN UGLY BUNCH OF STUPID, SELFISH BASTARDS.
THERE WAS THE PRIEST, A BLOODY MESS. I DIDN'T CARE...
...NO EXCUSE... I WAS IN WITH THE REST OF THEM, SHOVING, YELLING ABOUT FOOD AND GUNS...
THERE WAS NO PLAN, NOBODY FIGHTING THE FIRE...
FIRES ARE FOR THE FIRE DEPARTMENT. THAT'S WHY I PAY MY TAXES. WE HAD OURSELVES TO LOOK AFTER.
WE WERE HEADING EAST ON CHELSEA-- HIT THE GRAND UNION PARKING LOT...
...WHEN WE RAN INTO ANOTHER CROWD THAT'D GOTTEN THE SAME IDEA. LOOKED LIKE THEY CLEANED THE WHOLE STORE OUT--
--AND WANTED IT ALL FOR THEMSELVES.
ONE OF THEM MADE A MOVE FOR THE GUN. HE WAS BLACK-- I'M NO RACIST, BUT I THOUGHT HE MIGHT HAVE A KNIFE.
I DID WHAT ANYBODY WOULD'VE.
I STILL CAN'T BELIEVE IT GOT AS BAD AS IT DID. YOU'D NEVER HAVE KNOWN THAT JUST A FEW MINUTES EARLIER WE'D BEEN...
...I WAS STRANGLING SOMEBODY WHEN I HEARD THE HORSES...

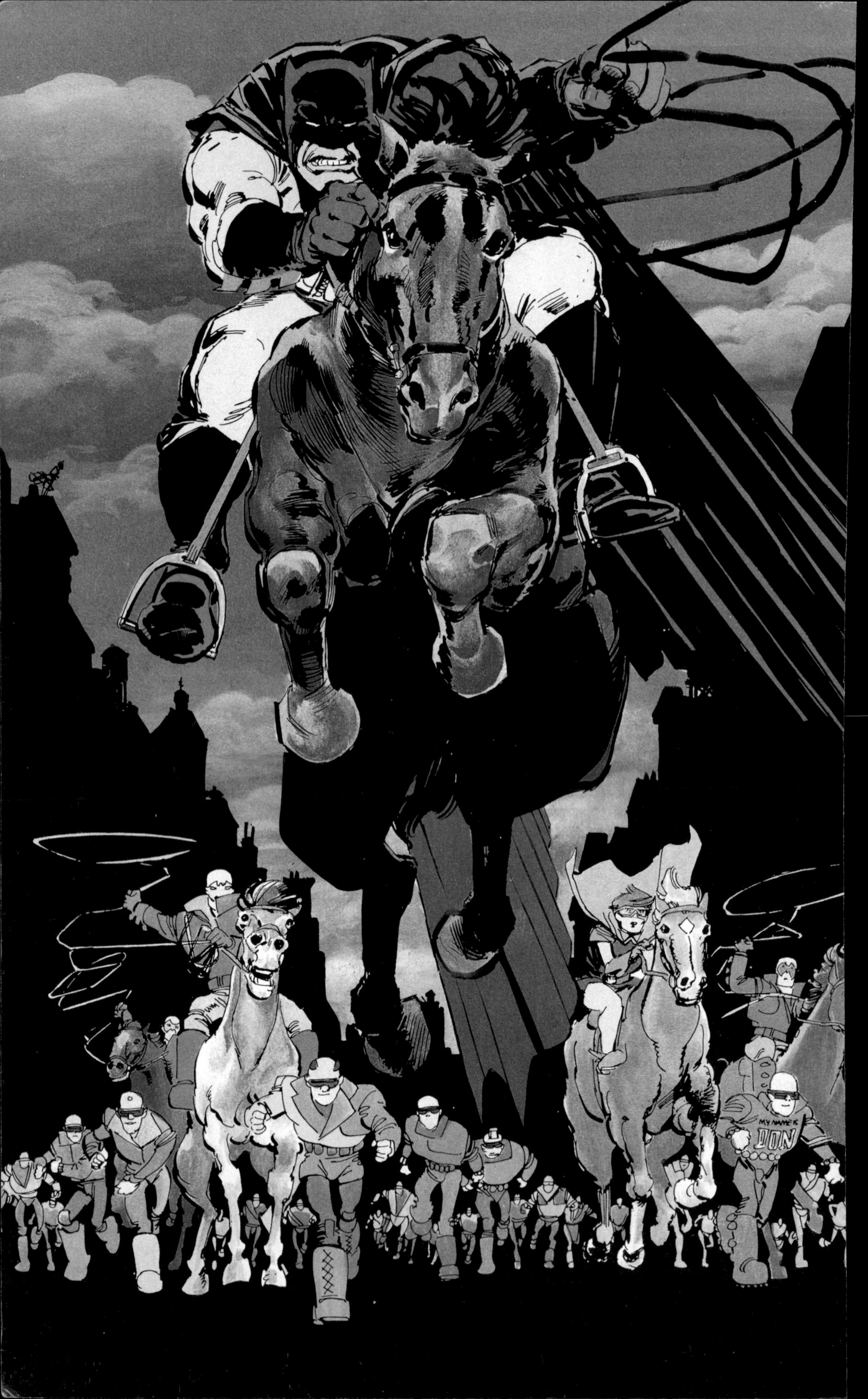
MY NAME IS
DON

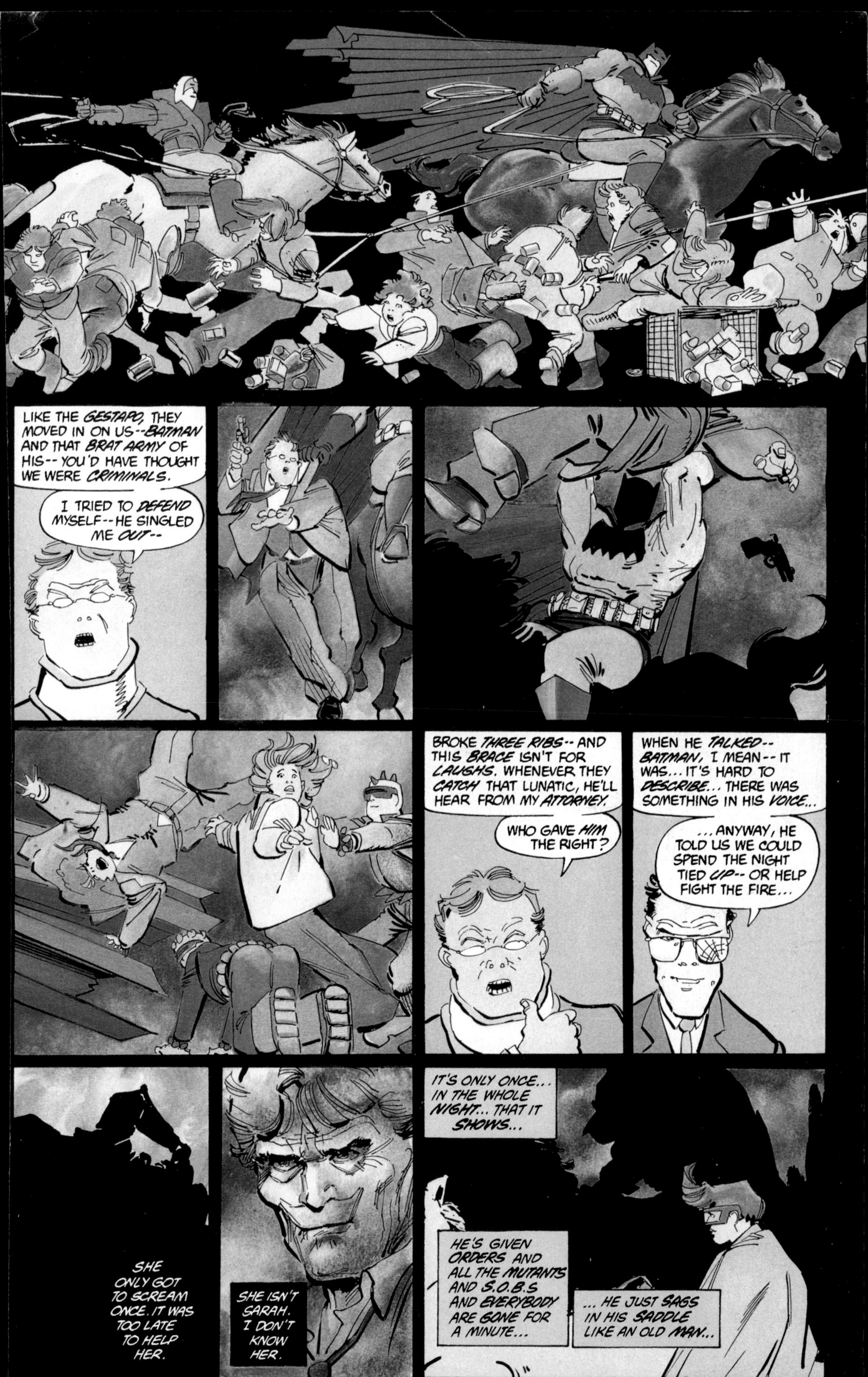

LIKE THE GESTAPO, THEY MOVED IN ON US--BATMAN AND THAT BRAT ARMY OF HIS-- YOU'D HAVE THOUGHT WE WERE CRIMINALS.
I TRIED TO DEFEND MYSELF--HE SINGLED ME OUT--
BROKE THREE RIBS-- AND THIS BRACE ISN'T FOR LAUGHS. WHENEVER THEY CATCH THAT LUNATIC, HE'LL HEAR FROM MY ATTORNEY.
WHO GAVE HIM THE RIGHT?
WHEN HE TALKED-- BATMAN, I MEAN-- IT WAS... IT'S HARD TO DESCRIBE... THERE WAS SOMETHING IN HIS VOICE...
...ANYWAY, HE TOLD US WE COULD SPEND THE NIGHT TIED UP-- OR HELP FIGHT THE FIRE...
SHE ONLY GOT TO SCREAM ONCE. IT WAS TOO LATE TO HELP HER.
SHE ISN'T SARAH. I DON'T KNOW HER.
IT'S ONLY ONCE... IN THE WHOLE NIGHT... THAT IT SHOWS...
HE'S GIVEN ORDERS AND ALL THE MUTANTS AND S.O.B.S AND EVERYBODY ARE GONE FOR A MINUTE...
... HE JUST SAGS IN HIS SADDLE LIKE AN OLD MAN...

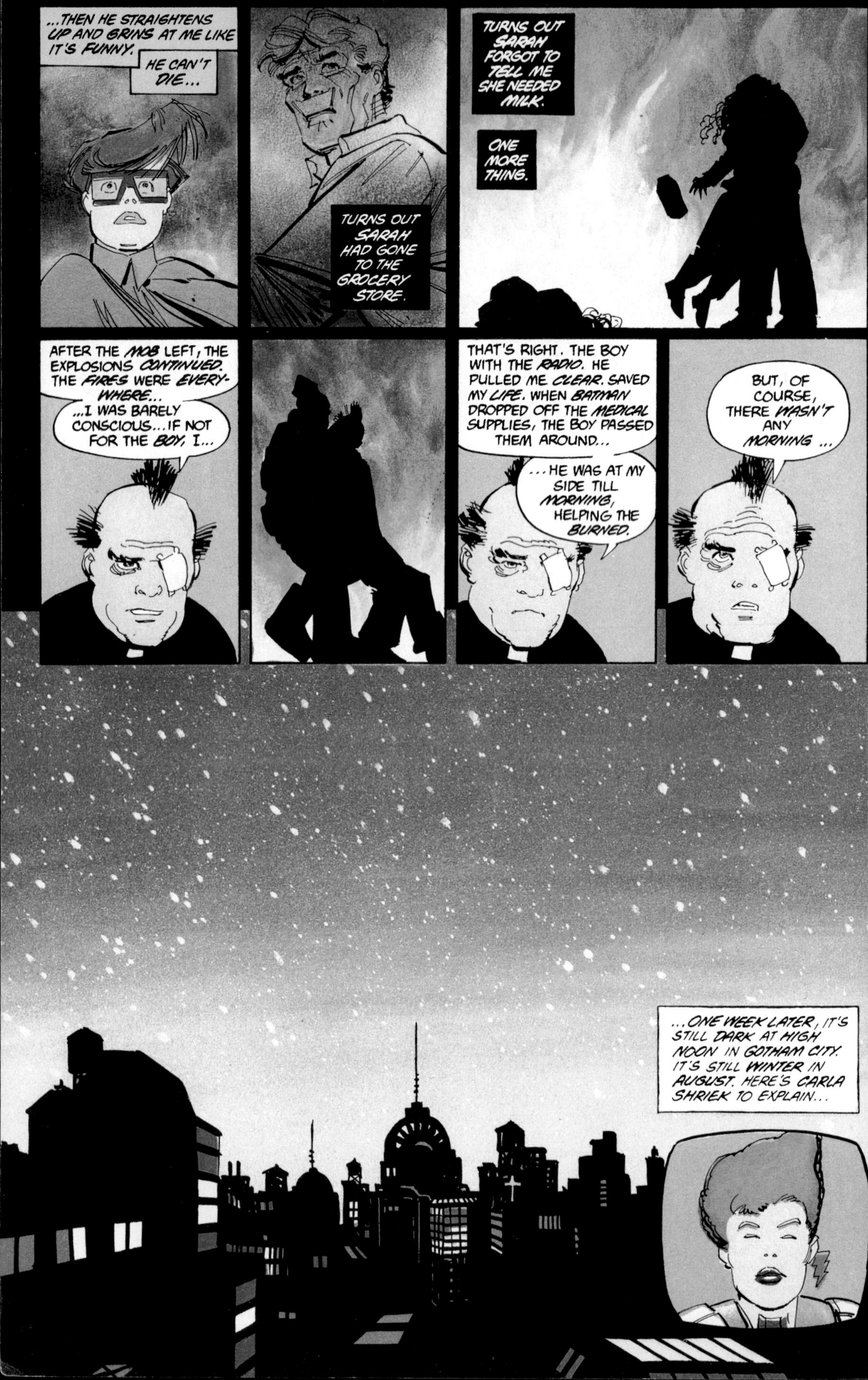
...THEN HE STRAIGHTENS UP AND GRINS AT ME LIKE IT'S FUNNY.
HE CAN'T DIE...
TURNS OUT SARAH HAD GONE TO THE GROCERY STORE.
TURNS OUT SARAH FORGOT TO TELL ME SHE NEEDED MILK.
ONE MORE THING.
AFTER THE MOB LEFT, THE EXPLOSIONS CONTINUED. THE FIRES WERE EVERY-WHERE...
...I WAS BARELY CONSCIOUS... IF NOT FOR THE BOY, I...
THAT'S RIGHT. THE BOY WITH THE RADIO. HE PULLED ME CLEAR. SAVED MY LIFE. WHEN BATMAN DROPPED OFF THE MEDICAL SUPPLIES, THE BOY PASSED THEM AROUND...
...HE WAS AT MY SIDE TILL MORNING, HELPING THE BURNED.
BUT, OF COURSE, THERE WASN'T ANY MORNING...
...ONE WEEK LATER, IT'S STILL DARK AT HIGH NOON IN GOTHAM CITY. IT'S STILL WINTER IN AUGUST. HERE'S CARLA SHRIEK TO EXPLAIN...

LOLA, THE SOVIET *COLDBRINGER* WAS DESIGNED TO *INDUCE* THE ENVIRONMENTAL EFFECTS OF *FULL-SCALE NUCLEAR WAR.* FIRST, IT GENERATED THE *PULSE* THAT BLACKED OUT--

ON THAT *PULSE*-- DON'T MISS OUR *SPECIAL* TONIGHT-- YOUR FAVORITE *STARS* ARE ASKED *"WHERE WERE YOU WHEN THE LIGHTS WENT OUT?"* CARLA?

LOLA, THE *PULSE* WAS ONLY THE *BEGINNING.* WEATHER PATTERNS ACROSS THE HEMISPHERE HAVE BEEN *COMPLETELY* DISRUPTED--

THEY SURE HAVE, CARLA. AND SO HAS MY *WARDROBE.* THIS IS THE *COLDEST* DAY OF THE YEAR. I DON'T KNOW *WHAT* TO WEAR THESE DAYS...

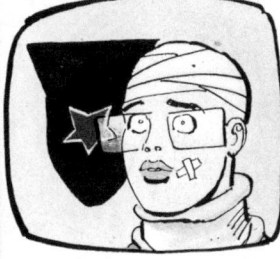   

THE COLDEST, LOLA-- UNTIL *TOMORROW.* THE BOMB'S *BLAST* THRUST *HUNDREDS* OF *MILLIONS* OF *TONS* OF *SOOT* INTO THE *STRATOSPHERE*--

--CREATING A *BLACK CLOUD* THAT COVERS THE *AMERICAS,* BLOTTING OUT THE *SUN*-- DEPRIVING US OF *LIGHT* AND *HEAT*...

STARVING

CUBANS WON'T *BUDGE*

RIOTS

CIVIL WAR IN THE MID-WEST

MEDIA PUSH

CREDIBILITY DISASTER

...NO, MR. PRESIDENT. I'M AFRAID HE'LL *NEVER* LET ME BRING HIM IN *ALIVE*...

...PEOPLE ARE *FREEZING* TO DEATH BY THE *THOUSANDS*... THE DAMAGE TO *CROPS* COULD WELL BRING ON A *FAMINE*...

I'M SURPRISED HE TOOK THE CHANCE OF COMING TO *AMERICA*-- WITH *CLARK* IN THE COUNTRY--

--BUT *OLIVER* HAS ALWAYS LIVED BY HIS *IMPULSES.*

THIS PARTICULAR *IMPULSE* I CAN *UNDERSTAND*...

YOU'VE ALWAYS HAD IT *WRONG,* BRUCE...

...GIVING THEM SUCH A BIG *TARGET.* SURE, YOU PLAY IT *MYSTERIOUS*-- BUT IT'S A *LOUD* KIND OF MYSTERIOUS, MAN. ESPECIALLY *LATELY.*

YOU GOT TO LEARN HOW TO MAKE THOSE SONS OF BITCHES WORK FOR YOU. LOOK-- IT'S BEEN *FIVE YEARS* SINCE I BLEW OUT OF *PRISON*--

--AND YOU *KNOW* I'VE KEPT *BUSY*--

... *COMPUTER FAILURE* WAS RESPONSIBLE FOR THE SINKING OF THE U.S. NUCLEAR SUBMARINE *VALIANT,* PENTAGON SOURCES DISCLOSED TODAY... NO HANDS WERE *LOST*...

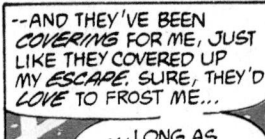

--AND THEY'VE BEEN *COVERING* FOR ME, JUST LIKE THEY COVERED UP MY *ESCAPE*. SURE, THEY'D *LOVE* TO FROST ME...

...LONG AS THEY CAN *DO* IT WITHOUT ADMITTING I *EXIST*.

SNAKT

BUT *YOU,* BRUCE--

--MAN, THEY *HAVE* TO KILL *YOU.*

OLIVER-- WHAT DO *YOU* WANT?

I ALWAYS *KNEW* IT'D GET DOWN TO *YOU* AND THE BIG BLUE *SCHOOLBOY.* PLANET'S TOO *BIG* FOR THE *TWO* OF YOU.

WHEN IT ALL COMES *DOWN...*

...I WANT A *PIECE* OF HIM. A *SMALL* PIECE WILL DO. FOR *OLD TIMES* SAKE, YOU KNOW...

...IT STILL *HURTS* WHEN IT'S *COLD...*

...NOTHING WE CAN'T HANDLE, FOLKS. WE'RE STILL *AMERICA*-- AND I'M STILL *PRESIDENT.*

WHO *WAS* THAT SPUD? TALKS LIKE MY *DAD.*

HE USED TO FIGHT *CRIME.*

...THE *PRESIDENT* HAS IMPOSED *LIMITED MARTIAL LAW,* THEREBY DEPLOYING *MILITARY* AID TO LAW-ENFORCEMENT AGENCIES AGAINST OUTBREAKS OF *VIOLENCE* AND *LOOTING...*

RIGHT *THERE*-- IN THAT *SADDLE*--IS ALL THE REASON I NEED...

...IT'S ALMOST *FRIGHTENING* HOW *QUICKLY* SHE'S LEARNING TO RIDE...

SHE HAS DECADES -- *DECADES,* LEFT TO HER...

... *NEW YORK, CHICAGO, METROPOLIS* -- EVERY CITY IN *AMERICA* IS CAUGHT IN THE GRIP OF A NATIONAL *PANIC*-- WITH *ONE* EXCEPTION. RIGHT, TOM?...

PANIC!

...THEN-- A *BLAST* OF *HEAT*--

--FROM THE *SKY*--

WHERE?

--AND IT *BEGINS...*

...THAT'S *RIGHT,* LOLA. THANKS TO THE *BATMAN* AND HIS VIGILANTE *GANG,* GOTHAM'S STREETS ARE *SAFE*-- UNLESS YOU TRY TO COMMIT A *CRIME...*

CRIME ALLEY.

...HEALING QUITE *POORLY,* MASTER BRUCE.

SHALL I PREPARE ANOTHER *STIMULANT?* WHY *DELAY* YOUR VERY FIRST *CARDIAC ARREST?*

OLIVER-- MAYBE OLIVER WAS RIGHT... ALL ALONG...

...CRAZY AS IT SOUNDS...

...BLOODY WALKING *HOSPITAL BED...*

THAT'S *ENOUGH,* ALFRED.

...IN THE PAST WEEK, *SEVENTY THREE* VIOLENT ATTACKS ON WOULD-BE *LOOTERS* HAVE BEEN ATTRIBUTED BY *WITNESSES* TO THE *BATMAN* AND HIS GANG...

...WHEN YOU *CAME* FOR ME... IN THE *CAVE...* I WAS JUST *SIX YEARS OLD...*

...YOU WERE *ANCIENT...* NOTHING COULD KILL YOU...

...BUT THE *WAR...*

...IT DID NOT *BEGIN* THEN...

NO... IT WAS... *TWO YEARS LATER...* WHEN HER *NECKLACE* CAUGHT ON HIS *WRIST...*

...WHEN HE SHOVED HIS *PISTOL* TO HER *JAW* AND PULLED THE *TRIGGER...*

...AND EVERYTHING MY MOTHER *WAS* STRUCK THE *PAVEMENT* AS A BLOODY *WAD...*

THAT *NIGHT...* BEGAN *THIRTY YEARS* OF HUNTING *THIEVES* AND *MURDERERS...*

...IS THAT WHAT YOU *INTENDED?...*

...COMMISSIONER YINDEL REFUSED TO COMMENT ON THE CHARGE THAT GOTHAM'S *POLICE* HAVE BEEN *LAX* IN PURSUING THE *MURDER CHARGE* AGAINST THE BATMAN...

SOMEWHERE IN THE ENDLESS *NIGHT...* LIKE A *BELLOW* FROM A WOUNDED *BEAR...*

...THE *ANSWER* COMES...

...*ARMY TROOPS* HAVE *EVACUATED* THE SLUM KNOWN AS *CRIME ALLEY*--NO EXPLANATION IS GIVEN--*NEWS* COVERAGE HAS BEEN FLATLY *DENIED--*

THE *TIMING...* MUST BE *EXACT...*

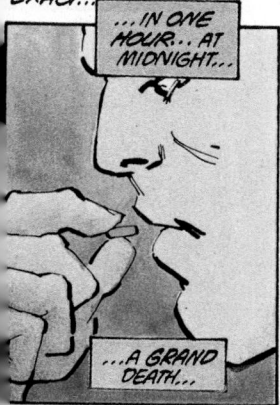

...IN ONE *HOUR...* AT *MIDNIGHT...*

...A *GRAND DEATH...*

RUMORS FLY-- ARMY *HELICOPTERS* HOVER OVER THE EMPTY STREETS OF *CRIME ALLEY*--IS THIS A *MILITARY EFFORT* TO CAPTURE THE *BATMAN--*

THIS ONE YOU *WON'T* BELIEVE, CLARK.

MY *BEST TRICK...*

--OR IS THIS THE FINAL *BATTLE* BETWEEN TWO *TITANS* -- THE LAST STAND FOR THE CAPED CRUSADER--FACING THE *MIGHT* OF THE MAN OF STE--

SKRIKK

DO NOT ADJUST YOUR SET

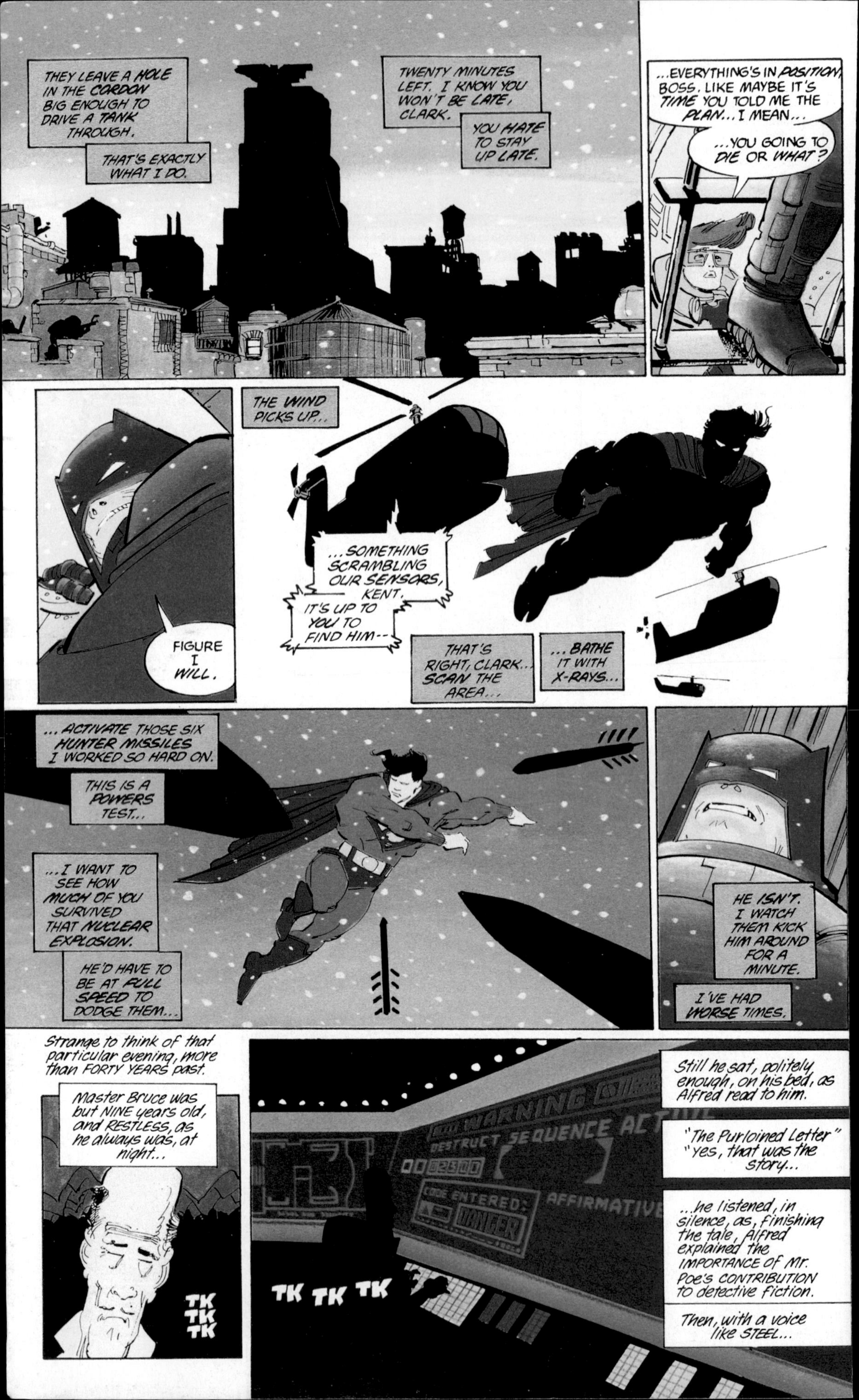

THEY LEAVE A HOLE IN THE CORDON BIG ENOUGH TO DRIVE A TANK THROUGH.
THAT'S EXACTLY WHAT I DO.
TWENTY MINUTES LEFT. I KNOW YOU WON'T BE LATE, CLARK.
YOU HATE TO STAY UP LATE.
...EVERYTHING'S IN POSITION, BOSS. LIKE MAYBE IT'S TIME YOU TOLD ME THE PLAN... I MEAN...
...YOU GOING TO DIE OR WHAT?
FIGURE I WILL.
THE WIND PICKS UP...
...SOMETHING SCRAMBLING OUR SENSORS, KENT.
IT'S UP TO YOU TO FIND HIM--
THAT'S RIGHT, CLARK... SCAN THE AREA...
...BATHE IT WITH X-RAYS...
...ACTIVATE THOSE SIX HUNTER MISSILES I WORKED SO HARD ON.
THIS IS A POWERS TEST...
...I WANT TO SEE HOW MUCH OF YOU SURVIVED THAT NUCLEAR EXPLOSION.
HE'D HAVE TO BE AT FULL SPEED TO DODGE THEM...
HE ISN'T. I WATCH THEM KICK HIM AROUND FOR A MINUTE.
I'VE HAD WORSE TIMES.
Strange to think of that particular evening, more than FORTY YEARS past.
Master Bruce was but NINE years old, and RESTLESS, as he always was, at night...
TK TK TK
WARNING
DESTRUCT SEQUENCE ACTIVE
CODE ENTERED:
DANGER
AFFIRMATIVE
TK TK TK
Still he sat, politely enough, on his bed, as Alfred read to him.
"The Purloined Letter" yes, that was the story...
...he listened, in silence, as, finishing the tale, Alfred explained the IMPORTANCE OF Mr. Poe's CONTRIBUTION to detective fiction.
Then, with a voice like STEEL...

...so frightfully FORMAL, his dark eyes FLASHING...

...Master Bruce asked -- no, DEMANDED... "the killer was CAUGHT. AND PUNISHED."

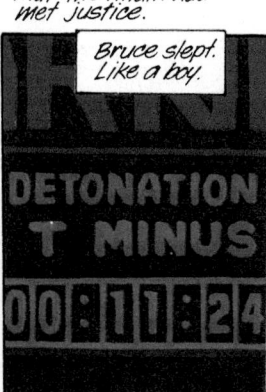

Alfred assured him that the villain had met justice.

Bruce slept. Like a boy.

DETONATION T MINUS

00:11:24

00:11:23

HE HITS THE GROUND ON SCHEDULE.

ONE BLOCK FROM ME.

BREATHING A LITTLE FAST--

IT'S ROBIN'S TURN--

THE CHARGE COULD SINK A BATTLESHIP. I THINK HE FEELS IT.

POOM

WHMP

SKREK

ISN'T TONIGHT A SCHOOL NIGHT?

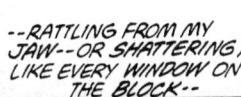

--RATTLING FROM MY JAW--OR SHATTERING, LIKE EVERY WINDOW ON THE BLOCK--

--WHEN I HIT HIM WITH THE SONIC.

A NOSEBLEED --SO SOON, CLARK--

DON'T DROP NOW-- THE NIGHT IS YOUNG--

AND I HAVE--SO MUCH PLANNED--

MORE WIND.

NOW HE'S TALKING-- TRYING TO REASON WITH ME. I CAN'T HEAR HIM, OF COURSE...

...NO, MY EARS ARE PROTECTED-- SO ALL I HAVE TO WORRY ABOUT IS MY TEETH--

--AND IT HAS TO END HERE-- ON THIS FILTHY PATCH OF STREET--

--WHERE MY PARENTS DIED...

...WHERE I CAN USE THE CITY'S POWER--

-EVERY WATT OF IT--

--TO FRY YOUR BRAIN--

--STILL TALKING-- KEEP TALKING, CLARK...

...YOU'VE ALWAYS KNOWN JUST WHAT TO SAY.

"YES"-- YOU ALWAYS SAY YES-- TO ANYONE WITH A BADGE-- OR A FLAG--

--NO GOOD--

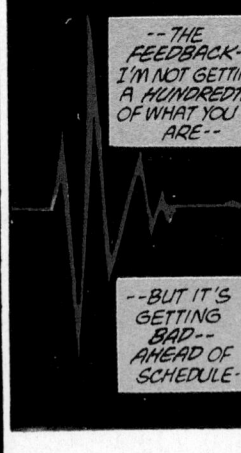

--THE FEEDBACK-- I'M NOT GETTING A HUNDREDTH OF WHAT YOU ARE--

--BUT IT'S GETTING BAD-- AHEAD OF SCHEDULE--

--WHAT DIDN'T HIT YOU-- AND ME-- FED THIS SUIT, CLARK--

--IT'S WAY PAST TIME YOU LEARNED--WHAT IT MEANS--

--TO BE A MAN--

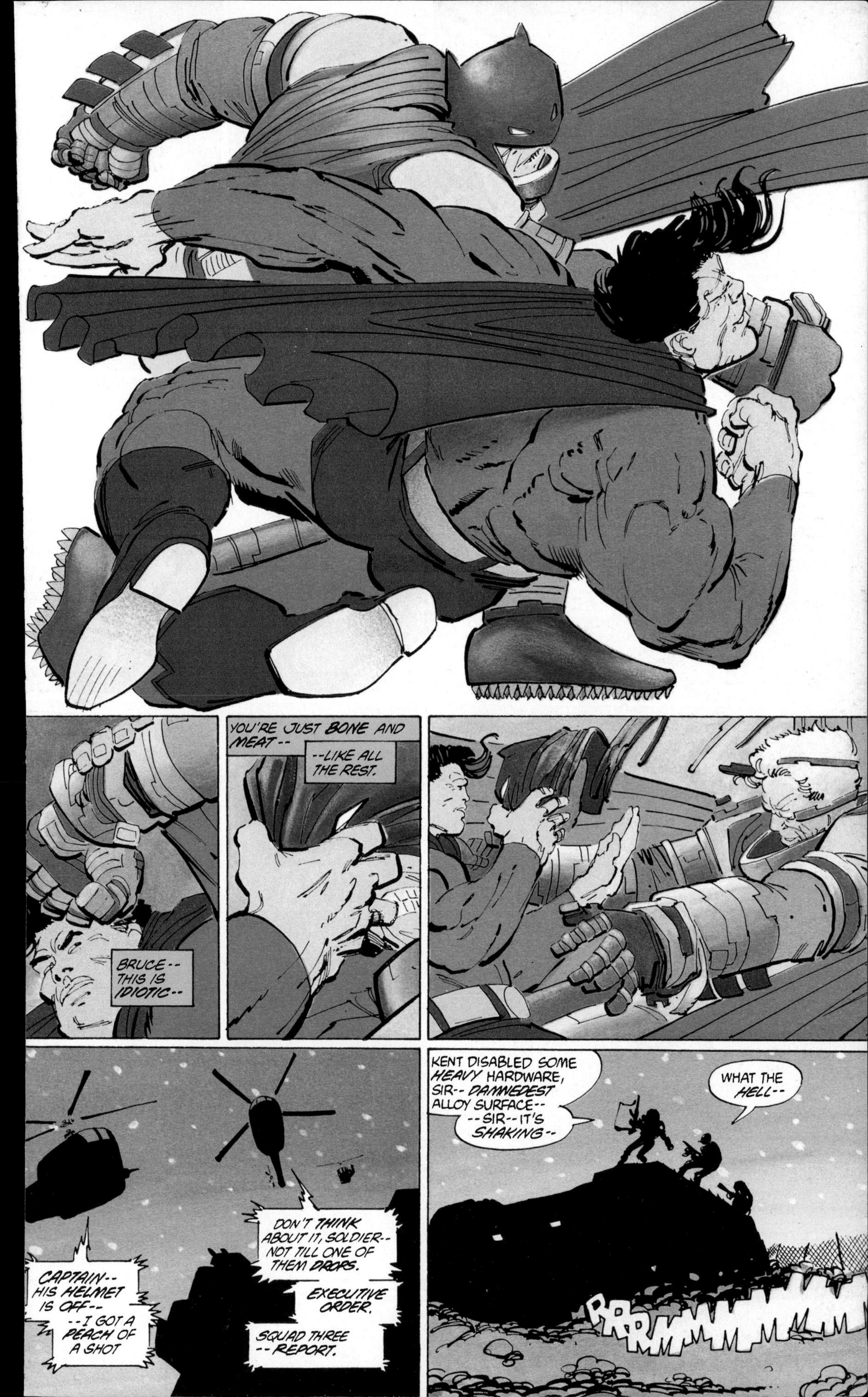
YOU'RE JUST BONE AND MEAT--
--LIKE ALL THE REST.
BRUCE-- THIS IS IDIOTIC--
CAPTAIN-- HIS HELMET IS OFF-- --I GOT A PEACH OF A SHOT
DON'T THINK ABOUT IT, SOLDIER-- NOT TILL ONE OF THEM DROPS.
EXECUTIVE ORDER.
SQUAD THREE --REPORT.
KENT DISABLED SOME HEAVY HARDWARE, SIR-- DAMNEDEST ALLOY SURFACE--
--SIR--IT'S SHAKING--
WHAT THE HELL--
RRRMMMMMMMM

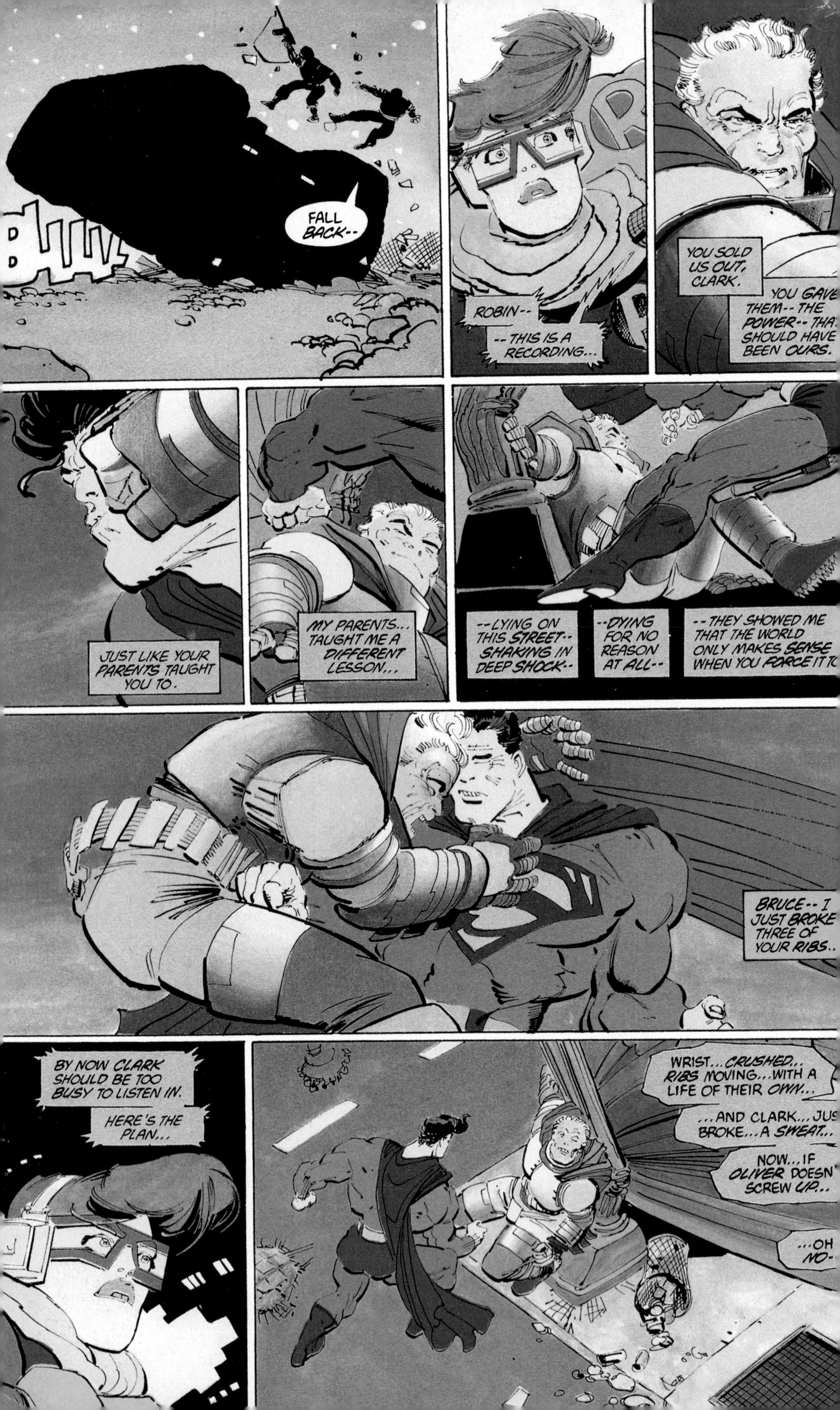

FALL BACK--
ROBIN--
--THIS IS A RECORDING...
YOU SOLD US OUT, CLARK.
YOU GAVE THEM--THE POWER--THAT SHOULD HAVE BEEN OURS.
JUST LIKE YOUR PARENTS TAUGHT YOU TO.
MY PARENTS... TAUGHT ME A DIFFERENT LESSON...
--LYING ON THIS STREET-- SHAKING IN DEEP SHOCK--
--DYING FOR NO REASON AT ALL--
--THEY SHOWED ME THAT THE WORLD ONLY MAKES SENSE WHEN YOU FORCE IT TO
BRUCE--I JUST BROKE THREE OF YOUR RIBS...
BY NOW CLARK SHOULD BE TOO BUSY TO LISTEN IN.
HERE'S THE PLAN...
WRIST... CRUSHED... RIBS MOVING... WITH A LIFE OF THEIR OWN...
...AND CLARK... JUST BROKE... A SWEAT...
NOW... IF OLIVER DOESN'T SCREW UP...
...OH NO--

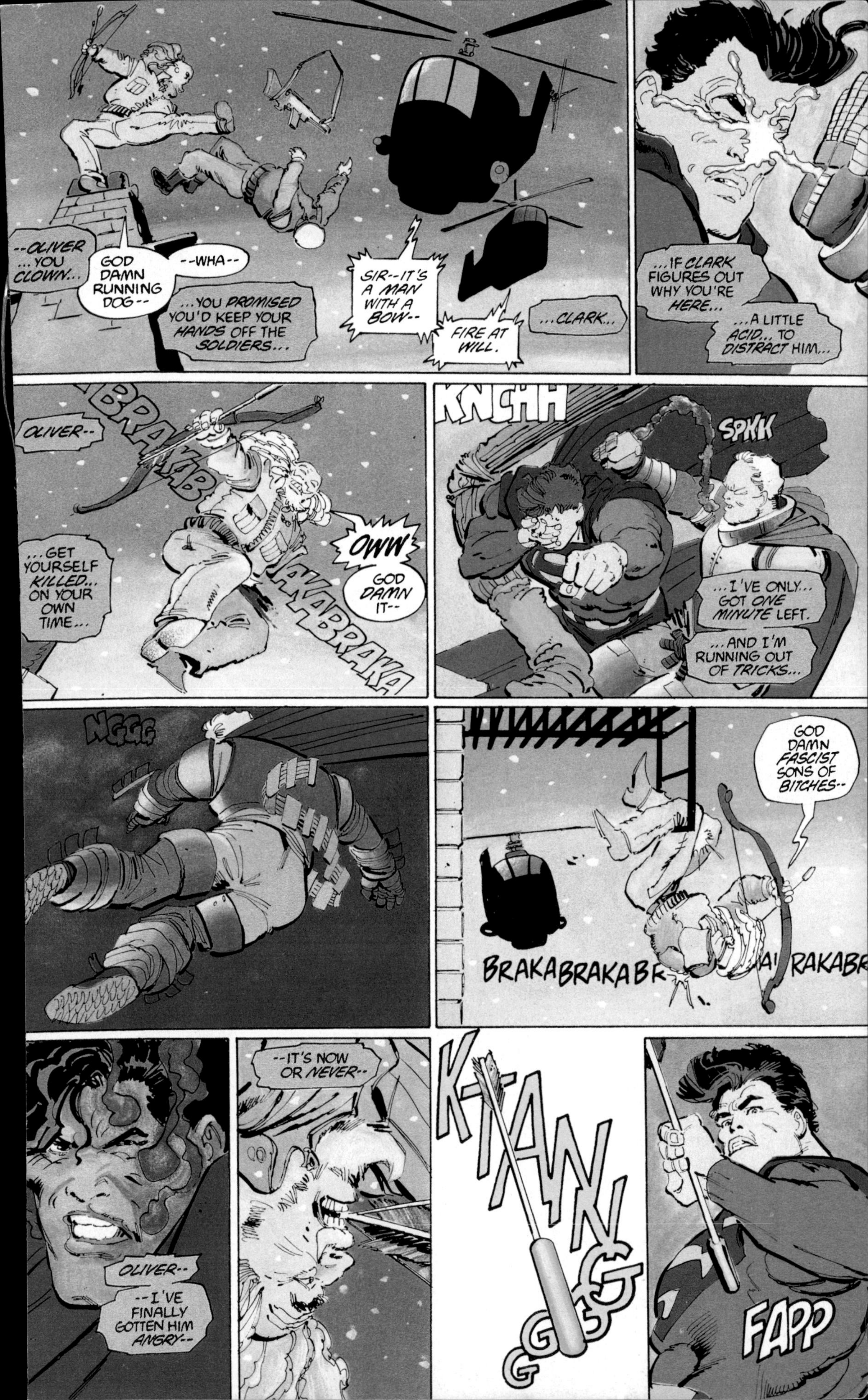
--OLIVER ...YOU CLOWN...
GOD DAMN RUNNING DOG--
--WHA--
...YOU PROMISED YOU'D KEEP YOUR HANDS OFF THE SOLDIERS...
SIR--IT'S A MAN WITH A BOW--
FIRE AT WILL.
...CLARK...
...IF CLARK FIGURES OUT WHY YOU'RE HERE...
...A LITTLE ACID... TO DISTRACT HIM...
OLIVER--
BRAKAB
...GET YOURSELF KILLED... ON YOUR OWN TIME...
OWW
GOD DAMN IT--
AKABRAKA
KNCHH
SPKK
...I'VE ONLY... GOT ONE MINUTE LEFT.
...AND I'M RUNNING OUT OF TRICKS...
NGGG
GOD DAMN FASCIST SONS OF BITCHES--
BRAKABRAKABR
RAKABR
OLIVER--
--I'VE FINALLY GOTTEN HIM ANGRY--
--IT'S NOW OR NEVER--
K-TANNGGGG
FAPP

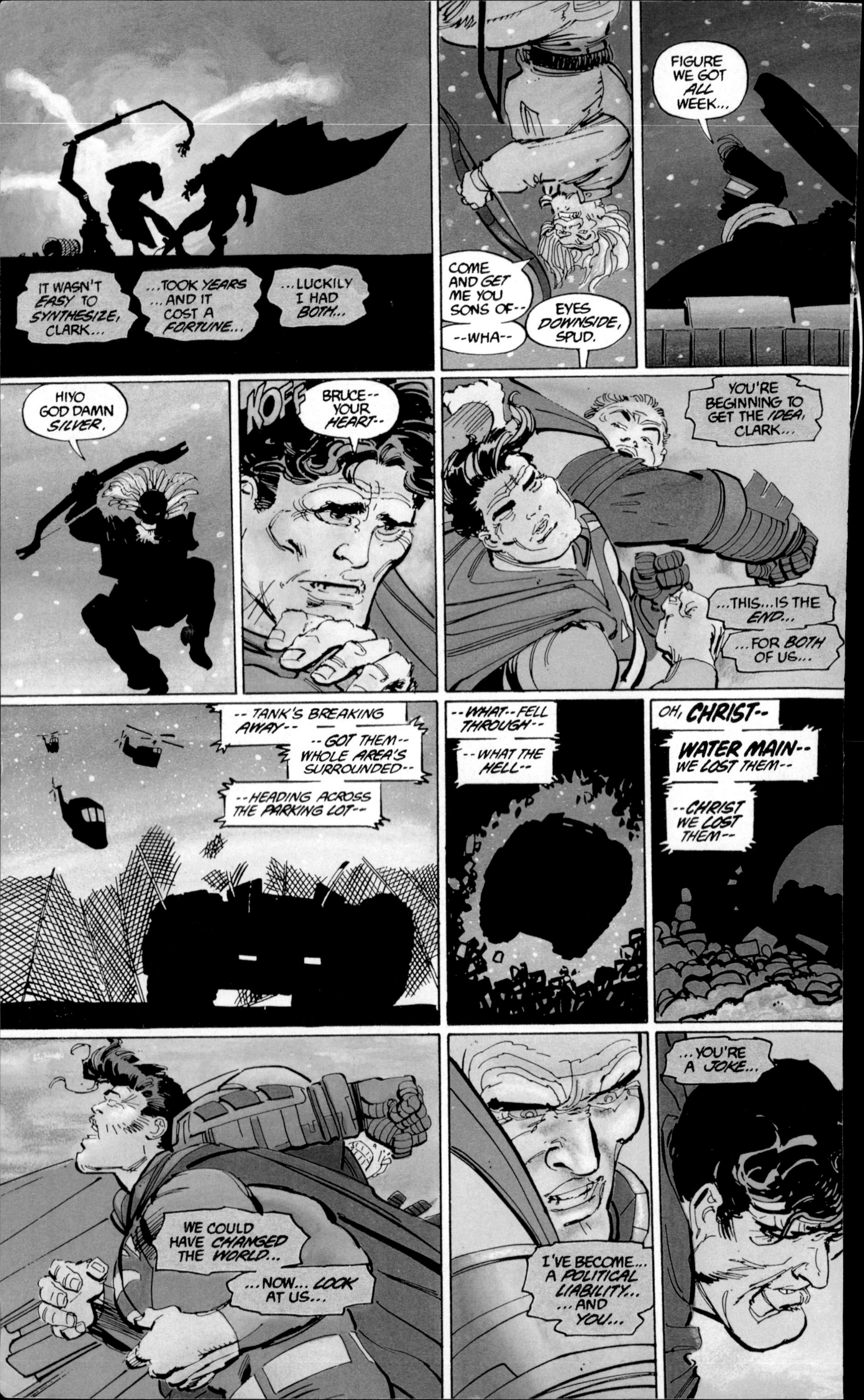
IT WASN'T EASY TO SYNTHESIZE, CLARK...
...TOOK YEARS ...AND IT COST A FORTUNE...
...LUCKILY I HAD BOTH...
COME AND GET ME YOU SONS OF--
--WHA--
EYES DOWNSIDE, SPUD.
FIGURE WE GOT ALL WEEK...
HIYO GOD DAMN SILVER.
KOFF
BRUCE-- YOUR HEART--
YOU'RE BEGINNING TO GET THE IDEA, CLARK...
...THIS...IS THE END...
...FOR BOTH OF US...
--TANK'S BREAKING AWAY--
--GOT THEM-- WHOLE AREA'S SURROUNDED--
--HEADING ACROSS THE PARKING LOT--
--WHAT--FELL THROUGH--
--WHAT THE HELL--
OH, CHRIST--
WATER MAIN-- WE LOST THEM--
--CHRIST WE LOST THEM--
WE COULD HAVE CHANGED THE WORLD...
...NOW... LOOK AT US...
I'VE BECOME... A POLITICAL LIABILITY... ...AND YOU...
...YOU'RE A JOKE...

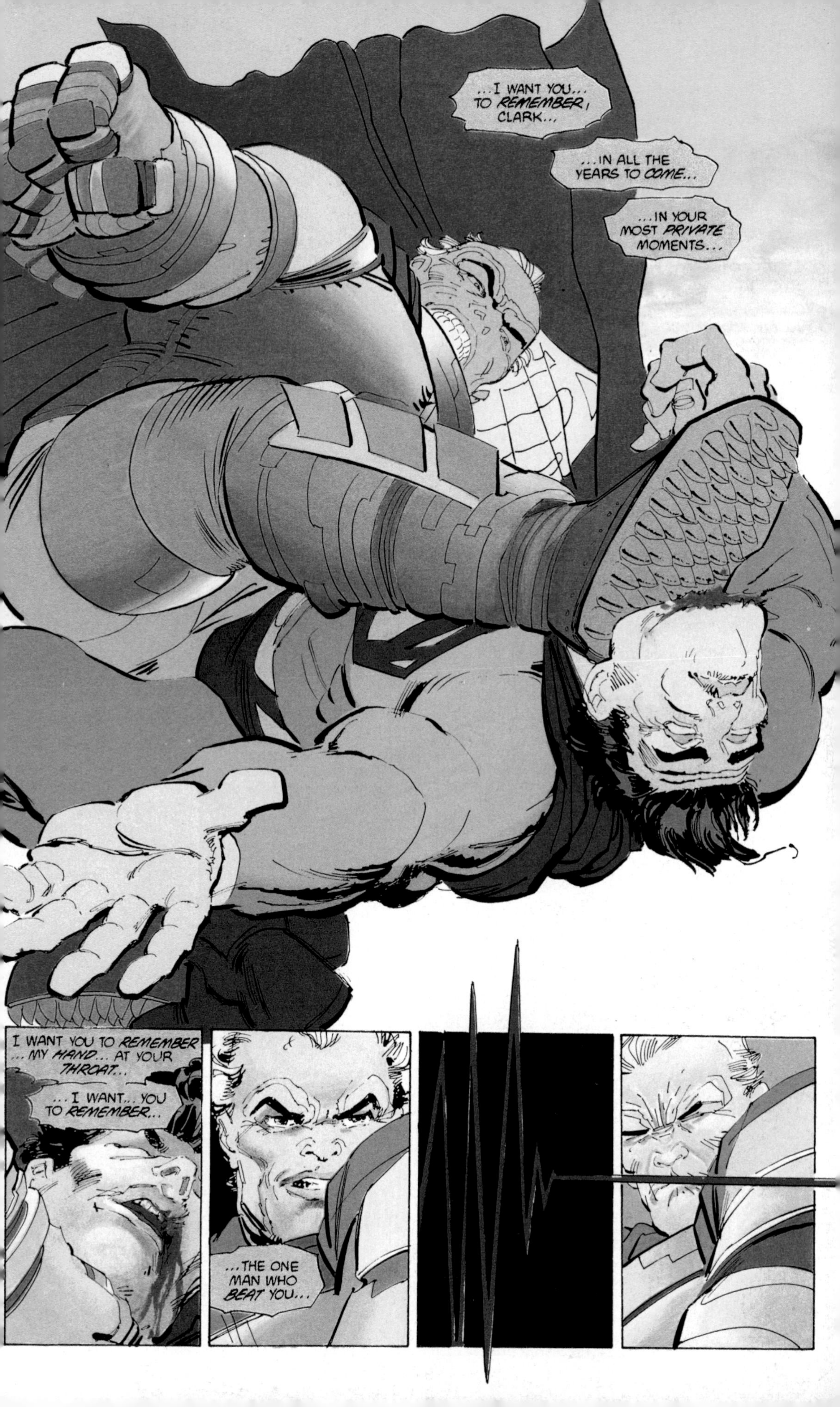

...I WANT YOU... TO REMEMBER, CLARK...
...IN ALL THE YEARS TO COME...
...IN YOUR MOST PRIVATE MOMENTS...
I WANT YOU TO REMEMBER ...MY HAND... AT YOUR THROAT...
...I WANT... YOU TO REMEMBER...
...THE ONE MAN WHO BEAT YOU...

The clock strikes TWELVE.

The ancient moor TREMBLES, beneath Alfred's feet.

Deep underground, COMPUTERS, holding every precious SECRET of the BATMAN, burst, and BURN...

Mrs. Wayne's priceless collection of PORCELAIN shatters, musically...

...the central mass of Wayne Manor SHUDDERS, as if ALIVE...

The world turns ruby RED. The manor roof RISES, madly, into the SKY, riding a pillar of FLAME.

A jolt travels the length of Alfred's SPINE. Of course, he thinks, as his head goes light.

...empty STABLES fly apart like toothpick models...

...then VANISHES in a FLASH, bright as the sun.

HOW utterly proper.

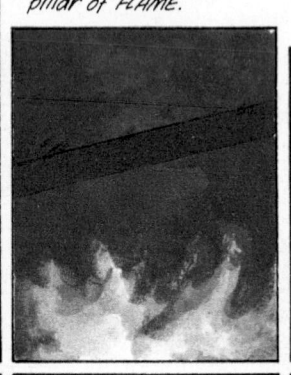

DON'T TOUCH HIM--

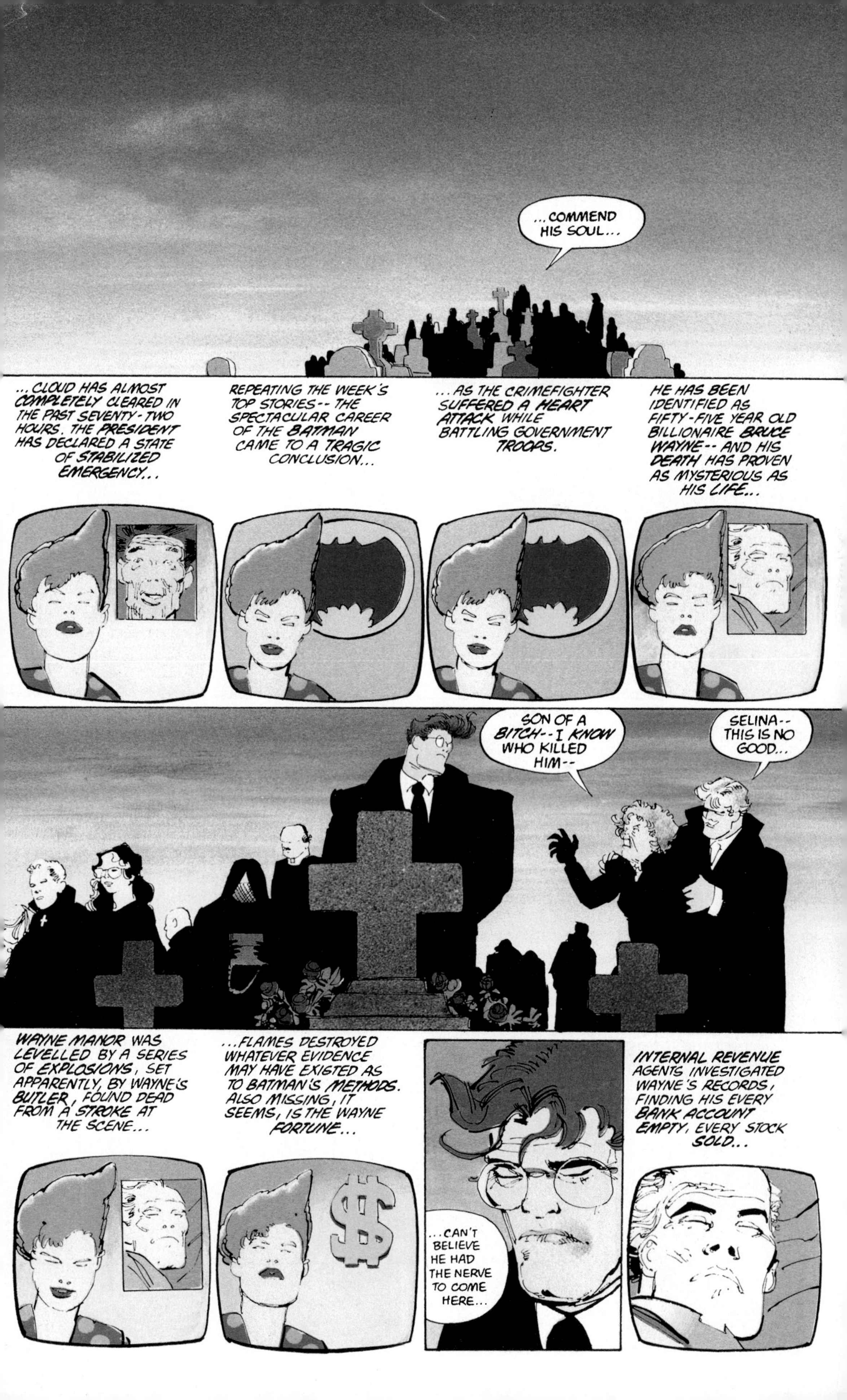
...COMMEND HIS SOUL...
...CLOUD HAS ALMOST COMPLETELY CLEARED IN THE PAST SEVENTY-TWO HOURS. THE PRESIDENT HAS DECLARED A STATE OF STABILIZED EMERGENCY...
REPEATING THE WEEK'S TOP STORIES-- THE SPECTACULAR CAREER OF THE BATMAN CAME TO A TRAGIC CONCLUSION...
...AS THE CRIMEFIGHTER SUFFERED A HEART ATTACK WHILE BATTLING GOVERNMENT TROOPS.
HE HAS BEEN IDENTIFIED AS FIFTY-FIVE YEAR OLD BILLIONAIRE BRUCE WAYNE-- AND HIS DEATH HAS PROVEN AS MYSTERIOUS AS HIS LIFE...
SON OF A BITCH--I KNOW WHO KILLED HIM--
SELINA-- THIS IS NO GOOD...
WAYNE MANOR WAS LEVELLED BY A SERIES OF EXPLOSIONS, SET APPARENTLY, BY WAYNE'S BUTLER, FOUND DEAD FROM A STROKE AT THE SCENE...
...FLAMES DESTROYED WHATEVER EVIDENCE MAY HAVE EXISTED AS TO BATMAN'S METHODS. ALSO MISSING, IT SEEMS, IS THE WAYNE FORTUNE...
...CAN'T BELIEVE HE HAD THE NERVE TO COME HERE...
INTERNAL REVENUE AGENTS INVESTIGATED WAYNE'S RECORDS, FINDING HIS EVERY BANK ACCOUNT EMPTY, EVERY STOCK SOLD...

...WHERE THE MONEY *WENT* IS ONE MORE SECRET WAYNE HAS TAKEN TO HIS GRAVE... HIS BODY WAS CLAIMED BY HIS ONLY LIVING RELATIVE, A DISTANT COUSIN...

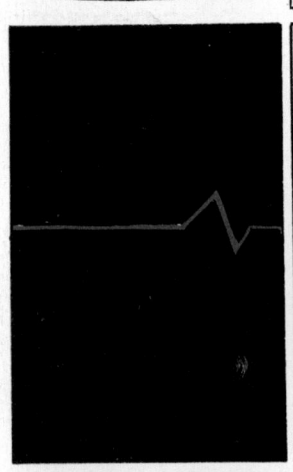

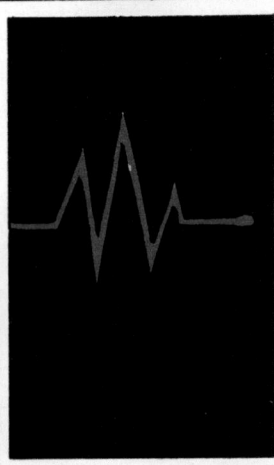

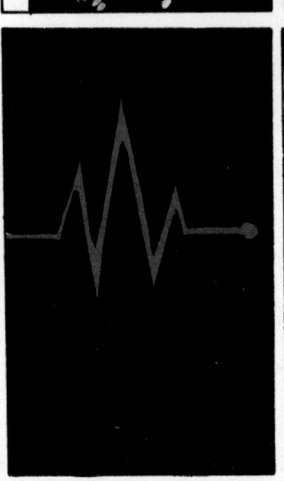

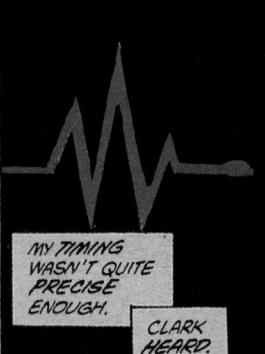

MY *TIMING* WASN'T QUITE *PRECISE* ENOUGH.

CLARK *HEARD.*

THAT WAS THE FIRST THING ROBIN *TOLD* ME--

--WHEN SHE *DUG* ME *UP.*

NOT THAT IT *MATTERED.* HE'D HAVE GUESSED *SOONER* OR *LATER.*

HE KNOWS HOW *GOOD* I AM WITH *CHEMICALS.*

I WAS *COUNTING* ON WHAT *OLIVER* SAID. AND WITH A *WINK--*

--CLARK PROVED OLIVER *RIGHT.*

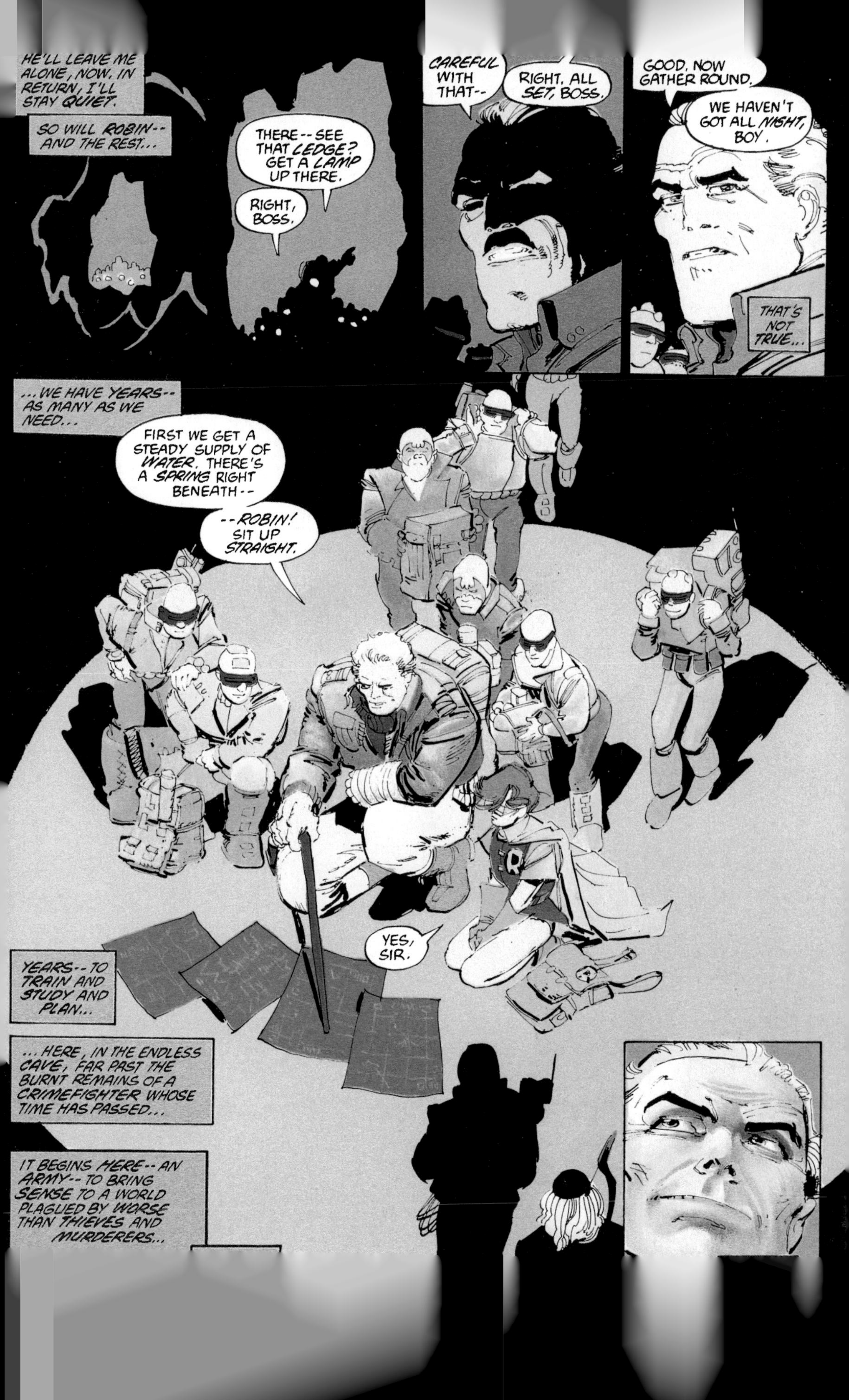
HE'LL LEAVE ME ALONE, NOW. IN RETURN, I'LL STAY QUIET.
SO WILL ROBIN-- AND THE REST...
THERE--SEE THAT LEDGE? GET A LAMP UP THERE.
RIGHT, BOSS.
CAREFUL WITH THAT--
RIGHT. ALL SET, BOSS.
GOOD. NOW GATHER ROUND.
WE HAVEN'T GOT ALL NIGHT, BOY.
THAT'S NOT TRUE...
...WE HAVE YEARS-- AS MANY AS WE NEED...
FIRST WE GET A STEADY SUPPLY OF WATER. THERE'S A SPRING RIGHT BENEATH--
--ROBIN! SIT UP STRAIGHT.
YES, SIR.
YEARS--TO TRAIN AND STUDY AND PLAN...
...HERE, IN THE ENDLESS CAVE, FAR PAST THE BURNT REMAINS OF A CRIMEFIGHTER WHOSE TIME HAS PASSED...
IT BEGINS HERE--AN ARMY--TO BRING SENSE TO A WORLD PLAGUED BY WORSE THAN THIEVES AND MURDERERS...

COVER
GALLERY

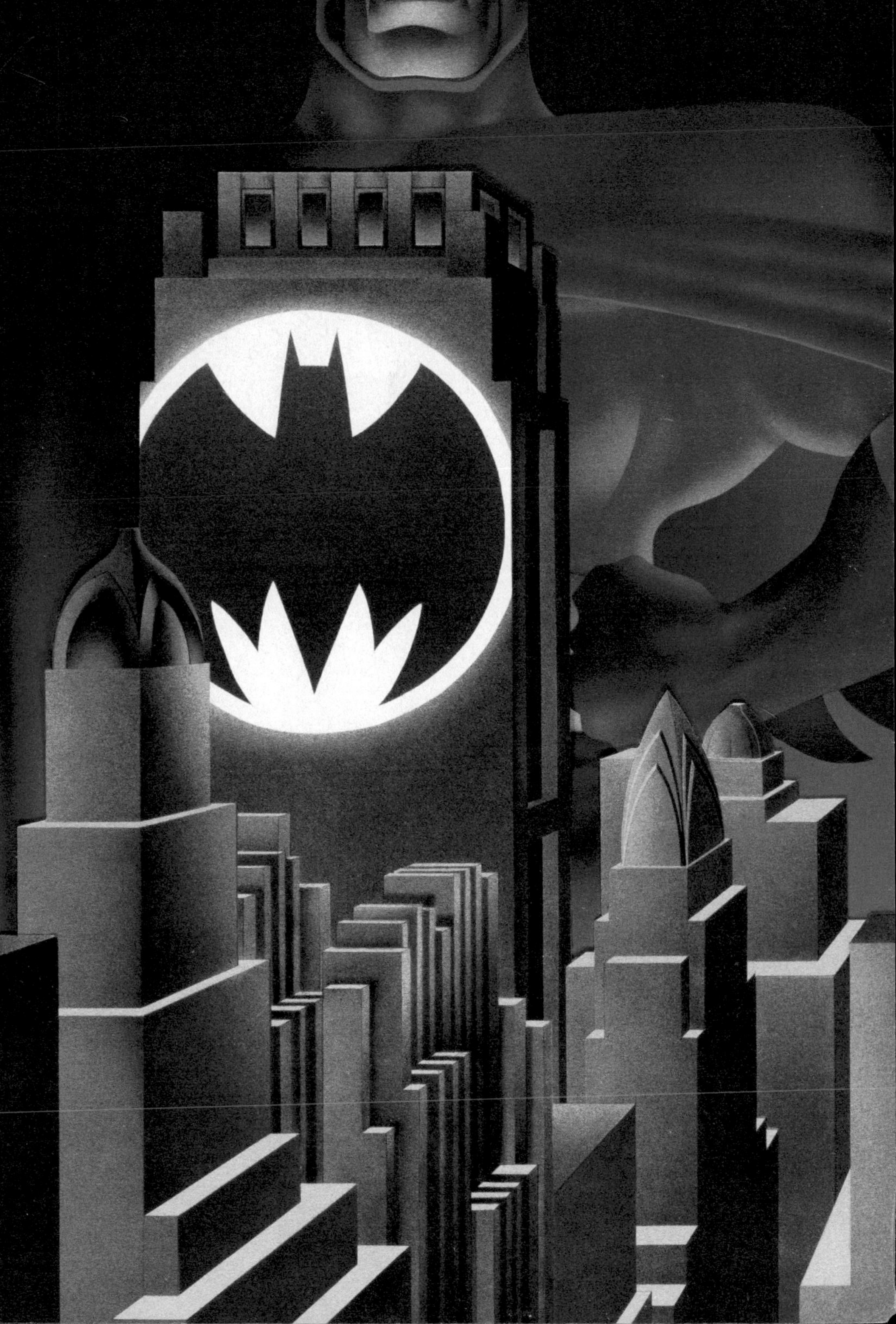

10TH ANNIVERSARY EDITION

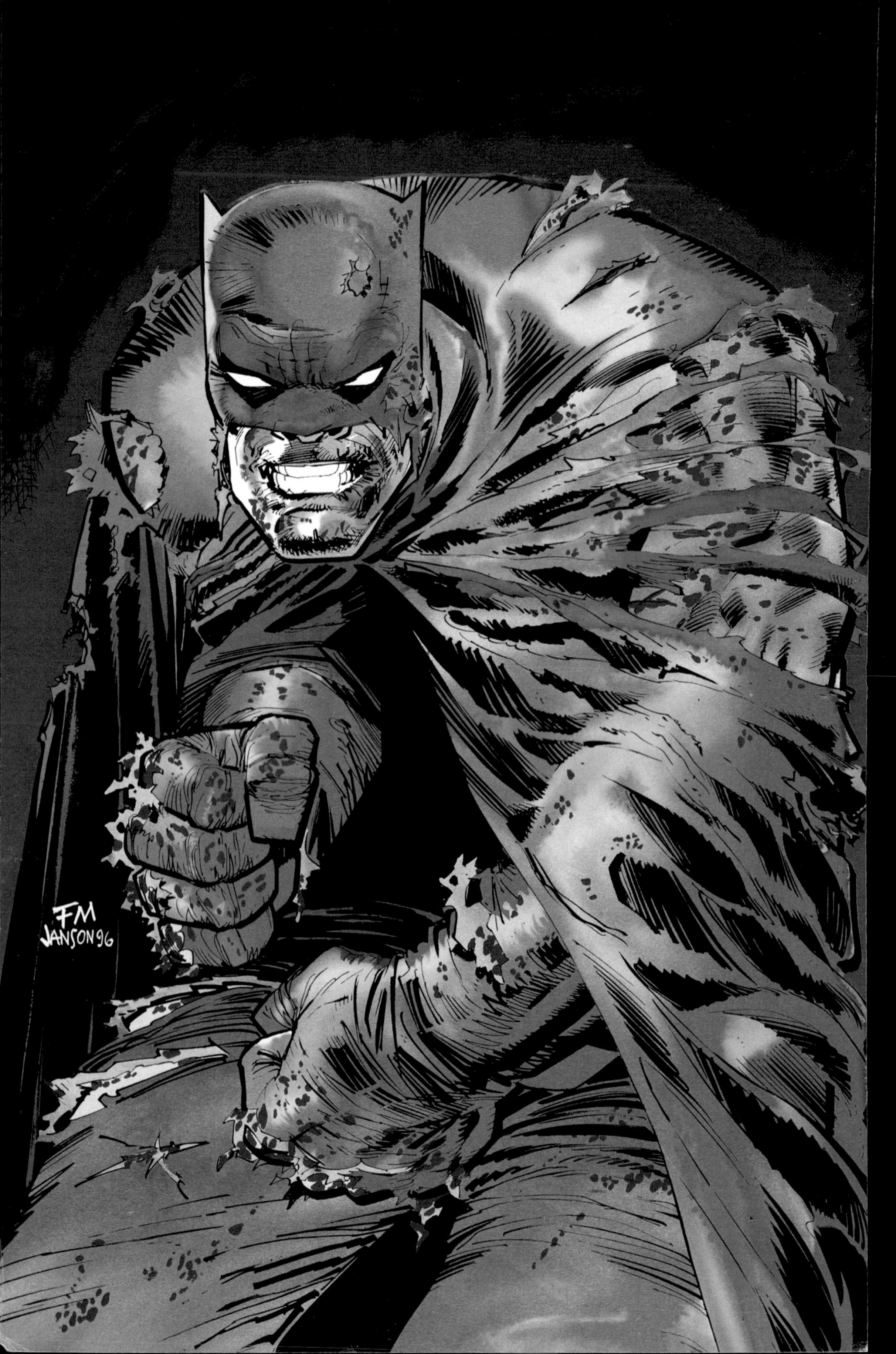
FM
JANSON 96

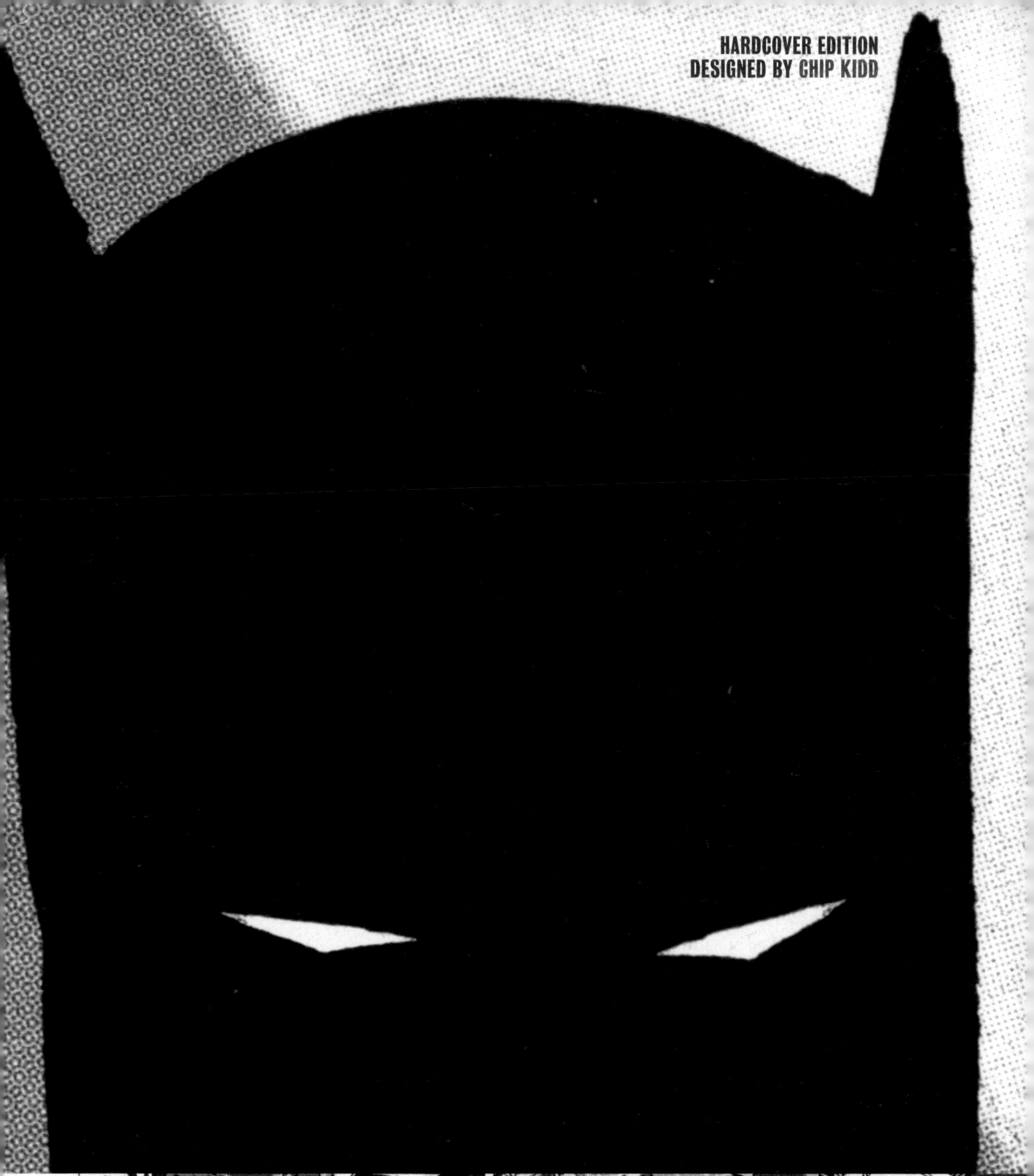
HARDCOVER EDITION
DESIGNED BY CHIP KIDD

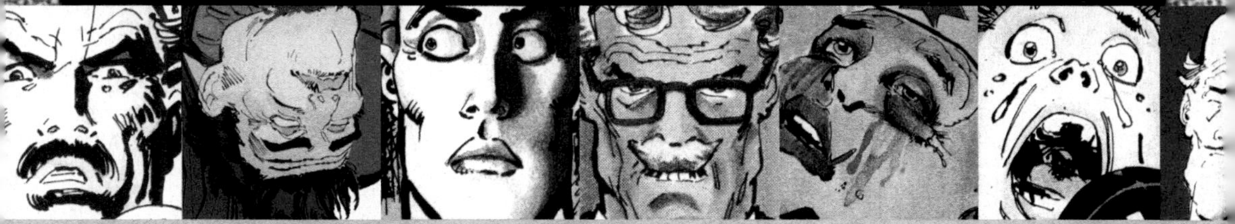

BATMAN®: THE DARK KNIGHT® RETURNS

FRANK MILLER

with KLAUS JANSON and LYNN VARLEY

"This is the first thing I ever called 'Dark Knight'—a proposal for a relaunch of Batman, it provided me backstory for DK 1 and much of the substance for BATMAN: YEAR ONE."

—FRANK MILLER

THE DARK KNIGHT

Original
Proposal 2/29/84

THE DARK KNIGHT

A DC Metropolis Comic

by Frank Miller

2/29/84

Episode One

WHO I AM

HOW I CAME TO BE

A violent thunderstorm batters stately Wayne Manor. Lightning

flashes, delineating an otherwise unlit study. We see a bloody

hand reach for a huge snifter of brandy, and bring it to a pair

of bruised and swollen lips. Bruce Wayne, age twenty-four, his face

battered almost beyond recognition, explains that he is afraid he

may have to die tonight.

A second lightning flash reveals that Bruce is speaking to a marble

bust of his father. Bruce speaks fondly of his early childhood.

He remembers how many times his father told him that his impetuous

nature would someday be the death of young Bruce.

... Bruce Wayne, age six, gleefully explores the grounds of

Wayne Manor. Faithful family retainer Alfred Pennyworth tries

to keep up with the athletic child, but Bruce tears off after

a rabbit, leaving Alfred behind. The rabbit ducks into

a hole, and Bruce recklessy follows. Almost immediately, the

earth gives way under Bruce, and he tumbles headlong into

darkness.

His scraped knees and the echo of his fall tell Bruce that he is in a large cave. Then, he hears screeching, and the flapping of thousands of wings. Bats come at him, then retreat as he swings his arms wildly. He looks about, his vision adjusting to the darkness, and sees one incredibly huge bat, hugging the floor, staring back at him, unwilling to retreat as his brothers did ...

Bruce continues to talk to his father. He's confused by the things he's finding himself thinking about tonight. He wants his father to help him find a way to go on. He has just lost, failed at the only thing that matters to him. So why is he thinking about Zorro, of all things?

... the black and white image of Douglas Fairbanks Jr. as Zorro flickers across a movie screen. Bruce, age seven, watches, wide-eyed and wondering, as Zorro routs a group of soldiers.

Bruce is ecstatic as they leave the theatre. His parents laugh and hold hands as Bruce jumps and dances, imitating his new hero. Father mentions that the movie was one of his old favorites. The Waynes are a happy, attractive couple in their late thirties. As they walk down the street, we see, huge in the foreground, footsteps following them.

A gunman comes up behind the Waynes, threatening, demanding Thomas
and Martha hand over their cash. Thomas turns, making a fist.
The gunman fires, once, and Thomas crumples to the pavement.
Bruce steps toward the gunman, his mouth forming a scream. The
gunman brings the barrel of his pistol across Bruce's face, stopping
the scream and knocking Bruce to the ground. Martha steps forward
to protect her child. The gunman grabs her by her diamond necklace,
then fires. The necklace comes free in his hand as Martha is
propelled backward, to fall across her husband.

Time seems to freeze as Bruce looks up at the gunman's face. He sees
a deadness in the man's eyes, the same deadness he'd seen in the
eyes of a man whose picture he'd seen in a newspaper. A man named
Oswald who was supposed to have shot the President. Bruce stares,
looking at what seems to be a demon, as the gunman points his
pistol at Bruce. Then, Bruce sees a glimmer of guilt in the
gunman's eyes, and knows that it is a man who shot his parents.
It's a sight he'll never forget. The gunman backs away, and
flees into the night.

That night, Bruce is barely conscious of a woman's kind attention,
and many questions from stern-faced policemen. Then all sense
of time is lost. Days and weeks of doctors and therapists float
by, all viewed as if from an immense distance by Bruce. He

hears himself described as traumatized, catatonic. But Bruce

knows that he has simply left the world, and will not return

until he finds a reason to.

Three months after his parents' murder, Bruce finds his reason. As

Alfred sits by his hospital bed, looking worried and old, Bruce

wakes. He calmly, solemnly tells Alfred that he is going to

devote his life to warring on all criminals. He asks Alfred if he

will help. Alfred quietly agrees.

Six months later, Bruce calls the family attorney into his father's

office. Bruce sits crosslegged in his father's huge chair, holding

a large book open in his lap. He explains that he wishes to enlist

the attorney's services, using his allowance, to keep orphanages,

guardians, and scholastic institutions out of Bruce's life. Alfred

will function as Bruce's guardian until Bruce is twenty-one. The

attorney tells Bruce that all this is impossible. Bruce says no, it

isn't. In fact, he's just figured out how to do it. He starts

reading from the book in his lap.

Briefly, we see Bruce studying with tutors, who seem amazed at his

aptitude and his intensity. Alfred watches, a little worried, a

little confused, and very proud. Bruce comments to Alfred, at one

point, that nothing in his studies contradicts the lesson he learned, when he was seven years old: that the world only makes sense when

you force it to.

Bruce, age twelve, lies in bed as Alfred reads him the concluding

lines of "The Purloined Letter". Alfred smiles, sets the book down,

and talks about the importance of the story in the development of

detective fiction. Bruce, jaw set, eyes open, asks quietly if

the killer was caught. And punished. Alfred assures him that he

was. Bruce closes his eyes and sleeps peacefully.

Bruce, age nineteen, stands on a mountain top in South America.

He and a dozen other men and women wear white karate robes. Bruce

is attacked by a hulk of a man. He easily smashes the man to the

ground, whirls, and brings his foot to the man's neck. His next

blow   would easily kill the man. Bruce steps back and smiles.

He turns to look at his teacher, a fierce-looking black man named

Jagger. Jagger strikes him roughly in the face, tells Bruce that

he is still too violent, too angry in his approach. Bruce argues,

saying that Jagger knows that Bruce is the finest student of Jagger's

eclectic fighting style. Jagger tells Bruce that his feelings are

interfering with his concentration, that rage ultimately robs him

of his real power. Bruce says that's rhetoric, embarrassing Jagger

in front of the class. Jagger decides to make an example of Bruce,

and kicks him twice, viciously, knocking him to the ground. Bruce looks up, grins, and says he'll show Jagger what his rage can do.

Bruce seems to fly from the ground, striking Jagger's chest and

stomach with powerful kicks, then using a kung fu punch to smash

Jagger's nose. Jagger collapses, nearly unconscious. He watches

Bruce leave, his face twisted with hate.

Bruce Wayne, age twenty-four, returns to Gotham City. He walks

calmly down the narrow street where his parents were murdered, and

stops, to lean casually against the streetlight that shines down

on the stretch of pavement where his parents lay, seventeen years

earlier. He can almost see them, and the face of a little boy whose

world was smashed to bits. And another face, of a man who was not

a demon ... From behind Bruce, we see three, then six pairs of feet

approach.

They circle him quickly, merrily. One asks him what an uptown boy

is doing in such a lousy neighborhood at such a late hour. Bruce,

almost distractedly, says he was born here. One of them draws a

nine millimeter pistol, and tells him to hand over his wallet. Bruce

says no, I don't think so. Then he leaps above the gun, lashing out

with a flying kick that sends the hood sprawling. Bruce drops to

the ground, snatching up the dropped pistol, and aims at the next

nearest hood. The pistol jams.

Then they are on him, kicking, stabbing, beating him horribly.
Bruce fights back, though outnumbered, wounding several of them. But
they win the fight, taking his wallet and leaving him a bloody, broken
mess on the sidewalk. After a long pause, he somehow begins an
agonizing journey back to Wayne Manor.

... Bruce sits, pleading with his father. He has learned, tonight,
that it is not enough to know how to fight, no matter how well. His
mission is that of one against thousands. He needs something –
something that will give him an edge. He pleads with his father.
Show me the way.

There is a deafening crack of thunder. A high casing window shatters
inward. For a moment everything is silent. Then, he hears the
flapping of wings. The huge bat from the cave he'd seen when he
was six years old glides into the study, hideous, frightening, and
powerful. It lands on his father's bust, its wings draped on either
side of his father's head. It stares at Bruce. Bruce looks deeply
into the eyes of the demon, and smiles.

Thank you, father, he says.

The unused first page from THE DARK KNIGHT RETURNS

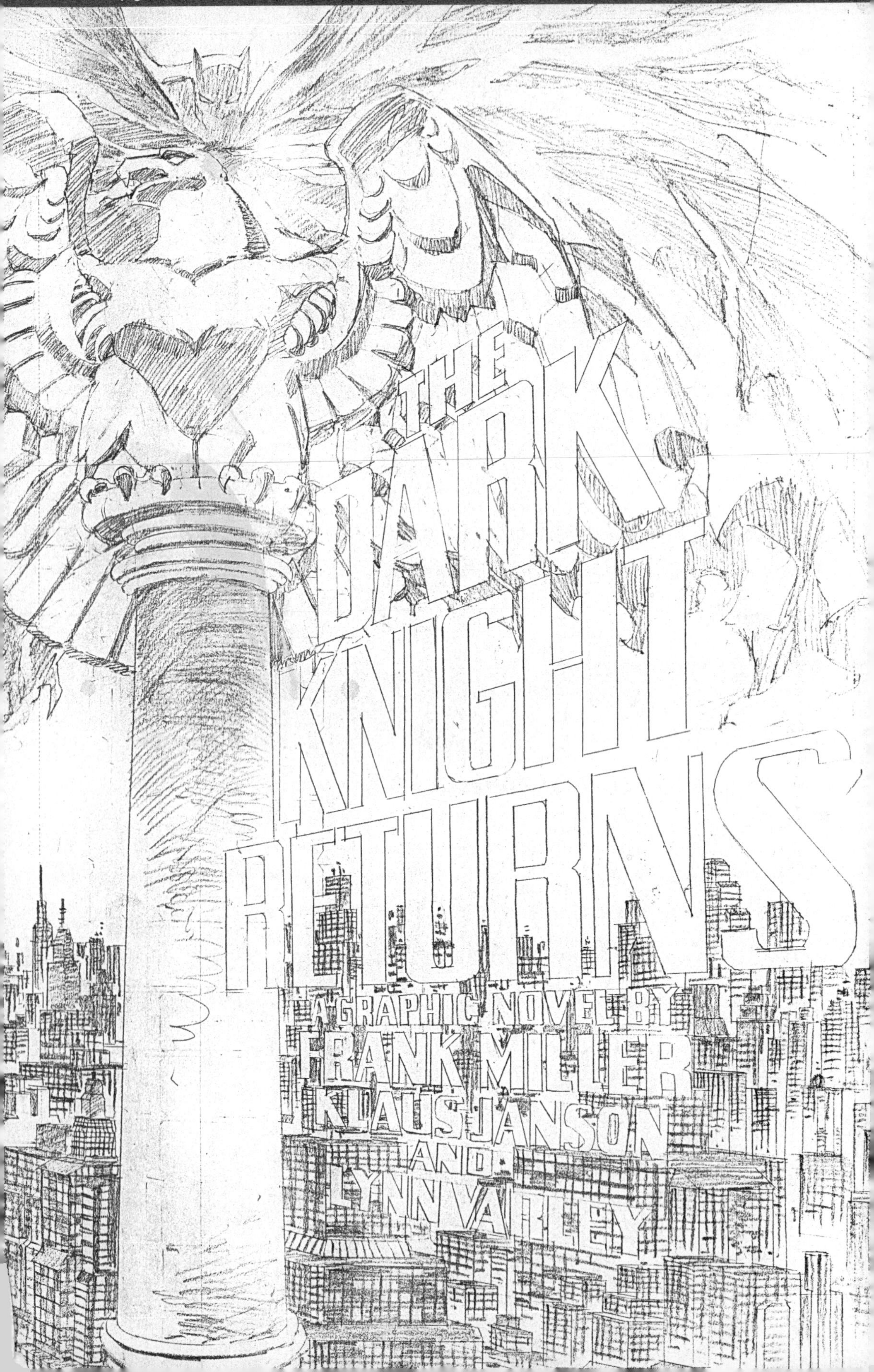
THE
DARK
KNIGHT
RETURNS
A GRAPHIC NOVEL BY
FRANK MILLER
KLAUS JANSON
AND
LYNN VARLEY

"Harlan Ellison sweet-talked me out of this original." —FRANK MILLER
BATMAN: THE DARK KNIGHT RETURNS #2, page 35

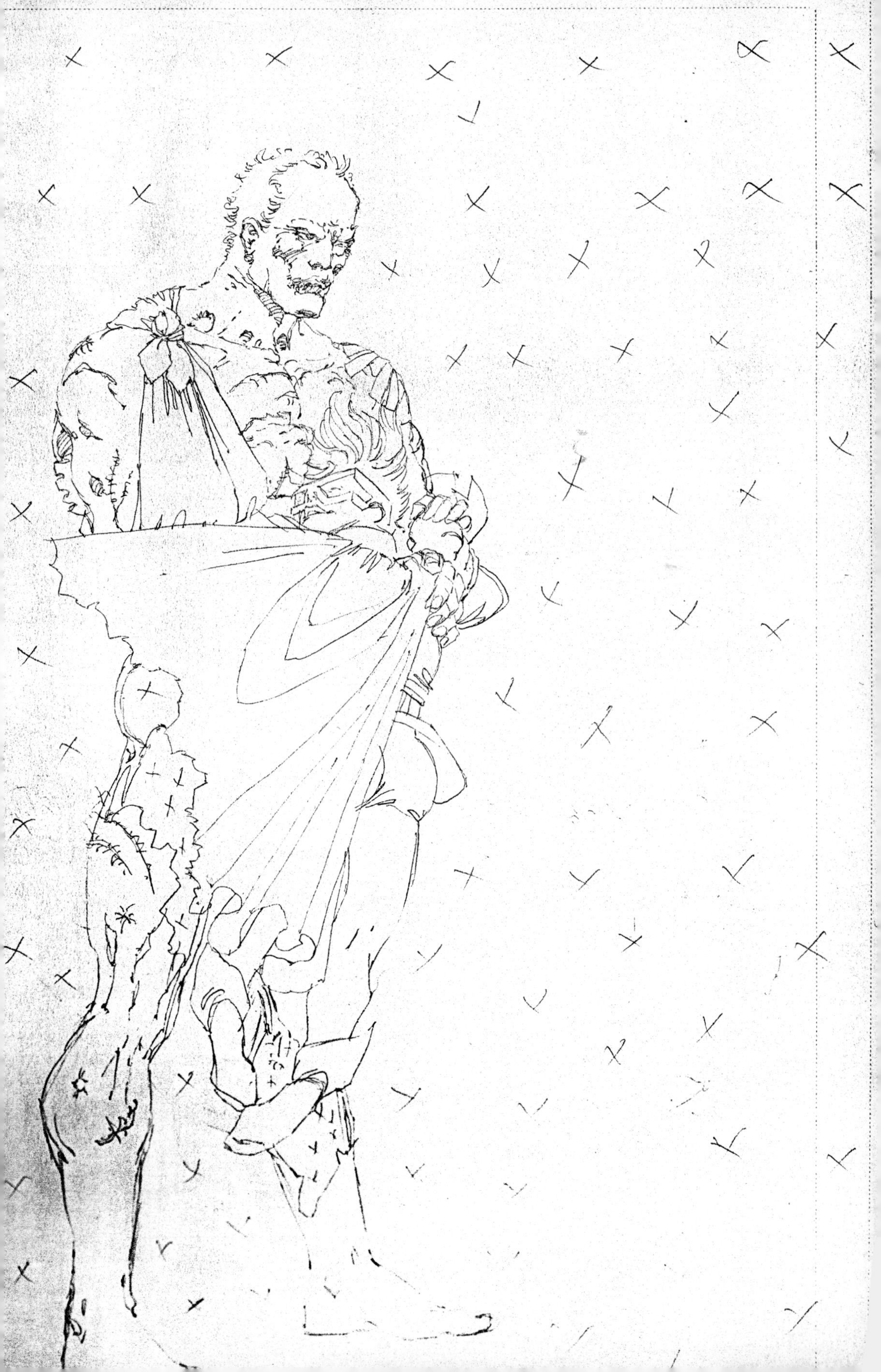

BOSS.. YOU'RE TURNING THE WRONG WAY..
HOLD ON..
SON OF A BITCH!
BLAM
YOU'RE HIT..
FLESH WOUND..
BANDAGE IT.. ON THE WAY..
SKREEKK
HOW MUCH LONGER.. HAVE I GOT...?
ALL UNITS.. CONVERGE ON KYLE ESCORT..
KLAUS: ROBIN'S CAPE NOT SILHOUETTED

"I love how Carrie makes Batman look gigantic."—FRANK MILLER
BATMAN: THE DARK KNIGHT RETURNS #3, page 37

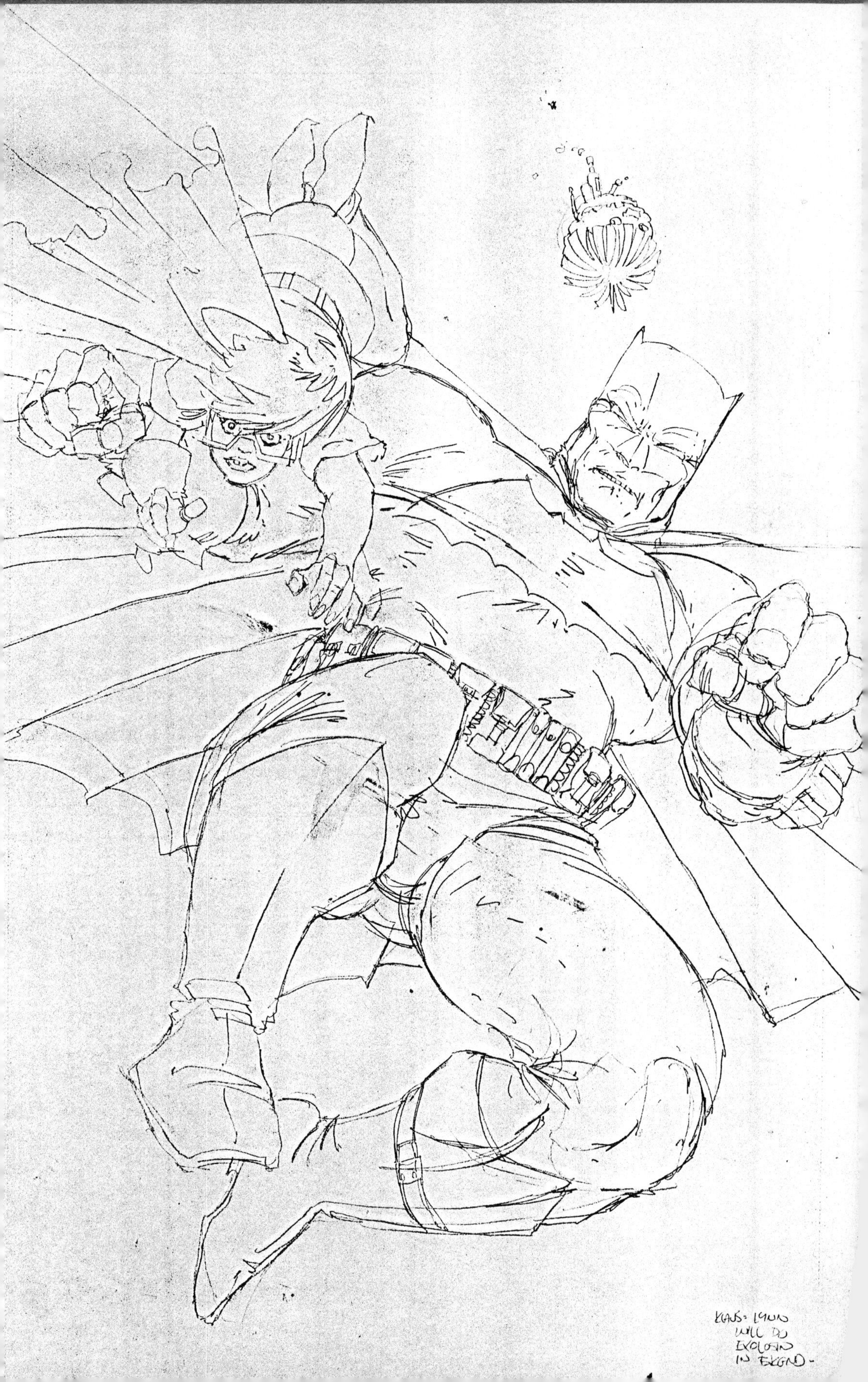
KLAUS= LYNN
WILL DO
EXPLOSION
IN BKGND-

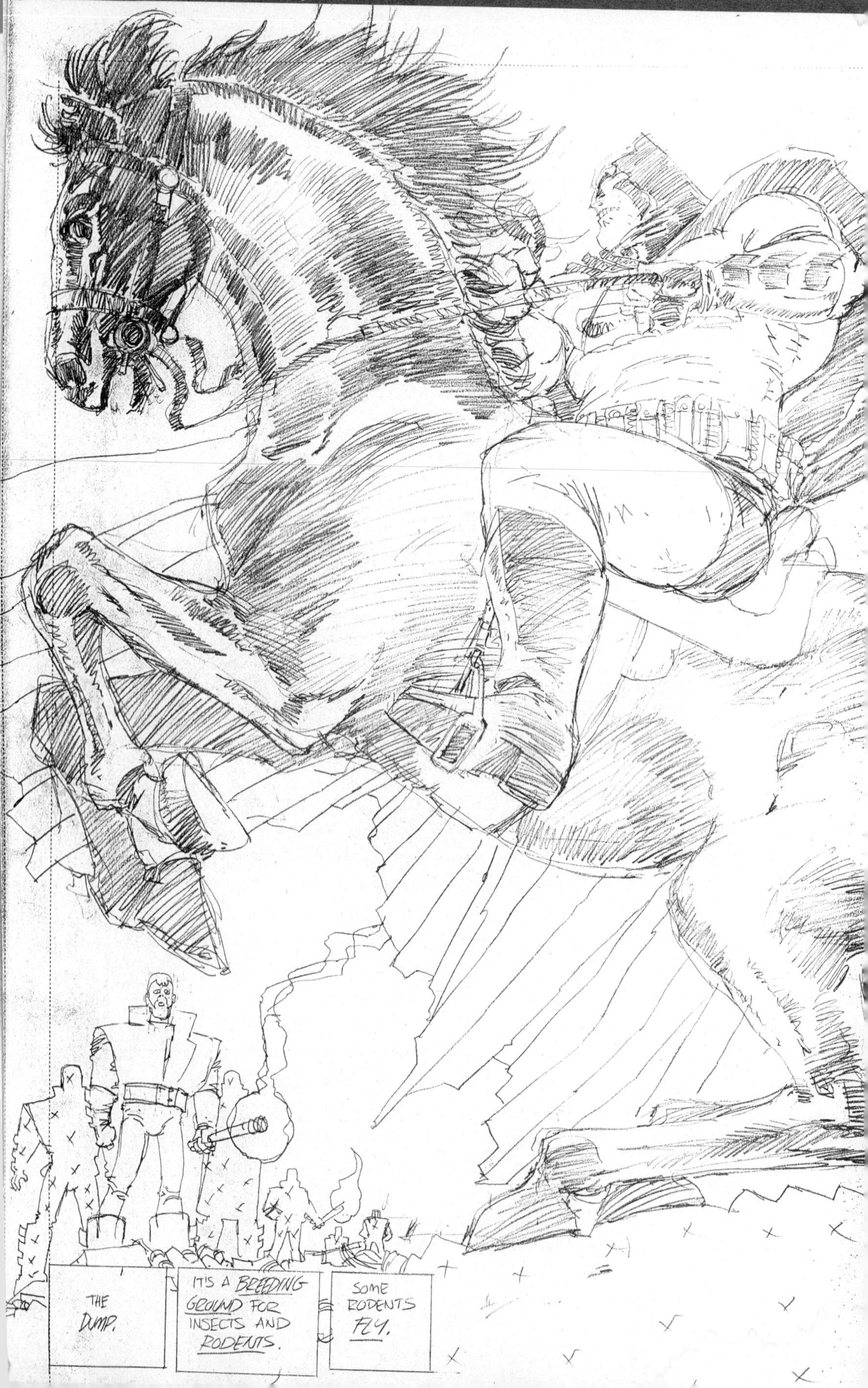
THE DUMP.
IT'S A BREEDING GROUND FOR INSECTS AND RODENTS.
SOME RODENTS FLY.

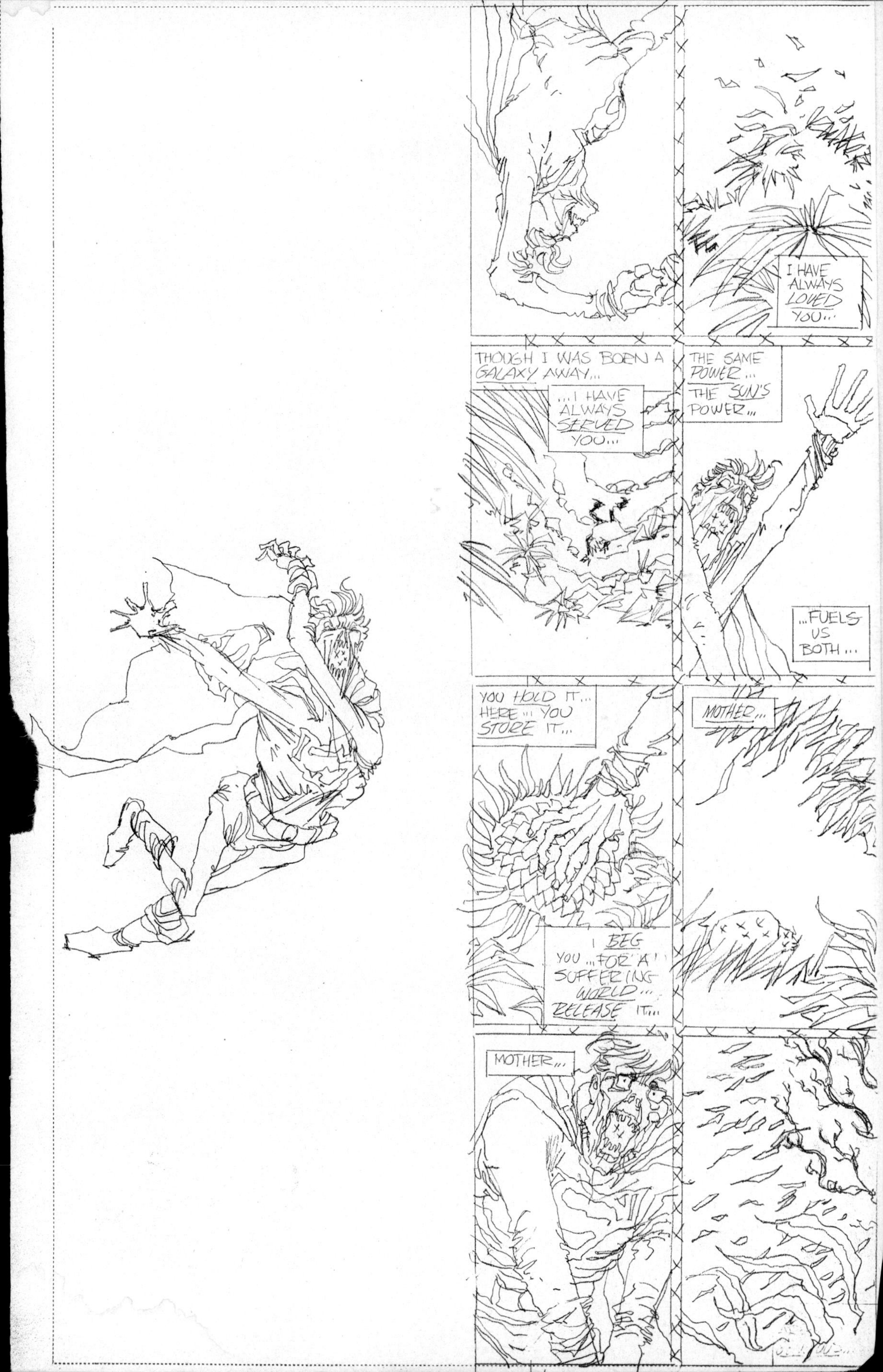
I HAVE ALWAYS LOVED YOU...
THOUGH I WAS BORN A GALAXY AWAY...
...I HAVE ALWAYS SERVED YOU...
THE SAME POWER... THE SUN'S POWER...
...FUELS US BOTH...
YOU HOLD IT... HERE... YOU STORE IT...
I BEG YOU... FOR A SUFFERING WORLD... RELEASE IT...
MOTHER...
MOTHER...

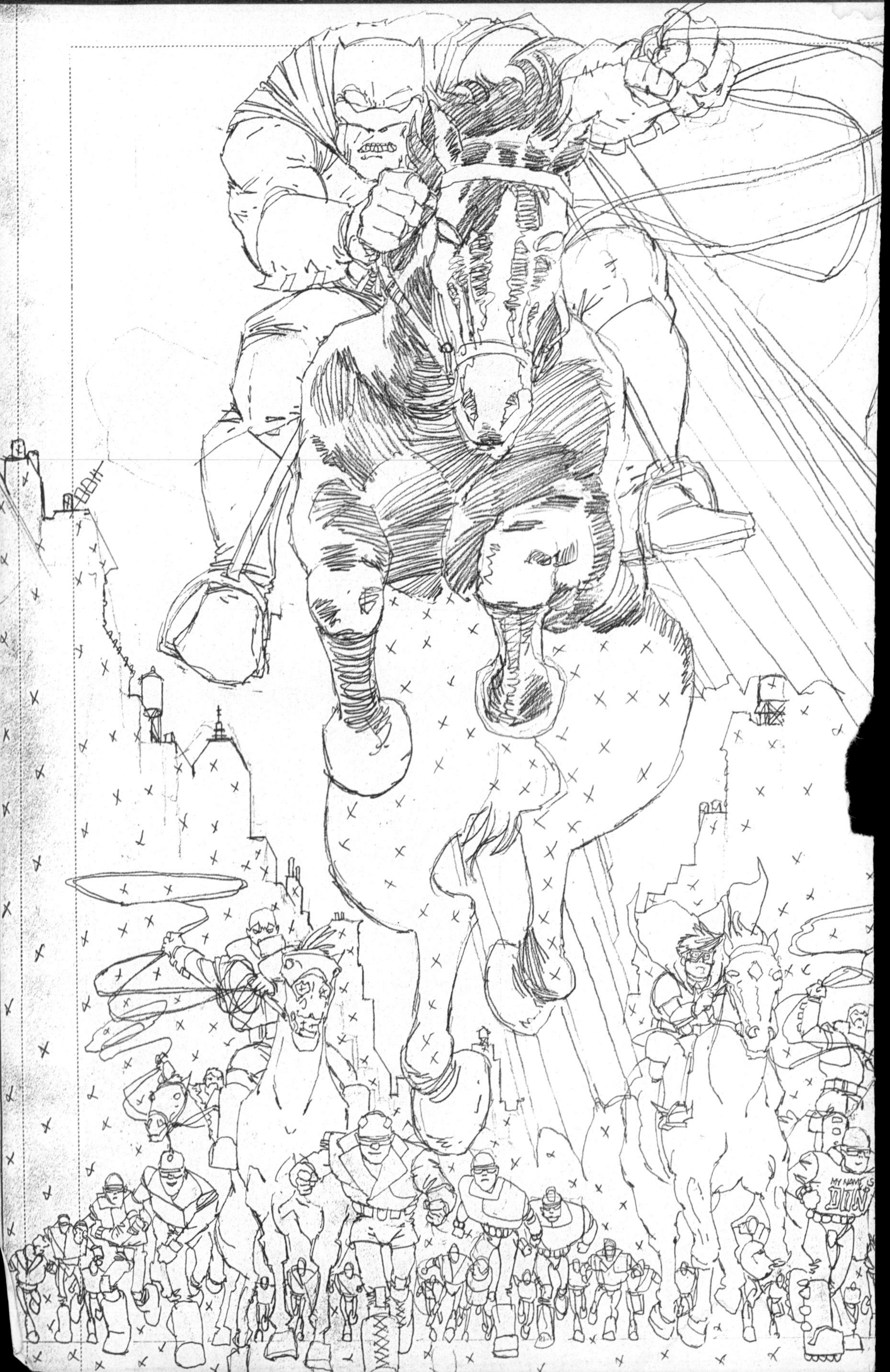
MY NAME IS
DON

...I WANT YOU... TO REMEMBER, CLARK...
...IN ALL THE YEARS TO COME...
...IN YOUR MOST PRIVATE MOMENTS...
I WANT YOU TO REMEMBER ...MY HAND ...AT YOUR THROAT...
...I WANT... YOU TO REMEMBER...
...THE ONE MAN WHO BEAT YOU...

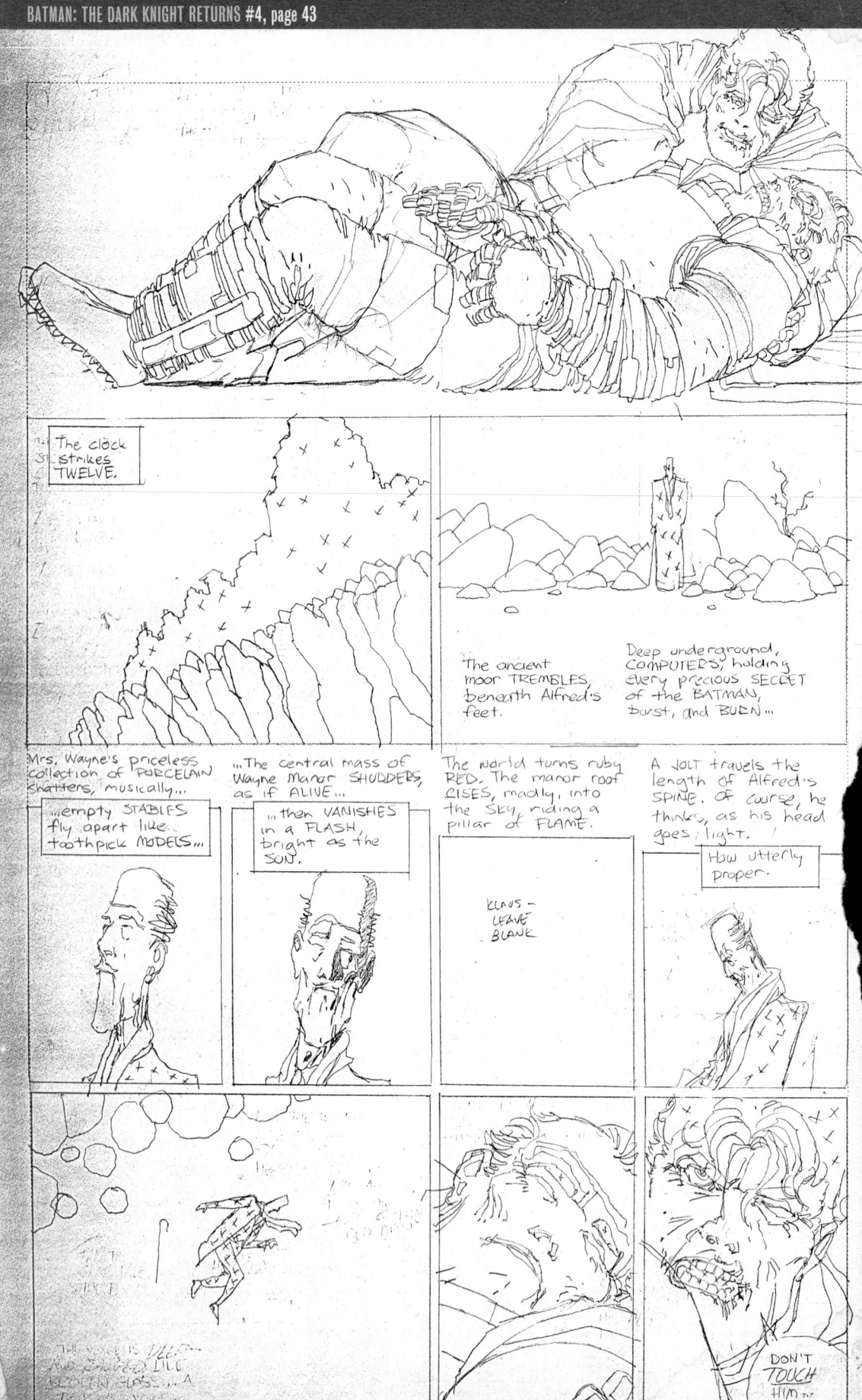

FRANK MILLER

Frank Miller began his career in comics in the late 1970s, first drawing then writing *Daredevil* for Marvel Comics, creating what was essentially a crime comic disguised as a superhero book. It was on *Daredevil* that Miller gained notoriety, honed his storytelling abilities, and took his first steps toward becoming a giant in the comics medium.

After *Daredevil*, Miller came to DC Comics, where he created RONIN, a science-fiction samurai drama that seamlessly melded Japanese and French comics traditions into the American mainstream; and after that, the groundbreaking and acclaimed BATMAN: THE DARK KNIGHT RETURNS and BATMAN: YEAR ONE, both of which not only redefined the classic character, but also revitalized the industry itself.

Finally able to fulfill his dream of doing an all-out, straight-ahead crime series, Miller introduced *Sin City* in 1991. Readers responded enthusiastically to Miller's tough-as-leather noir drama, creating an instant sales success.

His multi-award-winning *300* series from Dark Horse, a telling of one of history's most glorious and underreported battles, was brought to full-blooded life in 1998.

In 2001, Miller returned to the superhero genre with the best-selling BATMAN: THE DARK KNIGHT STRIKES AGAIN.

Frank Miller continues to push the medium into new territory, exploring subject matter previously untouched in comics, and his work consistently receives the highest praise from his industry peers and readers everywhere.

In 2005, with the hugely successful release of *Sin City*, co-directed with Robert Rodriguez, Miller added a director's credit to his already impressive résumé and introduced his characters to an entirely new legion of fans worldwide.

KLAUS JANSON

Klaus Janson was born in 1952 in Coburg, Germany, and came to America in 1957.

As a child growing up in Connecticut, he learned how to read and write the English language almost exclusively from Lois Lane and Superman comics.

Even at that early age, delusions of competence overtook him and he would cut apart the comics and paste them onto paper to construct new stories. This eventually led to the notion that drawing the stories outright and preserving the comics might be a more efficient way of approaching this medium.

A valuable and life-saving apprenticeship with his mentor Dick Giordano encouraged him to continue.

After many summers of portfolio reviews and rejections, Marvel Comics offered a part-time office job applying grey tones to the black and white horror comic reprints that were glutting the market.

Two things happened that would change that.

First, *Daredevil* with Frank Miller in the mid 1980s was a rare opportunity for two artists to work unconstrained by the typical expectations or oversight of corporate thinking. An anomaly for mainstream publishing, *Daredevil* was a struggle between artistic instinct and intellect that, at its best, resulted in that perfect balance. And that moment of perfection led to their next collaboration on THE DARK KNIGHT RETURNS.

The other step forward was teaching at The School of Visual Arts. Klaus believes that communication is the most powerful tool human beings possess. That ability to communicate can come in many forms but at its root is called storytelling.

Klaus lives in New York, where he writes, draws, inks, colors, teaches comics and where, from time to time, delusions of competence still overtake him.